SEVEN WHO SHAPED OUR DESTINY

A *Cass Canfield* BOOK

BOOKS BY RICHARD B. MORRIS

Seven Who Shaped Our Destiny (1973)
Harper Encyclopedia of the Modern World (*with Graham W. Irwin*)
    (1970)
The Emerging Nations and the American Revolution (1970)
John Jay, the Nation, and the Court (1967)
The American Revolution Reconsidered (1967)
The Peacemakers (1965)
Great Presidential Decisions (1960)
The Spirit of 'Seventy-six (*with Henry Steele Commager*) (1958, 1967)
Alexander Hamilton and the Founding of the Nation (1957)
The American Revolution: A Brief History (1955)
Encyclopedia of American History (*first edition*, 1953)
Fair Trial (1953)
A Treasury of Great Reporting (*with Louis L. Snyder*) (1949)
Government and Labor in Early America (1946)
The Era of the American Revolution (*editor*, 1939)
Studies in the History of American Law (1930)
A Guide to the Principal Sources for Early American History (*with Evarts
    Boutell Greene*) (1929)

(Volumes I and II of *The LIFE History of the United States*)
The New World (1963)
The Making of the Nation (1963)

SEVEN
WHO SHAPED OUR
DESTINY

The Founding Fathers as Revolutionaries

RICHARD B. MORRIS

HARPER & ROW, PUBLISHERS

New York, Evanston, San Francisco, London

A few portions of this book appeared in somewhat different form in the *New York Times Magazine*. Reprinted by permission.
Chapter I originally appeared in an abbreviated version in *American Heritage*.

Designed by Sidney Feinberg

Library of Congress Cataloging in Publication Data

Morris, Richard Brandon, 1904–
    Seven who shaped our destiny.
    Includes bibliographical references.
    1. United States—History—Revolution—Biography.
2. United States—History—Revolution—Causes.
I. Title.
E302.5.M67   973.3'092'2 [B]   73–4111
ISBN 0–06–013078–4

To My Beloved

CONTENTS

ILLUSTRATIONS

ACKNOWLEDGMENTS

The genesis of this book was an article in the *New York Times Magazine,* entitled "Seven Who Set Our Destiny," which benefited greatly from the editorial suggestions of Lester Markel. Since then, drawing upon the rich documentation of the Founding Fathers made available by the editorial staffs of the major national publication projects, upon whom I have drawn repeatedly for advice, I have reexamined the evidence in depth, and as a result the profiles in the present volume represent a substantial revision at numerous points of the original *Times* piece. In abridged form the chapter on Franklin appeared in *American Heritage.* For verification of research and documentation I have enlisted the services of David Goldberg, Wendy Rosan, and more especially my former student and research associate Dr. Mary-Jo Kline. Ene Sirvet has proven of invaluable assistance in preparing the manuscript for the press. Again, I have benefited from a critical and dedicated reading of the manuscript by my wife, Berenice Robinson Morris, from the literary advice and sage counsel of my editor, Cass Canfield, from whose fertile mind sprang the initial idea of the project, and, as always, from Beulah Hagen.

R.B.M.

SEVEN WHO SHAPED OUR DESTINY

A *Cass Canfield* BOOK

A TIME FOR LEADERSHIP

"I have known four and twenty leaders of revolt," sang Robert Browning. But in this book we are content with just seven. These men, extraordinary by the standards of their day as well as by our own, faced the sternest tests confronting our national history, the tests of achieving independence and building a durable nation. Incapable of self-delusion, they were prepared to assume the risks of revolution, confident that America would achieve its freedom from colonial rule and that a republic of free peoples would prosper and serve as an example to a world aching for liberty.

Seven Founders—Benjamin Franklin, George Washington, John Adams, Thomas Jefferson, John Jay, Alexander Hamilton, and James Madison—played central roles in determining the destiny of the new nation. Their task was immense and in certain respects incomparably greater than that confronting our statesmen today, for there was nobody before them to show them the way. As Madison commented to Jefferson in 1789, "We are in a wilderness without a single footstep to guide us. Our successors will have an easier task."

They thought of themselves, to use Jefferson's words, as "the Argonauts" who had lived in "the Heroic Age." Accordingly, they took special pains to preserve their papers as essential sources for posterity. Their writings assume more than dramatic or patriotic interest because of their conviction that the struggle in which they were involved was neither selfish nor parochial, but, rather, as Washington in his last wartime circular reminded his fellow countrymen, that "with our fate will the destiny of unborn millions be involved."

It has remained for this generation to launch a comprehensive

1

program of scholarly research and publication of the writings of the Founding Fathers, a project initiated by the National Historical Publications Commission. The enterprise, while not even close to completion, has already supplanted bowdlerized texts supplied by earlier editors with accurate ones, and provided the reader with scholarly annotations and commentary which add a dimension of depth and significance hitherto lacking. The result to date has been the unearthing of important historical documents, previously unknown or obscure, presenting the Founding Fathers in a fresh perspective as well as shattering numberless historical clichés about the American Revolution. The author, who is directing an editorial enterprise to publish the unpublished writings of one of the Seven Founders, John Jay, has levied heavily upon the editorial labors of others in the preparation of this set of profiles. These new editions bring us face to face with strong men holding strong opinions, frank to the point of being refreshingly indiscreet, yet withal essentially congenial minds whose agreements with each other proved more consequential than their differences.

Why just these Seven? Indubitably a case could be made for Samuel Adams, James Wilson, John Dickinson, Robert Morris, Thomas Paine, Patrick Henry, George Mason, and perhaps half a dozen others whose contributions to the making or the winning of the Revolution were noteworthy. On one ground or another they have failed the triple tests of charismatic leadership, staying power, and constructive statesmanship that the Seven Founders chosen for this volume passed with flying colors. Samuel Adams's and Patrick Henry's noblest efforts were largely confined to the preliminary stages of the Revolution. Thereafter they gave way to more constructive leaders; indeed, succumbed to mediocrity. George Mason's passion for privacy inhibited his public role. All the rest can be excluded on the ground that none filled the variety of high-level posts in state and nation that the Seven did, that none performed that amazing range of public services that stamp the Seven not only as indomitable but even exceptional in an age of versatility.

This book focuses on two questions: What made an elite, prosperous and conservative, members of the Establishment, one might say, turn against their king and start a revolution? Having made that irrevocable commitment, what difference did their leadership mean to the conduct and goals of the American Revolution; in what way did their participation invest that epochal conflict with a very special character? To answer these questions one must pierce the veil of privacy, seek in their private lives partial if not definitive solutions to an enigma not necessarily resolved by a study of their public professions. Fortunately, in all seven cases we have enough available documentation to see them on their own ground and judge them on their own terms.

Much has been said in recent years about a leadership crisis, even a leadership vacuum. Surely the appearance at the birth of the nation of a constellation of statesmen of first-rate abilities prompts the query as to why such a cluster of leadership talents has never appeared again in the American skies. Talented individuals, to be sure; but as a group even the remarkable team of Webster, Clay, and Calhoun pales in comparison.

To account for this phenomenon it has been suggested that the America of 1776 was an intimate and relatively homogeneous society, that it was possible in a young nation counting just two and one-half million people for a man with political ambitions to have a personal impact that seems inconceivable in a nation grown almost a hundredfold in numbers and perhaps threefold in territorial extent. Theirs was a society where the spirit of deference still prevailed, where an intellectual elite, or, if one prefers, a meritocracy, could rule. Yet the alleged homogeneity of ethnic origin and religious persuasion of the Revolutionary Americans has been exaggerated, nor was place found in this meritocracy for a half-million blacks.

It would be unrealistic to expect that an age of conformity such as our own would be likely to spawn that creative individualism that marked the leadership of the American Revolutionary era. Nor is an age of materialism calculated to encourage young people to abandon lucrative and prestigious career opportunities and dedicate themselves to the public service, as did the Founding Fathers. In a society that regards intellectuals seeking public office with suspicion, the Seven Founders, save perhaps Franklin, who knew how to mask his genius and take on the coloration of the common man, would find the climate uncongenial.

Some of the responsibility for the leadership gap must be borne by technology. The impact of immediacy which the communications media have thrust upon us places political leaders under furious pressure and fosters a certain type of talent for the glib answer, the bland statement, the technique of noncommittal, for what Learned Hand called the "reiterated suggestion" and the "consecrated platitude." At none of these talents would the forthright if deliberate Seven Founders excel. They read, they pondered, and they wrote, three activities which are rapidly going out of fashion. An age of jet travel and instantaneous communication not only allows less time for decisionmaking, but removes from subordinate officials dispatched to remote lands the opportunity for independent judgment. Time and distance conspired to augment the authority of the Seven Founders. Today these factors would work in reverse.

Finally, the question might well be raised as to whether there would be any role for the Seven Founders were they alive today? Do we really need the charismatic, individualistic leadership that the nation boasted in its infancy? Henry Kissinger has written that "a society that must produce a great man in each generation to maintain its domestic or international position will doom itself." As he sees it, the appearance and, even more, the recognition accorded a great man are to "a large extent fortuitous." Perhaps the twentieth century has had a surfeit of charismatic figures. Today we could do with honest ones. There was a time, however, when a fortuitous conjunction of character and destiny brought America a leadership unmatched throughout its history. And it is that leadership and the direction that it gave the new nation which are the subjects of this book.

I

DOCTOR FRANKLIN:

THE SENIOR CITIZEN

AS REVOLUTIONARY

As bedfellows they were curiously mismatched. Yet Benjamin Franklin and John Adams once shared a bed at a crowded New Brunswick inn, which grudgingly provided them with a room to themselves hardly larger than the bed itself. The room had one small window. Adams, who has recorded the night's adventure, remembered that the window was open. Afraid of the mild September night air, he got out of bed and shut it.

"Don't shut the window. We shall be suffocated," Franklin remonstrated. Adams explained his fears of the night air, but his senior companion reassured him: "The air within the chamber will soon be, and indeed is now, worse than that without doors. Come, open the window and come to bed, and I will convince you. I believe you are not acquainted with my theory of colds." With misgivings Adams agreed to open the window. While Franklin continued to expound his theory of the causes of colds, Adams fell asleep, remembering that the last words he heard were spoken very drowsily.[1] For this one night the testy Adams, who never relished being crossed or losing an argument, yielded to the diplomatic blandishments of Franklin, whose scientific experimentalism extended even to his code of personal hygiene. Neither caught colds that night.

Out of choice neither Adams nor Franklin would have picked the other as a companion with whom to spend that or any other night, but they had no choice. Dispatched in the late summer of 1776 by the Continental Congress, along with Edmund Rutledge, the young Carolinian, they were en route to a rendezvous with Lord Richard Howe, the British admiral, and Sir William Howe, the general, on

5

Staten Island for an informal peace conference. The hour was late. On the second of July the Congress had voted independence. At the end of August a vast amphibious force had routed the rebels on Long Island and was readying the trap for Washington's forces defending Manhattan. The three congressmen contested for space with soldiers thronging the Jersey roads to join Washington. What the Howes had to offer at the peace conference held on September 11 was no more than a pardon for those who had rebelled. It was too little and came too late. The war would be fought to a finish.

No one, least of all an Adams, could really get to know Franklin after a single night in bed with him. While Adams was to become increasingly disenchanted with the man with whom he was to work abroad for a number of years, he could take satisfaction in the knowledge that his prejudices were shared by a whole party in Congress that knew that Dr. Franklin was up to no good. To the rest of mankind (British officialdom and Tories excepted, of course), Franklin embodied the most admirable traits and was a truly great man.

Deceptively simple and disarmingly candid, but in reality a man of enormous complexity, Franklin wore many masks, and from his own time to this day each beholder has chosen the mask that suited his fancy. To D. H. Lawrence, Franklin typified the hypocritical and bankrupt morality of the do-gooder American, with his stress upon an old-fashioned Puritan ethic that glorified work, frugality, and temperance—in short, a "snuff-coloured little man!" of whom "the immortal soul part was a sort of cheap insurance policy." Lawrence resented being shoved into "a barbed-wire paddock" and made to "grow potatoes or Chicagoes." Revealing in this castigation much about himself and little insight into Franklin, Lawrence could not end his diatribe against the most cosmopolitan of all Americans without hurling a barbed shaft at "clever America" lying "on her muck-heaps of gold."[2] F. Scott Fitzgerald quickly fired off a broadside of his own. In *The Great Gatsby,* that literary darling of the Jazz Age indicted *Poor Richard* as midwife to a generation of bootleggers.

If Lawrence and Fitzgerald were put off by Franklin's commonsense materialism which verged on crassness or if Max Weber saw Franklin as embodying all that was despicable in both the American character and the capitalist system, if they and other critics considered him as little more than a methodical shopkeeper, they signally failed

to understand him. They failed to perceive how Franklin's materialism was transmuted into benevolent and humanitarian ends, how that
shopkeeper's mind was enkindled by a ranging imagination that set
no bounds to his intellectual interests and that continually fed an
extraordinarily inventive and creative spark.[3] They failed to explain
how the popularizer of an American code of hard work, frugality,
and moral restraint had no conscientious scruples about enjoying high
living, a liberal sexual code for himself, and bawdy humor. They
failed to explain how so prudent and methodical a man could have
got caught up in a revolution in no small part of his own making.

Franklin would have been the first to concede that he had in his
autobiography created a character gratifying to his own vanity. "Most
people dislike vanity in others, whatever share they have of it themselves," he observed, "but I give it fair quarter where I meet it."
Begun in 1771, when the author had completed a half-dozen careers
and stood on the threshold of his most dramatic role, his autobiography constitutes the most dazzling success story of American history.
The penniless waif who arrived in Philadelphia disheveled and
friendless, walking up Market Street munching a great puffy roll, had
by grit and ability propelled himself to the top. Not only did the
young printer's apprentice manage the speedy acquisition of a fortune, but he went on to achieve distinction in many different fields,
and greatness in a few of them. In an age when the mastery of more
than one discipline was possible, Franklin surpassed all his contemporaries as a well-rounded citizen of the world. Endowed with a
physique so strong that as a young man he could carry a large form of
type in each hand, "when others carried but one in both hands," a
superb athlete and a proficient swimmer, Franklin proved to be a
talented printer, an enterprising newspaper editor and publisher, a
tireless promoter of cultural institutes, America's first great scientist
whose volume on electricity turned out to be the most influential book
to come out of America in the eighteenth century, and second to none
as a statesman. Eldest of the Founding Fathers by a whole generation,
he was in some respects the most radical, the most devious, and the
most complicated.

From the available evidence, mainly provided by the subject himself, Franklin underwent two separate identity crises, when, as mod-
ern-day psychoanalysts suggest, the subject struggles for a new self
and a new conception of his place in the world. In adolescence

Franklin experienced a psychological crisis of the kind that Erik Erikson has so perceptively attributed to personages as disparate as Martin Luther and Mahatma Gandhi. Again, Franklin, the middle-aged man seeking a new image of himself, seems the prototype of Jung's classic case. As regards the first crisis, Franklin's autobiography reveals a sixteen-year-old rebelling against sibling rivalry and the authority of his household, using a variety of devices to maintain his individuality and sense of self-importance.

Born in Boston in 1706, the tenth son of Josiah and Abiah Folger Franklin, and the youngest son of the youngest son for five generations, Franklin could very easily have developed an inferiority complex as one of the youngest of thirteen children sitting around his father's table at one time. Everything about the home reduced Franklin's stature in his own eyes. When his father tried to make a tallow chandler and soap boiler out of him, he made it clear that his father's trade was not to his liking. His father then apprenticed the twelve-year-old lad to his brother James, who had started a Boston newspaper, the *New England Courant,* in 1721. For the next few years Benjamin was involved in one or another kind of rebellion.

Take the matter of food. Benjamin, an omnivorous reader, devoured a book recommending a vegetarian diet. Since his brother James boarded both himself and his apprentices at another establishment, Franklin's refusal to eat meat or fish proved an embarrassment to his elder brother and a nuisance to the housekeeper. Franklin, to save arguments which he abhorred, worked out a deal with his brother, who agreed to remit to him half the money he paid out for him for board if he would board himself. Concentrating on a frugal meatless diet, which he dispatched quickly, Franklin, eating by himself, had more time to continue his studies. While eating one of his hastily prepared meals he first feasted on Locke's treatise *On Human Understanding.*

A trivial episode, indeed, but this piece of self-flagellation forecast a lifelong pattern of pervasive traits. Benjamin Franklin did not like to hurt anyone, even nonhuman creatures. He avoided hostilities. Rather than insisting upon getting the menu he preferred, he withdrew from the table of battle and arranged to feed himself. This noncombative nature, masking a steely determination, explains much of Franklin's relation with others thereafter. Even his abandonment of the faddish vegetarian diet provides insights into the evolving

Franklin with his pride in rational decision. On his voyage from Boston to Philadelphia, he tells us, his ship became becalmed off Block Island, where the crew spent their idle moments catching cod. When the fish were opened, he saw that smaller fish came out of the stomachs of the larger cod. "Then, thought I," he confessed in his autobiography, "If you eat one another, I don't see why we mayn't eat you." With that, he proceeded to enjoy a hearty codfish repast and to return at once to a normal flesh-eating diet. With a flash of self-revelation, he comments, "So convenient a thing it is to be a *reasonable creature,* since it enables one to find or make a reason for everything one has a mind to do."

Franklin's rebellion against authority and convention soon assumed a more meaningful dimension. When, in 1722, his brother James was jailed for a month for printing critical remarks in his newspaper about the authorities, the sixteen-year-old apprentice pounced on the chance to achieve something on his own. He published the paper for his brother, running his own name on the masthead to circumvent the government. Continually quarreling with his overbearing brother, Franklin determined to quit his job, leave his family and Boston, and establish himself by his own efforts unaided. The youthful rebel set forth on his well-publicized journey to Philadelphia, arriving in that bustling town in October, 1723, when he was little more than seventeen years of age.

To carve out a niche for himself in the printing trade, Franklin had to keep a checkrein on his rebellious disposition. For weeks he bore without ill temper the badgering of his master Keimer. When the blow-up came, Franklin, rather than stay and quarrel, packed up and lit out. Once more he was on his own. "Of all things I hate altercation," he wrote years later to one of his fellow commissioners in Paris with whom he was continually at odds.[4] He would write sharp retorts and then not mail the letters. An operator or negotiator *par excellence,* Franklin revealed in his youthful rebellion against family and employers the defensive techniques he so skillfully utilized to avoid combat.[5] Yet there was little about Franklin's behavior which we associate with neurotics. He was a happy extrovert, who enjoyed the company of women, and was gregarious and self-assured, a striking contrast to Isaac Newton, a tortured introvert who remained a bachelor all his life. Suffice to say that Franklin never suffered the kind of nervous breakdown that Newton experienced at the height of his powers, and as a result his effectiveness remained undiminished until a very advanced age.

If Franklin early showed an inclination to back away from a quarrel, to avoid a head-on collision, if his modesty and candor concealed a comprehension of his own importance and a persistent deviousness, such traits may go far to explain the curious satisfaction he took in perpetrating hoaxes on an unsuspecting and gullible public. The clandestine side of Franklin, a manifestation of his unwillingness to engage in direct confrontation, hugely benefited by his sense of humor and satirical talents. An inveterate literary prankster from his precocious teens until his death, Franklin perpetrated one literary hoax after another. In 1730, when he became the sole owner of a printing shop and proprietor of the *Pennsylvania Gazette,* which his quondam boss Keimer had launched a few years earlier, Franklin's paper reported a witch trial at Mount Holly, New Jersey, for which there is no authority in fact.[6]

Franklin's greatest hoax was probably written in 1746 and perpetrated the following year, when the story ran in London's *General Advertiser.* Quickly it was reprinted throughout England, Scotland, and Ireland, and in turn picked up by the Boston and New York papers. This was his report of a speech of Polly Baker before a Massachusetts court, in defense of an alleged prosecution for the fifth time for having a bastard child. "Can it be a crime (in the nature of things I mean) to add to the number of the King's subjects, in a new country that really wants people?" she pleaded. "I own it, I should think it as praiseworthy, rather than a punishable action." Denying that she had ever turned down a marriage proposal, and asserting that she was betrayed by the man who first made her such an offer, she compared her role with that of the great number of bachelors in the new country who had "never sincerely and honourably courted a woman in their lives" and insisted that, far from sinning, she had obeyed the "great command of Nature, and of Nature's God, *Encrease and Multiply."* Her compassionate judges remitted her punishment, and, according to this account, one of them married her the very next day.

How so obviously concocted a morality tale as that one could have gained such wide credence seems incredible on its face. Yet the French sage, the Abbé Raynal, picked it up for his *Histoire Philosophique et Politique,* published in 1770. Some seven years later, while visiting Franklin at Passy, Raynal was to be disabused. "When I was young and printed a newspaper," Franklin confessed, "it sometimes happened, when I was short of material to fill my sheet, that I amused myself by making up stories, and that of Polly Baker is one of the number."[7]

When some years later Franklin's severe critic John Adams listed Polly Baker's speech as one of Franklin's many "outrages to morality and decorum,"[8] he was censoring not only Franklin's liberal sexual code but the latter's inability to throw off bad habits in old age. Franklin's penchant for pseudonymous writing was one side of his devious nature and evidenced his desire to avoid direct confrontation. He continued in later life to write a prodigious number of letters under assumed names which appeared in the American, English, and French press, some still undetected.[9] His sly "Edict by the King of Prussia," appearing in an English newspaper in 1773, was a parody, in which Frederick the Great threatened reprisals against England for failing to emancipate the colonists from Germany that originally settled the island. As commissioner in Paris Franklin reputedly wrote a vitriolic hoax, *The Sale of the Hessians,* in which a Count de Schaumbergh expressed delight that 1,605 of his Hessians had been killed in America, 150 more than Lord North had reported to him. This was a windfall, since he was entitled to a sum of money for every fatality suffered by the mercenaries he had sold to George III.[10] In the midst of delicate negotiations with the British to end the war of the American Revolution the irrepressible Franklin fabricated a hoax about the scalping of Americans by Indians in the pay of the British, and then printed it in the guise of a *Supplement to the Boston Independent Chronicle.* Gruesome propaganda indeed, but Franklin justified his deception to the censorious Adams by remarking that he believed the number of persons actually scalped "in this murdering war by the Indians to exceed what is mentioned in invoice."[11]

The image of himself Franklin chose to leave us in his unfinished autobiography was of a man on the make, who insincerely exploited popular morality to keep his printing presses running. Yet he himself, perhaps tongue in cheek, would have said that the morality of *Poor Richard* was foreshadowed by the plan of conduct Franklin had put down on paper on a return voyage in 1726 to Philadelphia from London, where he had spent almost two years in an effort to be able to buy equipment to set himself up as a printer. Later in life Franklin praised the plan as "the more remarkable, as being formed when I was so young, and yet being pretty faithfully adhered to quite through to old Age." The plan stressed the practice of extreme frugality until he had paid his debts, as well as truthfulness, industry, and the avoidance of speaking ill of others.[12]

Franklin, the sixteen-year-old apprentice, absorbed the literary styles of his brother James and other New England satirists running their pieces in the *Courant,* and he clearly used the *Spectator* as his literary model. He produced the Silence Dogood letters, thirteen in a row, until, he admitted, "my small fund of sense for such performances was pretty well exhausted." Until then even his own brother was not aware of the identity of the author. Typical was No. 6, which criticized pride in apparel, singling out such outlandish fashions as hoop petticoats, "monstrous topsy-turvy *Mortar-Pieces* . . . neither fit for the Church, the Hall, or the Kitchen," and looming more "like Engines of War for bombarding the Town, than Ornaments of the Fair Sex."[13]

If the Dogood letters satisfied Franklin's itch for authorship, *Poor Richard* brought him fame and fortune. Lacking originality, drawing upon a wide range of proverbs and aphorisms, notably found in a half-dozen contemporary English anthologies,[14] Franklin skillfully selected, edited, and simplified. For example, James Howell's *Lexicon Tetraglotton* (London, 1660), says: "The greatest talkers are the least doers." *Poor Richard* in 1733 made it: "Great talkers, little doers." Or Thomas Fuller's *Gnomolonia* (London, 1732): "The way to be safe is never to be secure"; this becomes in *Poor Richard,* 1748: "He that's secure is not safe." Ever so often one of the aphorisms seems to reflect Franklin's own views. Thus, *Poor Richard* in 1747 counseled: "Strive to be the *greatest* Man in your Country, and you may be disappointed; Strive to be the *best,* and you may succeed: He may well win the race that runs by himself." Again, two years later, *Poor Richard* extols Martin Luther for being "remarkably *temperate* in meat and drink," perhaps a throwback to Franklin's own adolescent dietary obsessions, with an added comment, *"There was never any* industrious *man who was not a* temperate *man."*[15] To the first American pragmatist what was moral was what worked and what worked was moral.

If there was any priggish streak in the literary Franklin it was abundantly redeemed by his bawdy sense of humor and his taste for earthy language. Thus, to *Poor Richard,* foretelling the weather by astrology was "as easy as pissing abed."[16] "He that lives upon Hope, dies farting."[17] The bawdy note of reportage guaranteed a good circulation for Franklin's *Gazette:* Thus in 1731:

> We are credibly inform'd, that the young Woman who not long since petitioned the Governor, and the Assembly to be divorced from her Husband, and at times industriously solicited most of the Magistrates on that Account, has at last concluded to cohabit with him again. It is said the Report of the Physicians (who in Form examined his *Abilities,* and allowed him to be in every respect *sufficient*) gave her but small Satisfaction; Whether any Experiments *more satisfactory* have been try'd, we cannot say; but it seems she now declares it as her Opinion, That *George is as good as de best.*[18]

Franklin's ambivalent views of women indubitably reflected his own personal relations with the other sex. In his younger days he took sex hungrily, secretly, and without love. One of his women—just which one nobody knows for sure—bore him a son in 1730 or 1731. It was rumored that the child's mother was a maidservant of Franklin's named Barbara, an accusation first printed in 1764 by a political foe of Franklin's, reputedly Hugh Williamson.[19] Whether it was this sudden responsibility or just the boredom of sowing his wild oats, Franklin came to realize that "a single man resembles the odd half of a pair of scissors." Having unsuccessfully sought a match with a woman who would bring him money, Franklin turned his thoughts back to Deborah Read, the girl he had first courted in Philadelphia and then jilted. Rebounding from that humiliation, Deborah married a potter named Rogers who quickly deserted her. Then she did not even bother to have the marriage annulled, relying instead on the rumor that her husband had left behind him a wife in England. Franklin, so he tells us in his autobiography, conveniently overlooked "these difficulties," and "took her to wife, September 1st, 1730." The illegitimate child, William, whether born before or after Franklin's common-law marriage to Deborah, became part of the household, a convenient arrangement for Franklin while a constant reminder to Deborah of her spouse's less than romantic feelings about her. Soon there arose between Deborah and William a coldness bordering on hostility.

The married Franklin's literary allusions to women could be both amicable and patronizing; he could treat them as equals but show downright hostility at times. He portrayed the widow Silence Dogood as frugal, industrious, prosaic, and earthy, but somehow retaining her femininity. Such inferiority as women appeared to have must be attributed to their inferior education. While believing in the moral equality of the sexes, Franklin did not encourage women to enter unconventional fields of activity. He stuffed his *Almanack* with female stereotypes, perhaps charging off his own grievances to the sex in general. He frequently jabbed at "domineering women," with Richard Saunders the prototype of all henpecked husbands and Bridget, his "shrewish, clacking" wife. Scolding, gossipy women and talkative old maids are frequent targets of Franklin's jibes. A woman's role in life, he tells us, is to be a wife and have babies, but a man has a more versatile role and therefore commands a higher value.

Franklin's bagatelles "On Perfumes" and "On Marriages," frequently if furtively printed, kept under wraps for years by the Department of State, attained a clandestine fame, but few in the nineteenth century dared to print either. With the sexual revolution of the twentieth century and the penchant for scatological vocabulary, Franklin's letter on marriages and mistresses attained respectability and wide circulation. In essence, Franklin, in a letter dated June 25, 1745, commended marriage as the state in which a man was "most likely to find solid Happiness." However, those wishing to avoid matrimony without forgoing sex were advised to choose *"old Women to young ones."* Among the virtues of older women he listed their more agreeable conversation, their continued amiability to counteract the "Diminution of Beauty," the absence of a "hazard of Children," their greater prudence and discretion in conducting extramarital affairs, and the superiority of techniques of older women. "As in the dark all Cats are grey, the Pleasure of corporal Enjoyment with an old Woman is at least equal, and frequently superior, every Knack being by Practice capable of Improvement." Furthermore, who could doubt the advantages of making an old woman *"happy"* against debauching a virgin and contributing to her ruin. Finally, old women are *"so grateful!!"*[20]

How much this advice reflected Franklin's own marriage of convenience remains for speculation. *Poor Richard* is constantly chiding cuckolds and scolding wives, and suggesting that marital infidelity is the course of things. "Let thy maidservant be faithful, strong, and homely." "She that paints her Face, thinks of her Tail." "Three things are men most liable to be cheated in, a Horse, a Wig, and a Wife."[21] Or consider poor Lubin lying on his deathbed, both he and his wife despairing, he fearing death, she, "that he may live." Or the metaphor of women as books and men the readers. "Are Women Books? says Hodge, then would mine were an *Almanack,* to change her every Year."[22]

Enough examples, perhaps, have been chosen to show that Franklin's early view of women was based on a combination of gross and illicit sexual experiences and a less than satisfying marriage with a wife neither glamorous nor intellectually compatible.

Abruptly, at the age of forty-two, Franklin retired from active participation in his printing business. He explained the action quite simply: "I flattered myself that, by the sufficient tho' moderate fortune I had acquir'd, I had secured leisure during the rest of my life for philosophical studies and amusements."[23] These words masked the middle-age identity crisis that he was now undergoing. Seeking to project himself on a larger stage, he did not completely cut his ties to a less glamorous past, including a wife who was a social liability, but conveniently eluded it. Now he could lay aside the tools of his trade and the garments of a petit bourgeois and enter the circles of gentility. Gone were the days when he would sup on an anchovy, a slice of bread and butter, and a half-pint of ale shared with a companion. His long bouts with the gout in later life attest to his penchant for high living, for Madeira, champagne, Parmesan cheese, and other continental delicacies. Sage, philanthropist, statesman, he became, as one critic has remarked, "an intellectual transvestite,"[24] affecting a personality switch that was virtually completed before he left on his first mission (second trip) to England in 1757. Not that Franklin was a purely parochial figure at the time of his retirement from business. Already he had shown that passion for improvement which was to mark his entire career. Already he had achieved some local reputation in public office, notably in the Pennsylvania Assembly. Already he had displayed his inventive techniques, most notably his invention of the Pennsylvania fireplace, and had begun his inquiries into the natural sciences.

Now, on retirement from private affairs, he stood on the threshold of fame. In the subsequent decade he plunged into his scientific investigations and into provincial politics with equal zest. Dispatched to England in 1757 to present the case of the Pennsylvania Assembly against the proprietor, he spent five of the happiest years of his life residing at the Craven Street residence of Mrs. Margaret Stevenson. Mrs. Stevenson, and especially her daughter Mary, provided for him a pleasant and stimulating home away from home. Reluctantly he returned to Philadelphia at the end of his five-year stay, so enraptured of England that he even contemplated settling there, "provided we can persuade the good Woman to cross the Seas."[25] Once more, in 1764, he was sent abroad, where he stayed to participate in all the agitation associated with the Grenville revenue measures. Snugly content in the Stevenson ménage, Franklin corresponded perfunctorily with his wife back in Philadelphia. Knowing that Deborah was unwilling to risk a sea voyage to join him in London, Franklin did not insist. And though he wrote his wife affectionate letters and sent her gifts, he never saw her again. She died of a stroke in December, 1774, without benefit of Franklin's presence.

It was in France after the American Revolution had broken out that Franklin achieved more completely that new identity which was the quest of his later years. There the mellow septuagenarian, diplomat, and peacemaker carried out a game with the ladies of the salon, playing a part, ironic, detached but romantic, enjoying an *amitié amoureuse* with his impressionable and neurotic neighbor, Mme. Brillon in Passy, flirting in Paris with the romantically minded Comtesse d'Houdetot, and then in the rustic retreat of Auteuil falling in love with the widow of Helvétius, whom he was prepared to marry had she been so inclined. In the unreal world of the salon Franklin relished the role of "papa." Still he avoided combat or confrontation even in his flirtation. Where he scented rejection, he turned witty, ironic, and verbally sexual.[26]

He found time, while engaged in the weighty affairs of peacemaking during the summer of '82, to draw up a treaty of "eternal peace, friendship, and love" between himself and Madame Brillon. Like a good draftsman, Franklin was careful to preserve his freedom of action, in this case toward other females, while at the same time insisting on his right to behave without inhibitions toward his amiable neighbor. Some months before he had written her:

> I often pass before your house. It appears desolate to me. Formerly I broke the Commandment by coveting it along with my neigh-

bor's wife. Now I do not covet it any more, so I am less a sinner. But as to his wife I always find these Commandments inconvenient and I am sorry that they were ever made. If in your travels you happen to see the Holy Father, ask him to repeal them, as things given only to the Jews and too uncomfortable for good Christians.[27]

Franklin met Mme. Brillon in 1777, and found her a beautiful woman in her early thirties, an accomplished musician, married to a rich and tolerant man, twenty-four years her senior. To Mme. Brillon Franklin was a father figure, while to Franklin she combined the qualities of daughter and mistress. Part tease, part prude, Mme. Brillon once remarked: "Do you know, my dear papa, that people have criticized the sweet habit I have taken of sitting on your lap, and your habit of soliciting from me what I always refuse?"[28] In turn, Franklin reminded her of a game of chess he had played in her bathroom while she soaked in the tub.

If Franklin was perhaps most passionately fond of Brillon, other ladies of the salon set managed to catch his eye, among them the pockmarked, cross-eyed Comtesse d'Houdetot, who made up in sex appeal what she lacked in looks. Unlike Rousseau, who cherished for the Comtesse an unrequited passion, which he widely publicized in his posthumous *La Nouvelle Héloise,* Franklin's relations with her never seemed to border on close intimacy. Contrariwise, Franklin carried on a long flirtation with the widowed Mme. Helvétius. Abigail Adams, John's straitlaced wife, was shocked at the open intimacies between the pair. Franklin complained that since he had given Madame "so many of his days," she appeared "very ungrateful in not giving him one of her nights."[29] Whether in desperation or because he really felt the need to rebuild some kind of family life, he proposed to her. When she turned him down, he wrote a bagatelle, recounting a conversation with Madame's husband in the Elysian Fields, as well as his own encounter with his deceased wife Deborah. He then dashed into print with the piece, an odd thing to do if he were deadly serious about the proposal. As Sainte-Beuve remarked of this episode, Franklin never allowed himself to be carried away by feeling, whether in his youth or in old age, whether in love or in religion. His romantic posture was almost ritualistic. He almost seemed relieved at the chance to convert an emotional rebuff into a literary exercise.[30]

Franklin's casual attitude toward sexual morality was shared by his son and grandson. Himself illegitimate, William, who sought to efface the cloud over his origin by becoming an arrant social climber and most respectable Tory, also sired an illegitimate son, William Temple Franklin, whose mother remains as much a mystery as William's own. Temple, engaged at Franklin's behest by the American peace commissioners as secretary in Paris, had an affair with Blanchette Caillot, a married woman by whom he had a child and whom he abandoned on his return to America.

If Temple was a playboy, that charge could never fairly be leveled at his grandfather. The Old Doctor, an irrepressible activist and dogooder, embodied in his own career that blend of practicality and idealism which has characterized Americans ever since. Convinced from early youth of the values of self-improvement and self-education, Franklin on his return to Philadelphia from his first trip to England organized the Junto, a society half debating, half social, attesting both to the sponsor's belief in the potentialities of continued adult education and to his craving for intellectual companionship not provided in his own home. Then came the subscription library, still flourishing in Philadelphia. Franklin's plans for an academy, drawn up in 1743, reached fruition a decade later, and were a positive outgrowth of his conviction that an English rather than a classical education was more suitable to modern man and that most colleges stuffed the heads of students with irrelevant book knowledge. Then, too, the Pennsylvania Hospital project drew upon his seemingly inexhaustible fund of energy, hospitalization being defended by him as more economical than home care.[31] So did his organization of a local fire company, and his program for a tax-supported permanent watch, and for lighting, paving, sweeping, draining, and deicing the streets of Philadelphia. Convinced of the virtues of thrift and industry, Franklin could be expected to take a dim view of poor relief, and questioned "whether the laws peculiar to England which compel the rich to maintain the poor have not given the latter a dependence that very much lessens the care of providing against the wants of old age."[32] Truly, this revolutionary, if he returned to us today, might well be aghast at the largess of the modern welfare state with its indifference to the work ethos.

Franklin evolved what he called his "moral algebra" to explain his code of ethics, a system which clearly anticipated Jeremy Bentham. In a letter to Joseph Priestley written in 1772 he outlined his method of marshaling all the considerations pro and con for a contemplated decision, setting them down in parallel columns, and then pausing for a few days before entering "short hints" for or against the measure. Subtracting liability from assets, one would come up with a moral or political credit or debit. Franklin never narrowed down the springs of human conduct to pain and pleasure, as did Bentham, but assumed a more complex set of motives.[33] Franklin's moral algebra stemmed in part from his bookkeeping mentality,[34] in part from his desire to reduce life to an orderly system.

That the oldest of American Revolutionaries should be committed to controlled, orderly change takes on larger significance when one seeks explanations as to why the American Revolution did not pursue the violent, even chaotic, course of the French. Nowhere is this better illustrated than in Franklin's evolving views about the Negro and slavery, in neither of which subjects did he show any active interest until well after middle life (after due allowance for the fact that as printer he published a few antislavery tracts in his earlier years). By shrewd calculation he demonstrated that the labor of a slave in America was dearer than that of an iron or wool worker in England. Embodying these calculations in what turned out to be a seminal paper on American demography,[35] written when he was forty-five, Franklin did not let himself get actively drawn into the Negro question for another twenty years, and then he agreed to serve as a trustee for an English fund to convert Negroes. As a Deist he could hardly have been passionately aroused by the prospect of saving souls, but may have consented to serve because of the degree of respectable public exposure involved. Earlier, in 1764, he was prepared to concede that some Negroes had "a strong sense of justice and honour," but it was not until 1772, when he was sixty-six years old, that he became aroused about the slave trade, that "detestable commerce." By the next year he was on record sympathizing with the movement to abolish slavery, and in 1787 he became president of the Pennsylvania Abolition Society, the oldest society of its kind in the world. He soon proposed a program for the education of free blacks in trades and other employment to avoid "poverty, idleness, and many vicious habits."

Franklin's last public act before his death was the signing of a memorial to Congress from his own Abolition Society asking for justice for the blacks and an end in the "traffic in the persons of our fellowmen." When Southern congressmen denounced the measure he sent to the press one of the last writings to come from his pen, a fictional account of an observation by an official of Algiers in 1687 denying a petition of an extremist sect opposing the enslaving of Christians. Accordingly, the divan resolved, in Franklin's tongue-in-cheek reporting, " 'The doctrine that plundering and enslaving the Christians is unjust, is, at best, problematical; but that it is the interest of this state to continue the practice, is clear: therefore let the petition be rejected.' "[36]

A man of the Enlightenment, Franklin had faith in the power and beneficence of science. In moments snatched from public affairs during the latter 1740's and early 1750's—moments when public alarms interrupted his research at the most creative instant—he plunged into scientific experimentation. While his lightning kite and rod quickly made him an international celebrity, Franklin was no mere dilettante gadgeteer. His conception of electricity as a flow with negative and positive forces opened the door to further theoretical development in the field of electromagnetism. His pamphlet on electricity, published originally in 1751, went through ten editions, including revisions, in four languages before the American Revolution. Honors from British scientists were heaped upon him, and when he arrived in England in 1757 and again in 1764, and in France in 1776, he came each time with an enlarged international reputation as a scientist whom Chatham compared in Parliament to "our Boyle" and "our Newton."[37]

Pathbreaking as Franklin's work on electricity proved to be, his range of scientific interest extended far beyond theoretical physics. He pioneered in locating the Gulf Stream, in discovering that northeast storms come from the southwest, in making measurements of heat absorption with regard to color, and in investigating the conductivity of different substances with regard to heat. A variety of inventions attested to his utilitarian bent—the Franklin stove, the lightning rod, the flexible metal catheter, bifocal glasses, the glass harmonica, the smokeless chimney. Indefatigable in his expenditure of his spare time on useful ends, he made observations on the nature of communication between insects, contributed importantly to our knowledge of the causes of the common cold, advocated scientific ventilation, and even tried electric shock treatment to treat palsy on a number of occasions.[38]

To the last Franklin stoutly defended scientific experimentation which promised no immediate practical consequences. Watching the first balloon ascension in Paris, he parried the question, "What good is it?" with a characteristic retort, "What good is a newborn baby?"

Committed as he was to discovering truth through scientific inquiry, Franklin could be expected to be impatient with formal theology. While not denigrating faith, he regretted that it had not been "more productive of Good Works than I have generally seen it."[39] He suggested that, Chinese style, laymen leave praying to the men who were paid to pray for them. At the age of twenty-two he articulated a simple creed, positing a deistic Christian God, with infinite power which He would abstain from wielding in arbitrary fashion. His deistic views remained unchanged when, a month before his death, Ezra Stiles asked him his opinion of the divinity of Jesus. Confessing doubts, Franklin refused to dogmatize or to busy himself with the problem at so late a date, since, he remarked, "I expect soon an opportunity of knowing the truth with less trouble."[40]

Unlike the philosophes who spread toleration but were intolerant of Roman Catholicism, Franklin tolerated and even encouraged any and all sects. He contributed to the support of various Protestant churches and the Jewish synagogue in Philadelphia, and, exploiting his friendship with the papal nuncio in Paris, he had his friend John Carroll made the first bishop of the Catholic Church in the new United States. He declared himself ready to welcome a Muslim preacher sent by the grand mufti in Constantinople, but that exotic spectacle was spared Protestant America of his day.

Although he fancied the garb of a Quaker, a subtle form of reverse ostentation that ill-accorded with his preachments about humility, Franklin was no pacifist. During King George's War he urged the need of preparedness upon his city and province, praising "that *Zeal* for the *Publick Good,* that *military Prowess, and* that *undaunted Spirit,"* which in past ages had distinguished the British nation.[41] Like most of the Founding Fathers he could boast a military experience regardless of its brevity, and in Franklin's case it lasted some six weeks. Following Braddock's disastrous defeat in December, 1755, Franklin as a civilian committeeman marched into the interior at the head of an armed force, directing an improvised relief program for the frontier refugees who had crowded into Bethlehem and seeing about the fortifying of the Lehigh gap. Back in Philadelphia he organized a defense force known as the "Associators," of which he was elected colonel. As in his other projects, he entered into these military arrangements with gusto, all to the annoyance of the proprietor, who regarded Franklin as a dangerous political rival and who regularly vetoed all tax bills which included military levies on the proprietary estates of the Penn family.

Once again, almost a decade later, he took command of a military force—this time to face down a frontier band known as the Paxton Boys who in 1764 set out on a lawless march to Philadelphia to confront the government with a demand for protection against the Indians. Franklin issued a blazing pamphlet denouncing the Paxton Boys for their attacks on peaceful Indians and organized and led a force to Germantown, where he confronted the remonstrants and issued a firm warning. The Paxton Boys veered off, and order was finally restored. "For about forty-eight hours," Franklin remarked, "I was a very great man, as I had been once some years before in a time of public danger."[42]

Franklin's brief exposure as a military figure, combined with his leadership of the antiproprietary party, and his general prominence and popularity had by now made him anathema to proprietor and conservatives alike. Standing out against the Establishment, Franklin was heartened by the enemies he had made. A thorough democrat, Franklin had little use for proprietary privileges or a titled aristocracy. In his Silence Dogood letters written as far back as 1723 he had pointed out that "Adam was never called *Master* Adam; we never read of Noah *Esquire,* Lot *Knight* and *Baronet,* nor the *Right Honourable* Abraham, Viscount Mesopotamia, Baron of Carian; no, no, they were plain Men."[43] Again, *Poor Richard* engaged in an amusing genealogical computation to prove that over the centuries it was impossible to preserve blood free of mixtures, and "that the Pretension of such Purity of Blood in ancient Families is a mere Joke."[44] With perhaps pardonable inconsistency Franklin took the trouble to trace his own family back to stout English gentry, but his basic antiaristocratic convictions stood the test of time. When, in the post-Revolutionary years, the patrician-sounding Society of the Cincinnati was founded in America, Franklin in France scoffed at the Cincinnati as "hereditary knights" and egged on Mirabeau to publish an indictment of the Order which set off an international clamor against its hereditary character.[45]

For courts and lawyers, defenders of property and the status quo, Franklin reserved some of his most vitriolic humor. His *Gazette* consistently held up to ridicule the snobbery of using law French in the courts, excessive legal fees and court costs, and the prolixity and perils of litigation. For the lawyers who "can, with Ease, Twist Words and Meanings as you please," *Poor Richard* shows no tolerance.[46] Predictably, Franklin took the side of the debtor against the creditor, the paper-money man against the hard-currency man.[47]

Franklin's support of paper money did not hurt him in the least. As a matter of fact, the Assembly gave him the printing contract in 1731 for the £40,000 in bills of credit that it authorized that year.[48] This incident could be multiplied many times. Franklin ever had an eye for the main chance. Whether as a poor printer, a rising politician, or an established statesman-scientist, he was regarded by unfriendly critics as a man on the make of dubious integrity. One of the improvements Franklin introduced as deputy postmaster general of the colonies was to make the carrying of newspapers a source of revenue and to compel his riders to take all the papers that were offered. On its face a revenue producer and a safeguard against monopoly, the ruling could hardly damage Franklin, publisher or partner of seven or eight newspapers, a chain stretching from New York to Antigua, and even including a German-language paper in Pennsylvania.[49]

Accumulating a tidy capital, Franklin invested in Philadelphia town lots, and then, as the speculative bug bit him, plunged into Nova Scotian and western land ventures. His secretive nature seemed ideally suited to such investments, in which he followed a rule he laid down in 1753: "Great designs should not be made publick till they are ripe for execution, lest obstacles are thrown in the way."[50] The climax of Franklin's land speculations came in 1769 when he joined forces with Samuel Wharton to advance in England the interests of the Grand Ohio Company, which was more British than colonial in composition. This grand alliance of speculators and big-time politicians succeeded in winning from the Privy Council on July 1, 1772, a favorable recommendation supporting their fantastic dream of a colony called Vandalia, to be fitted together from the pieces of the present-day states of Pennsylvania, Maryland, West Virginia, and Kentucky. There Franklin's love of order would replace that frontier anarchy which he abhorred.[51]

Standing on the brink of a stunning success, the Vandalia speculators were now put in jeopardy by Franklin's rash indiscretion in turning over to his radical friends in Massachusetts some embarrassing letters of Governor Thomas Hutchinson which had been given to him in confidence. Indignant at Franklin's disloyalty, the Crown officers refused to complete the papers confirming the grant to the Grand Ohio Company. With his usual deviousness, Franklin, in concert with the banker Thomas Walpole, publicly resigned from the company.[52] In reality Walpole and Franklin had a private understanding by which the latter would retain his two shares out of the total of seventy-two shares of stock in the company. As late as April 11, 1775, Franklin, Walpole, and others signed a power of attorney authorizing William Trent to act on their behalf with respect to the grant, hardly necessary if Franklin was indeed out of the picture. In the summer of 1778 Franklin had a change of heart and decided to get back his original letter of resignation. When Walpole complied, Franklin added thereto a memorandum asserting: "I am still to be considered as an Associate, and was called upon for my Payments as before. My right to two shares, or two Parts of 72, in that Purchase still continues . . . and I hope, that when the Trouble of America is over, my Posterity may reap the Benefits of them."[53] Franklin's posterity, it should be pointed out, stood a much better chance were England to retain the Old Northwest and the Crown validate the Grand Ohio claim than were title thereto to pass to the new United States, whose claim to that region Franklin would be expected by Congress to press at the peacemaking.[54] Such an impropriety on Franklin's part was compounded by his casual attitude about his carrying on a correspondence with a British subject in wartime while officially an American commissioner to France.

Franklin's critics denounced his penchant for nepotism, his padding the postmastership payroll with his relatives, the pressure he exercised on his fellow peace commissioners to have the unqualified Temple Franklin appointed as secretary to the Commission, and his willingness to have his grandnephew Jonathan Williams set up as a shipping agent at Nantes. Franklin's conduct of his office in France continued to supply grounds for ugly charges. What is significant is not that Franklin was guilty as charged but rather that the suspicion of conflict of interest would not die down despite his own disclaimer. At best, Franklin in France was untidy and careless in running his office.

What can be said about a statesman whose entourage numbered a secretary who was a spy in British pay, a maître d'hôtel who was a thief, and a grandson who was a playboy![55] Only a genius could surmount these irregularities and achieve a stunning triumph. And Franklin had genius.

Because of Franklin's prominence in the Revolutionary movement it is often forgotten that in the generation prior to the final break with England he was America's most notable imperial statesman, and that the zigzag course he was to pursue owed more to events than to logic. As early as 1751 he had proposed an intercolonial union to be established by voluntary action on the part of the colonies.[56] Three years later, at Albany, where he presented his grand design of continental union, he included therein a provision for having the plan imposed by parliamentary authority.[57] A thorough realist, Franklin by now saw no hope of achieving union through voluntary action of the colonies, and, significantly, every delegate to the Albany Congress save five voted in favor of that provision. Twenty years later a number of these very same men, chief of them Franklin himself, were to deny Parliament's authority either to tax or to legislate for the colonies.

Franklin's Plan of Union conferred executive power, including the veto, upon a royally appointed president general, as well as the power to make war and peace and Indian treaties with the advice and consent of the grand council. That body was to be chosen triennially by the assemblies of the colonies in numbers proportionate to the taxes paid into the general treasury. Conferring the power of election upon the assemblies rather than the more aristocratic and prerogative-minded governor's councils constituted a notable democratic innovation, as was his proposal for a central treasury for the united colonies and a union treasury for each colony.

Each intensely jealous of its own prerogatives, the colonial assemblies proved cool to the plan while the Privy Council was frigid. As Franklin remarked years later, "the Crown disapproved it as having too much weight in the democratic part of the constitution, and every assembly as having allowed too much to the prerogative; so it was totally rejected." In short, the thinking of the men who met at Albany in 1754 was too bold for that day. In evolving his Plan of Union Franklin had shown himself to be an imperial-minded thinker who placed the unity and effective administration of the English-speaking world above the rights and rivalries of the separate parts. Had Franklin's Plan of Union been put in operation it would very likely have obviated the necessity for any Parliamentary enactment of taxes for the military defense and administration of the colonies.

If Britain did not come up with a plan of union of her own soon enough to save her old empire, the Americans did not forget that momentous failure of statesmanship. Franklin's plan constituted the basic core of that federal system that came into effect with the First Continental Congress and, as proposed in modified form by Franklin in 1775, provided a scheme of confederation pointing toward national sovereignty. While the Articles of Confederation drew upon notions embodied in the Albany Plan, such as investing the federal government with authority over the West, it rejected Franklin's proposal to make representation in Congress proportional to population, a notion which found recognition in the federal Constitution. Writing in 1789, Franklin was justified in his retrospective judgment about his Albany Plan of Union. His was a reasonable speculation that had his plan been adopted "the different parts of the empire might still have remained in peace and union."[58]

Franklin's pride in the Empire survived his letdown in 1754. In April, 1761, he issued his famous Canada pamphlet, "The Interest of Great Britain," wherein he argued the case for a plan which would secure for Great Britain Canada and the trans-Appalachian West rather than the French West Indian islands, arguments upon which Lord Shelburne drew heavily in supporting the Preliminary Articles of Peace of 1762 that his sponsor Lord Bute had negotiated with France.[59]

For Franklin, 1765 may be considered the critical year of his political career. Thereafter he abandoned his role as imperial statesman and moved steadily on a course toward revolution. Some would make Franklin out as a conspirator motivated by personal pique,[60] and while one must concede that Franklin's reticence and deviousness endowed him with the ideal temperament for conspiracy and that his public humiliation at the hands of Crown officials provided him with all the motivation that most men would need, one must remember that, above all, Franklin was an empiricist. If one course would not work, he would try another. Thus, Franklin as agent for Pennsylvania's Assembly in London not only approved the Stamp Act in advance, but proposed many of the stamp collectors to the British government. To John Hughes, one of his unfortunate nominees who secured the unhappy job for his own province, Franklin counseled "coolness and steadiness," adding

> . . . a firm Loyalty to the Crown and faithful Adherence to the Government of this Nation, which it is the Safety as well as Honour of the Colonies to be connected with, will always be the wisest Course for you and I to take, whatever may be the Madness of the Populace or their blind Leaders, who can only bring themselves and Country into Trouble and draw on greater Burthens by Acts of rebellious Tendency.[61]

But Franklin was a fast learner. If the violence and virtual unanimity of the opposition in the colonies to the Stamp Act took him by surprise, Franklin quickly adjusted to the new realities. In an examination before the House of Commons in February, 1766, he made clear the depth of American opposition to the new tax, warned that the colonies would refuse to pay any future internal levy, and intimated that "in time" the colonists might move to the more radical position that Parliament had no right to levy external taxes upon them either.[62] Henceforth Franklin was the colonists' leading advocate abroad of their rights to self-government, a position grounded not only on his own eminence but on his agency of the four colonies of Pennsylvania, New Jersey, Massachusetts, and Georgia. If he now counseled peaceful protest, it was because he felt that violent confrontations would give the British government a pretext for increasing the military forces and placing the colonies under even more serious repression.[63] A permissive parent even by today's lax standards, Franklin drew an interesting analogy between governing a family and governing an empire. In one of his last nostalgic invocations of imperial greatness, Franklin wrote:

> Those men make a mighty Noise about the importance of keeping up our Authority over the Colonies. They govern and regulate too much. Like some unthinking Parents, who are every Moment exerting their Authority, in obliging their Children to make Bows, and interrupting the Course of their innocent Amusements, attending constantly to their own Prerogative, but forgetting Tenderness due to their Offspring. The true Act of governing the Colonies lies in a Nut-Shell. It is only letting them alone.[64]

A hostile contemporary, the Tory Peter Oliver, denounced Franklin as "the *instar omnium* of Rebellion" and the man who "set this whole Kingdom in a flame." This is a grotesque distortion of Franklin's role. While he was now on record opposing the whole Grenville-Townshend-North program as impractical and unrealistic, the fact is that his influence in government circles declined as his reputation in radical Whig intellectual circles and in the American colonies burgeoned. It must be remembered that, almost down to the outbreak of hostilities, he still clung to his post of absentee deputy postmaster general of the colonies, with all the perquisites thereto attached. All that dramatically changed in the years 1773–74, a final turning point in Franklin's political career.

Franklin had got his hands on a series of indiscreet letters written by Thomas Hutchinson and Andrew Oliver, the governor and lieutenant governor of Massachusetts Bay respectively, and addressed to Thomas Whately, a member of the Grenville and North ministries. The letters, which urged that the liberties of the province be restricted, were given to Franklin to show him that false advice from America went far toward explaining the obnoxious acts of the British government. Tongue in cheek, Franklin sent the letters on to Thomas Cushing, speaker of the Massachusetts House of Representatives, with an injunction that they were not to be copied or published but merely shown in the original to individuals in the province. But in June, 1773, the irrepressible Samuel Adams read the letters before a secret session of the House and later had the letters copied and printed.

The publication of the Hutchinson-Oliver letters, ostensibly against Franklin's wishes, caused an international scandal which for the moment did Franklin's reputation no good. Summoned before the Privy Council, he was excoriated by Solicitor General Alexander Wedderburn. The only way Franklin could have obtained the letters, Wedderburn charged, was by stealing them from the person who stole them, and, according to one account, he added, "I hope, my lords, you will mark and brand the man" who "has forfeited all the respect of societies and of men." Henceforth, he concluded, "Men will watch him with a jealous eye; they will hide their papers from him, and lock up their escritoires. He will henceforth esteem it a libel to be called a man of letters; *homo trium literarum!*" Of course, everyone in the audience knew Latin and recognized the three-lettered word Wedderburn referred to as "fur," or thief.[65]

Discounting Wedderburn's animosity, the solicitor general may have accurately captured the mental frame of mind of Franklin at this time when he remarked that "Dr. Franklin's mind may have been so possessed with the idea of a Great American Republic, that he may easily slide into the language of the minister of a foreign independent state," who, "just before the breaking out of war . . . may bribe a villain to steal or betray any state papers." There was one punishment the Crown could inflict upon its stalwart antagonist, and that was to strip him of his office as deputy postmaster general. That was done at once. Imperturbable as was his wont, Franklin remained silent throughout the entire castigation, but inwardly he seethed at both the humiliation and the monetary loss which the job, along with his now collapsed Vandalia scheme, would cost him. He never forgot the scorching rebuke. He himself had once revealingly remarked that he "never forgave contempt." "Costs me nothing to be civil to inferiors; a good deal to be submissive to superiors."[66] It is reported that on the occasion of the signing of the treaty of alliance with France he donned the suit of figured blue velvet that he had worn on that less triumphal occasion and, according to an unsubstantiated legend, wore it again at the signing of the Preliminary Peace Treaty by which Great Britain recognized the independence of the United States.[67]

Believing he could help best by aiding Pitt in his fruitless efforts at conciliation, Franklin stayed on in England for another year. On March 20, 1775, he sailed for America, convinced that England had lost her colonies forever.[68] On May 6, 1775, the day following his return to Philadelphia, he was chosen a member of the Second Continental Congress. There he would rekindle old associations and meet for the first time some of the younger patriots who were to lead the nation along the path to independence.

An apocryphal story is told of Franklin's journey from Nantes to Paris, to which he was to be dispatched by Congress. At one of the inns in which he stayed, he was informed that the Tory-minded Gibbon, the first volume of whose *History* had been published in the spring of that year, was also stopping. Franklin sent his compliments, requesting the pleasure of spending the evening with the historian. In answer he received a card stating that notwithstanding Gibbon's regard for the character of Dr. Franklin as a man and a philosopher, he could not reconcile it with his duty to his king to have any conversation with a rebellious subject. In reply Franklin wrote a note declaring that "though Mr. Gibbon's principles had compelled him to withhold the pleasure of his conversation, Dr. Franklin had still such a respect for the character of Mr. Gibbon, as a gentleman and a historian, that when, in the course of his writing a history of the *decline and fall* of empires, the *decline and fall* of the British Empire should come to be his subject, as he expects it soon would, Dr. Franklin would be happy to furnish him with ample materials which were in his possession."[69]

II

GEORGE WASHINGTON:

SURROGATE FATHER TO

A REVOLUTIONARY GENERATION

In portraiture and sculpture George Washington never smiled. When he did in real life, the artist, whether by accident or design, failed to record the memorable occasion for posterity. Washington himself recounts the story of his posing for a life mask by Joseph Wright, the young American artist who was first to sculpture the General from life. "With some reluctance" the subject consented. "He oiled my features over," the General recalled, "and, placing me flat upon my back upon a cot, proceeded to daub my face with the plaster. Whilst in this ludicrous attitude, Mrs. Washington entered the room, and seeing my face thus overspread with the plaster, involuntarily exclaimed. Her cry excited in me a disposition to smile, which gave my mouth a slight twist or compression of the lips that is now observable in the busts which Wright afterwards made."[1] The result was not a smiling Washington, but a General whose mouth was peculiarly constricted.

Other artists may have been better craftsmen, but their results were no less solemn. Consider the work of Charles Willson Peale, whose portrait of young Washington as an officer of the French and Indian War (Washington's earliest known) depicts the subject as stiff, serious, and unsmiling. Indeed, Washington confessed that the sittings found him in "so grave—so sullen a mood" that the artist would be hard put to it "in describing to the world what manner of man I am."[2] The result was little different on his canvas of the General in his brief moment of triumph at Princeton, noble carriage but solemn visage, or, again, in Peale's depiction of the rather tight-lipped, determined delegate to the Constitutional Convention. Or observe how Houdon's classic bust of a virile hero froze the features in an austere mold, while Gilbert Stuart, in painting his exceptionally stiff portrait, was additionally handicapped by the new set of ill-fitting false teeth which his subject wore.[3]

However much Washington might ordinarily control his impulses, we do know, for the General admitted it himself, that he did have "a disposition to smile." In his autobiography Charles Biddle tells of being with a friend at the theater and of the latter's seeing Washington, an inveterate playgoer, seated in one of the boxes and obviously enjoying the performance. The friend exclaimed, "See how he laughs; by the Lord, he must be a gentleman."[4] If George Washington smiled like a gentleman, it was because he had been taught in childhood to refrain from boisterous guffaws. As a boy he had to make a copy of a set of rules of civility that were observed by English gentlemen and were enjoined on those professing to be Virginia gentlemen. Among them was the injunction not to laugh at one's own jokes, and more specifically, "Laugh not aloud, not at all without occasion."[5] This was but one of a cluster of admonitions that the young Washington took with the utmost seriousness.

If the artists made the General seem grave, they also froze him in the classic image of patriot-statesman. Washington himself sensibly objected to Houdon's depicting him dressed as Cincinnatus in ancient toga and reminded Jefferson that Benjamin West had successfully defied convention by painting his subjects in contemporary dress,[6] but he could stop neither Congress from explicitly commissioning sculpture of him in the classic mode[7] nor the host of sculptors who followed Houdon. Typically, Canova, in a statue ruined by fire, dressed Washington in Roman armor, while Horatio Greenough, in a colossal statue of the General unveiled in front of the Capitol in 1858, presented Washington like Phidias's Zeus, seated on a carved throne, naked to the waist, the rest of his anatomy covered with drapery, and his feet shod with Roman sandals. Significantly, the observers were shocked not by the classic pose but by the nakedness. "Did anybody ever see Washington nude?" Nathaniel Hawthorne asked, and others would have agreed with him when he added, "He had no nakedness, but I imagine was born with his clothes on, and his hair powdered, and made a stately bow on his first appearance in the world."[8]

Aside from hagiographers and mythmakers like Parson Weems,

Washington's contemporaries had contributed immensely to the conception of him as proper and serious, if not priggish, truly a selfless patriot in the Greek or Roman mold. Fisher Ames, the Federalists' foremost orator, likened him to Epaminondas, the Theban patriot, whose nobility of character Plutarch eulogizes.[9] Washington himself seemed to prefer the roles of Cincinnatus, the virtuous Roman and sensible husbandman returned to the plow—in this case to his "villa," as he described Mount Vernon—or the younger Cato of Addison's play, which both Washington and his elder brother Lawrence were fond of quoting.[10] All this playacting and mythologizing fixed upon the public the notion of the Father of the Country as a man devoid of deep affection and passion, aloof and unapproachable, austere, correct, humorless, with impenetrable dignity and steely reserve. This largely fictional portrayal bears only partial resemblance to the man and far less to the youth who became the man.

It is hard to conceive of two personalities more disparate than Benjamin Franklin and George Washington. Yet both reacted in much the same way to the circumstances of their origin and family relationships, and both underwent two separate identity crises, one in adolescence, the other in maturity. In both cases the public interest proved the gainer. Just as Franklin rebelled against family pressures, so Washington sought to escape the cloying control of his mother and to carve out for himself a career of importance, one in which he would secure the recognition he felt his due. In youth, insecure, aggressive, striving, goaded by a sense of the inferiority of his station, Washington was headstrong, uninhibited, and quite self-centered. In short, he was not too lovable. He never grew an extra coating to protect his extremely thin skin and remained throughout his life hypersensitive to criticism and inclined to ascribe the worst motives to his critics. He did manage, though, to bridle his aggressiveness, to subordinate his self-interest to a cause larger than self, and to build a reputation for character and integrity. The hot temper remained, but in later years it was under steely control—almost but not always. His documented outbursts in maturity proved infrequent, but when they occurred they were volcanic in dimension. Above all, that instinct for command, that talent for leadership which he demonstrated as a youth, enlisted loyalty and support in the trying days of Revolution and nation building. Washington's great height, his impenetrable dignity, his faith in himself and his country, conferred on him a charismatic power that few others of this nation's leaders have enjoyed.

Nothing in the nineteenth-century hagiography of Washington explains how this young man, with an impulsive gesture, touched off a world war, why on the eve of his marriage he would dispatch an ardent profession of love to the flirtatious wife of his good friend and neighbor, how he incessantly and, to others, tediously sought the military preferment that was his due and sulked in his tent when he did not get it, and how indefatigable he was to satiate his land hunger and to respond to the deep speculative strain that dominated so many of his early moves.

Washington's deep insecurity as a youth, his early strident claims for recognition, and his hunger for affection were rooted in his origins and early family relationships. Like all Virginians of his day, his was an immigrant family. The first Washington to venture to America was George's great-grandfather John. Possessed with the passion for acreage which was to brand the family, John also felt a need to acquire wives, three in quick succession. The two last were sisters who came recommended to him when he sat as a justice of the peace. One was charged with keeping a bawdyhouse, the other with being the governor's whore, although the disposition of the defamatory charges cannot be determined.[11] George's grandfather raised the level of respectability of the family in his role as a lawyer, and on his death his second son, Augustine, was dispatched to England by his stepfather to be educated. Planter and businessman, with a keen interest in ironworks, this blond giant outlived his first wife and in 1731 married Mary Ball, a self-willed possessor of a tidy estate. Eleven months later George was born, the first of three children of this second marriage. In a sparsely settled region where Little Henry Creek ran into the Potomac, Augustine Washington built a farmhouse, on the present site of Mount Vernon.

When George was eleven his father died. To an admiring son this was a catastrophe, for he had no rapport whatsoever with his mother. Left in straitened circumstances by her husband's death, the semiliterate Mary Ball Washington showed little concern about her eldest born's education. Imperious, self-centered, possessive, grasping are a few of the adjectives that describe her, not only in her early days of widowhood but when she basked in the reflected glory of her famous son. Throughout his life Washington put up with his mother's bid for attention and money. The latter he regularly doled out to her, being scrupulous about entering all such sums in his account books; attention, if not affection, he seems to have bestowed more sparingly,[12] and he was even more niggardly in displaying his affections.

In striking out on an adventurous career remote from smothering home influences, Washington counted on the moral support and even conspiratorial help of his older half-brother Lawrence, whom he idolized, and the Fairfaxes, that distinguished aristocratic family that lived close by. What he did he did on his own, but along the route he found helping hands and friends at court.

George was perhaps six years old when he first met Lawrence, whose military career he followed with fascination. Lawrence served as a captain in the Virginia contingent that participated in Admiral Edward Vernon's amphibious campaign against New Granada (modern Colombia). Lawrence returned home with nothing but contempt for British generalship which had turned the expedition into a fiasco, but undiminished admiration for his admiral, after whom he named the estate he inherited from his father. In the four-way split of Augustine's property Washington received a minor share, Ferry Farm, which his mother clung to for thirty years, and some scattering lots—hardly enough to assure a prosperous future as a planter.

What to do with this fast-growing and restless adolescent was a family concern. Lawrence proposed to his stepmother that George be permitted to go to sea after having put out feelers about securing a midshipman's commission for him. Mary Washington, less than enthusiastic about the prospect, solicited advice from her half-brother Joseph in England. In a strongly worded reply Ball squelched the notion. "I think he had better be put apprentice to a tinker," he remarked, "for a common sailor before the mast has by no means the common liberty of the subject." Warming up to his theme, he added: "They will press him from a ship where he has fifty shillings a month and make him take three and twenty; and cut him and staple him and use him like a Negro, or rather, like a dog." Far better, Ball concluded, to be master of three hundred acres of land and three or four slaves than master of a ship.[13] And that spelled finis to George Washington's intentions toward the Royal Navy. One dare not speculate on what direction his life would have taken had he gone to sea as a midshipman, nor on the fate of the whole revolutionary struggle had Washington found himself on the king's side.

If Mary Washington wished to keep her gangling oldest son tied to her apron strings, it was not because she was especially concerned about his education. What education George received was of an indifferent sort, possibly at the hands of tutors whose names are unrecorded and more likely for a time at a little school in Fredericksburg. Washington quickly revealed a talent for ciphering, and a close application to mathematics laid the foundation for his early career as a surveyor. He diligently applied himself to his reading and writing exercises. His reading was always heavily utilitarian, weighted toward military treatises and books on agriculture, for example, but he was stirred by novels and especially dramatic literature, an enthusiasm which later turned him into an ardent theatergoer, and to some extent by history. His favorite historian was Catherine Macaulay. He applauded her liberal principles and entertained her in later years at Mount Vernon, after which the two carried on a correspondence. While not a speculative mind like Jefferson, Washington collected a library of some nine hundred volumes, which contained such representative British Enlightenment figures as Burgh and Hume.[14]

Not an avid reader himself, Washington believed that a continuing reading program was requisite for a soldier-statesman. When he took command of the Virginia Regiment he admonished his officers to read books on warfare,[15] and urged upon his major "in the strongest terms" the necessity of his qualifying himself by reading for the discharge of his duties as an officer. At the end of the Revolution he tactfully reminded Lafayette that great figures patronized great poets, implying thereby that the French officer might well pay more attention to literature.[16] Education transcended book learning, of course, but Washington considered "a knowledge of books" as "the basis upon which other knowledge is to be built."[17]

Washington worked at his writing all his life. His spelling and grammar improved to the point where he attained a proficiency equal to his contemporaries who had enjoyed more formal schooling. At times his diary entries could be spritely and colorful, but he lacked a reportorial sense and the kind of ego projection one associates with a John Adams, a born diarist. Too often, when great issues were in the air, Washington confined himself to routine weather and farm data. Nonetheless he developed into a powerful stylist. He drew equally upon the revolutionary rhetoric to which he was exposed, upon a moral fervor which expressed his special religiosity, and upon apt biblical metaphor to hammer home his message. The man who wished that "the most atrocious" speculators be hung "upon a gallows five times as high as the one prepared by Haman,"[18] who looked forward to the day "when every man could sit under his own vine and his figtree, and there shall be none to make him afraid,"[19] and could hail the West as "the *second land of promise*,"[20] appreciated the resources of his Bible. A talented phrase maker and equally gifted phrase snatcher, "to bigotry no sanction, to persecution no assistance,"[21] Washington felicitously rephrased Hamilton's "original Draft" of the Farewell Address and eschewed Hamilton's wordiness. Thus, Hamilton: "Why quit our own ground to stand upon foreign ground?" Washington: "Why quit our own to stand upon foreign ground?" Again Hamilton: "Permanent alliances, intimate connection with any part of the foreign world is to be avoided; so far, (I mean) as we are now at liberty to do it." Washington: "It is our true policy to steer clear of permanent alliances with any portion of the foreign world, so far, I mean, as we are now at liberty to do it."[22] How much better the corrected prose than the original.

Like so many other self-made men who moved ahead without the advantages of a formal or extensive education, Washington always put a high, perhaps overly high, estimate on its potentialities. He assumed the responsibility for the education of his stepchildren, and helped underwrite the schooling of a number of other relatives and the children of friends as well. Later in life he was to come out in favor of a national university and to provide a bequest to what became Washington and Lee University. As he stated in his will, it had been his "ardent wish to see a plan devised on a liberal scale which would have a tendency to spread systematic ideas through all parts of this rising Empire."[23] His Farewell Address urged promoting "as an object of primary importance, institutions for the general diffusion of knowledge," for, "in proportion as the structure of a government gives force to public opinion, it is essential that public opinion should be enlightened."[24]

Travel is presumed to broaden one's intellectual horizons, and Washington, indisputably the Founding Fathers' foremost traveler, whom every hostelry on the Atlantic seaboard would claim as an overnight guest, owed much of his liberation from Southern parochialism and his burgeoning continental outlook to this activity. Surprisingly, though, he left the continental colonies only on one occasion, and that was when as a lad of nineteen he accompanied his half-brother Lawrence to Barbados. Lawrence, wasting away with tuberculosis, was under the illusion that the semitropical climate of that island would bring about a cure. During the stay, as his diary reveals, Washington "was strongly attacked with the small Pox."[25] A bout of almost a month's duration left him with the telltale pockmarks, but conferred upon him an immunity to a disease that decimated the ranks of the Continental and British armies during the Revolution.

When Lawrence died in July, 1752, on his return to Virginia, Washington was not bereft of influential friends and counselors. Some nine years earlier his stepbrother had married Anne Fairfax, the daughter of Colonel William Fairfax, the cousin and agent of the prestigious proprietor of the Northern Neck, Thomas Fairfax, the sixth baron. Indeed, this Fairfax connection proved crucial to his initial occupation as a surveyor (at the age of fifteen Washington was already earning small fees in that activity); the colonel invited him to go with a party that was to survey Baron Fairfax's land west of the Blue Ridge. To the adventure-stricken Washington that first journey from home and initial contact with the frontier started a love affair with the West which lasted all his life. It fortified his sense of self-reliance and inspired some of his most colorful prose. His diary records a stay at a backwoods cabin where his bed was "nothing but a little Straw Matted together, without Sheets, or anything else, but only one thred bear blanket with double its Weight of Vermin, such as Lice, Fleas, etc." As soon as he could, he put on his clothes and lay down on the floor instead. The next day, at better lodgings, he reported, "We cleaned ourselves (to get rid of the game we had catched the night before)." Soon he encountered a party of thirty Indians, whooping it up with only one scalp among them, and on another occasion some German squatters, who appeared to him "as Ignorant a set of People as the Indians they would never speak English, but when spoken to they speak all Dutch."[26] If young Washington did not miss his lack of training in foreign languages, that deficiency would soon bring him immense embarrassment.[27] Hard upon his return Washington was appointed a surveyor of the newly created Culpeper County, and through Lawrence he became interested and then involved in the Ohio Company, organized to exploit Virginia's claims to the western country.

Lawrence's death left George one of his half-brother's executors,

and under the terms of the will he was to acquire Mount Vernon, succeeding to it on the death of the testator's daughter and wife in that
order, a double eventuality that young Washington must have thought
very remote indeed.[28] He also assumed Lawrence's duties as an adju-
tant of the colony, one of four such officers charged with training the
militia. What he learned and what he taught of the discipline of
military musters and drills might prove of dubious value in forest
warfare, but he himself was psychologically prepared for the risks of
combat. Thus, suddenly at the age of twenty Washington had a military career thrust upon him at a time when war was expected
momentarily. That war, in which Washington by a reckless action
involved two great powers in direct confrontation, plunged him into
a cluster of crises, both emotional and physical, stretching over a
period of some five years. In the course of it he would outgrow the
strong-willed youth kept within reach of an overprotective mother
and patronized by wealthy and influential neighbors. He was to dis-
close a talent for military heroics and command, a penchant for high-
level quarrels, and an unquenchable thirst for recognition. From this
experience he would emerge matured, chastened, and highly publicized.

It was to Washington that Lieutenant Governor Robert Dinwiddie
turned in 1753 to head a mission to warn the French not to encroach
upon the English (i.e., the Virginia) lands in the Ohio country and
to promote friendly relations with the Six Nations. Washington, with
a party of six frontiersmen, reached the forks of the Ohio in late
November, only to find that the French had withdrawn for the
winter. At Logstown on the Ohio he held a futile council with some
of the Six Nation chiefs, who were not inclined to put much stock in
English assurances when the French were already on the ground and
in force. The Indian confrontation elicited one of Washington's
special talents. Not given to public speaking, he seemed to have a gift
for Indian-style oratory, and his speeches might have won acclaim
from his long-departed great-grandfather, John, whom the Indians
had named Conoticarius, a fearsome compliment meaning "devourer
of villages." When Washington reached Venango, he found the
French officer in command unwilling or unauthorized to receive
Dinwiddie's message. Through winter-clogged swampland Washington trekked a hundred miles farther to reach Fort Le Boeuf, near the
shore of Lake Erie. There he was met by firm politeness. The French

declined to pull out. For Washington the return journey, accompanied by his guide Christopher Gist, proved to be one of the most dangerous and mettlesome in a military career crammed with perils. He was shot at by a prowling Indian, forced to push on by foot over frozen terrain when his horses gave out, almost drowned crossing the ice-choked Allegheny in an improvised raft, and then nearly froze to death from exposure. His report in the form of a "Journal" was printed by the governor and created a stir here and abroad.[29]

Determined not only to build a fort on the site Washington had proposed—the present Pittsburgh—but to see that it was properly reinforced, Dinwiddie commissioned Washington a lieutenant colonel and ordered him to march to the Forks. With 150 militiamen Washington headed north, only to learn that the French had beaten him to the punch, swooped down on the newly built fort, and captured it. Henceforth, Washington, with single-minded resolve, was determined to destroy Fort Duquesne, as the French had renamed it, and that refrain runs through his correspondence over the next four years. *Delenda est Carthago!* "The cause of all our troubles must first be removed."[30]

Aware of the inadequacy of his small force for a siege, Washington began to widen a trail at a point some forty miles from Fort Duquesne, confident that Dinwiddie would supply the needed troops to utilize it. He stopped at Great Meadows, Pennsylvania, long enough to construct an entrenched camp which he called Fort Necessity. Informed that a French party was nearby, Washington staged a surprise attack, in the course of which ten Frenchmen were killed, including the officer in charge, Sieur de Jumonville. The clash occurred on May 27, 1754, at a time when peace, not war, was the official state of affairs between England and France. Washington did not wait to determine the business of the French party, whose survivors later claimed to be that of a friendly "embassy." Jumonville's instructions were sufficiently ambiguous to raise doubts. He was to warn the English to get out of French territory while at the same time reconnoitering their positions. Deeming the French seizure of the fort at the Forks to constitute an act of war, Washington held the French to be the aggressors and looked upon Jumonville as being engaged in espionage. "In strict justice," he wrote Dinwiddie, "they ought to be hanged as spies of the worst sort."[31] Not only had Washington's party fired the first shots of the undeclared French and Indian War (with hostilities not formalized until two years later), but without hesitation Washington had chosen personally to lead the attack on the right wing, which was exposed and would receive the brunt of the enemy's fire, while he assigned the left to his senior captain, Adam Stephen, with the Indians taking up the rear. Washington's baptism under fire (the earlier Indian incident excepted) proved a heady experience. "I heard the bullets whistle," he wrote a relative, "and, believe me, there is something charming in the sound."[32] This letter, published in the *London Magazine,* elicited from George II the shrewd observation that young Washington would not consider the sound of bullets charming "if he had been used to hear many."[33] In later life a sobered Washington would have agreed with George II. To an acquaintance who asked him if it was true that he found charm in the whistling of bullets, he is reputed to have replied, "If I said so, it was when I was young."[34]

If Washington's easy victory led him to underestimate the enemy,[35] his headstrong course brought prompt retribution. The French, in reprisal for the capture of Jumonville's party, advanced in force. Washington fell back to Great Meadows, and after a ten-hour siege in a heavy downpour which flooded his entrenchments, he gave up the post. Apparently without realizing what he was admitting, Washington signed a water-soaked paper stating that Jumonville had been "assassinated." However inept his Dutch translator may have been, it is hard to believe anyone could have mistaken a word which is substantially the same in French and English. Washington's explanation, placing the blame on his interpreter,[36] though lame, was accepted by the governor and assembly, but in England his admission was denounced as "the most infamous a British subject ever put his hand to."[37]

Having been "soundly beaten," to use Washington's own phrase, and then having compounded his mistake by assuming the blame for touching off the war, the young colonel might have been expected to remove himself from the limelight until the notoriety had died down. After all, he had prejudiced the moral position of the English, had lost face with the Indians, and shown himself foolhardy in defending an indefensible post when he had the time to withdraw and await reinforcements.[38] Instead, Washington anticipated his critics by pouncing on minor grievances and giving himself the airs of martyrdom. On the eve of the siege of Fort Necessity he did have two complaints. He and his men were paid far less than the regular troops. Dinwiddie gave him the option of serving as a volunteer, presumably without pay. Washington chose instead to continue to accept the per diem stipend of 12s. 6d. But what especially rankled was the dispatching to him of reinforcements in the form of an "Independent Company," incorporated in the British establishment, with James Mackay, a well-born Scot, as captain. Mackay, who had seniority in years and military service, at once contended that *any* royal commission outranked *all* colonial ones, and that he, not Washington, would give the orders. Nor would the Scot order his men to work on the road, a task which Washington exacted of his own troops. That regulars would "march at their ease whilst our faithful soldiers are laboriously employed" constituted an indignity that so prideful a soldier as Washington, one so concerned with equal justice in the army, could not abide.[39] Somehow, confronted with the common peril, Mackay and Washington fought together in defense of Fort Necessity, and the British officer had the dubious honor of signing the capitulation first.

Worse news awaited Washington on his return to Williamsburg. He was no longer an asset to Governor Dinwiddie, and that worthy found a device guaranteed to remove Washington and his tedious complaints from the scene. Washington had constantly raised the issue of equivalent rank as between colonial and British officers, reminding the governor that "the rank of officers . . . to me, Sir, is much dearer than the pay."[40] In order to settle the matter, the Virginia Regiment was broken up into companies, with no officer higher than captain. Rather than accept demotion from colonel, Washington resigned his commission. Spurning the proposal that he keep his colonelcy as an honorary title, he tossed off an irate letter to an aide of Maryland's Governor Horatio Sharpe, newly appointed to head a frontier expedition and no admirer of Washington. "If you think me capable of holding a commission that has neither rank nor emolument annexed to it, you must entertain a very contemptible opinion of my weakness, and believe me to be more empty than the Commission itself."[41] Only a man who was emotionally unhinged by a combination of bitter wrangling, military defeat, and the final humiliation of demotion could have penned so gratuitously biting a letter. On the plus side the series of episodes contributed tremendously to Washington's education. He now had learned at first hand that the British imperial system demanded a degree of subordination from colonies and colonists alike, a lesson that was to be repeated enough times for Washington to learn it thoroughly.

Washington's letter of declination indicated his confused state of mind at leaving the service. "My inclinations are strongly bent to arms," he had confessed. What lay ahead for the retired warrior? His mother clearly could not be dislodged from Ferry Farm, and he of necessity looked to Mount Vernon. Lawrence's daughter had died, and the absent widow leased the estate to him. Would he now settle his mind toward farm management? Not when war on a bigger scale than ever before seemed imminent. Accordingly, when Major General Edward Braddock sailed into Virginia's waters heading an expedition to take Fort Duquesne, Washington dashed off a congratulatory letter which at the same time called attention to his own qualifications. The hint was acted upon. Braddock invited him to join his personal staff "by which all conveniences" of rank should be "obviated."[42] Washington stalled, was inclined to say yes, held off out of deference to his mother's wishes, and finally accepted on condition that he could join the expedition later at Wills Creek and leave when the main objective was obtained.[43] Since he had agreed to serve as a volunteer without pay, Washington made a point of letting his intimate friends, including John Robinson, speaker and colony treasurer, know the sacrifice he was making. "The sole motive wch invites me to the Field, is the laudable desire of servg. my Country; and not for the gratification of any lucrative ends; this I flatter will manifestly appear by my going a Volunteer, without expectation of reward, or prospect of attaining a Command."[44] Truly reputation was the supreme reward, but in establishing his own, Washington was fashioning a literary formula that he would utilize on a more famous occasion twenty years later. As regards forgoing all rewards, Washington must have acted impulsively, because he showed himself tenacious in getting his due. Since Speaker Robinson was a principal in one of the great embezzlements of American history, a complicity disclosed only after his death, he may have taken with a grain of salt his young friend's pious professions of disinterestedness.

Arriving at Wills Creek stockade, Washington was cordially welcomed and quickly appointed an aide-de-camp to General Braddock. The young Virginian was elated. "I am thereby freed from all commands but his, and give Orders to all, which must be implicitly obey'd." Nor would he make light of the potential contacts which might be "serviceable hereafter, if I can find it worth while pushing my fortune in the military way."[45] Ironically, among these new contacts were Lieutenant Colonel Thomas Gage, to be accused of cowardice for quitting the field and in a later day Washington's chief adversary in the siege of Boston,[46] and that stormy petrel, Lieutenant Charles Lee, a chief critic of the General on the Patriot side in the early years of the Revolution.

Out of the ashes of the Braddock disaster Washington almost miraculously emerged with his reputation greatly enhanced. The tragic events stamped themselves indelibly upon his memory. As he recalled the rout thirty years later—and his and other contemporary reports provide substantiation of his later recollection—the British vanguard had just crossed the Monongahela, with the rear still in the river when a mixed force of French, Canadians, and Indians let loose a barrage. The front lines fell into "irretrievable disorder." Mowed down minute by minute by an invisible enemy, unhinged by hair-raising Indian war whoops, the troops, despite the exhortations of their officers, fled in panic. Washington offered to head a force of provincials to "engage the enemy in their own way," but so sensible a plan was not adopted until it was too late. Braddock received a fatal wound, and Washington, the only aide to come out unscathed, had "one horse killed and two wounded under him. A ball through his hat, and several through his clothes." Placing Braddock in a small covered cart, Washington had him brought across the first ford of the Monongahela and by the general's order rode forward to halt the retreat and then to cover it, sending forward food and drink to the retreating and wounded men. His efforts "took up the whole night and part of the next Morning," and left him, worn out with dysentery, torn by anxiety, and still pushing himself to the final limits to discharge his remaining duties, including the burial of the general in an unmarked grave in the center of the road, with every trace of its location hidden. Looking back upon the nightmare, Washington spoke of the "shocking Scenes" of the night's march: "the dead,—the dying—the groans,—lamentation and crys along the Road of the wounded for help."[47] Back at Wills Creek, George was amused by reports of his own death and even an account of his dying words. He rushed off letters to his family to assure them that he was "in the land of the living by the miraculous care of Providence that protected me beyond all human expectation."[48]

If Washington's previous military experience had imbued him with deep dissatisfaction over the inferior role colonial officers were expected to play in contradistinction to officers holding British commissions, the disaster along the Monongahela earned his contempt for British regularly enlisted men, who, in Washington's words, "behaved with more cowardice than it is possible to conceive." Most of the casualties, he charged, came not from enemy fire, but "from our own cowardly English soldiers who gathered themselves into a body, contrary to orders, 10 or 12 deep, would then level, Fire, and shoot down the Men before them." That done, "they broke and run as Sheep pursued by dogs," and efforts to halt their flight met "with as much success as if we had attempted to have stop'd the wild Bears of the Mountains." As for the Virginia troops, they "behaved like men and died like soldiers."[49]

Braddock's defeat left the frontier more exposed than ever, and made Washington appear more indispensable than ever to fill the breach. In the fall of 1755 Dinwiddie appointed him colonel and commander in chief of all Virginia forces. The hardened veteran of twenty-three assumed the impossible task of defending a mountainous frontier some three hundred miles in extent with what amounted to a force of one man per mile. He would accept, he explained to his mother, "if the Command was press'd upon me by the gen[era]l voice of the Country." To refuse suitable terms would reflect "eternal dishonor" upon him and cause his mother "greater cause of uneasiness" than his going.[50] The truth of the matter was that Washington drove a hard bargain. The proffered terms included payment for past expenditures, 30s. a day salary, £100 a year expenses, and a 2 percent commission on all purchases he made, along with complete freedom to pick his own staff and field officers.[51]

In most respects this last stretch of service on the frontier proved the most galling and frustrating of Washington's career. Again he was confronted with the problem of British officers subordinate in rank who not only would not take his orders but began to give orders to him. Washington reacted with cold fury to the airs of Captain John Dagworthy, commander of a pocket army of thirty Marylanders holed up in Fort Cumberland. Appealing in vain for redress to Dinwiddie and Speaker Robinson, he set out in February, 1756, for Boston to place his case before Braddock's successor in command, Governor William Shirley, an imperial-minded statesman of vision whom the young warrior admired. Shirley dodged the major issue. With Solomonic wisdom he ruled that Dagworthy, now acting under a Maryland commission, was under Washington's orders,[52] but avoided the larger issue of the conflict of command between colonial and British officers. A cheerful card-playing companion, Shirley let Washington know that Governor Sharpe of Maryland, a Dagworthy sympathizer, was now in command of the entire Southern theater of operations. As the Virginia colonel's friend and fellow officer, Adam Stephen, summed it up, Washington had taken a big journey, his first extensive trip in fact to the big urban areas along the Atlantic seaboard, only to be treated in the way that one might "Expect from persons Conversant at the Courts of Princes."[53]

True, his situation was becoming increasingly untenable, but Washington would not quit his post while the frontier was ablaze, while he was a constant witness to scenes that tore at his heart. "The supplicating tears of the women and moving petitions from the men, melt me into such deadly sorrow," he avowed to Governor Dinwiddie, that he would willingly "sacrifice" his own life "to the butchering enemy" if he could contribute to the people's security. With mounting despair, he exclaimed: "If bleeding, dying! would glut their insatiate revenge, I would be a willing offering to savage fury, and die by inches to save a people!" If frontier warfare instilled in the young commander a loathing of the Indians, he was hardly ready to embrace the white population of the western settlements as less than craven, nor could he conceal his contempt of militiamen conscripted for service who vanished from the scene at the first sniff of danger.[54]

He went so far as to hang two hardened offenders on a gallows forty feet high as a warning to others so inclined. Toward his fellow officers, however, he was usually amiable and tolerant of minor peccadilloes such as card playing or bringing mistresses to camp. Where the girl complained of appeared to be someone else's white indentured servant, Washington seemed mollified so long as the master was reimbursed for the loss of his property rights.[55] If he boiled over when his officers were criticized by stay-at-homes, he was acutely sensitive to charges that he himself had chosen to live snugly in the comparative safety of Winchester and had to be ordered to move his headquarters to the front line at Fort Cumberland.[56]

Lord Loudoun, Shirley's successor as commander in chief, was less diplomatic than the Massachusetts governor, and best renowned for his utter mediocrity. When he showed little inclination to take Washington's military advice, the colonel went to Philadelphia to confront him in person. The trip was a fiasco. Washington was rudely snubbed, never invited to military conferences, and ushered in to Loudoun's presence merely to receive orders. When it was perfectly clear at last that Loudoun had no intention of transforming the Virginia Regiment into a royal establishment, as Washington had repeatedly urged, Washington in righteous indignation expostulated to Dinwiddie, *"We can't conceive that being Americans should deprive us of the benefits of British subjects."*[57] Thus, as early as 1757 Washington began to think of himself no longer as an Englishman, not exclusively as a Virginian, but in terms of budding continental nationalism and as an *American*. Perhaps, more significant, his remark anticipated the major line of embattled colonial ideologues from James Otis down to John Dickinson.

Washington's burgeoning Americanism could not conceal the Virginia-style ruffles peeking through his jacket sleeves. That ardent championing of Virginia interests would soon plunge him into the most stubborn and wrong-headed controversy of his entire career. The issue over the most suitable route for transporting men and supplies over the mountains toward Fort Duquesne was precipitated by that change of strategy and commanders which signalized William Pitt's dynamic direction of the British war effort in America. Loudoun was recalled, and for the campaign against Fort Duquesne, another Scotsman, Brigadier General John Forbes, was picked. Washington was placated by Pitt's order that colonial officers should command all regulars of inferior rank, but still hoped to be singled out by the new commander in a manner that would distinguish him "from the *common run* of provincial officers."[58] When it came to making decisions, however, Forbes proved to be his own man. After careful review Forbes was persuaded by Philadelphians to run the road from Rayston to Fort Duquesne, entirely through Pennsylvania. The new road had the advantage over the old Braddock Road of being not only forty miles shorter but of avoiding the perilous crossing of both the Youghiogheny and the Monongahela, which proved the undoing of

Braddock's forces. Still, Washington marshaled every argument on behalf of the Braddock Road, which, starting at Fort Cumberland, or Wills Creek, at the headwaters of the Potomac, and meandering west and northwest, joined Virginia to the western country. This route he had first explored back in 1753. How many long years before that must have seemed! Only an imputation of self-interest could explain how so knowledgeable an explorer as Washington could have persistently pressed for so wrong-headed a proposal.[59] Behind the desire for restoring and enlarging the old Braddock Road lay the concerns of a Virginia land company with claims to the West, a company for whom hope seemed to spring eternal and one which claimed Washington as a member.[60] It is harder still to understand why, when the decision was made against his choice, Washington should have been so emotional about the matter. The "New way to the Ohio," he exclaimed, meant "all is lost! All is lost by Heavens!"[61] Forbes regarded Washington's meddling and politicking on this issue as "Singularly Impertinent," and deemed his behavior "a shame for any officer to be Concerned in."[62] A loser for himself and for Virginia, the dispirited Washington, victimized at the time by dysentery and suffering from a pulmonary ailment which he feared might have been the tuberculosis which proved fatal to his stepbrother, now felt that all hope of glory had vanished. If the commanders were obvious "dupes," he put it down to "Pennsylvania Artifice,"[63] nor was he ever reconciled to the project.[64]

Washington sulked, but he did not quit. As Forbes advanced toward the frontier, a strong party of Virginians under Lieutenant Colonel Mercer was detached to reconnoiter the enemy. Hearing "hot firing" and fearing his troops were getting the worst of it, Washington went to their aid with a small volunteer force. Making their way through wooded terrain in twilight, Washington's men soon found themselves under fire, which they returned. Tragically, Virginians were firing on each other, mistaking their targets for the enemy. As Washington recalled it, he dashed "between two fires, knocking up with his sword the presented pieces." Before the senseless shooting stopped, fourteen men were killed, twenty-six wounded, and Washington had been in perhaps the most dangerous situation of his entire military career. Happily, the reconnaissance was fruitful, for evidence had been gathered that the French garrison was small and the Indian allies had pulled out.[65] On Christmas eve came news that the enemy had burned and abandoned the fort. Thus by anticlimax the great prize of the western frontier was secured without firing a shot.

Boiling over at the shabby way his Virginians had been treated in the campaign, filled with a sense of injustice both to his men and to himself, dimly conscious that his expertise had been shown faulty and his pushy tactics exasperating to his superiors, badly run down physically, Washington quit the service. The British army had lost him forever. He would not return to military life for seventeen years, and when he did it was in a situation in which he would not have to take orders from British regulars, nor from any other officer for that matter.

Washington's obnoxiously self-assertive behavior, combined with an emotional imbalance, evidenced some deep void in his private life which, perhaps, a wife and a home might fill, but not his mother. Her comment when George returned from the service was characteristic of her total concern with self. There had been "no end to my trouble while George was in the army, but he has now given it up," she remarked.[66] Hence, January 6, 1759, constituted a landmark in his life. On that day he married Martha Dandridge Custis. A rich widow, pretty, plump, and diminutive, senior to the groom by eight months, Martha brought to the marriage a substantial estate in land, slaves, and securities, instantly converting a minor planter into a major one. In addition, she brought along a son and daughter to whom the new stepfather was intensely devoted. "Patsy" Custis's death in 1773 was a terrible shock to Washington,[67] while the sobering problem of educating the nonstudious idler "Jackie" made the stepfather something of an expert in educational counseling as well as bringing home to him the generation gap as it then must have loomed to exasperated parents. An amiable wife and charming hostess who never tired of extending gracious hospitality to that endless stream of visitors who would turn Mount Vernon into a hostelry, Martha built into the marriage a certain serenity and stability which was reflected in Washington's life thereafter.

Washington was so obviously fond of children, had so deep a yearning for children and grandchildren of his own, that speculation has never ceased as to why he was childless. Since he was sexually potent he never seems to have accepted the probability of his own sterility.[68] But as he more and more assumed the father image which his country fixed upon him, he could not escape the personal fate of lacking offspring. With the assistance of Colonel David Humphreys, the literary wit, he would one day draft a presidential inaugural address, which he then discarded. Therein was an extraordinary personal revelation for a proposed state paper. "It will be recollected," Washington observed, "that the Divine Providence hath not seen fit that my blood should be transmitted or my name perpetuated by the endearing, though sometimes seducing, channel of immediate offspring. I have no child for whom I could wish to make a provision—no family to build in greatness upon my country's ruins."[69]

We do know he was a masculine man, attracted to women all his life. Stand-offish to men, he was ever the gallant to the ladies. As one woman remarked, "downright impudent sometimes—such impudence, Fanny, as you and I like."[70] Indubitably some of the barracks-room humor to which he was long exposed brushed off on him. His campmate, Captain Mercer, wrote him from Charleston about his disappointment with "the fair Ones," utterly lacking in "those enticing, heaving throbbing alluring plump breasts common with our Northern Belles," while a letter from a French-born officer included the tantalizing comment, "I imagine you By this time plung'd in the midst of Dellight heaven can afford, and enchanted By Charms even stranger to the Ciprian Dames."[71]

Washington enjoyed jokes about sex and at times made his own contribution to the subject. In later years he wrote of his former aide, Colonel Joseph Ward, as being "under the influence of vigorous passions." From military experience Ward should "have learnt how to distinguish between false alarms and a serious movement" and "like a prudent general" to have "reviewed his *strength,* his arms, and ammunition before he got .involved in an action." Otherwise, "let me advise him to make the *first* onset upon his fair del Toboso, with vigor, that the impression may be deep, if it cannot be lasting."[72] As a farmer, he could be expected to take a barnyard view of animal passion. Concerning a young jackass he received as a gift from the king of Spain, Washington remarked to Lafayette: "The Jack . . . in appearance is fine; but his late royal master, tho' past his grand climacteric, cannot be less moved by female allurements than he is; or when prompted, can proceed with more deliberation and majestic solemnity to the work of procreation." A jenny presented by the Marquis to Washington acted more responsively when bred to a stallion of Washington's friend Richard Sprigg, behaving, as the

General reported, "like a true female"; not "terrified at the disproportionate size of her paramour," she "renewed the conflict twice or thrice."[73] Perhaps another autobiographical revelation? Indeed, when he spoke about sex his words carried the authority of experience. As he remarked to a lady in 1783, "When once the Woman has tempted us and we have tasted the forbidden fruit, there is no such thing as checking our appetites, Whatever the consequence may be."[74]

Before carrying off Martha Custis to Mount Vernon in what must have been a whirlwind courtship, Washington, like any sensible young chap, seems to have looked over the field. Never a misogynist, he had been involved in a succession of flirtations, from his teenage crush on a still unidentified "low Land Beauty" to a few probes at serious courting that did not come off. Still others inspired callow poetry redolent of romantic ardor and were recorded in cryptic references found in his surveyor's record book.[75] At the age of twenty he twice proposed to Betsy Fauntleroy, the daughter of a prosperous Virginia burgess, only to be twice rejected.[76] Four years later, stopping over in New York en route to Boston, he set tongues wagging by squiring Mary Eliza Philipse around the town. That tall, slim, sensuous beauty, heiress to a great estate, would have been a capital match by the standards of the time, but Washington, who harbored notions of matrimony,[77] failed to press his suit, put off perhaps by the lady's imperious manner. It is a fair speculation that had George Washington successfully laid siege to one Philipse and John Jay not been turned down by two Delanceys, the Tory side might have been greatly strengthened by the addition of two principal colonial personages who were destined to become Founding Fathers.

In the case of Mary Eliza, Washington may well have beeen more interested in the pursuit than the capture, for at this very time he was head over heels in love with the wife of his good friend George William Fairfax. The only known portrait of that lady, less than flattering, captures none of the coquetry that must have proved so irresistible to a young frontier soldier, but suggests a slender, lithe, intense young matron with hidden depths. How long Washington harbored more than neighborly thoughts about her it is impossible to say, but we now know that the acquaintance went back more than a decade, when she came to Belvoir, the Fairfax mansion, as a bride of eighteen and he was an impressionable sixteen. Each time he came back from the wars he visited the Fairfaxes, and they corresponded when he returned to camp. Gradually his letters to Sally became more and more admiring and even indiscreet, and their tone obliged Sally to request that he desist from writing her directly.[78]

Not long after his engagement to Martha Custis, and some months before his marriage,[79] he wrote Sally, obviously overjoyed that their two-way correspondence had been resumed. Whether it was vanity or something deeper, Sally kept the letter. It was located a century ago, then vanished, only to surface in 1958, when the Houghton Library of Harvard University acquired it. One biographer of Washington argues that the lady "in the case" was Martha Custis, but the internal evidence makes clear that it was Sally Fairfax. Acknowledging with joy Sally's letter of September 1, Washington reveals how his feelings had overcome his discretion or sense of propriety:

> If you allow that any honour can be derived from my opposition to our present System of management you destroy the merit of it entirely in me by attributing my anxiety to the annimating prospect of possessing Mrs. Custis.—When—I need not name it.—guess yourself—Should not my own Honour and Country's welfare be the excitement? Tis true, I profess myself a Votary of Love—I acknowledge that a Lady is in the Case—and further I confess, that this Lady is known to you.—Yes Madam as well as she is to one who is too sensible of her Charms to deny the Power, whose Influence he feels and must ever Submit to. I feel the force of her amiable beauties in the recollection of a thousand tender passages that I could wish to obliterate, till I am bid to revive them—but experience alas! sadly reminds me how Impossible this is.—and evinces an Opinion which I have long entertained, that there is a Destiny, which has the Sovereign controul of our Actions—not to be resisted by the strongest efforts of Human Nature.—
>
> You have drawn me my dear Madam, or rather have I drawn myself into an honest confession of a Simple Fact—misconstrue not my meaning—'tis obvious—doubt in [it?] not, nor expose it,—the World has no business to know the object of my Love,—declared in this manner to—you when I want to conceal it—One thing above all things in this World I wish to know, and only one person of your Acquaintance can solve me that or guess my meaning.—but adieu to this, till happier times, if ever I shall see them.

The prospective bridegroom then confesses that he is in a "melancholy" mood.[80] Sally's reply has not been found, but that she did answer is clear from Washington's letter to her of two weeks later: "Do we still misunderstand the true meaning of each other's letters? I think it must appear so, tho' I would feign hope the contrary as I cannot speak plainer without, But I'll say no more, and leave you to guess the rest," and then inserting "most unalterably" before his conventional closing, "Your Most obedient and Obliged G. Washington."[81]

If Washington's marriage was indeed one of convenience, if when he took the nuptial vows he was in love with another woman who happened to be a neighbor, he clearly kept his feelings toward Sally under some control, and Sally, though she could be tantalizing, was also prudent, providing her husband with no real ground for suspicion. Both families exchanged frequent visits, and Washington remained an intimate friend of Sally's husband, faithful indeed to all the Fairfaxes even when, as King's sympathizers, they found it expedient to leave Virginia before the Revolution began. As Washington himself phrased it, he would not permit his friendship with them to suffer any "diminution from the difference in our political Sentiments."[82] After the war Washington visited the ruins of Belvoir, which had burned down. He wrote George William, "When I viewed them, when I considered that the happiest moments of my life had been spent there, when I could not trace a room in the house (now all rubbish) that did not bring to my mind the recollection of pleasing scenes, I was obliged to fly from them; and came home with painful sensations, and sorrowing for the contrast."[83] Finally, years after the death of her husband Sally received a note from ex-President Washington, near the close of his own life, in which he confessed to her that none of the great events of his career, "nor all of them together, have been able to eradicate from my mind the recollection of those happy moments, the happiest [of] my life, which I have enjoyed in your company."[84]

If this perhaps was pushing gallantry to extremes, and if it shows how as general and President he was still carrying the torch some forty years after his own marriage, one is not justified in drawing the inference that Washington was unhappily married. Never expecting from his marriage those moments of exquisite ecstasy which he recalled having shared with Sally Fairfax, Washington was content with the serenity and stability which Martha brought to his life, and the evidence suggests that each cleaved faithfully to the other. During the Revolutionary War years the enemy stooped to brazen falsification of intercepted letters and forgery of alleged documents to spread scandalous stories about Washington's love life, notably the tale of a liaison with a Tory girl from New Jersey named Mary Gibbons. That splenetic scandalmonger Major General Charles Lee added his bit, but none of these stories in fact could ever be substantiated, nor did they have the remotest ring of plausibility.[85]

Washington found no difficulty in making the adjustment to civilian life. Plantation management posed a real challenge, which he took up with enthusiasm, revealing unsuspected talents as agronomist and entrepreneur. He had remembered his visit to Barbados and the careful way in which the West Indian planters had handled manures. As he was later to write the great English agricultural expert Arthur Young, farming in Virginia was unscientific and haphazard. Tobacco and corn were planted year after year "without any dressing; till the land is exhausted; when it is turned out without being sown with grass-seeds, or any method taken to restore it; and another piece is ruined in the same manner."[86] In his region Washington pioneered crop rotation and the planting of grasses, sowing legumes, now called alfalfa, as early as 1760. He ordered the latest farm books from abroad and as much assorted grass seed as could be got.[87] His methods were disclosed by such careful journal entries as one for the spring of 1760, in which he recorded that he filled ten boxes with different kinds of soil and different kinds of manures, and planted three grains of wheat, three of oats, and three of barley in each. Recognizing that the soil of the area was not suited to producing anything better than average tobacco leaf, he dared to turn to wheat, stamping himself at once as a controversial innovator. Quickly discovering that the men who were handling his crop were making a profit by selling it to millers, he decided to become a miller himself and launched upon a program of making his plantation part industry, part farm. He also had an establishment for manufacturing woolen, cotton, and linen cloth, employing at least one white woman and five Negro girls, and producing by 1768 some 2,000 yards of such cloths; and, when President, he set up a distillery producing rye whiskey. He improved his meadowlands, again differing from his fellow planters in raising draft animals and sheep instead of cattle, hogs, and riding horses. His fascination with sheep stemmed from his interest in the wool rather than the mutton. Overlooking no chance for exploiting his property's resources, he kept a seine which was lowered in the Potomac whenever fish appeared to be running, thereby securing substantial catches of herring and shad.

No absentee proprietor or armchair manager, Washington could be seen in the fields, his coat off, sleeves rolled up, giving a hand to the work force when needed. He showed considerable ingenuity in improving a plow at hand and inventing a farm implement which was something like a seed drill. He treated his seed to prevent smut and experimented to protect his grain from rust and the Hessian fly.

Applying to farm management the mathematical outlook of the surveyor and the discipline of the soldier, Washington ran his work force with system and efficiency. He seems to have been an innovator of time-and-motion studies and, upon taking over personal management of his plantation, carefully calculated the number of feet of plank each of his carpenters ought to saw for a full day's work, "from Sun to Sun," noted how many cradlers were sufficient to keep the rest of his hands employed in harvesting wheat, and the advantage of splitting the cradlers up into at least three gangs to cut down stops and delays.[88]

Washington's military service had exposed him to the injustice of the British army's systematic discrimination against colonials. Likewise his operations as a producer of farm staples and an importer of British goods furnished him with a whole new set of grievances against the discrimination which he found implicit in the empire's trade and navigation program. His correspondence with the English firm of Robert Cary and Company constitutes a veritable roster of complaints. He had to pay higher freight rates than other shippers; his insurance premiums were excessive; his tobacco was damaged by being placed on a leaky vessel; and the prices the Cary firm obtained for his tobacco were in four out of five years higher in Virginia than in England. When the farm equipment he ordered from England arrived, it often proved defective. Goods, poorly packed, arrived broken or damaged, cloth came moth-eaten, seeds were ruined, and cargoes reached him too late to be used. "We often have Articles sent us," he informed his correspondent with thinly veiled sarcasm, "that could only have been used by our Forefathers in the days of yore. 'Tis a custom . . . with many Shop keepers and Tradesmen in London

when they know Goods are bespoke for Exportation to palm sometimes old, and sometimes very slight and indifferent Goods upon Us,
taking care at the same time to advance 10, 15, or perhaps 20 per cent
upon them." When ordering a spinet, he asked Cary as a personal
favor not to let it be known that it was being purchased for export,
but to give the seller the impression that it was for himself or an
English friend.[89] This background of distrust and resentment explains Washington's enthusiastic support for nonimportation. That
scheme involved retaliating against British merchants and factors
for what he and his fellow Virginians felt they had suffered at their
hands for much too long.

As a substantial slaveowner and purchaser of slaves, Washington,
at least prior to the Revolution, took the institution in stride. True, he
shared with George Mason the sponsorship of the Fairfax County
Resolves of 1774, which coupled a recommendation for a ban on
importing slaves into the continental colonies with a condemnation of
that trade as "wicked, cruel, and unnatural."[90] But it was the commerce in slaves, not the institution, which elicited his criticism.
Indeed, if slavery was a moral evil, this Virginia planter failed to
make a point of it. A concerned slaveowner, he was also a strict
disciplinarian, and in a few cases sold intransigent slaves to the West
Indies as a lesson to the rest. What aroused his fierce indignation was
the proclamation of Virginia's last royal governor, Lord Dunmore,
issued in November, 1775, declaring as free all indentured servants
and slaves who were willing and able to bear arms.[91] Excoriating
Dunmore as an "arch-traitor to the rights of humanity," who must be
"instantly crushed," Washington deplored what he felt might be the
snowball effect of his proclamation "if some expedient cannot be hit
upon to convince the slaves and servants of the impotency of his
design."[92] Fearing that free Negroes might flock to the British
colors, Washington licensed their enlistment in the Continental
army.[93] Pressed by Colonel John Laurens and his father Henry to
add blacks to the Southern army so badly in need of reinforcement,
Washington as late as 1779 expressed the view that the policy of
arming slaves was "a moot point unless the enemy set the example."[94]
Speaking as a planter rather than as a general, he remarked that it
would make those slaves who had not been recruited feel that they
were discriminated against. Washington had closed his eyes to enlistment of slaves in Rhode Island, but deferring to the deep-rooted

planter prejudice, especially in the Lower South, he walked a cautious line. When John Laurens confessed to him in 1782 that his "black project" to raise Negro soldiers in the Lower South was voted down in South Carolina and was likely to be defeated in Georgia as well, Washington comforted him by remarking that the "spirit of Freedom" and personal sacrifice at the start of the war had "long since subsided" and in its place "every selfish Passion" ruled. Regretfully, he added, "it is not the public, but the private Interest, which influences the generality of Mankind nor can the Americans any longer boast an exception."[95]

Prolonged exposure to the Northern climate of antislavery and frequent contact with black troops indubitably shaped Washington's later views of slavery. He was prepared to see that slaves who had enlisted under a promise of freedom would not be returned to their masters,[96] while at the same time he saw no inconsistency in making sure that the British did not, in violation of the Preliminary Peace Treaty, carry away any of his own slaves when they embarked from New York.[97] Within a few years he was known to favor the gradual emancipation of slaves "by legislative authority,"[98] a position that he clung to until the end of his life.[99] He never was converted to abolition, and found the Quaker propagandists an intolerable nuisance. As President he was obviously relieved when Congress decided that under the Constitution it could not interfere with the slave trade until 1808.[100] At his death he owned 124 slaves, another 153 (the dower Negroes) belonged to Martha, and some forty others were leased from a neighbor.[101] By his will Washington provided for the manumission of all slaves he held of his own right upon his wife's death. He felt it impracticable for the emancipation to take effect during Martha's life because of the intermarriage of his and the "dower Negroes." He also enjoined his heirs to provide for the basic needs of the aged and infirm and to bind out until they reached the age of twenty-five minors whose parents were either no longer living or could not care for them. Washington regarded this as a solemn obligation, adding, "I do, moreover, most pointedly, and most solemnly enjoin it upon my Executors hereafter named, or the Survivors of them, to see that *this* clause respecting Slaves, and every part thereof be religiously fulfilled at the Epoch at which it is directed to take place; without evasion, neglect or delay," adding as a prudent planter, "after the Crops which may then be on the ground are harvested." To his faithful black servant William Lee, who had been at Washington's side throughout the Revolution, he offered a choice of immediate freedom or his current status, with an annuity of thirty dollars for the rest of his life.[102]

Up to his armpits in wheat, clover, and manures, Washington had not forgotten the West. That region's future had seemed to him to be inextricably tied to the objectives of the Ohio Company, over which his stepbrother Lawrence had presided for a time.[103] Other stockholders included Governor Dinwiddie, influential Virginians, and prominent Englishmen. In 1749 the company had received a grant from the King of 200,000 acres on condition that it build a fort and settle one hundred families on the land within seven years.[104] As a first step the company set up a base of operations on Wills Creek. To men like Dinwiddie and the Washingtons there seemed to be an identity rather than any conflict of interests of King, Virginia, and the Ohio Company. Accordingly, when the French threatened the tract of land between the Youghiogheny and the Monongahela which the company had fixed upon for development, Dinwiddie dispatched Washington to warn them that they were trespassing and to build a fort on the forks of the Ohio to forestall them. Significantly, the French built their fort on the exact spot where the Ohio Company planned to build their own—the forks of the Ohio. That dedication to King, Virginia, and Ohio Company in which he had a stake had prompted Washington to press so persistently for the road northwest from Wills Creek, which the company had long wanted, rather than the more suitable road through Pennsylvania that Forbes chose.

Washington's involvements in the prospects of the Ohio Company served only to whet his appetite for western lands, wherein his speculations and operations exposed an acquisitive, even avaricious streak, an inclination to circumvent legal technicalities, and a bold vision about the future of what he was to call the "American Empire."

Aside from his speculative interest in the Ohio Company, Washington had an additional stake in the 200,000-acre bounty lands on the Ohio which Dinwiddie had promised the officers and men of the Virginia Regiment back in 1754. He bided his time, and in 1769 petitioned Lord Botetourt, Dinwiddie's successor, to make good on the pledge as quickly as possible before squatters settled on the land.[105] Although the governor and Council insisted that the entire bounty be located and surveyed before claims could be filed, Washington was prepared to assume the responsibility. Appointing a surveyor, he journeyed down the Ohio in the fall of 1770, accompanied by a fellow veteran, Dr. James Craik, covering well over two hundred miles from Fort Pitt to the Great Kanawha. At the junction of the two rivers he made surveys of the bottomlands and put up boundary markers. Ultimately he secured title to 30,000 acres, or fifteen percent, of these bounty lands for himself, "river low-grounds," he described them, "of the first quality."[106] Acting as manager for a small group of veterans, Washington had no hesitancy in awarding himself and Dr. Craik "the cream of the Country," as he later described it.[107] They were entitled to the choicest lands, he said defensively, because they had taken both the initiative and the risk of exploitation. Toward critics he exhibited his usual thin-skinned exterior, rebuking one veteran complainant for his "drunkenness, stupidity and sottishness," and adding his regret that he "ever engag'd in behalf of so ungrateful and dirty a fellow as you are."[108] In carving out for his own portion so extensive a stretch of bottomland, Washington had ignored an old Virginia statute which forbade tracts more than three times as long as they were deep.[109] He even persuaded Governor Dunmore to grant him a colonel's share of 5,000 acres of lands on the basis of still another land bounty offer which technically should not have applied to him because he resigned his commission some years before the Virginia Regiment was disbanded. That he knew his claim was dubious is apparent from a letter he wrote his brother Charles, asking him to buy up rights for him, but adding two cautions. First, he was to make sure that he dealt only with soldiers who had served to the end of the war. Second, he should suggest buying "in a joking way, rather than in earnest at first," and then to buy in his own name "for reasons I shall give you when we meet."[110]

Washington saw the Treaty of Paris of February, 1763, ending the war between France and Britain, as providing him with the opportunity to feed his grandiose western ambitions. According to that treaty France renounced all its claims to territory east of the Mississippi except for the town and island of New Orleans. Washington moved fast. Joining with his brother John Augustine, various members of the Lee clan, and other Virginians, he set up the Mississippi Company, which in September of that year petitioned the King for a twelve-year option on 2,500,000 acres of Crown land in an area both north and south of the Ohio River and including some of the best lands in what are the present states of Illinois, Indiana, Ohio, Kentucky, and Tennessee. The petitioners agreed to settle two hundred families in that time period unless prevented by "the savages" or a "foreign enemy."[111] Before they could formally present the petition to court, the Royal Proclamation of 1763 was issued, temporarily reserving lands west of the Alleghenies for the Indians.

How did a law-abiding subject of the Crown feel about the Proclamation? His private view was clear from his orders to his surveyor William Crawford to locate "valuable" lands in the prohibited area and stake them out. "I can never look upon that proclamation in any other light (but this I say between ourselves)," he wrote Crawford, "than as a temporary expedient to quiet the Minds of the Indians." It could be expected to "fall" in a few years, since the Indians would be consenting to occupation. "Any person, therefore who neglects the present opportunity of hunting out good Lands and in some measure marking and distinguishing them for their own (in order to keep others from settling them) will never regain it," Washington warned. He enjoined Crawford "to keep this whole matter a profound Secret" lest he be censured for having an opinion adverse to the King's proclamation, while at the same time alerting other speculators with clashing claims "before we could lay a proper foundation for success ourselves." Both these pitfalls Crawford could avoid if he could manage his operation "snugly" and "under the pretence of hunting other Game."[112] Again, when news came of the Privy Council Order of April 7, 1773, forbidding the issuance of warrants or patents for land grants beyond the Proclamation Line of 1763 without special order, Washington hastened to advertise his leaseholders in the Ohio Country.[113] Nothing would come of the Mississippi grant, nor of a rival claim of Pennsylvania speculators organized as a Grand Ohio Company and including Washington in their far more grandiose scheme for some twenty million acres in the same general area.

In short, the Washington record in acquiring undeveloped western lands, his shrewd wire pulling, and his less than scrupulous deception does lend credence to the uncharitable characterization of the General by a Tory minister who knew him well. The Reverend Bennet Allen referred to Washington as having been "avaritious under the most

specious appearance of disinterestedness, particularly eager in engrossing large tracts of land."[114]

There is a brighter side to the coin, however. Absorbed though
Washington may have been in acquiring pieces of real property, he
found natural obstacles to their settlement, obstacles such as mountains and swamps, a challenge to his capacities as surveyor and
engineer to surmount them. One such challenge was posed by the
Dismal Swamp, a vast area stretching between the lower James River
and Albemarle Sound. His conviction that the swamp could be
drained was confirmed by his exploration of the area in 1763, when
he paddled across its inundated lands. Heading a group of investors,
he secured an exclusive option to survey and patent up to 180,000
acres in the area. In order to get around the royal instructions restrict-
ing governors to grants of not more than one thousand acres to any
one person,[115] the petitioners padded their list with 138 dummies to
secure the desired acreage. Careful to see that the option was renewed,
Washington made at least seven trips to the area between 1763 and
1768, and kept getting back to the project throughout his lifetime.
Eventually, after his death, a canal was completed from Norfolk and
the swamp drained for about three-fourths of its 2,200 square miles,
but even before he died the investment had proved rewarding if only
for its valuable standing timber.[116]

As time passed, Washington was able to reconcile his national
outlook with the interests of his own state. Perhaps the best example
was his valiant effort to open a water route between the West and
Virginia's Tidewater by connecting the Potomac and Ohio rivers. An
enterprise of vision initiated before the canal-building craze, it was
doomed to lose out to a competitive route connecting the Hudson and
the Great Lakes.[117] In the course of feverish planning, Washington
quickly came to realize that only a federal government with effective
powers could carry out a large-scale interstate water transportation
system tying the trans-Appalachian region to the coastal states. To
this end he took the initiative in setting up the Mount Vernon Conference of 1785, the first link in the chain leading to the Constitutional Convention.

Washington's dream of becoming a great landed proprietor in the
West was never fully realized. Settlers were not excited about the
prospect of acquiring from him not freehold but leases which would

expire after "three lives."[118] His huge stake in the Mississippi and Grand Ohio companies vanished into thin air with the coming of the Revolution, his settlement on the Great Kanawha was destroyed, his mill at Perryopolis, Pennsylvania, went to rack, while squatters occupied the choicest sites of his western holdings. Still, at his death these properties constituted perhaps the greatest portion of his estate, exceeding in extent 49,000 acres.[119]

As a realist Washington could not have failed to observe how every phase of his career as soldier, planter, land speculator, and entrepreneur was enormously affected by political decisions. Save perhaps for Franklin, no colonial could rival Washington in the range of his contacts with royal officialdom. He had worked closely with Dinwiddie and was on terms of social intimacy with Fauquier and Dunmore. He exchanged hospitality with Governor Eden of Maryland. On a trip north he had dined with Governor Penn of Pennsylvania, Governor William Franklin of New Jersey, and his old comrade-in-arms General Gage, commander in chief in British America. With his activist temperament Washington could be expected to try to get to the heart of decisionmaking—politics. As early as 1755 his friends, apparently without his knowledge, ran him as a candidate for the burgesses from frontier Frederick. He ran a poor third then, lost again in 1757, but persisted. In 1758 his friends put up a vigorous campaign on his behalf, dispensing liquid "hospitality" in liberal portions on election day, as was the custom of the time. Even though Washington did not "show his face," as his friends had advised him to do, remaining on duty at Fort Cumberland, he won easily, and thereafter represented Fairfax instead of Frederick in the burgesses.[120]

Washington, who had found imperial decisions so constraining in his own private affairs, went along with his fellow burgesses in opposing the tax and trade measures of the Grenville ministry. He reacted first like a businessman rather than an ideologue. When, in 1764, Parliament forbade paper money emissions in Virginia, Washington found it difficult to collect what was owed him locally. He informed his British creditors that their opposition to paper money in Virginia was "ill-timed," predicting that it would "set the whole Country in Flames." For himself he remained open-minded, professing a willingness to "suspend his further opinion of the matter."[121] While not abandoning his concern with the economic impact of the ministry's tax measures, he saw the Stamp Act in Whig constitutional terms, deploring it privately as an "unconstitutional method of Taxation" while appearing to distinguish "the Speculative part of the Colonists" with tough-minded realists like himself. If, indeed, American liberties were being subverted, it was apparent to him that England was cutting off her own nose, since "whatsoever contributes to lessen our Importations must be hurtful to their Manufacturers." The eyes of the people were opened, Washington warned, and they would dispense with British luxuries and turn to their own manufactures.[122] Then and thereafter Washington lined up squarely behind nonimportation. In April, 1769, upon learning of the agreements entered into by merchants in Philadelphia and Annapolis not to import certain goods from England as long as the Townshend Acts were in force, he turned to his neighbor at Gunston Hall, the Whig theoretician George Mason, and asked him how to proceed. Some three weeks later Mason sent him a proposed Association, which borrowed heavily from that of Philadelphia but included a "few alterations" of his own which in the main Washington endorsed. Washington then persuaded the Assembly to adopt them, even though that defiant body had been forced to convene at Raleigh Tavern after Governor Botetourt had dissolved the Assembly for its intransigence.[123]

Washington had by now emerged as a full-fledged political activist and militant, one of that breed whom the hireling Samuel Johnson was soon to denounce as "zealots of anarchy, dictators of sedition," and "croakers of calamity."[124] Ridiculous as it might seem at first glance to lump a solid, property-conscious gentleman like George Washington in the same camp with a Patrick Henry and a Samuel Adams, it must be conceded that an increasingly incendiary rhetoric characterizes Washington's content and style henceforth. To appreciate the full extent of his ideological transformation one should compare his address to the troops during the French and Indian War with some of his letters written hardly a dozen years later. On the former occasion, in August of 1756, he had urged his troops "to show our willing obedience to the best of kings, and by a strict attachment to the royal commands, demonstrate the love and loyalty we bear to his sacred person."[125] Now, in the spring of 1769, he would denounce "our lordly Masters in Great Britain" who would "be satisfied with nothing less than the deprivation of American freedom." As Washington saw it, it was a time for action to "maintain the liberty which we have derived from our ancestors." But what would be the most appropriate tactics? He dismissed as ineffectual addresses to the King and petitions to Parliament. That left an armed confrontation or economic retaliation. At that date Washington preferred the latter. "Arms," he insisted, should be "the last resource." Rather should the colonies try "starving their Trade and manufactures." Realizing full well that the execution of nonimportation would be hampered by "clashing interests, and selfish designing men," he argued that the lead should be taken by "the Gentlemen" in Virginia's counties who should take pains "to explain matters to the people." This was to be a protest directed by the elite, but with a popular base of support, and calculated to deter "Factors from their importations." True, the British government might restrict colonial manufacturing, but in Washington's mind, the risk would be worth taking, especially since, in consideration of the heavy indebtedness of colonials to Great Britain, nonimportation would lift the whole country "from the distress it at present labours under." Prudence would dictate economy and even force the planters to start living within their means.[126] A principal sponsor of the agreement which was adopted in Williamsburg, Washington vowed to "adhere religiously to it," setting his artificers at Mount Vernon to redouble their spinning, weaving, and iron forging.[127]

Arms in one's own defense was one matter; destruction of property quite another. Washington, as a property owner and by his own lights a law-abiding one, could not bring himself to approve the Boston Tea Party. Neither would he disown Boston, but hailed its cause as "the cause of America" and, charging that the ministry was forging "the Shackles of Slavery" upon the colonists, warned that Americans would "never be tax'd without their own consent."[128] The government's punishment of Boston was hasty and the Intolerable Acts unjustified, he asserted. Before closing the port of Boston, the government, as Washington saw it, should have demanded payment for the tea destroyed and been refused. By the summer of '74 he was convinced of the existence of "a fixed and uniform plan to tax us," while excoriating General Gage's conduct in Boston as "more becoming a Turkish bashaw, than an English governor." Infatuated by his own rhetoric, he went so far as to castigate the military regime in Boston as "an unexampled testimony of the most despotic system

of tyranny, that ever was practiced in a free government." Respond-
ing to the heat of his own arguments, he decried any further petitions
to England. "Shall we, after this, whine and cry for relief, when we
have already tried it in vain? Or shall we supinely sit and see one
province after another fall a prey to despotism?"[129]

A prideful activist like George Washington could not be expected
to "supinely sit." When he sent off these comments to Byron Fairfax
he had just worked out in consultation with his house guest George
Mason the details of the Fairfax Resolves. That major state paper,
wherein Mason incorporated the gist of their conversations and
dressed them up in his own distinctive style,[130] declared the principle of government by consent of the governed to be "the most
important and valuable Part of the British Constitution." To ampu-
tate this part of the Constitution would, they insisted, lead to government's degenerating "either into an absolute and despotic monarchy,
or a tyrannical Aristocracy," with the consequent annihilation of the
people's freedom. Mason and Washington denied that the American
colonists were or could be from their situation represented in the
British Parliament and insisted that the legislative power in the colonies could be exercised only by their own provincial assemblies "or
parliaments" subject to the "Assent or Negative" of the Crown.
While conceding it to be the "duty" of the colonies to contribute in
proportion to their abilities to the necessary expenses of the empire
"of which We are a Part," they denied Parliament's right to tax the
colonies and denounced as extortion "without our consent" the claims
"lately assumed" by Parliament to legislate for the colonies. Not only
were such claims diametrically opposed to the "first principle" of the
Constitution, but they were "totally incompatible with the Privileges
of a free People, and the natural Rights of Mankind." The exercise
of such powers by the House of Commons would, if continued, establish "the most grievous and intollerable Species of Tyranny and
Oppression, that ever was inflicted upon Mankind." Denouncing both
the revenue measures and the recent Intolerable Acts, the Resolves
proposed that the colonies take common measures to redress grievances and offer to contribute toward compensating the East India
Company for the tea destroyed in Boston Harbor, while excoriating
that company as "the Tools and Instruments of Oppression," and
proposed a boycott on tea sold by the company and the sequestration
of tea cargoes until Parliament repealed the tea duty.

Significantly, Mason and Washington shared with such advanced political thinkers as Jefferson and James Wilson the constitutional doctrine which denied to Parliament legislative supremacy over the colonies. That same month Jefferson's *Summary View* would be published, followed some weeks later by Wilson's *Considerations on the Nature and Extent of the Legislative Authority of the British Parliament*. Beyond expounding constitutional theory, the Fairfax Resolves called upon the colonies to send deputies to a congress "to concert a general and uniform Plan for the Defence and Preservation of our common Rights," while continuing the connection and "dependence" of the colonies on Great Britain "under a just, lenient, permanent, and constitutional Form of Government." Not the first of many calls for an intercolonial congress, a movement initiated in Providence, Rhode Island, on May 17,[131] the Resolves lit a fire under the Southern political leadership and evidenced the formation of a united front transcending regional differences. The chief business for such a congress, Mason and Washington urged, was the promotion of a "solemn Covenant and Association" on nonimportation and nonexportation, noncooperating colonies or towns to be boycotted by the rest. This would mean forgoing luxuries and all extravagance, an example to be set by "Men of Fortune" in offering premiums for promoting manufactures. Finally, the two slaveowners proposed a ban on slave importations throughout the British mainland colonies and in language that smacks more of Mason than of Washington went on record "declaring our most earnest Wishes to see an entire Stop for ever put to such a wicked, cruel, and unnatural Trade."[132]

Washington did more than give his blessing to the Fairfax Resolves. He enthusiastically endorsed them both privately and publicly. He reminded one dissident that the right of taxation was an essential part of the English Constitution and that Parliament "hath no more right to put their hands into my pocket, without my consent, than I have to put my hands into yours for money."[133] He bludgeoned the Resolves through the July 18 meeting at Alexandria over which he presided. As the Fairfax delegate to the Convention in Williamsburg, he presented the Resolves to that body and, according to repute, made a fiery speech endorsing them, in which he declared: "I will raise 1000 Men, subsist them at my own Expense, and march myself at their Head for the Relief of Boston."[134] Finding Washington's enthusiasm contagious, the Convention adopted the resolves and won from John Adams, normally chary with compliments, a comment on the "prodigious" spirit of the people and a characterization of their resolves as "really grand."[135] As one of the Virginia delegates to the First Continental Congress in Philadelphia, Washington had the satisfaction of seeing the Fairfax Resolves serve as the essential basis for the Continental Association,[136] the initial mechanism of inter-colonial independent government. Still red hot for retaliation and putting Parliament down a notch or two, Washington, as did other Founding Fathers at the time, felt called upon to refute the charges that the colonies thirsted after independence. This was false, he charged, but he coupled his denial with a warning that blood would be shed if the ministry was determined to push matters to an extremity.[137]

So far as Washington was concerned, Lexington and Concord resolved the dilemma. He had now aligned himself clearly on the side of the radicals, considering further petitions as futile and demeaning. As he saw it, the colonies were contending not for a favor but a right. "The once happy and peaceful plains of America are either to be drenched with Blood, or Inhabited by slaves." A slaveowner himself, he could hardly be expected to accept the latter alternative without putting up a fight. The moral issue seemed clear. "Can a virtuous Man hesitate in his choice?"[138]

One virtuous man did not. Six years before the outbreak of hostilities he had remarked that "no man shou'd scruple, or hesitate a moment to use arms." Like other leading Patriots who moved from moderation to insurrection, he had scrupled. But now, the only delegate in military dress at the Second Continental Congress, his buff and blue uniform of the Fairfax militia gave to his intentions a high degree of visibility. The hint was not lost on the delegates. John and Samuel Adams realized that Washington's leadership would transform a local conflict into a continental struggle, and Washington himself was fully cognizant of the political factors entering into his appointment.[139] On June 15, 1775, he was elected "to command all the Continental forces raised or to be raised for the defense of American liberty."[140]

Forty-three years old at the time he assumed command, Washington looked every inch the general. Six feet three in his stocking feet, he towered over the Philadelphia assemblage or any other gathering for that matter. Broad-shouldered, flat-chested, and narrow-waisted, limbs sinewy and well proportioned, Washington seemed the model of physical fitness. Blue-gray eyes looked out penetratingly from a round, slightly pockmarked face. Reddish brown hair worn in a cue matched his fair, even florid, complexion. Before the war was over he was to wear reading glasses and have a few false teeth. Whether afoot or in the saddle, he was a graceful, athletic figure. As a personality he possessed a charismatic quality that inspired awe, even reverence, and often affection.

If in physical stamina Washington was equal to the demands that lay ahead, he was psychologically unprepared. In fact, the awesome challenge and responsibility of leading the ragged Continentals in a struggle against a great world power threw him into a second crisis of identity. Having now arrived at the top, he had to prove himself worthy of the trust. At the start he was riven by self-doubts, but not about the justice of his cause, which he embraced with religious zeal, first as a fight for survival, and then as a war for independence. Rather did he question his own capacity to perform the prodigies expected of him. If his early military moves were marked by vacillation and irresolution, he now possessed the saving grace of a healthy humility sadly lacking in his youth. On crucial matters he was ready to abide by the judgment of a Council of War. In his handling of Congress and his deference to their judgment, he showed himself a master politician, a character abundantly demonstrated in his later civilian career. Counting as he did on a vast reservoir of popular support, he was able to defuse criticism and face down his ambitious rivals.

Above all, he never temporized on the political goals of the war. When he learned that peace commissioners were on their way early in 1776 he urged the American people to stand firm. "I would not be deceived by artful declarations, nor specious pretences," he wrote.

I would tell them, that we had borne much, that we had long and ardently sought for reconciliation upon honorable terms, that it had been denied us, that all our attempts after peace had proved abortive, and had been grossly misrepresented, that we had done everything which could be expected from the best of subjects, and that the spirit of freedom beat too high in us to submit to slavery, and that, if nothing else could satisfy a tyrant and his diabolical ministry, we are determined to shake off all connextions with a state so unjust and un-natural. This I would tell them, not under covert, but in words as clear as the sun in its meridian brightness.[141]

He never wavered. When the British launched a second big peace offensive in 1778, Washington wrote: "Nothing short of Independence can possibly do."[142]

When Parliament closed the port of Boston, Washington wrote: "Ought we not . . . put our virtue and fortitude to the severest test?"[143] In his early career Washington had managed to combine selfish interest with public virtue. He was now concerned that he should from the start project an image of selfless patriotism and integrity. Accordingly, Washington, in accepting his appointment as commander, made a point of assuring Congress that "no pecuniary consideration could have tempted" him from taking the post "at the expense" of his "domestic ease and happiness." "I do not wish to make any proffit from it," he stipulated. "I will keep an exact Account of my expences. Those I doubt not they will discharge, and that is all I desire."[144] Washington had issued such self-denying ordinances before, but this time he meant it. At a time when it was standard practice for military officers to feather their own nests in the procurement of supplies, Washington never took the least personal advantage of his exceptional powers.[145] Meticulously entering his expenses by including secret service accounts, his totals were inflated by the large number of aides whose expenses he covered, and he justified including Martha Washington's trips to his encampment on the ground that throughout the war he had never taken a furlough to visit Mount Vernon. The figures are further inflated by the devaluation of Continental currency. If Washington did not make a profit on his expense account, it is clear from the items and the figures that he and his staff may have practiced austerity but not frugality.[146]

Indeed, expenses aside, Washington stood as a symbol of Revolutionary austerity. He advocated hunting down as "pests of society" the "most atrocious" and stringing them up.[147] He adopted a tough line toward the Tories—those "wretched creatures," he called them. He had no qualms about arresting royal governors if necessary,[148] or about hanging the plotter Thomas Hickey, involved in the conspiracy to turn New York over to the British and kidnap and perhaps assassinate the General.[149] When mutiny struck he had no hesitancy in ordering "the principal incendiaries executed on the spot" as a lesson to the rest.[150] Toward the talented Major John André, trapped in Benedict Arnold's treason plot, Washington refused to temper justice with mercy. "Remorseless," Washington was called, for he not only upheld the sentence of André to death as a spy, but insisted that the manner of André's death be by hanging, considered an ignominious end in those days.[151] The case of Captain Charles Asgill gives further insight into the severe side of Washington as a war leader. Washington had ordered that, in retaliation for the execution by the Tories of an American Patriot, Joshua Huddy, a British prisoner be selected by lot and put to death. The choice fell on young Asgill, one of the thousands of prisoners surrendered at Yorktown. The Asgill case quickly became an international cause célèbre. Only under great pressure did Washington stay the execution, and finally Congress, on the intervention of no less than Louis XVI, voted the British officer's release. Again, as in the André case, Washington had insisted on strict compliance with the laws of war. To his mind, the failure of the British commander, Sir Henry Clinton, to deliver up Huddy's murderers left him no alternative but retaliation.[152] He was equally prepared to retaliate against British prisoners when American prisoners were improperly treated.[153]

Nothing became Washington more than the style in which he left the war. A military man but never a militarist, he eschewed uncurbed adventurism and "untrammelled ambition,"[154] and in these respects was the very antithesis of his military aide Alexander Hamilton. If anyone doubted his devotion to republican institutions and his concern that the civil arm of the government must remain supreme over the military, they had merely to consider both his frequent comments on that score and his decisive actions.

Two incidents toward the close of the war reveal his very modest pretension for himself and his complete dedication to the civil republic. In the spring of 1782, with an enemy threat no longer imminent, the morale of the army was lowered by sterile inactivity and long payless periods. At this time Colonel Lewis Nicola of the Invalid Regiment proposed a plan to use the army to set up Washington as king, a notion which Nicola claimed was popular in camp. Washington, in a withering blast, denounced the scheme, banishing for good and all the phantom of monarchy.[155]

The threat of a military coup had not ended, however. Washington's moment of decision arrived when he was confronted with the proposals of the Newburgh conspirators. Late in 1782 a number of officers, headed by Major General Alexander McDougall, presented Congress with a petition from the Continental army encamped at Newburgh, New York. Fearing that Congress in its bankrupt condition would repudiate a promise that had been made in 1780 of half-pay pensions, the petitioners offered to accept a compromise in the form of a lump sum payment, coupling their petition with a warning that any further testing of the army's patience might have "fatal effects."[156] The nationalists led by Robert Morris viewed the army as providing new ammunition to support the impost that Congress had never been able to enact, owing to the stubbornness and self-interest of particular states. To the arch-nationalist Hamilton the army presented itself now as "a powerful engine."[157] As events unrolled, it appeared that the principal activists were prepared to use force to achieve their ends.[158] Knowing Washington's deference to Congress and his sense of moderation, the conspirators were even prepared to turn to Washington's old discredited rival, General Horatio Gates. In a circular letter that breathed fire and brimstone, they revealed their hand. Washington, realizing that the officers were about to plunge "themselves into a gulph of civil horror,"[159] acted swiftly. He confronted the officers in person, with Gates in the chair, and proceeded to denounce their summons to a meeting as "unmilitary" and "subversive of all order and discipline." Was it conceivable, he asked, that the army would turn its swords against Congress, plotting the ruin of both, by sowing the seeds of discord and separation "between military and civil?" "My God!" the General exclaimed. "What can this writer have in view, by recommending such measures? Can he be a friend to the army? Can he be a friend to this country? Rather is he not an insidious foe?"[160] Shaken by the confrontation, the officers spontaneously recoiled; some openly wept.[161] The plan was shattered; civilian control of the nation had been preserved. Jefferson paid the most fitting tribute to Washington's role when he observed that "the moderation and virtue of a single character has probably prevented this revolution from being closed as most others have been by a subversion of that liberty it was intended to establish."[162]

Washington had done more than secure independence in a victorious war. He had by this action preserved the republic.

III

JOHN ADAMS:
THE PURITAN AS
REVOLUTIONARY

"The History of our Revolution will be one continued Lye from one end to the other," Adams once ruefully predicted. "The essence of the whole will be *that Dr. Franklins electrical Rod, smote the Earth and out sprung General Washington."* Continued Adams: *"That Franklin electrified him with his rod—and thence forward these two conducted all the Policy, Negotiations, Legislatures and War."* In other words there would be no place left for John Adams. "Mausauleums, Statues, Monuments will never be erected to me," he bemoaned, "nor flattering orations spoken to transmit me to Posterity in brilliant Colours."[1]

In his own mind John Adams never played second fiddle to anyone, nor would he "willingly suffer blockheads," whom he had "a right to despise," elevated above him.[2] Nevertheless, in each of the great events with which he was associated—the organization of insurgency in Massachusetts, the declaring of independence, the winning of the peace—he seemed fated to be overshadowed by another participant. Obliged to seek refuge in England, Thomas Hutchinson, Massachusetts' Tory governor, had an audience with the King upon his arrival.

"I have heard of one Mr. Adams, but who is the other?" asked the King.

"He is a lawyer, Sir," Hutchinson replied.

"Brother to the other?"

"No, Sir, a relation."[3]

Thus, if George III could be pardoned for confusing John with his more notorious second cousin Samuel Adams, others, even less informed about America, could be expected to mix up the Adamses. In France it was the same story. When John Adams went abroad he had the mortification of having to tell the French that he was not *"le fameux Adams."* The French first thought him overmodest, a quality which could never fairly be charged to John. Since he was not the famous Adams, on second thought they felt he must be a "nobody," a "cypher," an impression which was at least in Adams's own mind accentuated by his weak French, poor figure, and unstylish dress.[4]

Adams cherished such incidents as long-remembered slights. A driven man, he was thirsty for fame and greedy for applause,[5] seemingly obsessed with his reputation and how it could be enhanced. As a young man he entered this self-questioning in his diary, almost in despair: "How shall I gain a reputation! How shall I spread an opinion of myself as a lawyer of distinguished genius, learning, and virtue!"[6] Combining enormous self-esteem with a very special talent for denigrating his rivals, he exploited his first-rate mind and abundant energy to propel himself forward on his career. Ever so often, however, he was beset by self-doubt and would succumb to a state of depression, exhibiting to the external world his peevish and fretful side. Inclined to dramatize his role, he alternately saw himself as a prime mover of events or a wretched failure whom greatness would always elude. As is not unusual with activists, his depression was wont to follow an outburst of prodigious energy, intellectual or physical. "My life has been a continued scaene of fatigue, vexation, labour and anxiety," he confessed in 1774 to his wife, who knew about it at first hand. "I have done the greatest business in the province. I have had the very richest clients in the province: yet I am poor in comparison with others." Of course, he was no money manager. He had spent his surplus income on books and a town house in Boston, leaving himself little cash to weather the several interruptions of his law practice stemming from pre-Revolutionary events. Aside from work on his farm or garden and occasional horseback rides, Adams had never learned to play. Eschewing cards, balls, assemblies, and concerts, he was relaxed and happiest with his family and a few close like-minded friends, with a book, or at the writing desk. In a typically morose mood he fancied himself a "recluse" on the way to becoming a "hermit." His Puritan conscience left him impervious even to the heady seductions of Paris, which he described to his wife with relish.[7] Fortunately for the history of the American Revolution these moods did not linger, because Adams possessed an inner resiliency that enabled him to bounce back from humiliation and frustration.

As a young teacher in Worcester, Adams expressed concern that he was fated "to live and die an ignorant, obscure fellow."[8] He once confessed to a friend: "I look so much like a small boy in my own eyes, with all my vanity, I cannot endure the sight of the picture."[9] Alfred Adler would have labeled Adams's strong feelings of insecurity and the overcompensatory drives such feelings aroused as an inferiority complex. In a revealing piece of self-diagnosis Adams spoke of "this passion for superiority," which he found to be the "predominating principle" of human nature at every stage of life.[10] But whatever the explanation of Adams's own insecurity, the effects were patently abrasive in his relationships with his peers. Perhaps the most infuriating quality of John Adams was his belief not only that he had a monopoly on truth but that everyone else required instruction from him. Thus, he could be insufferably didactic and deplorably indiscreet. Never having learned to conceal his feelings, he was outspoken to the point of being downright quarrelsome.

John Adams was constantly reminding himself of his shortcomings. At twenty-one years of age he entered this confession in his extraordinary diary:

> Oh! that I could wear out of my mind every mean and base affection, conquer my natural Pride and Self Conceit, expect no more defference from my fellows than I deserve, acquire that meekness, and humility, which are the sure marks and Characters of a great and generous Soul, and subdue every unworthy Passion and treat all men as I wish to be treated by all.[11]

But whether at twenty-one or at eighty-one, he seldom succeeded in curbing his vanity or in finding a charitable spot in his heart for those who outshone him or differed with him. His latter-day reconciliation with Thomas Jefferson is perhaps the notable exception.

Adams's huge bump of envy was aroused by the good fortune of foe and friend alike. He castigated the Hutchinsons and the Olivers for monopolizing the top offices in Massachusetts Bay,[12] but he had no qualms about seeking posts for his own family, friends, and in-laws.[13] He nominated Washington for the post of commander in chief, but as he watched Washington, mounted grandly on his horse, take his departure for his post, he confessed to his wife, "I, poor Creature, worn out with scribbling, for my Bread and my Liberty, low in Spirits and weak in Health, must leave others to wear the Lawrells which I have sown; others, to eat the Bread, which I have earned."[14] Later, joining Franklin in a diplomatic mission abroad, he was introduced everywhere as "le collègue de Monsieur Franklin," and constantly reminded that whether at court, among the intellectuals, or with the populace, Franklin, not Adams, was their favorite. Thus Adams found fault with Franklin's morals, with his habits of sloth and indolence, he distrusted Franklin's associates, and he was infuriated by his reticence, a quality which Adams never learned to acquire. No, he was not envious. As he wrote his friend James Warren, he would rather be infected with the French pox, "contracted here by an Acquaintance with the elegant Nymphs of the Boulevards," than with envy.[15]

Propelled by ambition, inflated with self-esteem, and bitten with envy, Adams could have been a morose and unlikable human being, but his correspondence reveals an entirely different side. He had a wonderful apprehension of sensuous experience, was extraordinarily responsive to the physical qualities of life, and possessed an ability to dramatize situations, a keen ear for dialogue and, surprisingly, a spontaneous and even irrepressible sense of humor founded in large measure on his recognition of the ridiculous. A compulsive writer like all the Founding Fathers, Adams proved to be the most uninhibited, the most amusing, as a diarist the most self-revealing, and as a correspondent the saltiest.

Writing came naturally to him, and as he confessed, it was one of his greatest pleasures.[16] There was an earthiness about his writing that would never be found in a Jefferson, a Jay, or a Madison, but which he shared with Franklin and Washington. He preferred plain speech and eschewed euphemism. This quality he captured at an early age, and it never eluded him. Along with his Puritan morality, it gave a distinct cast to his literary output. Let others "waste the bloom of life" at cards or billiards, the twenty-one-year-old schoolteacher exclaimed, let them get drunk, assault people, or debauch young girls. He derived more pleasure from contemplating the future careers of his pupils than changing places with some rich parasite. What prompted these reflections? As his diary tells us, a "fine gentleman" with "laced hat and wast coat" propositioned a girl on the street and asked her to come into the stable with him. "The Girl relucted a little, upon which he gave her 3 Guineas, and wished he might be damned if he did not have her in 3 months. Into the horse Stable they went. The 3 Guineas proved 3 farthings—and the Girl proves with Child, without a Friend upon Earth that will own her, or knowing the father of her 3 farthing Bastard."[17]

Not even Ben Franklin could pack as much barnyard philosophy into one brief paragraph as John Adams when the spirit moved him. In his writing one is confronted with an overpowering personality, who wielded a sledgehammer to drive home metaphor upon metaphor, so that even his redundancies impart a flavor of the intentionally absurd. None could surpass him in giving class overtones to the Revolutionary struggle. "The dons, the bashaws, the grandees, the patricians, the sachems, the nabobs, call them by what name you please, sigh, and groan, and fret, and sometimes stamp, and foam, and curse, but all in vain. The decree is gone forth, and it cannot be recalled, that a more equal liberty than has prevailed in other parts of this earth, must be established in America."[18] The "whole affair" of the peace commission to Lord Howe he described as "a buble, an ambuscade, a mere insidious manoeuvre, calculated only to decoy and deceive, and it is so gross, that they must have a wretched opinion of our generalship to suppose that we can fall into it."[19] Adams always made sure that his reader got the point.

Commenting retrospectively on his role in the American Revolution, John Adams declared, "I was borne along by an irresistible sense of duty."[20] This was unconscious tribute to that Puritan spirit which animated his entire career. An intense Puritan morality fortified Adams's fierce integrity and channeled him into Revolutionary politics. Puritanism was in his blood and in the air he breathed. He was born in Braintree (later Quincy), Massachusetts, on October 19, 1735. His forebears were thrifty, hard-working Puritans who had accumulated a few acres of land, a few head of cattle, some household goods. They had been town clerks, constables, selectmen. His father, John Adams, Sr., a farmer and local politician, had raised the social position of the family a notch by marrying Susanna Boylston, of a prominent Bay Colony family. The meetinghouse, at which the elder John served as deacon, was the focus of both spiritual and social activity, while the town meeting, that nursery of democratic politics, was managed in no small measure by John, Sr., a selectman for a number of years and a lieutenant in the town militia. As a youngster Adams enjoyed performing farm chores and, above all, hunting, but as an eldest son (his two brothers, Peter Boylston and Elihu, were each three years younger in turn), he was destined for the ministry, not the plow. Suffering local tutors whom he detested, John went to Harvard, already a famous school for the ministry, graduating a few months before his twentieth birthday.

In what was supposed to be an interlude before entering on his theological studies, John Adams taught school at Worcester. In that outpost of western civilization he soon had a surfeit of theological discourse, and at the end of a year's teaching decided he wanted to be a lawyer. For two years he combined schoolmastering and law studies under a local lawyer named James Putnam, a highly permissive, even neglectful, tutor. Then he left Worcester for good and all. As he related in his autobiography, he "panted for the want of the breezes from the sea." Admitted to the Boston bar in 1758, he decided to settle down in his ancestral town of Braintree. With clients at first widely spaced, he had time to translate Justinian by day and read Gilbert's *On Tenures* at night.

Somehow he managed time for much other reading, a good deal concerning Puritanism. He soon soaked himself in the history of the revolution of Cromwell's time, and references to John Milton and Puritan political and military figures of the "grand rebellion" come much more frequently in his writings than do those to Locke.[21] He called upon the memories of Hampden and Sidney, of Burnet and Hoadley, not only to deny that armed resistance "against usurpation and lawless violence" did not constitute "rebellion by the law of God or the land," but also to assert the superior virtues of republican government.[22] Rather than shrink from Cromwell, he eulogized him for establishing a government "infinitely more glorious and happy to the people than Charles's," though perhaps not "as free as he might and ought."[23] So encrusted were his writings with allusions to the Commonwealth days that the British in Boston were to call him "John the Roundhead."[24] His admiration extended even to late-sixteenth-century Dutch Calvinists, and he urged upon young John Quincy Adams a study of the means by which the United Provinces of the Netherlands "emancipated themselves from the domination of Spain."[25]

Adams drew upon his Puritan heritage for not only his stout

republicanism but his obsession with virtue. His fears that the American people would be addicted to corruption, idleness, and luxury, and his timid response to aesthetic experience, stemmed from that pervasive Puritan approach to life. Virtue to him meant more than an avoidance of sin. It dictated a concern for the welfare of society above self-centered aims.[26] It combined respect for industry with a sense of discipline. When, in 1776, Congress sought his advice for a seal, he proposed the figure of Hercules, representing the young republic, leaning on his club. On one side stood Virtue urging him to ascend the mountain; on the other, Sloth, "wantonly reclining on the ground, displaying the charms, both of her eloquence and person, to seduce him into vice." Fortunately, the idea did not seduce Congress, and even Adams admitted that the design was too cluttered for a seal or medal.[27]

Adams's proposal revealed a disdain for the arts when they did not serve a didactic or even propaganda role of which he approved. What disturbed him most about the arts was his conviction that from earliest times they had been "on the side of despotism and superstition."[28] He was perfectly prepared, however, to exploit the arts for the right cause as he saw it. While he was not inclined to meddle with history, he felt that "painting, sculpture, statuary, medalling, and poetry ought to assist in publishing to the world, and perpetuating to posterity, the horrid deeds of our enemies."[29]

To Adams the Puritan there was something decadent about the arts. He felt a sense of guilt when in opulent and magnificent surroundings. "I cannot help suspecting," he wrote pompously to his wife Abigail, "that the more elegance, the less virtue, in all times and countries."[30] Concerned as he always was about the "bewitching charms of luxury" and the "siren song of sloth," he asked Jefferson in a series of letters exchanged between the pair in their old age, "Will you tell me how to prevent luxury from producing effeminacy, intoxication, extravagance, vice and folly?"[31]

What kept Adams from being a dour Puritan stereotype was an irrepressible sense of humor, a readiness to recognize even the ridiculous side of himself. Urging in later years that a painting be made of the famous Writs of Assistance Case of 1761, at which he was a spectator and reporter, he remarked, "John was the youngest; he should be painted looking like a short thick archbishop of Canterbury, seated at the table with a pen in his hand."[32] Looking back on his early career as a Patriot, he described his service in the militia in the spring of 1770 thusly: "I had the honor to be summoned, in my turn, and attended at the State House with my musket and bayonet, my broadsword and cartridge-box, under the command of the famous Paddock. I know you will laugh at my military figure."[33] With time his figure became even more rounded, prompting partisan jesters to confer the honorific title "His Rotundity" upon him when he became Vice President.

Spontaneous humor bubbled to the surface of almost any page to which Adams put his pen. Take the account of his interview with the Tripolitan minister to London: "I took the Pipe with great Complacency, placed the Bowl upon the Carpet, for the Stem was fit for a Walking Cane, and I believe more than two Yards in length, and Smoked in aweful Pomp, reciprocating Whiff for Whiff, with his Excellency. . . . The two secretaries, appeared in Raptures and the superiour of them who speaks a few Words of French cryed out in Extacy, Monsieur votes êtes un Turk."[34]

The tradition of Puritan resistance to tyrannical government found expression in one of Adams's earliest writings, his "Dissertation on the Canon and the Feudal Law," written and published in 1765. This "speculation" came out of a discussion at a lawyers' club in Boston, known as the Sodality, to which Adams belonged. The discussion had focused on the irrelevancy of the English feudal system to American conditions. In Adams's preliminary draft he found an "infernal conspiracy," uniting the feudal and ecclesiastical systems, and culminating in the reign of the Stuarts. "Almost in despair" a resolution was formed "by a sensible people . . . to fly to the wilderness, for refuge from the temporal and spiritual principalities and powers, and plagues and scourges of their native country." Adams's admiration for these founding Puritans was unabashed. "I always consider the settlement of America with reverence and wonder—as the opening of a grand scene and design in Providence, for the illumination of the ignorant and the emancipation of the slavish part of mankind all over the earth,"[35] he confessed.

Adams allowed his admiration for the republican virtues of the Puritan founders to affect profoundly his retrospective view of the American Revolution. Time and again he was to say that the American Revolution "began as early as the first plantation of the country," or was "in the minds of the people" and effected in the fifteen years "before a drop of blood was drawn at Lexington." When Adams was in this mood, the war to him "was no part of the Revolution," only a consequence thereof. Independence of church and Parliament, in his mind, had been "a fixed principle" as far back as 1620, "as it was of Samuel Adams and Christopher Gadsden in 1776."[36] To Adams, the Puritans had effected the Revolution, and the Patriots merely secured its benefits.

Time and again John Adams captured much of the Hebraic spirit that animated the founding Puritans. He saw, and he was by no means alone in this,[37] a parallel between "the case of Israel" and that of America, between the conduct of Pharaoh and George III. If one pressed the parallel a little harder, one might conceivably find John Adams in Moses's role. Writing in May, 1776, to his wife, Adams remarked, "Is it not a saying of Moses, 'Who am I, that I should go in and out before this great people?' " Considering the events which had transpired and the still greater happenings to come, could he perhaps be pardoned for considering himself as being "instrumental in touching some springs, and turning some small wheels, which have had and will have such effect"? Reflecting upon his role, Adams was filled with a profound sense of "awe."[38] Possessing this admiration for the ancient Hebrews, Adams would later take up the cudgels against Voltaire for his scurrilous attacks upon the Jews and his "ribaldry against the Bible." Rather than portraying them "in such a contemptible light," Adams eulogized the Jews as "the most glorious nation that ever inhabited this earth" and "the most essential instrument for civilized nations."[39] This admiration, however, seemed reserved for the "People of the Book" rather than for his Jewish contemporaries.[40] It is significant that when Adams founded an academy in 1822, he recommended the inclusion in the curriculum not only of the classical languages but also of Hebrew—to teach at least the "rudiments" of the grammar and lexicon so that in later life students might "pursue the study to what extent they pleased."[41]

A Puritan, he found doctrinaire Calvinism too much for him in his youth and denied its orthodox tenets in his old age when he professed Unitarianism. Never bewitched by Roman Catholicism, he was no less unsympathetic to atheism, and on the occasion of the French Revolution was prompted to remark, "I know not what to make of a republic of thirty million atheists."[42] Still, he came to take a strong position in favor of separation of church and state, opposed legislation punishing those denying the divine authority of the Bible, and at the Massachusetts Convention of 1820 proposed equal protection of the laws for "all men, of all religions."[43]

As with most of the Founding Fathers, Adams was largely self-educated. In the main what he learned was from books. He was an omnivorous reader and, from early manhood, an indefatigable book collector. Ten years of law practice had given him sufficient competence to build a substantial library. What end would be answered by it? he asked in 1768. Perhaps fame, fortune, power; perhaps "the service of God, country, clients, fellow men." "Which of these lie nearest my heart?" Adams asked himself, but did not stop for an answer.[44]

By 1771 he was recklessly ordering from London "every book and pamphlet, of reputation, upon the subjects of law and government as soon as it comes out."[45] With such a blanket order to his booksellers, one can understand why three years later he had already spent £400 sterling, "an estate in books," and he never could curb this one extravagance. His library of some three thousand titles, excluding gifts he made and thefts he suffered, was perhaps half the number of items in the collection Jefferson sold to the Library of Congress in 1815, but it represented an extraordinary range of interests. Aside from the law books, he appears to have read many others at leisure long after acquisition. Thus the choice collection of the works of the eighteenth-century English and French philosophes was largely purchased during the years of his wartime mission to France, but most of the items seem to have been read during his vice-presidency and presidency, turned to again in retirement, and extensively annotated by him.[46]

Adams's attention to modern languages exemplifies his views on the importance of adult postgraduate self-education. Confronted with a mission abroad, he pursued his study of French assiduously, aiming to supplement his youthful knowledge of French grammar and vocabulary with skill in conversation.[47] Adams had a system of his own for mastering a foreign language in a year. That involved close contacts with people, visits to the law courts, to the Comédie, and to church, along with "diligent study" of grammars, dictionaries, "and reading of their best authors." Inspired by some after-dinner conviviality at L'Orient, Adams added this pithy observation: "There are two ways of learning French commonly recommended," he remarked. "Take a mistress and go to the comedy." When asked his opinion as to which system worked best, he conceded facetiously that "perhaps both would teach it soonest; to be sure, sooner than either."[48] That Adams never seemed to have surmounted his pedestrian gifts as a French conversationalist may well be laid to his choosing the latter method and not combining it with the former.

Although Adams was something of a prig and very much the grind, there was a gayer, sensuous, not entirely repressed side to his nature which proved especially responsive to the fair sex. As a young teenager he confessed to having idled a good part of each week "gallanting the girls," and only a timely interruption spared him from making a proposal which would have caught him up in the coils of matrimony with Hannah Quincy, an imperious coquette who would have been quite wrong for him.

Adams had been acquainted with Parson William Smith of neighboring Weymouth for some years, and although on first acquaintance a sixteen-year-old slip of a daughter named Abigail seemed anything but provocative, Adams soon found himself head over heels in love. Theirs was a long and thorny courtship. The Smiths, related to the blue-blooded Quincys, thought Adams beneath their daughter socially, and Abigail's mother interposed one obstacle after another even though it must have been embarrassingly obvious that the couple hungered for each other. On the occasion of one separation during the courtship, Abigail wrote her beloved, "All alone . . . a mere nun I assure you," and one whom John might easily lead "into temptation."[49] After courting Abigail for some years, Adams wrote her that a snowstorm which prevented his coming to Weymouth was probably a blessing in disguise, for he was prevented from flying to her like steel to a magnet, "and Aches, Aches, Agues and Repentance might be the Consequence of a Contact in present Circumstances."[50]

Their correspondence as "Lysander" and "Diana" revealed a hot-blooded romance, and set the mold for their lifelong relationship. Adams, who could always spare the time to tell others what was wrong with them, dispatched to Abigail an itemized list of her frailties, including her lack of talent as a singer, her tendency to hold hands of cards awkwardly, her failure to develop a "stately strutt," her crime of sitting cross-legged and hanging her head "like a bulrush." Knowing her man and appreciating that tact was never his strongest point, Abigail took it all in good humor. While freely acknowledging her deficiencies, she pointed out that "a gentleman has no business to concern himself about the leggs of a lady."[51] The truth, as she confessed, is that all her life she feared "more than any other person on earth" the disapproval of John Adams.

Abigail could not much longer be held in a state of enforced virginity. Having undergone the terrible rigors of smallpox inoculation and the discomforts of quarantine, and having put his law practice on a serious footing, Adams managed to overcome the family opposition to the match. They were married in October, 1764, the bride just under twenty on her wedding day, the groom some ten years her senior. She was to be her spouse's companion, co-warrior, and sustainer through fifty-four eventful years.

Abigail and John shared much in common: a Puritan background and temperament, an intellectual approach to life, a love of the classics, a didactic and at times even a pompous streak, an identity of political views clothed in identical political rhetoric. Though mentally a well-mated pair, physically they seemed disparate even to themselves. "My good man is so very fat that I am lean as a rale," Abigail bemoaned.[52] While she managed the household and the farm, and reared a brood of three sons and two daughters, John was off making a mark for himself, at the law courts, in Philadelphia on the business of Congress, and for a long spell beginning in 1778 abroad on diplomatic missions. Indeed, the early part of their marriage was marred by many long and painful separations. The theme of longing and lonesomeness runs like a refrain through Abigail's noncomplaining letters to her man. "How ardently I long for your return." "I want a companion a nights," she pleaded. "Many of them are wakefull and lonesome."[53] John's letters sustained her in her solitary, desolate, and even terrified moments. She once wrote him to Philadelphia about a letter of his penned at Princeton. "It really gave me such a flow of spirits that I was not composed eno' to sleep till one oclock."[54] Adams, in turn, was kept in suspense about the welfare of his wife and children when the mails were held up.[55]

Despite the unglamorous role that was to be her lot as the marriage partner of a political celebrity, Abigail was uncomplaining and heroic—even John conceded the latter point.[56] "Methinks I am like the poor widow in the Gosple, having given my mite, I sit down disconsolate," she once remarked.[57] When her husband and eldest son left for France in 1778, Abigail confided, "None know the struggle it has cost me."[58] Still she encouraged John in his political career, putting the public good above her own needs for his companionship and consortium. When John was first elected to the Massachusetts legislature, he told Abigail, with his customary exaggeration, that the post would be his ruin and the ruin of his family. As he recalled, she burst into tears and then exclaimed, "Well, I am willing in this cause to run all risks with you, and be ruined with you, if you are ruined." That was the kind of supportive role that Abigail played in the times her husband described as having "tried women's souls as well as men."[59] Unlike their mutual friend, James Warren's wife, who talked her husband out of accepting appointment to the bench of the Massachusetts Superior Court,[60] Abigail backed John all the way. She herself struggled with a growing household, managed a farm with hands scarce and dear, fought the housewife's daily battle with rampant inflation,[61] and still found time to give her spouse moral support and to be intellectually responsive.

Unlike Jefferson, who felt uncomfortable with intellectual women, Adams did not shy away from bluestockings. He married one to start with, encouraged her political speculations, and took good-naturedly her jibes at male superiority and governance. Abigail, a committed feminist, often baited her husband about the undue subordination of women at the law and in education. While you men in Congress are busily "emancipating all nations," she wrote to him in Philadelphia, you are insisting "upon retaining an absolute power over wives."[62] John gave the expected male answer. Men had "only the name of masters," he rejoined, and for them to renounce the title "would compleatly subject us to the despotism of the petticoat." To preserve this fiction, all men, from General Washington down, would have to fight, he threatened.[63] But Abigail's jibes carried a sting, and John felt obliged to justify a system of government resting, as it professed, upon the consent of the people, but which in fact excluded women from participation, along with the propertyless and minors. These groups were excluded quite arbitrarily, he conceded, but on a rule of convenience and in deference to Harrington's principle "that power always follows property." In addition, women's delicacy and suitability for household and child-rearing functions rendered them unfit for the public service or warfare.[64] Clearly Adams, who could be a persuasive advocate when he set his mind to it, had advanced a pretty lame argument to support the male establishment. His views as expressed to his wife and their mutual friend, the writer Mercy Otis Warren, reveal him to be a strong advocate of the education of women and fully cognizant of their potential in civic affairs.[65]

Rather than be stuck in an interior town teaching dull pupils or preaching to still duller adults and, as Adams himself put it, "sleep away" his "whole seventy years," he chose the law.[66] Entering this arena, he could anticipate no end of excitement, build a reputation, and get involved in causes that could capture his imagination. At the threshold of his career he asked himself, "Shall I look out for a Cause to Speak to, and exert all the Soul and all the Body I own, to cut a flash, strike amazement, to catch the Vulgar. In short shall I walk a lingering, heavy Pace, or shall I take one bold determined Leap."[67]

Admitted to practice the previous year, Adams had already taken the leap, but he was to find at the start a minimum of glamour and much drudgery in the service of his exacting mistress, many oafish clients with weak cases, the enforced company of "bauling lawyers, drunken squires, and impertinent and stingy clients."[68] Much of his time was consumed in bread-and-butter work—collecting debts, drawing wills, foreclosing mortgages, suing on marine insurance, protesting bills of exchange, and getting caught up in contests over thatch banks and clam diggings. Nonetheless, he did have more than his share of causes célèbres. If he was to become the busiest lawyer in the province, it was because he was willing not only to defend notorious smugglers and plead the causes of rich landed proprietors, but also to undertake the defense, not always successfully, of poor debtors, mental defectives, putative fathers facing bastardy charges, and persons who Adams felt were victims of "insane, wild" accusations of defamation.[69]

With a wonderful ear for dialogue, Adams recorded the evidence in some choice domestic relations actions, including a Negro's eyewitness testimony relating exactly how a New England fisherman was cuckolded by his wife's lodger while he was away in Newfoundland.[70] Adams seemed to relish recording the details of a scuffle outside a Boston barber shop. The defendant had accosted what presumably was a young, seductive girl, only to find out to his humiliation that the subject of his ardor was a man dressed in female clothes. In outrage the victim of the prank opened up a hole in the scalp of the plaintiff, allegedly the instigator of the impersonation.[71] Involved as counsel in a family feud on Martha's Vineyard, Adams commented retrospectively, "It was impossible for human sagacity to discover on which side justice lay."[72]

Adams's pleading book, Commonplace book, and fugitive papers along with the extant trial records reveal him as an attorney learned in both the common and the civil law. Although his arguments bristled with citations of English law reports, he was prepared to deviate from the English law when colonial practice and precedent so dictated. He and his associates at the bar were not afraid to simplify the ancient real property actions or to ignore the fictitious character of historic writs, and simplify pleading and practice encrusted with hallowed terminology and beset with countless traps for the unwary. In the absence of published law reports for the province, Adams and his colleagues were forced to turn to the English cases, thereby making an unwitting contribution to the large-scale reception of the common law in America.

Adams's dedication to the law gave his revolutionary zeal a very distinctive character. While lawyers traditionally have tended to view every inroad upon habit as a catastrophic revolution, here was a respected member of the bar who somehow managed to reconcile change with stability, to reform as well as to conserve. That there was an ambivalent character about Adams the lawyer, with his concern for order, precedent, security, and civil rights, and Adams the revolutionary, bent on overturning the political system, was manifest throughout his law practice. That ambivalence made it possible for him to defend Tory victims of mobbism, on the one hand, and Patriot merchants prosecuted for smuggling, on the other, to serve as counsel for the Crown in prosecuting those who cut down white pine trees marked with the King's broad arrow and to defend loggers charged with identical acts. He gave his talents unsparingly to a shipowner of Tory or neutralist coloration whose ship and cargo had, according to Adams's argument (to be upheld many years later on appeal to the United States Supreme Court), been wrongly seized by a New Hampshire Revolutionary privateer.[73] He even was retained by the owners of the tea ships to give legal advice just before "King" Hancock, Samuel Adams, and their Mohawk braves issued invitations to their famous tea party.[74] Yet on behalf of a renowned Patriot he assidu-

ously pursued a hated Tory printer for a debt and collected every last
farthing he could get his hands on.[75]

A stout defender of law and order and of the obligations of
contract, Adams condemned equally mobbist acts by overzealous
Patriots and the tactics of debtors who would exploit a Revolutionary
situation to avoid payment of their debts. In his defense of the British
soldiers at the Boston Massacre trial, Adams criticized the "unlawful
assembly" that crowded into King Street on March 5, 1770. In his
summation he said: Let us call a spade a spade. This was a mob.

> We have been entertained with a great variety of phrases, to avoid
> calling this sort of people a mob. Some call them shavers, some call
> them geniuses. The plain English is, gentlemen, most probably a
> motley rabble of saucy boys, negroes and mulattoes, Irish teagues and
> outlandish jack tarrs. And why we should scruple to call such a set of
> people a mob, I can't conceive, unless the name is too respectable for
> them.[76]

This may have been clever defense tactics, but it came from the
depths. On the very eve of his departure for the First Continental
Congress, when traveling the "eastern circuit" for the last time,
Adams saw mobbism's consequences and did not like what he saw. In
a letter to Abigail he described how in Scarborough, Maine, some dis-
gruntled neighbors of Richard King, a merchant, vented their dislike
of their creditor's political leanings by breaking into his house in the
middle of the night, rifling his papers, and terrifying his pregnant
wife, children, and servants. Expressing his detestation of "private
mobs," Adams, who took on King's suit for damages, called it "a
famous cause," and it certainly was a protracted one, as the mobbing
had occurred eight years earlier during the Stamp Act troubles.
Adams minced no words about his attitude toward unrestrained and
undisciplined mobbism. "These private mobs," he asserted, "I do and
will detest." Adams differentiated between private and public mobbism. "Commotions" of the latter variety and in defense of the
Constitution could be justified in his opinion "only when funda-
mentals are invaded," nor then unless for absolute necessity and with
great caution. For tarrings and featherings and housebreaking "by
rude and insolent rabbles in resentment for private wrongs or in
pursuit of private prejudices and passions" must be discountenanced,
he sternly declared. Whether as Patriot lawyer shocked by his

wretched client's plight at the hands of a mob, as a diplomat abroad chagrined to learn of Shays's insurgency in his home state, or as President obliged to deal sternly with tax rioters, Adams remained consistent to the last in his adherence to the rule of law.[77]

In his autobiography Adams recorded in 1775 "an event of the most trifling nature in appearance, and fit only to excite laughter in other times." But in this time of political crisis, it made Adams profoundly depressed. A quondam client of his, described as "a common horse jockey," came up to Adams in court and greeted him thusly: "Oh! Mr. Adams, what great things have you and your colleagues done for us! We can never be gratefull enough to you. There are no Courts of Justice now in this Province, and I hope there never will be another!" Adams recoiled in righteous indignation. "Is this the object for which I have been contending?" he asked himself. How many people in America shared the horse jockey's sentiments? Perhaps, for all Adams knew, "half the nation are debtors if not more." He concluded gloomily, "If the power of the country should get into such hands, and there is danger that it will, to what purpose have we sacrificed our time, health and every thing else?"[78]

Adams never disavowed these principles. When, during the preliminary peace negotiations in Paris in 1782, the issue of debts owing to British creditors came up, Adams, without advance consultation with either of his colleagues, Franklin or Jay, blurted out, "I have no notion of cheating anybody!" That settled it, and Adams persuaded his colleagues to accept a formula under which Congress would recommend that the states open their courts of justice for the recovery of all just debts. Creditors would still find insuperable obstacles to collecting moneys owing them in America, but that was no fault of John Adams.[79]

Adams enjoyed playing a dual role at the bar. Always the advocate, he fancied himself on occasion an instrument of political justice. Only consider the contrasting parts he played in defending John Hancock against smuggling charges and in serving as counsel to the prisoners tried for the Boston Massacre. In the first case he was defending a zealous Patriot from a vexatious and politically inspired prosecution at the hands of the Crown; in the other, hated "lobsterbacks" who had offended his town and people.

Hancock was not only a leading merchant, but a Boston selectman and representative to the General Court. He had bullied, boasted, and snubbed the customs commissioners, who were determined to even the score. On the ground that he had connived at the alleged smuggling of wine from his sloop *Liberty,* the customs officers seized the ship and, in the face of a defiant mob, towed her out into the harbor under the guns of a British frigate. The vice-admiralty court declared the ship forfeit, and she served until 1769 as a revenue cutter until the mob seized her and burned her in Newport. Not satisfied with the forfeiture, the customs commissioners now prosecuted Hancock for treble damages of the value of the smuggled cargo, as authorized by the revenue laws. Although Adams complained that the case was "a painful drudgery," his conduct as Hancock's counsel constitutes a classic example of his talent for lifting a sordid argument over casks of wine or barrels of oil onto the plane of fundamental rights. In insisting that a penal statute conflicting with basic principles should be construed in every instance in favor of the subject, Adams manipulated political theory within a legal framework. He managed to reach two different audiences—the courtroom in which his arguments were presented and the public forum in which broader constitutional issues were debated. Finally, the Crown took the road of political expediency and dropped the case.[80]

The courage of John Adams and Josiah Quincy, Jr., in undertaking the unpopular defense of Captain Preston and the British soldiers charged with culpability for the Boston Massacre of March 5, 1773, seems an imperishable part of the mythology of the Revolution. More than three decades later Adams recorded that, when asked to assume the defense of Captain Preston, he answered unhesitatingly, "Counsel ought to be the very last thing that an accused person should want in a free country." When Josiah Quincy's father taunted him for taking the case ("Great God! Is it possible?"), the son replied that his critics should have "spared a little reflection on the nature of an attorney's oath and duty." That is the tradition, but the actual role of the Patriot trial lawyers was more subtle and less forthright than these historic remarks might indicate. Recent researches have disclosed a number of new facts about the conduct of the defense.[81]

First of all, despite the efforts of Samuel Adams and other hotheads to press for an immediate trial, John Adams and others for the defense, doubtless in cahoots with the Tory-minded lieutenant governor, Thomas Hutchinson, saw to it that the trial was postponed until some of the excitement had died down. Second, the defense made the

crucial but sensible decision to sever the trials in order to avoid the
risk of mass convictions. Captain Preston was tried first. His acquittal
made the trial of the soldiers anticlimactic.

It may destroy some illusions, but the evidence now in shows that
the jury was packed, that five of the twelve jurors were later Loyalist
exiles and were doing business with the British army well before the
trial. Surely Adams knew this, if he had not connived at it. Hero or
no, in going to the defense of a hated British officer, Adams prudently toned down the slashing cross-examination that his co-counsel
Quincy had planned because he did not want the conduct of the town
of Boston to be blackened, and some pointed questions to Crown
witnesses would have placed the Boston town fathers in an embarrassing posture. As a Patriot he was less than anxious to bring out on
cross-examination evidence showing that the expulsion of the British
troops from the town of Boston was a plan concocted by the towns-
people. Indeed, his relatively gentle treatment of Crown witnesses
raises a nice ethical question. How far should a lawyer permit his
political ties and loyalties to color his judgment of the most effective
means of conducting a trial in his client's best interest? In this case
John Adams enjoyed the best of two worlds. He added luster to his
rising reputation as a lawyer by securing his client's acquittal, but he
prudently avoided damaging his standing as a Patriot. Had the case
gone the other way, Adams might have been justifiably the subject of
serious censure.

Finally, and without seeking to detract from Adams's defense
tactics, the prosecution, as is so often the case, was managed incompe-
tently, and the defense shone brilliantly by comparison. The town of
Boston had previously gathered depositions to show that the soldiers
had been consistently provocative, had abused the populace time on
end, and had quarreled with journeymen and apprentices in their
efforts to get civilian jobs in their spare time. Only a third of the
ninety-five deponents actually testified at the ensuing trials, and the
prosecution signally failed to elicit much pertinent testimony bearing
on motive and provocation.[82] Although Adams pulled his punches on
cross-examination, his closing arguments expertly marshaled the law
("Self-defense," paraphrasing Blackstone for the jurors, "is the primary canon of the law of nature") and mercilessly dissected the evidence for the prosecution. He managed to turn the Crown witnesses'
words around. He tactfully refrained from accusing one impressive

prosecution witness of perjury and merely suggested that he must have been mistaken. "It must be this," Adams told the jury. "The Captain said 'Fire by no means' when the people spoke to him, but the witness heard only 'Fire.' "

What John Adams participated in was in effect a show trial. With a jury safely packed and the defendants confident, if convicted, of securing reprieves or pardons, Adams must in conscience have been embarrassed about the whole affair. In 1772 he declined to give the annual Boston Massacre Day oration, the big propaganda occasion for the Patriots. "I should only expose myself to the lash of ignorant and malicious tongues on both sides of the question," he felt.[83] One can understand why, years later, when Captain Preston and Adams met on a London street, they passed without speaking.[84]

If the law made John Adams famous, it also turned him into a revolutionary while providing him at the same time with that grounding in the business of government so essential to successful revolutionaries. He had been practicing barely a little more than two years, and with a handful of cases to show for his efforts at that, when he was first caught up in the great constitutional struggle which ended in separation from England. The year was 1761; the occasion, the Writs of Assistance case, a dress rehearsal for the contests over revenue jurisdiction and revenue duties precipitated by the enforcement of old laws and the enactment of a batch of new ones. To plug up the wholesale violations of the Acts of Trade which the French and Indian War had made notorious, the Crown officials in Boston sought general search warrants, permitting them to enter any house by day and search for smuggled goods without special application to a court. These writs of assistance, as they were called, had been issued in the course of the war, but with the accession of George III to the throne in 1760 it was necessary for the customs officers to procure new ones. Their issuance was now contested by a group of Boston merchants, who engaged James Otis, Jr., and Oxenbridge Thacher as their counsel. Otis, fashioning a new law of privacy, argued that a general writ violated the fundamental principle that a man's house is his castle. He proceeded to lay the basis for a path-breaking principle of American constitutional law by urging that a statute violative of fundamental law was void. Otis's eloquent warning anticipated the midnight visitation by totalitarian police which would terrify a later era less sensitive than his was to individual freedom.

Years later John Adams remarked that on the day that Otis expounded his memorable argument against the writs, "the Child Independence was born."[85] Granted the oral argument delivered before a relatively small audience did not have the inspirational effect on the public that Adams retrospectively attributed to it, it would seem that young Adams himself was from that instant inspired with a zeal for the Patriot cause, a prudent zeal, to be sure. Adams hastily took down notes of the trial, and then published a more elaborate abstract of the argument which was circulated among the members of the bar and published more than a decade later in a Boston newspaper.[86] It is in Adams's more elaborate abstract that he seems to have combined his notes and impressions of the larger questions, to have pruned legal complexities and added fervor. The result was an important piece of political propaganda, the first from a master hand.

Neither Otis's eloquence nor Adams's literary skill prevailed at that time, for the court, after some delay to find out about the practice in England, went on to issue the writs. The controversy burst out anew a half-dozen years later when, as a result of the efforts of customs officers to obtain writs of assistance explicitly authorized under the later Townshend Acts of 1767, widespread resistance to general search warrants developed. Once more was the issue revived, leading ultimately to the safeguards against unreasonable searches and seizures embodied in some of the Revolutionary state constitutions, notably that of Massachusetts which Adams authored, and to its prohibition in the Fourth Amendment to the Constitution.[87]

Truly in his first public advocacy had Adams ridden the wave of the future. As for Otis, his mental infirmities and erratic behavior were soon to forfeit whatever claims he may have had to colonial leadership. Within four years of the Writs of Assistance argument, Adams wrote of him: "His imagination flames, his passions blaze. He is liable to great inequalities of temper—sometimes in despondency, sometimes in a rage. The rashness and imprudences, into which his excess of zeal have formerly transported him, have made him enemies, whose malicious watch over him, occasion more caution, and more cunning and more inexplicable passages in his conduct than formerly."[88] To John Adams, Otis was no longer a hero.

John Adams made no bones about the fact that the Stamp Act caused him economic hardship. With that ability to personalize abstract measures, he denounced "this execrable project" as having been "set on foot for my ruin as well as that of America in General, and of Great Britain."[89] This was perfectly true, even though Parliament did not have John Adams directly in mind when it passed that misguided revenue measure. Since the courts refused to operate without stamped paper, and there was none to be had, Adams and the rest of the bar found themselves without clients and without cases. In September of 1765 Adams drew up a set of "Instructions" for the town of Braintree's representative. Therein the Stamp Act was denounced as both burdensome and unconstitutional. As a lawyer Adams targeted "the enormous penalties, to be prosecuted, sued for, and recovered at the option of an informer, in a court of admiralty, without a jury." Ill-timed to coincide with a postwar business recession, the Stamp Act duties, Adams charged, "would drain the country of its cash, strip multitudes of all their property, and reduce them to absolutely beggary." Finally, in picking up a refrain heard throughout the colonies, Adams argued that to be taxed by Parliament without being represented therein was "inconsistent" not only with the spirit of the common law but also with "the essential fundamental principles of the British Constitution."[90] Not long thereafter the town of Boston asked Adams to join with Jeremy Gridley and James Otis to request the governor to reopen the courts. Adams, in his argument, took a strong constitutional stand. "The Stamp Act," so he insisted, "was made where we are in no sense represented, therefore no more binding upon us, than an act which should oblige us to destroy one half of our specie." He went so far as to claim that "a Parliament of Great Britain can have no more right to tax the colonies than a Parliament of Paris."[91] The argument was wasted, and for the time the courts stayed shut. Adams held Hutchinson, the chief victim of the Stamp Act riots, to be the architect of a policy of "political finesse" which kept the courts closed down, and by so doing lost the respect of the populace and many members of the bar. "Can we," Adams asked, "be sufficiently amazed at the chickanery, the finess, the prevarication, and insincerity, the simulation, nay the lyes and falsehoods of the judges of the Superior Court. These are harsh words, but true. The times are terrible, and made so at present by Hutchinson C. J."[92]

In sum, the year 1765 had proved to be a critical year both for the American colonies in general and for John Adams in particular. During the enforced and unwelcome lull in his practice, he used his time to indict the social, legal, and constitutional structure of Great Britain by preparing and publishing a series of powerful articles, instructions, and arguments. He had now joined forces with Samuel Adams, the leader of Boston's radical opposition, and rejoiced at the unanimity of denunciation which the Stamp Act had aroused. "Our presses have groaned, our pulpits have thundered, our legislatures have resolved, our towns have voted," Adams noted, adding gleefully, and "the Crown officers have every where trembled, and all their little tools and creatures, been afraid to speak and ashamed to be seen."[93]

By himself Adams kept the presses groaning. In January, 1766, he published three letters under the pseudonym "Clarendon," demolishing the notion of absolute Parliamentary supremacy over America, and reminding his readers that the violation of rights so fundamental as trial by jury and representation in the legislature must be defended at all costs.[94] Exactly a year later he engaged in a duel of the pens with his longtime companion at the bar and intimate Jonathan Sewall, the latter writing as "Philanthropus" to defend Governor Bernard's refusal to administer the oath of office to two representatives elected from Newburyport, and Adams, appropriately, as "Governor Winthrop." To Adams the old founding Puritans would have applauded the resistance to the Stamp Act and would have joined him in warning that liberty was too precarious a blessing to be hazarded. "The world, the flesh, and the devil have always maintained a confederacy against her." On the point at issue, Adams argued forcefully that the legislature should be the sole judge of its own membership.[95]

Still, in the years immediately following the Stamp Act controversy Adams was to strike his most effective blows on behalf of constitutional liberty and due process in the courtroom. In the case of Hancock's sloop *Liberty*, wherein he attacked a penal statute as violative of fundamental rights, he would borrow that portion of his arguments relating to the right to jury trial and incorporate it in the Instructions of the Town of Boston to their Representatives, which he prepared in May, 1769. Their publication kept basic constitutional issues at the forefront of the running controversy with the home government.[96]

Hard on the heels of his defense of Hancock on smuggling charges, Adams undertook to defend four sailors charged with killing the executive officer of the frigate *Rose*, who had sought to impress them. The officer, according to the evidence, defied the crew, stepped over a line of salt they had drawn under the weather deck, and for his presumption was struck in the jugular by a harpoon wielded by one of the sailors, Michael Corbet, and instantly killed. In a trial before a Special Court of Admiralty in 1769 Adams argued that the killing was justifiable homicide. Possessing an unrivaled collection of the old law books, he dug up an old statute presumably barring impressment in America. An embarrassed court recessed, and then brought in a decree of justifiable homicide, setting the prisoners at liberty. Adams had managed to turn a murder trial into a forum to consider two great legal issues—the right of juries in the colonies and the right of the Royal Navy to impress seamen. In Adams's own judgment this case outranked the Boston Massacre trial in importance. As regards the basic issues at law, he was indubitably correct. Little did Adams realize, as he elicited from the British sailors forthright testimony revealing their abhorrence of the press gang, how persistently this nagging issue of impressment would embroil England and her former colonies on this side of the Atlantic.[97]

In the course of his classic Speech on Conciliation with America delivered in Parliament in March of '75, Edmund Burke remarked on the grounding that Americans had in the law, and hinted that "when great honors and great emoluments do not win this knowledge to the service of the state, it is a formidable adversary of government." The Crown authorities were no more likely to take a hint from Burke on how to win over the colonial opposition than was Parliament calculated to vote down the bill for restraining the trade of New England, a bill like the other coercive measures that Burke opposed. Sour Loyalists and humiliated Crown officials found it easiest to attribute sordid motives to the resistance of Whig lawyers to the power of the prerogative. Thus, the charge was commonly made that James Otis's public course was dictated solely by revenge for his father's disappointment at not being made Chief Justice. To that allegation Josiah Quincy aptly rejoined at a later time that it might "be classed with Disraeli's insinuation that John Hampden's refusal to pay ship money was occasioned by an ancient grudge against the sheriff who levied it."[98]

That is not to say that the Whig lawyers, and not least among them John Adams, did not become increasingly resentful of a policy which saw them systematically discriminated against in awarding lucrative and influential places to men of no greater competence, a policy which crested in the impolitic and greedy nepotism of the clan Hutchinson. Adams, who was not infrequently bitten by the worm of jealousy, complained: "Is not this amazing ascendancy of one family foundation sufficient on which to erect a tyranny? Is it not enough to excite jealousies among the people."[99] That three of his most intimate friends—Jonathan Sewall, Samuel Quincy, and Daniel Leonard— were "seduced from his bosom" by Hutchinson merely enkindled his discontent.[100]

Was it too late to win Adams over to the side of the Crown? In 1768, at the height of his reputation and practice, he was proffered the advocate-generalship in the Court of Vice-Admiralty. No more tactful and persuasive way of handling John Adams could have been devised. Jonathan Sewall, then attorney general, came to dinner at the Adamses, a visit which, Adams confessed, gratified him, because although they were longtime friends they were, as he put it, "at antipodes in politics." You are the best man for the post, Sewall told him. Sorely tempted as Adams might have been to obtain "a sure introduction to the most profitable business in the province" and to take "a first step" up the ladder of royal favor, he courteously replied that his political principles, friendships, and connections prevented him from accepting. Sewall was persistent, and returned three weeks later, only to learn that Adams's declination was unalterable.[101] Hutchinson put the refusal down to Adams's having been passed over by Governor Bernard for a commission of justice of the peace on an earlier occasion, but this information he gathered at second hand as an exile in London a decade after the events he was reporting.[102]

Sewall made a final effort to seduce Adams to the royal cause, or at least to keep him out of trouble. In July of '74, on the eve of Adams's departure for Philadelphia to represent his province at the First Continental Congress, the pair after court at Falmouth took a last walk together on Munjoy's Hill overlooking Casco Bay. For years they had been divided politically, but still remained friends. Sewall now made an eloquent effort to dissuade Adams from going to Congress. You will ruin your career, he warned, set brother against brother, and in the long run see England triumph. Adams remained inflexible. He intended to go to Congress and *"with my friends,"* repeating the last phrase for emphasis. "I have passed my Rubicon. I will never change. Sink or swim, live or die, survive or perish, I am with my country from this day on." To the two fast friends the parting was tragic. "You may depend upon it," Adams told Sewall. "This adieu is the sharpest thorn on which I ever set my foot."[103]

The pair embraced, and did not meet again for at least a dozen years, and then under utterly different circumstances. Adams went on to fame and victory, Sewall to embittered exile in England, finally to die in Nova Scotia. Typical of Adams's ability to make the friendly and impulsive gesture was the visit he paid Sewall in London in 1787 when he was there as the American minister to the Court of St. James's. Their reunion, despite all that had elapsed, was cordial. Sewall's later comment showed remarkable insight into his friend. "Adams has a heart formed of friendship and susceptible of its fondest feelings. He is humane, generous and open, warm in his friendly attachment, though perhaps implacable to those whom he thinks his enemies." His ambitions both for his country and himself fulfilled, Adams, Sewall now felt, was out of his element abroad and truly missed "those happy days, when in a snug house, with a pretty farm about him at Braintree, he sat quiet, in the full possession of domestic happiness." Sewall shrewdly observed how miscast Adams appeared in a diplomatic role:

> He was an honest lawyer as ever broke bread but he is not qualified, by nature or education, to shine in courts. His abilities are undoubtedly equal to the mechanical parts of his business as ambassador, but this is not enough. He cannot dance, drink, game, flatter, promise, dress, swear with the gentlemen and talk small talk and flirt with the ladies. In short, he has none of the essential arts or ornaments which constitute a courtier.[104]

Even had Adams possessed the clairvoyance to see the trouble that would accompany his triumphs, it is clear that duty, ambition, and vanity would have kept him on his course. As a lawyer his resistance to Crown and Parliamentary usurpation was a matter of principle; as a householder of Boston, where he established a residence on Brattle Square, he found the arrival of British Redcoats in that town in the year 1768 an infernal nuisance, what with "the spirit stirring drum and the earpiercing fife" waking up his household at an unearthly hour.[105] Troops parading in front of his door only confirmed him in the view that there was a calculated attack on the liberties of his colony, stemming from a "conspiracy." He had warned back in 1765 that a party "consisting chiefly *not* of the descendants of the first settlers of this country" was dedicated to the overthrow of Puritan cultural values and that Parliament intended "an entire subversion of the whole system of our fathers."[106] In his "Novanglus" letters he would elaborate upon the notion of a plot to subvert the colonial constitution, this time charged to the Tories.[107]

Still, Adams sedulously avoided the sulfurous language of an Otis or a Samuel Adams. If he was a partisan, he was by no means a rabid one, nor was he yet committed to a complete severance of the cord to the mother country.

What brought John Adams back into the fray was the storm stirred up by the announcement that henceforth the salary of the judges in Massachusetts would be paid by the Crown. In February, 1773, Adams engaged in a newspaper exchange with the Tory-minded William Brattle to defend the principle that judges should hold office during good behavior and to denounce the power of the Crown to remove judges at their own whim as a menace to the Constitution and the rights of Englishmen and Americans.[108] Adams also seems to have had a hand in the preparation of two state papers emanating from the House of Representatives and expounding the theory of the Constitution that he was later to elaborate in the "Novanglus" letters. America, the House insisted, was subject to the king but outside the realm and thereby not under the direct legislative authority of Parliament.[109]

The Boston Tea Party of December, 1773, proved the event that precipitated Adams's ultimate commitment to the Patriot cause. Deeply opposed as he had always been to riots and mobbism, he acclaimed the "sublimity" of the tea dumping and applauded the populace for having "passed the river and cut away the bridge."[110] Here, indeed, was a violation of a basic right that, in Adams's eyes, justified direct action. Now should a standard arise and a camp be formed, he divulged to his good friend Mercy Otis Warren, she should not be surprised to find John Adams there.[111] Always looking toward constitutional means of protest rather than violent ones, Adams now proposed to the leading Patriots that the House of Representatives impeach the judges before the governor and council for high crimes and misdemeanors. There were precedents, to be sure, the great impeachment trials during the Puritan Revolution, but Adams went so far as to assert that if no precedents could be found, "it is now high time that a precedent should be set."[112] While the governor and Council, as anticipated, refused to receive the impeachment, the indictment by the House was printed in the newspapers, and thereafter no jurors would serve under the impeached judges. Perhaps Adams melodramatized the effects in retrospect when he asserted that "the royal government was from that moment laid prostrate in the dust."[113]

On one more occasion did John Adams have cause to reprove mobbism. That was when in June of 1774 he served as moderator of the Boston town meeting. When the crowd howled down a wealthy merchant for his presumption in proposing that the town make a voluntary payment to the East India Company for the tea destroyed, Adams reproved the meeting with a favorite quotation from Milton:

> I did but prompt the age to quit their clogs
> By the known rules of ancient liberty,
> When straight a barbarous noise environs me
> Of owls and cuckoos, asses, apes, and dogs.[114]

Adams constantly talked about crossing the Rubicon, but that stream still lay before him. Even after word reached him of his designation as one of the five delegates to the First Continental Congress, he felt unsure both of his own capacity for so awesome a role and of what stand he ought to take. On the one hand, as he confessed in his diary, he felt himself "unequal to this business," not sufficiently versed in affairs other than law and policy. "The objects before me are too grand and multifarious for my comprehension," he wrote. "We have not men fit for the times. We are deficient in genius, in education, in travel, in fortune, in every thing. I feel unutterable anxiety. God grant us wisdom and fortitude!" Death would be "less terrible" than submission.[115] If he was not sure of himself, he was understandably chilled at the thought of sharing the fate of those revolutionaries of Puritan times—Hampden, Sidney, and Harrington.[116]

The midsummer days of '74 saw John Adams pulled in one direction by his resolve to avoid "in councilling, or aiding or abetting any tumult or discords" and in the opposite direction by a zeal for liberty which he found it increasingly difficult to choke off. He realized full well that failure to conceal his inner feelings might "prove fatal to the fortune and felicity of my family." Truly, said Adams, borrowing a line from Otis, "The zeal-pot boils over,"[117] and it required superhuman discipline to pursue the even tenor of one's ways while being drawn more and more to the extremist wing in his own party. By this date he was reported to have concurred with the view of Samuel Adams that the boycott being proposed for the coming Congress would be neither sufficient nor decisive, and that "we shall have to resist by force."[118]

The great assemblage at Philadelphia convened in September of 1774 transported Adams from his own narrow, parochial, but relatively harmonious circle to a wider and more cosmopolitan world, brought him face to face with men of more moderate inclinations than his own, and provided him with an opportunity to take their measure. As the acerbic comments in his diary reveal, he relished the chance. To begin with, Adams found himself in a Congress of moderates ("Hutchinsonian Addressers," he labeled them) anxious to patch up the quarrel and radicals like himself determined upon resistance. Among these "strangers" he confessed feeling uncomfortable and found his companions "jealous of each other—fearfull, timid, skittish."[119] He and his fellow delegates from Massachusetts quickly made common cause with the radical-minded Virginians. This alliance straddled the touchy middle colonies with their Toryish and faint-hearted spirits and gave to the men of rash measures a continental-wide façade.

Hardly had the delegates settled in their seats when a batch of radical resolves brought down from Boston and known as the "Suffolk Resolves" were submitted for endorsement. The resolves pulled no punches, indicted Parliamentary acts, especially as related to Massachusetts, declared that no obedience was due such measures, opposed the payment of taxes until the government of the province was placed once more on a constitutional foundation, and proposed severing trade relations with Great Britain. Finally, and on the touchiest point of all, they avowed their determination "to act merely upon the defense," only so long as supported by reason and the principle of self-preservation, "but no longer." Without stopping to weigh the consequences of adopting it but as a vote of sympathy for the plight of suffering Boston, Congress quickly endorsed the resolution. Adams, who had reported that "the spirit, the firmness, the pride of our province are vastly applauded," exultingly noted that evening in his diary: "This was one of the happiest days of my life.

In Congress we had generous, noble sentiments, and manly eloquence. This day convinced me that America will support the Massachusetts or perish with her."[120]

Congress went a step further, when five days later it spelled out a
specific request of the Suffolk convention by recommending a suspension of commercial intercourse with Great Britain "until the sense of
Congress, on the means to be taken for the preservation of the
liberties of America, is made public." John Adams was not yet ready
for precipitate action, and counseled a compatriot in Boston that it
would be wiser for Massachusetts "to live wholly without a legislature and courts of justice as long as will be necessary to obtain relief"
rather than defiantly to set up a countergovernment. Congress, as
Adams interpreted that body, was telling Massachusetts: "Stand still,
bear, with Patience, if you come to a Rupture with the Troops all is
lost."[121]

Wined and dined on a scale that no Puritan before him had ever
been regaled, including one dinner with "Turttle, and every other
thing—Flummery, Jellies, Sweetmeats of 20 sorts, Trifles, Whipped
syllabubbs, floating Islands, fools, etc., and then a Desert of Fruits,
Raisins, Almonds, Pears, Peaches," topped off with excellent wine
and Madeira which he consumed "at a great Rate," Adams, who was
prepared to "Eat Potatoes and drink Water" rather than "submit to
the unrighteous," feared he would be "killed with Kindness in this
Place."[122] He was impatient for action and found the endless
wrangling "tedious beyond expression." The wrangling proved
worth it, though, for Congress, in no small part as a result of John
Adams's prodding, voted down the conciliatory Plan of Union proposed by Joseph Galloway, adopted a Declaration of Rights incorporating a section written by Adams denying Parliament any authority
over the colonies except for the regulation of external commerce,[123]
and finally entered into a solemn agreement to pursue a rigid policy
of nonintercourse with Great Britain until the grievances complained
of should be redressed. After an evening of congenial leave-taking at
the City Tavern, following adjournment on October 26, the delegates
set out for their respective homes, Adams to Boston, as he himself
records it,

Took our departure, in a very great rain, from the happy, the
peaceful, the elegant, the hospitable, and polite city of Phyladelphia

It is not likely that I shall ever see this part of the world again, but I shall ever retain a most gratefull, pleasing sense of the many civilities I have received in it. And shall think myself happy to have an opportunity of returning them.[124]

For Adams this was to be no final leave-taking. He was back in Philadelphia in the spring of '75 as his colony's delegate to the Second Continental Congress, and this time for a much longer stay. Not all the same faces were there to greet him, but Adams, to be sure, did not miss the absence of Tories like Joseph Galloway. To make up for the absentee conservatives he had the opportunity of meeting for the first time the renowned Benjamin Franklin and the learned Scotsman James Wilson of Pennsylvania, along with a red-headed scholarly lawyer from Virginia named Thomas Jefferson.

Between October of '74 and May of '75 John Adams's world had turned upside down. He himself in a series of a dozen letters published in the Boston *Gazette* during the winter of '75 under the pseudonym of "Novanglus" had totally denied the authority of Parliament over the colonies except in the area of trade, where the colonies had consented to Parliament's legislation. He even denied that the colonies were constituent members of the British Empire, since they were not an extension of the realm. In fact, the colonial legislatures, he had contended, were supreme within their respective colonies, and the shore of America was the boundary line between colonial and Parliamentary authority.[125]

The publicity accompanying the "Novanglus" letters had contributed to John Adams's growing reputation, if not notoriety, as a leader of the irreconcilable faction, a member of the firm of "Adams & Adams." Despite the shooting war which Lexington and Concord had now triggered, the junior partner found that Congress was still disposed "to keep open the door of reconciliation—to hold the sword in one hand and the olive branch in the other." Adams was losing patience fast. While still paying lip service to reconciliation on a constitutional basis, but one that the British authorities could hardly be expected to accept, Adams now diagnosed the "cancer" as "too deeply rooted and too far spread to be cured by anything short of cutting it out entire." But, taking into consideration the vastness of the continent and the multiplicity of interests represented at the Congress, Adams realistically admitted, "We cannot force events."

In his dedication to the business of Congress Adams proved indefatigable. He served on at least ninety committees of Congress between September, 1774, and November, 1777, and chaired some twenty-five. Aside from his heavy load of committee work, Adams managed to find himself in the thick of almost every debate, and to keep the pressure on Congress. At his initiation Congress authorized a sizable army and picked George Washington to command it (with Adams pulling strings behind the scenes and making the seconding speech). Shrewd enough to see the necessity for picking a Southerner to head a war being fought down East,[126] Adams chuckled maliciously in recalling in his old age that when he pronounced the name of Washington, he "never remarked a more sudden and sinking change of countenance" than in the face of the president of Congress. "Mortification and resentment were expressed as forcibly" as Hancock's visage could exhibit them.[127]

So far, so good. But even after Bunker Hill, Adams reported "a strange oscillation between love and hatred, between War and Peace— Preparations for War and Negociations for Peace."[128] The chief target of Adams's animadversions was John Dickinson, sponsor and drafter of the Olive Branch Petition to the King, which Congress adopted on July 5. Exasperated by the petitions and manifestoes, and throwing that little discretion he possessed to the wind, Adams wrote his friend James Warren later that month: "In confidence. I am determined to write freely to you at this time. A certain great fortune and piddling genius, whose fame has been trumpeted so loudly, has given a silly cast to our whole doings. We are between Hawk and Buzzard."[129] Rather than petition and remonstrate, Adams scolded, Congress should have seized control of the entire governmental structure of the continent, drawn up a model Constitution, raised a navy, opened the ports, "arrested every Friend to Government on the Continent and held them as Hostages for the poor Victims of Boston, and then opened the Door as wide as possible for Peace and Reconciliation."[130] A committed activist, Adams assigned civil liberties a secondary rank in the hierarchy of revolutionary values.

Alas for John Adams, his letter was intercepted by some British officers and quickly found its way into the newspapers. Everybody recognized the "piddling genius" as John Dickinson, who was not amused. The next time the pair met on the street, Adams bowed and pulled off his hat. Dickinson "passed haughtily by." Since it would turn out that the King would not even deign to receive Dickinson's Olive Branch Petition, the satisfaction that Adams took from his accurate prophecy must have soon effaced the embarrassment of the snub. Adams never changed his mind about Dickinson's literary effort, characterizing the Olive Branch Petition in his autobiography as a "measure of imbecility that embarrassed every exertion of Congress."[131]

Indeed, activists like John Adams were slowly but surely getting their way. Congress rejected Lord North's proposals of conciliation, authorized the issuance of bills of credit, and as a result of Adams's virtually single-handed efforts authorized both a navy and privateers. Here, as at the peacemaking in Paris, Adams, whose wide acquaintance with fishing and whaling captains was acquired in attendance at county seats in seafaring towns, demonstrated his exceptional knowledge of the American fishing industry and its longer-range potential for the nation. In addition, he drew up a set of "Rules" for the regulation of the navy which Congress adopted and published.[132] He also drafted the mechanism of judicial trial for cases of prize and capture, allowing for an appeal to Congress—an area with which he was to have more firsthand activity than perhaps he anticipated.[133] Indeed, looking back on his frenzied career during the Revolution, Adams regarded his service on the Naval Committee of Congress as "the pleasantest part" of four years' attendance at Congress.[134]

John Adams was moving toward independency at a faster speed than most of his colleagues. Back in June of '75 he had sponsored a move to have Congress draw up a plan for the civil governments for the colonies, expressing the opinion that Congress should recommend the calling by "the people of every colony" of conventions to set up such governments, "for the people were the source of all authority and original of all power," views which when first expressed in Congress seemed "new, strange and terrible doctrines to the greatest part of the members."[135]

At that time Adams, according to his recollection, was ready for extreme measures, believing there was great wisdom in the adage, "When the sword is drawn, throw away the scabbard." The opportunity came again when, in October, New Hampshire, finding herself in a "convulsed state," asked Congress for advice on governance. This gave Adams the moment for which he was long waiting. "I embraced with joy," he wrote at a later time, "the opportunity of haranguing on the subject at large," and of urging Congress to call conventions and institute regular governments. When pressed to describe the kind of government he would advise the people to set up, he was ready with the answer:

> A plan as nearly resembling the governments under which we were born and have lived as the circumstances of the country still admit. Kings we never had among us. Nobles we never had. Nothing hereditary existed in the country: Nor will the country require or admit of any such thing: but governors, and councils we have always had as well as representatives. A legislature in three branches ought to be preserved, and independent judges.

But where and how will you get your governors and councils? he was pressed. "By elections." How, who shall elect? he was asked. "The representatives of the people in convention will be the best qualified to contrive a mode."[136]

Thus was conceived one of the most innovative and profound of the mechanisms of government to stem from the American Revolution. One can draw a straight line from the response to New Hampshire in the fall of '75 to the summons to the states in May of '76 to set up their own governments, a call climaxed by the Constitutional Convention and popular ratification, by which Massachusetts adopted her Constitution of 1780, of which Adams was the principal author. Truly did Adams's brain stock an overflowing inventory of plans. "I had in my head and at my tongue's end," he declared, "as many projects of government as Mr. Burke says the Abbe Sièyes had in his pigeon-holes," but, when he got down to it, his advice was sensible and suitable.

Meanwhile the move toward independence was less than irresistible, even after the Parliamentary act of December, 1775, removing the colonies from the protection of the Crown, prohibiting trade with them, and authorizing seizure of American ships at sea. Adams in a letter to Horatio Gates referred to it as "the Act of Independency." Here was a gift from Parliament, and Adams could not understand why Americans should hesitate to accept it, why they should consider "independency" as "a Hobgoblin of so frightful Mien that it would throw a delicate person into Fits to look it in the Face."[137]

One answer to the British Restraining Act was to throw open the ports, a step which the timid considered as "a bold step to independence," the very reason why Adams urged it. But Congress followed his leadership and took the step on April 6.

Would there be conciliation, or a final break? "We continue still between Hawk and Buzzard," Adams wrote James Warren on April 2. Overhanging Philadelphia was the report that peace commissioners were on the way. Their arrival Adams described as "a messiah that will never come." "I have laughed at it,—scolded at it,—grieved at it," he wrote Abigail in mid-April, "and I don't know but I may, at an unguarded moment, have rip'd at it—but it is vain to reason against such delusions."[138] The impatience of the firm of Adams & Adams was now ill-concealed. "Have We not been independent these twelve Months, wanting Three days?" John Adams wrote James Warren on April 16. Have we not passed privateering resolves and opened our ports to all nations? "What more would you have?"[139] Just one thing more: a declaration of independence. In January the clarion call had been sounded loud and clear by Thomas Paine in his pamphlet *Common Sense*. Henceforth the current ran swift and unchecked. Except in the middle colonies, the radicals had won control of the machinery of government, and one state after another was making a commitment to independence. Early in May the Provincial Congress of Massachusetts sounded out the opinion of the towns on the great question. In meeting after meeting, in town after town, the freemen voted for independence. On John Adams's prodding, Congress on May 10 adopted a resolution instructing every colony to adopt such government "as shall best conduce to the happiness and safety of their constituents in particular, and America in general," to which was prefixed a preamble which was a sort of trial run for independence. Exultantly, Adams wrote Abigail that "Great Britain has at last driven America to the last step, a compleat separation from her; a total absolute independence, not only of her Parliament, but of her Crown, for such is the amount of the resolve of the 15th."[140] On May 20 Adams reported, "Every post and every day rolls in upon us Independence like a torrent."

What were Adams's "Sensations"[141] when he saw Congress passing resolutions which he himself had "most earnestly pressed for against Wind and Tide Twelve Months ago"? How did he feel to see "the Farmer [Dickinson] himself now confessing the Falsehood of all his Prophecies, and the Truth of mine, and confessing himself, now for instituting Governments, forming a Continental Constitution, making Alliances with foreigners, opening ports and all that," and admitting that the defense of the country had been neglected in consequence of "fond delusive hopes and deceitful Expectations"? A veteran Adams watcher would not have been surprised at the mixed emotions of smugness and humility, of exultation and trepidation, that his object exhibited. "The gloomy Prospect of Carnage and Devestation" that now presented itself was "too affecting" to give him pleasure.[142] Independence was inevitable, and probably could not await the establishment of governments by the states, Adams advised Patrick Henry early in June. The pride of a few monopolizing families would now be brought down "to the confines of reason and moderation"; then, drawing upon his Puritan morality, he observed that their downfall would do them good, for "pride was not made for man, only as a tormentor."[143]

Once the fateful resolutions for independence had been introduced by Richard Henry Lee on June 7, Adams pressed feverishly for the final break. Everybody conceded that America was independent, but still some raised objections. Taking that last step was absolutely essential, Adams cogently argued. Only then would the states complete the forming of their new governments, act against the Tories and the Tory press, push armaments and privateering, win foreign aid, and galvanize the activities of both the civil and military arms.[144]

When the Lee resolutions for independence came up for debate in Congress on July 2, it was only fitting that John Dickinson, speaking in opposition and at great length, should be answered by the self-confessed "author of all the mischief," and that Adams should prevail.[145] It was only fitting, too, that Congress should name Adams to a committee to draft the declaration of independence. For once Adams took a back seat on the advice of the Pennsylvania delegation, who urged the men of Massachusetts to let Virginia take the lead. Jefferson, deferring to his senior in years and in reputation as a chief architect of independence, asked Adams to make the draft. Adams declined, and when pressed for his reasons, according to his very late recollection, stated: "Reason first—You are a Virginian, and a Virginian ought to appear at the head of this business. Reason second—I am so obnoxious and unpopular. You are very much otherwise. Reason third—You can write ten times better than I can."

Clearly the pressure brought upon Adams by the delegates from Pennsylvania produced lasting dividends. Adams confessed himself delighted with the document's "high tone" and "the flights of oratory with which it abounded," especially the denunciation of Negro slavery which he knew Jefferson's "Southern brethren" would most certainly delete. Despite reservations, he cordially endorsed it. A few phrases rubbed him the wrong way, notably the allusion to the King as a "tyrant." Adams thought this "too personal," and later insisted that he never had regarded George "to be a tyrant in disposition and in nature," but rather "deceived by his courtiers on both sides of the Atlantic and, in his official capacity only, cruel." He thought Franklin and Sherman would strike the phrase out, but when they let it stay he went along. "I do not now remember that I made or suggested a single alteration."[146] No debater, Jefferson left the defense of the Declaration to Adams, who, Jefferson wrote in 1813, "was the pillar of its support on the floor of Congress, its ablest advocate and defender against the multifarious assaults it encountered."[147]

To Adams, the adoption of the Declaration of Independence on the Fourth of July was anticlimactic. The great moment had been July 2, when the resolution so eloquently sponsored by Adams was adopted, and thenceforth he would regard the Second rather than the Fourth as "the great anniversary festival," one which should be commemorated "as the Day of Deliverance by solemn acts of devotion to God Almighty. It ought to be solemnized with pomp and parade, with shews, games, sports, guns, bells, bonfires and illuminations from one end of this continent to the other, from this time forward forevermore."[148] Hailed by Richard Stockton, the New Jersey signer, as "the Atlas of American Independence," a triumphant Adams, humble in his greatest moment of victory, little realized that he would prove premature by two days, and that Mr. Jefferson, not Mr. Adams, would be the man ever identified with that occasion.

For John Adams, this was no time for exultation, but rather for quiet confidence. "I am well aware of the toil and blood and treasure that it will cost us to maintain the Declaration," he averred to Abigail, "yet through all the gloom I can see rays of ravishing light and glory." Posterity would triumph "in the day's transaction."[149]

Adams was not only in the forefront of the struggle to have the colonies declare their independence, but the indisputable leader of the movement to have the states establish their own governments. Back in June of '75 he had urged that state governments be set up through the innovative device of a constitutional convention. He felt the urgency of independent governments for two reasons: first, because he was dedicated to a system by which the people ruled, and perhaps equally because he feared the vacuum of power created by the lack of a permanent government at a time of revolution. Such a vacuum of authority was calculated, in Adams's view, to "injure the morals of the people and destroy the habits of order and attachment to regular government."[150] As a stout Puritan that was the last thing he wanted to occur.

In the spring of '76 Adams was solicited by prominent Patriots in a number of states, notably in Virginia, for his ideas about state constitutions. Accordingly, he prepared his "Thoughts on Government," written in effect to refute Thomas Paine's advocacy of a unicameral legislature which he embodied in his celebrated pamphlet *Common Sense*. On the futility of reconciliation with Great Britain, Adams embraced Paine's views, while rejecting his constitutional notions, which, to Adams's mind, showed up Paine as better "at pulling down than building."[151] Maintaining that the foundation of the ideal government was virtue rather than fear, which kept most operating, he laid out a plan for constituting a representative assembly. Therein he expounded his idea of equal representation, by which he insisted that "equal interests among the people should be equal interests in it." He had already articulated the notion that the lower house should mirror society, "think, feel, act and reason like the people," whereas the upper house should be differently structured and should have a negative on the lower.[152]

Adams seized the opportunity to put his ideas in practice when he was selected in 1779 to draft the Massachusetts Constitution adopted the next year.[153] Therein he incorporated his commitment to separation of powers and to annual elections of the legislature and the chief executive officers. Stating axiomatically that "very few men who have no property have any judgment of their own,"[154] Adams saw to it that the property franchise for voting was retained. In fact, however, as a result of the widespread ownership of property then prevailing, very few adult males were barred by this qualification.[155] Contrariwise, the upper house membership was based upon the amount of taxes paid in special senatorial districts rather than simply upon population, and much more clearly represented the property interests of the commonwealth.

John Adams never had and never would subscribe to the notion of "one man, one vote" for both houses of the legislature. The distortions of constitutional history with which the cluster of decisions stemming from *Baker* v. *Carr* abound would have elicited from him a lion's roar of dissent.

Ever lurking in Adams's mind was his fear of mob rule, a conviction he shared with Abigail, that an unchecked populace would be as oppressive as an uncurbed monarchy, and that men in all ages preferred a life of ease and pleasure to liberty. To preserve liberty, political bulwarks would have to be erected. In short, it was the Puritan, with his deep pessimism about man and his Puritan stress on moral values, that gave so distinctively conservative a cast to Adams's revolutionary thought.[156] When he wrote in 1788 that "there can be no liberty without some balance,"[157] he was not repudiating his earlier revolutionary ideas but merely reiterating them. His convictions were set forth at length in that curious panorama of the republican systems throughout the ages entitled *The Defence of the Constitutions of Government of the United States of America,* which he began in October, 1786, and completed just as the opening shots of the French Revolution were fired. The *Defence* reflected Adams's characteristic perturbation about "factious rages" and "delirious enthusiasm" prompted by Shays' Rebellion.[158] Conservative as it may have sounded even when it was written, and unfashionable as it appears today, it was not inconsistent with either Adams's "Thoughts on Government" or his draft of the Massachusetts Constitution. Favoring separation of powers and a strong executive with an absolute veto, Adams sought to provide the kind of mixed government best exemplified in his mind by the English Constitution, although he later said that his real preference was "an attachment to their old colonial forms."[159] Convinced of the merits of balanced government, he was equally convinced of the inevitability of inequality in society. His was a stout and undeviating republicanism, no longer in tune with that more democratic society whose feasibility and safety he doubted. Indeed, it was the tragedy of Mr. Adams that while he stood still, the American people as a whole had pressed on beyond his basic political assumptions.[160]

Sensitive as he was to currents of thought, Adams realized that he seemed as archaic as one of the prehistoric artifacts that his friend Jefferson took pleasure in collecting. He professed not to care. "Popularity was never my Mistress, nor was I ever, or shall I ever be a popular Man," he wrote at the time his *Defence* first appeared.[161] In his old age he lamented to Benjamin Rush, "From the year 1761, no more than fifty years, I have constantly lived in an enemies country."[162] Hamilton in his latter years shared the same feeling.

If this Puritan revolutionary often marched out of step with his own side, he managed at the same time to contain in one brain a maze of seemingly contradictory attitudes. One of the staunchest advocates of "Independence Now," he sternly disapproved of grass-roots movements, of what he denigrated as "the rage for innovation," and felt that a watchful eye should be kept on popular conventions. To Adams, Shaysite leaders like Lem Shattuck and Daniel Shays himself were "as great" tyrants as a Bernard or a Hutchinson.[163]

Author of the Massachusetts Bill of Rights with its lofty declaration in Article I to the effect that "all men are born free and equal, and have certain natural, essential, and unalienable rights" (a far more cautious statement than the Declaration of Independence), Adams did not believe that all men *remained* equal. In a marginal comment on Rousseau's *Essay on Inequality* he disposed of the notion that at a given point in a state of nature, "all equality vanished." "What equality was there before?" he asked. "Was the child equal to the mother? And the mother to the father? Not in strength, swiftness, understanding or experience." To Adams, inequality was natural, and its implications were profoundly political as well as social.[164]

Viewing the greatest of all inequalities, slavery, John shared his wife's views of the "iniquitous" character of the institution, but never took a strong public stand on the issue. In his old age he declared: "I have, through my whole life, held the practice of slavery in such abhorrence that I have never owned a Negro or any other slave, though I have lived for many years in times when the practice was not disgraceful."[165] Privately he conceded that the slave trade went back to Adam[166] and that many slaveowners inherited burdens not necessarily of their own choosing. What concerned him most of all about slavery were the divisions that he foresaw for the country and the fears of a black insurrection.[167] During his life he was a gradualist, not an advocate of immediate abolition, but had he lived one might hazard the guess that he would have taken pride in the heroic stand of his son, "Old Man Eloquent," on behalf of the right of antislavery groups to petition the Congress.[168]

Adams tinctured his own brand of nationalism with a vigorous, distinctively isolationist pigment. The combination buttressed his revolutionary convictions. He saw "something very unnatural and odious in a government one thousand leagues off." Contrariwise, he deemed exemplary a government "of our own choice, managed by persons whom we love, revere, and can confide in."[169] Abigail, who shared his sentiments on most political matters, referred to "our country" as "a Secondary God," and "the first and greatest parent,"[170] a notion pretty close to the *Vaterland* concept of modern nationalisms, given a new lease on life in the synthetic nationalism of emerging nations. A continentalist like Hamilton, who hoped every man would be imbued with "a more exalted love for his country,"[171] Adams had abiding roots which the New Yorker could not claim. In this case it was New England which he loved dearly, and one would be put to it to rank New England and America in their respective order of attachment in Adams's own mind.

In his diary for May 3, 1785, he recorded this conversation with a foreign diplomat in Paris:

> One of the foreign Ambassadors said to me, "You have been often in England?"
> "Never but once in November and December 1783."
> "You have relations in England no doubt."
> "None at all."
> "None, how can that be? You are of English extraction?"
> "Neither my father or mother, grandfather or grandmother, great grandfather or great grandmother nor any other relation that I know or care a farthing for have been in England these 150 years. So that you see, I have not one drop of blood in my veins, but what is American."
> "Ay, We have seen," says he, "proofs enough of that."

The concluding comment pleased Adams no end.[172]

His partiality to New England did not blind him to the imperfections of his own countrymen. In the years abroad, he was often homesick for the land of his birth. Bogged down at the Hague in a sticky but ultimately triumphal diplomatic mission among the cheese-loving Dutch, Adams wrote home: "Oh peace! When wilt thou permit me to visit Penns-hill, Milton-hill, and all the blue hills? I love every tree and rock upon all those mountains."[173]

As a nationalist John Adams was perhaps the pioneer America-Firster. With France he wanted neither a political nor a military connection, "only a commercial connection." When on instructions of the Congress he drafted a "Plan of Treaties" in 1776, he "carefully avoided every thing that could involve us in any alliance more than a commercial friendship." Recalling his notions at the time, he observed years later: "My principle was perpetual peace, after that war should be concluded, with all powers of Europe, and perfect neutrality in all their future wars."[174] In the course of his role as a negotiator of the preliminary and definitive peace treaties with Great Britain at the end of the American Revolution, Adams pointed out to the British emissaries that, having for so long "been a foot-ball between contending nations, it ought to be our rule not to meddle" in European affairs. Later, in a conversation with the Russian plenipotentiary in Paris, he reputedly declared that America did not plan to have "intimate relations" with any European power.[175] When at a later date, shortly after being inaugurated President, Adams declared, "We will have neither John Bull nor Louis Baboon," he was voicing a New England Puritan's feelings of moral repulsion for the corruption and political intrigue of the Old World and a commitment made almost a quarter-century earlier to withdraw from foreign involvements as soon as feasible and to keep aloof.[176]

To call Adams irrelevant for our own time, as have some critics, because his political views of balanced government are no longer fashionable, is to ignore his durable claims to the nation's gratitude for a long and honored career in the public service. Nothing in his entire life became him so much as his courageous efforts as President to wind down the quasi-war with France. With a priceless sense of timing and a zest for drama, he "electrified the public," as he put it to Abigail, when he sent to the Senate a nomination for a minister plenipotentiary to be dispatched to the French Republic, and did so without consulting or informing his disapproving cabinet, whose members were plotting behind his back. He followed up this move with a series of measures to bring the quasi-naval war with France to an end. Verily, Adams's model for ending an undeclared war has special relevance in times of long and seemingly endless undeclared warfare.[177]

If John Adams is irrelevant today, then the love of freedom is irrelevant. It was he who wrote on the first of July, 1776, that "freedom is a counterbalance for poverty, discord, and war, and more."[178] It was he who wrote his son, young John Quincy Adams, in April of that same year, to share with his family their rejoicing in the repossession of Boston by the Patriots. What he said was meant not only for his immediate family but for all the young people of Revolutionary America.

> I hope you and your sister and brothers will take proper notice of these great events, and remember under whose wise and kind providence they are all conducted. Not a sparrow falls, nor a hair is lost, but by the direction of infinite wisdom. Much less are cities conquered and evacuated. I hope that you will all remember, how many losses, dangers, and inconveniences, have been borne by your parents, and the inhabitants of Boston in general for the sake of preserving freedom for you, and yours—and I hope you will all follow the virtuous example if, in any future time, your countrys liberties should be in danger, and suffer every human evil, rather than give them up. —My love to your Mamma, your sister and brothers, and all the family. I am your affectionate father,
>
> John Adams.[179]

Those who still cherish freedom might take heart from these eloquent words addressed by one future American President to another.

IV

THOMAS JEFFERSON:

THE INTELLECTUAL

AS REVOLUTIONARY

When the Revolutionary War ended, the author of the Declaration of Independence considered himself a tragic failure. Resigning the governorship of his state because of public clamor against his administration, Thomas Jefferson confessed: "I had folded myself in the arms of retirement, and rested all prospects of future happiness on domestic and literary objects." Then came the tragic death of his wife. "A single event wiped away all my plans and left me a blank which I had not the spirits to fill up."[1] He grasped momentarily at a chance to join the peace delegation in Paris and put the Atlantic Ocean between himself and matters he wished to forget.

Jefferson was to leave two other major public posts under a cloud. He resigned his office of Secretary of State when it was embarrassingly clear that his pro-French policies had boomeranged, and he finished his second term in the Presidency with the country on the edge of a needless war and at a time when he had expended most of the vast fund of popularity which he had enjoyed in his early years as chief executive.

Jefferson's career as an administrator was spotty; as a principled statesman he was a model of inconsistency; as a private man he could be both charming and withdrawn, blissfully happy at times; at others, a tortured and ambivalent soul. Yet, without the arts one now associates with politicians he was the most successful politician of his age. More than any other statesman he gave to the Revolution a special stamp which explains its relevance to the contemporary world, while his pronouncements have fueled that continuing revolution which has reshaped American society in our own century.

Paradoxically, the man who constantly inveighed against the Established Order and professed a special empathy for rebels and revolutions is rated by today's young people as neither an enlightened liberal nor a radical in quest of the future. Instead, they label him a slaveowner, racist, and equivocator, who sought to perpetuate the conservative values of rural society. His ambivalence in the matter of slavery is put down to sectional expediency at best; at worst, to hypocrisy. If Jefferson no longer occupies a niche in the radical left's pantheon of folk heroes, it is because his recent critics have overlooked the full record and the complete man, for Jefferson, like other Founding Fathers, but perhaps more so, was a complex man who defies easy categorizing.

Like so many later critics of the Established Order, Jefferson was very much a part of it, but his feelings toward the upper class were ambivalent. His father, Peter Jefferson, was a self-made man, a pioneer in the western region, a rugged and adventurous surveyor, who had risen from the overseer class but married Jane Randolph of the well-entrenched Randolph family and became a great landowner. The Randolphs, Jefferson tells us in his autobiography, could "trace their pedigree far back in England and Scotland," adding, cryptically, "to which let every one ascribe the faith and merit he chooses."[2] That Jefferson preferred his father to his mother is no secret, and, as a Jefferson rather than a Randolph, he seems to have felt some compulsion to secure a Jefferson coat of arms from the College of Heralds, if one such existed.[3] Despite his egalitarian leanings, he was not without a strain of snobbishness, a belief that he, his family, and his friends were the equal of, if not better than, the rest of mankind. He believed that governing should be entrusted to a natural aristocracy of virtue and talents, but since he also believed in rotation in office and low salaries,[4] the effect in practice was to give preference to men of wealth. He was to find fault with John Adams for employing in the minor post of diplomatic courier "one Humphreys, the son of a ship carpenter."[5] As President he took "standing in society" into consideration in making appointments to office and rejecting nominations by party stalwarts,[6] and, if anything, his pride in lineage burgeoned with the years, a concern with genealogy which one does not normally associate with Jeffersonian democracy.[7]

Like other Virginia planters, Peter Jefferson had provided in his will for all his children,[8] but he allowed his eldest son to choose between properties to divide with his only brother, Randolph. None of the property was entailed. This lesson was not lost on Thomas.[9] When his father died, Jefferson at fourteen took over the household as the eldest son. That household comprised a mother, four sisters, and Randolph, with whom he never had much in common.[10] Behaving much as eldest sons had behaved in the British aristocracy for centuries, Jefferson did not ignore his father's example. Peter Jefferson's concern for his entire family, one which Thomas shared, helps explain why, though an eldest son and a gentleman both by lineage and by cultural inclination, Jefferson would one day topple entails and the common law rule of descent to the eldest son prevailing in Virginia in the case of intestate succession,[11] why he would tilt a lance against outmoded feudal rules and privileges which were still perpetuated, why he would pose as the principal advocate of an aristocracy not of blood or class but of virtue and talent. With an inheritance of land and slaves, which were greatly increased by his own marriage, Jefferson could indeed afford the luxury of a life centered on politics and on cultural and aesthetic satisfactions.

As a boy Jefferson had leaned heavily upon his father, and when the latter died he made his own decisions, ran the farm and household, and at the age of seventeen notified his guardian that the time had come for him to go to college at Williamsburg, which he entered in March, 1760.[12]

Seeking little or no advice from his mother, about whom he remained reticent, Jefferson hungered for the affection and approval of older men, whether his Scottish professor, Dr. William Small, mathematician and philosopher, or the figures at the "familiar table" to which Small introduced him. Presided over by genial Governor Francis Fauquier, the table included, in addition to Small, George Wythe, the noted law teacher and jurist under whom Jefferson would prepare himself for the practice of his profession. In much later life Washington may have provided that authoritarian father figure. In addition to wishing the security and guidance of older men, Jefferson kept a tight rein on his highly competitive urges. He may well have sought to prove to the world that a Jefferson was as good a man as a Randolph. Since Hamilton possessed similar, even more intense cravings, one could predict that a confrontation of the two uncongenial personalities might engender formidable competition and animosity, not only over issues of principle, but as rivals for the approval of a surrogate father.[13]

As a youth Jefferson was blessed with social and seemingly economic security as well as superb physical health. Tall, lanky, loose-jointed, with long limbs and huge hands and feet, young Jefferson, with his ruddy and freckled complexion, his thin lips, angular nose, and strong chin, presented to the world a thoughtful rather than a handsome countenance. An excellent horseman, Jefferson still preferred walking to all other forms of exercise. Even down to old age he kept all his teeth, enjoyed good hearing, and did not use glasses until late in life, when he wore them only to read at night.[14] The "violent headaches" which he experienced could have been migraine attacks, seemingly touched off by emotional stress.[15]

If the Randolphs were born to the purple and could afford to profit by events not necessarily of their own making, the Jeffersons, notably Peter, had achieved their success by enormous industry. These traits of hard work and stern perseverance, which Jefferson admired in his father, he adopted for himself. In truth, Jefferson was an obsessive-compulsive personality. A Puritan in matters of sensual pleasure, he was doubly so in his hostility to idleness of mind or body. He took a meticulous interest in the proper and judicious use of words, and though, ironically, he turned out to be a poor historian, he scrupulously recorded to the last penny all his personal expenditures and collected a variety of historical archives. While his Virginia contemporaries employed their idleness in drinking and gambling, Jefferson in his leisure moments brought his mind to bear upon every branch of knowledge. For Jefferson leisure had to be purposeful. As he wrote his daughter Martha years later, "Of all the cankers of human happiness, none corrodes it with so silent, yet so baneful a touch as indolence," adding the caution, "If at any moment, my dear, you catch yourself in idleness, start from it as you would from the precipice of a gulph."[16]

A true product of the world of the Enlightenment, Jefferson cultivated his restless mind in every known branch of knowledge. When fire destroyed his mother's house in 1770, he lost his papers and precious library, which he valued at £200 sterling. "Would to God it had been the money," he sighed. Undaunted, he rushed off letters to his bookseller abroad to collect another, the "Great Library," one of the most valuable owned by any American of his time, which he sold—or "ceded," as he preferred—to the Congress in 1815.[17] A voracious reader, he drenched himself in the classics, studied Latin and Greek and even the American Indian languages, and enjoyed bilingual puns.[18] An aficionado of the natural history of North America, which he defended against its detractors, Jefferson was assiduous in collecting prehistoric bones and searching out Indian artifacts. His curiosity aroused by the Indian mounds that were repositories of their dead, he opened up such a mound in his neighborhood, intuitively pursuing a technique of excavation that is now a foremost tool of all archaeologists, the determination of the age of remains by the strata in which they are located.[19] Concerned likewise with meteorology, he kept a temperature diary and recorded two readings daily.

Jefferson sought knowledge not merely for utility, but for its own sake. He advised his daughter to acquire "that degree of science which will guard you at all times against ennui, the most dangerous poison of life."[20] An amateur and dilettante, Jefferson, in his enthusiasm for music and architecture, particularly the latter, possessed a dedication which is the stamp of a professional. He was enamored of the violin, and his passion was doubtless encouraged by Governor Fauquier's musicales. At the Palace Jefferson played in a quartet which the governor himself assembled. Whenever he could, he devoted three hours daily to practicing the fiddle. He acquired John Randolph's Cremona by Amati after elaborate negotiation.[21] And he kept up his practice until he broke his wrist in the latter 1780's. He ordered a handsome piano from abroad, paying for it with the first tobacco he would get to the warehouse in the fall.[22] Jefferson lamented to a foreigner that, while music was "the favorite passion of my soul," "fortune" had cast his lot "in a country where it is in a state of deplorable barbarism."[23] As a builder and architect, Jefferson proved more creative than as a musician. He adapted the Greco-Roman and baroque styles to his home at Monticello, which was well into the planning stage by 1767. His exquisite home and his designs for the state capitol at Richmond and the buildings of the University of Virginia would set the course of architecture in America for a half-century.[24]

In turning to the law as a profession Jefferson did what seemed perfectly natural for an intellectually gifted member of the country gentry, so much of whose time was consumed with legal instruments such as land surveys, patents, bills, and accounts. Furthermore, by the eve of the Revolution the law seemed the quickest road to politics. Yet in Jefferson's case the choice was by no means obvious, for by temperament and tastes he was hardly cut out for a trial lawyer. He had little of the qualities of an extrovert and too much exquisite sensitivity. He was unlikely to relish a face-to-face encounter with an adversary or take that sadistic satisfaction that some lawyers derive from a savage cross-examination of a squirming witness. Thin-skinned and hypersensitive, with a shyness in public that was legendary, Jefferson was to prefer the role of office lawyer.

Jefferson prepared under Wythe for the practice of the law. He plodded through the law books, finding the task a drudgery, as did his contemporaries. "I do wish the Devil had old Cooke, for I am sure I never was so tired of an old dull scoundrel in my life," he confessed.[25] In addition to a wide variety of books from both the common and the civil law,[26] Jefferson gave special attention to the history of English law, whose Anglo-Saxon origins were to exercise a compelling fascination on his thinking. Admitted to the bar in 1767, Jefferson drew his clients from relatives, neighbors, and other members of the gentry. Although half his practice was in the county courts to which he rode circuit, Jefferson never relished dealing with the pettifoggers who clogged the courts with small claims and, as he was to complain, "consume the harvest." Later he tried to reform the practice of the law by separating practice in the county courts from admission to the bar of the General Court at Williamsburg,[27] but his colleagues at the bar would not go along with what amounted to transplanting to these shores a distinction maintained in England between the solicitor and the barrister.

Basically a scholar and law reformer, Jefferson contrasted markedly with his radical associate Patrick Henry, who relished adversary proceedings and flaming oratory before country juries. Still, Jefferson worked at it and made a respectable living. By 1773 his case load had peaked to five hundred cases, a considerable physical burden for a man without a partner, and he grossed perhaps $2,000 a year from his practice, a respectable sum, neither inconsiderable nor exceptional by the standards of his time. Despite his case load he took the time to report the judicial decisions handed down in the General Court when he attended, along with an earlier period whose opinions he had unearthed, reports which provided a major source of judicial opinions for the pre-Revolutionary period and made Jefferson a pioneer American law reporter.[28] And like every other lawyer, he was concerned about his fees, subscribing to a notice, along with five of his colleagues, including Patrick Henry, in which the attorneys refused to give an opinion or prosecute or defend a suit unless the tax and one-half the fee were paid in advance, excepting those cases where they chose to act gratis.[29]

Jefferson practiced until the eve of the Revolution, when his activist political role compelled him to abandon the law as a profession, as did John Adams and John Jay. The imprint of his legal training is found in all his state papers. The Declaration of Independence is really a bill of indictment. In many of the papers he drafted, the hand of the advocate pleading a cause is ill-concealed. Jefferson always proved resourceful in finding authorities to support his position, and he manhandled history like an advocate choosing what he needed and discarding or ignoring what would embarrass or contradict his case.

The imperial crisis did not confront a Virginia lawyer like Jefferson with the same kind of dilemma that it posed for a New York lawyer like John Jay. On its face the risk-taking for the former seemed rather remote. By espousing the radical case, Jefferson, unlike Jay, ran no danger of losing clients, friends, or votes. Jefferson could be fashionably radical in Virginia, where the elite, certainly on this issue if not on others, showed a remarkable unity in support of the Revolution. The ideological rhetoric may have concealed their motivations, but the tobacco-planting elite shared certain common grievances. In the early 1760's they had been prepared to contest their ministers' claim to back pay, not only because they felt that church affairs should be largely left to the control of the parish rather than the Anglican authorities abroad but also because they bitterly resented the powers of disallowance exercised by the King in Council in this case.[30] Patrick Henry's strenuous courtroom oratory on that occasion, even though it carried revolutionary overtones, was widely applauded. The entire Virginia elite were heavily involved in western land speculation, an enterprise to be seriously hampered if not jeopardized by Crown regulatory measures, and, most significantly, that same elite were heavily in debt to English and Scottish merchants who had advanced them credit against future tobacco shipments.[31] Jefferson himself by the eve of the Revolution had piled up a rather formidable indebtedness. By the time he entered politics, power had shifted to the younger gentry of the Piedmont and Potomac regions, whose leaders were firebrands like Patrick Henry and Richard Henry Lee. The prestige of the old guard had been damaged by a scandal which rocked the colony, when it was disclosed upon the death in 1766 of Speaker John Robinson how that worthy had embezzled some £100,-000 in paper money from the Virginia treasury to help his friends in distress, included among whom had been Jefferson's father and father-in-law.[32]

Just as John Adams confessed that he was stirred by Otis's passionate oratory in the Writs of Assistance case, so Jefferson, according to his later recollection, was inflamed by Patrick Henry's controversial "treason" speech delivered in protest of the Stamp Act. "He appeared to me to speak as Homer wrote," Jefferson recalled, and he credited Henry with setting "the ball of revolution" in motion.[33] Hence, by affinity of age, inclination, and conviction, Jefferson, when he entered politics, aligned himself with the rising younger gentry.

One could hardly charge so diffident a person as Jefferson with actively thirsting after political leadership. Rather, leadership was thrust upon him by a society wherein such direction seemed naturally to devolve upon the community's social leaders, whose dominance in politics went largely uncontested, a society which was a Spartan-type democracy by and for landholders.[34] Elected to the House of Burgesses in 1769, Jefferson, on the first day of his first session, was given the task of drafting an innocuous address to Governor Botetourt.[35] He voted for the resolves criticizing the Townshend Act, and joined his fellow burgesses (now ex-burgesses, as the governor had dissolved the House for its temerity) in adopting a nonimportation agreement.[36] Thus Jefferson was initiated in the war of commercial coercion, an experience which was to shape profoundly his later views on commerce and diplomacy. To this weapon he would turn in the post-Revolutionary years to right the trade balance with the mother country, a weapon which his adversary Alexander Hamilton would render impotent.

Truly a war of sorts had been initiated, and for Jefferson there was no wavering. No public speaker, he did his best work behind the scenes. He shared in the draft of a resolution creating the Virginia Committee of Correspondence. He rummaged through revolutionary precedents going back to the English Civil War to help in drafting a resolution for the celebration of a fast day on the date when the Boston Port Act was to go into effect[37] (a resolution which led to another dissolution of the Burgesses), supported an association of members of the dissolved Burgesses condemning the Tea Act and calling for a general congress to meet annually and "to deliberate on these general measures which the united interest of America may from time to time require,"[38] and held out to the Bostonians the prospect that their Virginia compatriots would join them not only in nonimportation but at some future day in nonexportation as well, should the British government pursue its "odious" measures.[39]

By midsummer of 1774 Jefferson's facile pen established him as a leading advocate of the radical position and a proponent of intercolonial union. Later in July he drafted a declaration of rights which he sent to the Virginia Convention, along with a draft of instructions to the Virginia delegates to the Continental Congress, combining a nonimportation agreement with an assertion of constitutional rights. A bout of dysentery had laid Jefferson low, and he was not present when, as Edmund Randolph recalled, his proposed instructions were read at the home of Peyton Randolph. There was considerable feeling that Jefferson had gone too far in denying Parliament the right of external taxation which John Dickinson's *Letters of a Pennsylvania Farmer* had some years earlier conceded. The division seemed to be on age lines. "The young ascended with Jefferson to the source of those rights; the old required time for consideration, before they could tread this lofty ground, which, if it had not been abandoned, at least had not been fully occupied, throughout America."[40] Heeding the senior advisers, the Convention adopted a more temperate set of instructions. Jefferson felt that they were flawed in at least two respects. The association that was set up had too many loopholes, and the instructions committed Virginia to conform only to such resolutions as her deputies assented to, a provision which, as Jefferson saw it, "totally destroys that union of conduct in the several colonies which was the very purpose of calling the Congress." In short, to the radical nationalist, "we have left undone those things which we ought to have done. And we have done those things which we ought not to have done."[41]

Although rejected by the Convention, Jefferson's draft resolution and instructions were printed by his friends in pamphlet form, appearing in the early fall of '74 as *A Summary View of the Rights of British America*. It soon achieved a continental circulation and was reprinted in London by the end of the year. Therein Jefferson denied all Parliamentary authority over the colonies whatsoever and claimed that the only tie with Great Britain was supplied by the King, to whom the colonists had voluntarily submitted. By now he had moved to an insistence upon both the revindication of Anglo-Saxon liberties, which he had discovered in a remote past, as well as upon "rights as derived from the laws of nature." Jefferson's conception of the British empire was too advanced for a Dickinson or a Jay, but was shared contemporaneously by a Scottish lawyer from frontier Pennsylvania named James Wilson, and within a few months espoused by John Adams, a rising politician from Braintree, Massachusetts, and a King's College student from New York, a young unknown named Alexander Hamilton, whose principles history does not normally intertwine with the Jeffersonian ideology.[42]

It was the tone as much as the substance of *A Summary View* that had come as a shock to the more temperate-minded among the burgesses. Jefferson spoke of the "treasonable crimes" of the House of Stuart which brought on them "the exertion of those sacred and sovereign rights of punishment, reserved in the hands of the people for cases of extreme necessity"—a more legal-minded paraphrase of Patrick Henry's irresistible, if disputed, allusion to "Charles the First his Cromwell. . . ." Denouncing the Navigation Laws and other Parliamentary legislation as "that rapid and bold succession of injuries," he warned: "Single acts of tyranny may be ascribed to the accidental opinion of a day; but a series of oppressions, begun at a distinguished period, and pursued unalterably thro' every change of ministers, too plainly prove a deliberate, systematical plan of reducing us to slavery." In short, while Jefferson explicitly denied Parliament's legislative authority over the colonies and condemned that legislature as "a body of men foreign to our constitutions, and unacknowledged by our laws," he refused to acquit the King of complicity in the results. He denounced him for disallowing laws for "the most trifling reasons, and sometimes for no conceivable reason" and for making "the civil subordinate to the military," a phrase that reappears in the Declaration of Independence, where the King is charged with having "affected to render the Military independent of and superior to the Civil Power." All this the King had done "by force," but he should remember, Jefferson warned, "that force cannot give right." Appealing to the King to stop sacrificing the "rights of one part of the empire to the inordinate desires of another," Jefferson asserted that it was neither the wish nor the interest of the colonies to separate from Great Britain, but rather to form part of a union in which commercial preference would be enjoyed by all its members without barring the colonies from other markets and without subjecting colonial property to being taxed or regulated "by any power on earth but our own." Then Jefferson closed on a warning note: This was the last plea to the King to redress grievances. If Jefferson had had his way this would indeed have been the last, but more moderate spirits like Dickinson and Jay persuaded the Congress the following year to transmit a final plea, known as the Olive Branch Petition.

Jefferson had every reason to take pride in the momentum he had given to the commercial boycott, but, ironically, he was one of the very first persons to get entangled in the new restrictive regulations. In May, when only tea had been the subject of a proposed boycott in Virginia, Jefferson had ordered fourteen pairs of sash windows from England, along with some spare glass for replacements. When the more comprehensive association was adopted in August, Jefferson wrote abroad to countermand the order, only to learn that the goods were already shipped. Lacking "the spirit of prophecy," Jefferson certainly could not have foretold this eventuality, and to set a proper example he agreed to having these goods placed at the disposal of the local committee.[43]

Like other patriots, Jefferson felt impelled to refute the repeated charge that revolutionary ardor had been fanned by the conspiratorial activity of the radical leaders. As he saw it, Lexington had "cut off our last hopes of reconciliation; and a phrenzy of revenge seems to have seized all ranks of people." In a section of a letter he later struck out, he argued that this fact disproved the government's contention that the ferment had been stirred up by "a few principal men in every colony." First he had written "hot headed demagogues." In fact, "the utmost efforts of the more intelligent people" had "been requisite and exerted to moderate the almost ungovernable fury of the people."[44] Thus, as the resort to violence was becoming seemingly irreversible, Jefferson sought to get on the record for old friends whose opinion he respected evidence that he himself was a moderate and reasonable man, being pushed to extremes by an obtuse government and an aroused populace. From radicals like Jefferson to conservatives like Jay, leaders of every spectrum of colonial protest chose retrospectively to deny that they had started the Revolution or had plotted separation.

Immersed as he was in public affairs, Jefferson managed to spend more time on his beloved plantation and with his immediate family than did most contemporary political leaders. How much his family bolstered his morale is by no means clear, however, since Jefferson chose to absent himself from some of the most crucial votes or debates, whether as a delegate to the Virginia Convention or to the Continental Congress, and was confined to his mountain retreat burdened with family cares.

Jefferson's views of women, sex, and marriage are shrouded in reticence, but ever so often a small flicker of light comes through the chinks of privacy. To start with, Jefferson had a repressed or prudish streak, a deep-seated belief in the inherent danger of female passion, if uncontrolled, coupled with a conviction that sexual promiscuity was the ultimate corruption. Fearing women as sexual aggressors, he counseled Madison in 1786 that the punishment of castration for rape was "indecent and unjustifiable," as women would be tempted "to make it the instrument of vengeance against an inconstant lover, and of disappointment to a rival."[45] No American, he counseled a young friend, should come to Europe "under thirty years of age." For, if he does come, he will be inevitably "led by the strongest of all human passions into a spirit for female intrigue destructive of his own and others happiness, or a passion for whores destructive of his health, and in both cases learns to consider fidelity to the marriage bed as an ungentlemanly practice and inconsistent with happiness."[46]

As a youngster the views he expressed on sex and women were quite conventional,[47] but it would be only fair to say that he did not care particularly for the society of women, nor were they particularly attracted to him. He first paid court to Rebecca Burwell, a sixteen-year-old orphan, sister of a college mate, but his was less than a whirlwind courtship, and when he did come face to face with his inamorata, he stammered a few irrational phrases.[48] In fact, Jefferson never put the categorical question to her, but merely asked for time on the ground that he planned to go abroad to study. Rebecca, who never seems to have been responsive to his overtures, had no intention of waiting around. Instead, she married Jacquelin Amber, and the news gave Jefferson the first of those "violent headaches" accompanying the receipt of bad news.[49] The daughter of Rebecca and Jacquelin would marry John Marshall, and Jefferson's intense dislike for that jurist may well have, unconsciously, sprung from this relationship. After all, but for the vagaries of female passion, Marshall might have been his own son-in-law!

His one-sided romance ended, Jefferson consoled himself with misogynous outbursts, and turned to the companionship of men. Henceforth the only women to whom he was to be attracted were either married or once married. The first of these was Mrs. John Walker, the wife of a friend and neighbor, to whom by his own later admission he had made improper, if clumsy, advances in Walker's absence from home. It speaks volumes for Jefferson's own marriage that, as Walker later charged, he continued to make such advances over a period of seven years after he himself had taken a wife. Nothing really happened, except that the lady, after long suffering in silence, told her husband, curiously delaying the revelation more than fifteen years after the first seduction attempt allegedly took place. Walker, exploiting the political rancor of a later day, touched off a full-scale scandal timed to embarrass Jefferson in his first term as President. Jefferson privately admitted that he had behaved improperly, an admission limited to acts committed before his own marriage. "I plead guilty to one of their charges, that when young and single I offered love to a handsome lady. I acknolege its incorrectness."[50]

Ten years after his blighted romance with Rebecca Burwell and some four years after his initial attempts to share Mrs. Walker's bed, Jefferson married a twenty-three-year-old widow, Martha Skelton Wayles. By marriage Jefferson not only doubled his acreage but saddled himself with his father-in-law's debts. He had found a mate who shared his enthusiasm for literature and music and brightened his temper. That conical little mountain peak a mile outside Charlottesville which, in a misogynist mood he had called "The Hermitage," he now renamed "Monticello," a more romantic-sounding Italian villa.

As his spirits soared, Jefferson optimistically pushed forward with his plans for his Monticello home where he and Martha could hopefully live out their lives together. Fate decreed otherwise. Martha bore him six children, one a boy. Four died in infancy, and two daughters survived. Throughout the marriage Jefferson's wife suffered ailing health and was a constant source of anxiety to him. Whatever sense of heightened physical excitement had accompanied the courtship, honeymoon, and early marriage days perished after a brief flicker. Martha's death in 1782, after only ten years of marriage, left him shattered with grief and consumed with self-pity. Atop her grave on a slab of white marble Jefferson recorded her birth, then:

> Intermarried with
> Thomas Jefferson
> January 1st, 1772;
> Torn from him by death
> September 6th, 1782:
> This monument of his love is inscribed.

Then follow two lines in Greek from the *Iliad:*

> Though the dead forget their dead with Hades in the grave
> Even there I shall remember my sweet friend.[51]

In retrospect, Jefferson may not have found his married life completely satisfying. He destroyed all correspondence with Martha and most memorabilia concerning her. From this insistence on the privacy of his feelings each person is free to draw his own conclusion. He warned James Monroe that "matrimony illy agrees with study,"[52] and after his defeat for the Presidency in 1796 he wrote Edward Rutledge that he did not regret it, that "the honeymoon would be as short in that case as in any other, and moments of extasy would be ransomed by years of torment and hatred."[53] Strong words indeed for one who was so devoted to his wife's memory that he remained a widower for the last forty-two years of a long life! It is evident that anxiety and torment had in Jefferson's mind transformed the bonds of matrimony into a bruising chain and left him with memories of tension, anxiety, and heavy responsibilities.

Jefferson, on his wife's death, assumed the role of both father and mother to his two daughters, Martha (Patsy) and Mary (Maria), to whom he was deeply attached. While minister to France he put his daughters in a convent school. According to tradition, Martha wrote her father for permission to become a nun. His reply was to withdraw both daughters from the school and to remain determinedly reticent on the subject thereafter.[54] Martha, on her return, married a second cousin, Thomas Mann Randolph, and Maria would marry John

Wayles Eppes, a first cousin. In the education of both of these male kinfolk Jefferson had long taken a keen interest, and he was especially fond of Eppes, who had been brought up in the Jefferson household. In the picking of mates who were long a part of the intimate family circle—indeed, one might say "kissing cousins"—Jefferson's daughters might have shown a trifle more independence, but they could scarcely have married men more suitable from their father's point of view.

When, during his presidency, Mary died at the age of twenty-four, Jefferson poured forth his grief to the friend of his boyhood, John Page. "I, of my want, have lost even the half of all I had. My evening prospects now hang on the slender thread of a single life. Perhaps I may be destined to see even this last cord of parental affection broken!"[55] This gloomy prophecy was not borne out, but on his death Jefferson left his surviving daughter a mountain of debts, and Martha was driven penniless and propertyless from the land of her birth.

The closest Jefferson ever came to having a love affair as a mature man took place in Paris, where in pursuit of his diplomatic duties he also pursued Maria Cosway. Maria was different from the forward intellectual types that crowded the Paris salons, and Jefferson, after a number of years of exposure to French ladies, remarked that he preferred home-loving American "Angels" to foot-loose French Amazons who neglected "their nurseries" in their endless hunt for pleasure.[56] Jefferson had a consuming flirtation, and drew back on the brink when no further obstacles seemingly interposed themselves.

Maria Cosway, born in Florence of English parents and a devout Catholic, possessed of beauty and artistic talent, had married a vain and foppish but rich miniaturist named Richard Cosway, considerably older than herself and a head shorter. Jefferson first met her in the summer of 1786. Maria, then twenty-seven, had a baby-doll face and a rosebud mouth. Her slim and graceful figure was strikingly set off by a mass of golden hair. Not least of her enticements was a musical voice and a vivacity matched by her skill at coquetry. For weeks Jefferson and Maria Cosway were constant companions. Not far from their day of parting, Jefferson, according to one version, took Maria for a walk along the Seine. Coming to a fence, Jefferson in a moment of boyish exuberance ventured to vault it, perhaps intending to help his lady cross from the far side. But at the most luckless moment the agility and skill of his youth deserted him. He took an awkward tumble, and, in trying to break his fall, fractured his right wrist. The fracture was never set properly. For weeks he was immobilized, and for the rest of his life he had difficulty writing normally. How much the self-revelation that he was no longer a dashing young blade contributed to dampening his ardor is pure speculation. Finally, the Cosways left Paris, with Jefferson accompanying them as far as St.-Denis.

That evening he sat down and, with his left hand, wrote one of the most unusual, as well as revealing, love letters. It took the form of a dialogue between his "Head" and his "Heart," a debate between reason and emotion, with history helping the latter's cause. "If our country when pressed with wrongs at the point of the bayonet had been governed by its heads, instead of its hearts, where should we have been now?" the Heart asked, but the Head claimed the final word, comforting itself with the expectation of the return of Maria in the spring, as she had promised. "I should love her forever, was it only for that."

To Maria, London without Jefferson, despite the social whirl, seemed dull. On Christmas of 1786 Jefferson wrote Maria, referring to the legend of Fortunatus, who possessed a magic cap permitting him to wish himself wherever he might want to be. If he had such a cap, Jefferson said, "I question if I should use it but once. I should wish myself with you, and not wish myself away again."

Jefferson had his wish, for in August, 1787, Maria turned up in Paris, this time without her husband and for a four months' stay. But nothing really happened. The couple spent little time together, and Jefferson even came late for a farewell breakfast with Maria, only to find a note instead from his beloved. The exciting events of the fall of '87, in which Jefferson was involved, doubtless provided him with the excuse if he needed one for having studiously avoided her. As Maria pouted when she got back to London, "My forcing you would have [been] unkind and unfriendly as it would be cruel to pretend in what is totally disagreeable to you." Jefferson returned to America in 1789, and the love affair never got beyond a further exchange of letters, ending some years later when Maria retired to a convent.

The lady had provided him with every opportunity, but Jefferson proved evasive. "The day we went to St. Germains was a little too warm, I think, was it not?" the Heart had at one point admitted. And that is all that is on the record to suggest that the affair was not unconsummated. Jefferson's wariness, as in all other encounters of passion, reveals that he was never all consumed. For Jefferson, a liaison or possibly even a marriage with one so vain, self-centered, and incorrigible as Maria might have been a personal tragedy. To have publicly flaunted a liaison with a married woman and devout Catholic to boot might have been *comme il faut* in Paris, but in the less cosmopolitan reaches of Virginia it would have spelled finis to the public career of Thomas Jefferson. Save, perhaps, for Franklin Delano Roosevelt's decision not to seek a divorce from Eleanor, no American national public figure ever came so close to the brink and drew back before it was too late.[57]

It is somewhat extraordinary that the two future political rivals, Alexander Hamilton and Thomas Jefferson, should have had their later careers muddied by accusation of illicit sexual affairs. By admitting his relations with Mrs. Reynolds, Hamilton virtually closed the book on that sordid episode, while Jefferson, by maintaining his customary reticence in all matters involving his private life, succeeded only in fanning the flames of scandal over his alleged liaison with "Dusky Sally."

Fourteen years old when she accompanied Polly Jefferson to France, Sally Hemings was an attractive, very light-colored slave, one of twelve slave children mothered by the prolific mulatto slave Betty Hemings. Jefferson acquired Betty and her brood in the settlement of the estate of his father-in-law, John Wayles. According to oral tradition, Betty was Wayles's concubine and he was the father of the six youngest children she brought to Monticello. If this is true, Jefferson must have felt a special concern for the illegitimate half brothers and sisters of his own wife, whose presence in her new home must have caused her acute embarrassment. Trained to household work or the crafts, they received favored treatment, and two were freed. As for Sally's children, one daughter was freed at the age of twenty-one, and Jefferson by will provided for the boys' apprenticeship to their uncle, and emancipation at twenty-one.

At Monticello there always was talk about the Hemings and their favored position, but it was a scandalmonger and character assassin named James Thomas Callender who spread the Sally Hemings story in the Richmond press during the summer and fall of 1802, at the height of Jefferson's first term in the presidency. Callender charged that Sally Hemings, the "African Venus" as he called her, was the mistress of the President. The Federalist press and antislavery organs hammered home the charges with choice bits of salacious poetry, like this stanza to the tune of "Yankee Doodle":

> Yankee doodle, who's the noodle?
> What wife were half so handy?
> To breed a flock of slaves for stock,
> A blackamoor's the dandy.

And the theme was strummed ad nauseam:

> In glaring red and chalky white,
>   Let others beauty see;
> Me no such tawdry tints delight—
>   No! *black's* the hue for me!

Jefferson never deigned to answer the charge publicly, nor is he known to have even mentioned it privately. Two circumstantial sets of facts have been adduced to support the probabilities of the relationship. Sally gave birth to five children between 1795 and 1808, and although Jefferson was away from Monticello about two-thirds of the time, he was at home nine months prior to each birth.[58] Second, some of Sally's children bore a striking resemblance to Jefferson, and one of them, Madison Hemings, claimed years later that he was the son of the President.[59] The likeness has been explained by one tradition, according to which Sally was the mistress of Peter Carr, a favorite nephew of Jefferson's, and her sister Betsey was the mistress of Peter's brother Samuel, whom one of Jefferson's granddaughters described as "the most notorious good-natured Turk that ever was master of a black seraglio at other men's expense."[60] Speculation notwithstanding, a secret liaison with an attractive household slave is not inconsistent with Jefferson's guilt feelings in matters of sex, his fear of rejection, his view of women as sexual aggressors, and of blacks as sexually more animal than whites, as persons to whom love was "only an eager desire, not a tender delicate excitement, not a delicious foment of the soul."[61]

Black or white, the female was regarded by Jefferson as the more dangerous sex, the less trustworthy, the one governed by emotion rather than reason. In short, from any review of Jefferson's relations with women, he emerges as a full-fledged antifeminist who had not the slightest wish to have women share with men that equality of which he was the nation's most eloquent exponent.

Abigail Adams excepted, Jefferson detested intellectual women. Annoyed by the political chatter of women in Parisian salons, he wrote home expressing the hope that "our good ladies . . . are contented to soothe and calm the minds of their husbands returning ruffled from political debate."[62] Even that comforting but restricted objective found no place in Jefferson's vast educational structure. He had no plans to prepare women for civic responsibilities, but merely to educate them in genteel pursuits and to perform their functions as wives and mothers.[63] A hint from Albert Gallatin, his Secretary of the Treasury, that the President might consider women for the public service, elicited this sharp rejoinder from Jefferson: "The appointment of a woman to office is an innovation for which the public is not prepared, nor am I."[64] Even the purest of democracies, so Jefferson pointed out in old age, would find it necessary to exclude women from the suffrage "to prevent depravation of morals and ambiguity of issue."

So much for Jefferson and "women's lib"!

Jefferson's personal life impinges perhaps more intimately upon his public role than was the case with most of the Revolutionary leaders. Moods of anxiety and depression, not unmitigated by guilt feelings, brought on interludes of disorientation from the public service. Fortunately for the cause he served, these moods never for too long were allowed to dampen his dedication to the Revolutionary movement. On June 2, 1775, he arrived in Philadelphia to take his seat in the Second Continental Congress. Quickly he was propelled to the center of the national stage. Two days after he arrived he was appointed to a committee of five to draw up a "Declaration of the Causes and Necessity for Taking Up Arms," which Washington was to publish on his arrival at the American encampment at Cambridge. Jefferson prepared a preliminary draft, which, as he later recalled, was "too strong for Mr. Dickinson," still hopeful of reconciliation with the mother country. Dickinson made a new statement, retaining much of the Jefferson material. As William Livingston put it, both Jefferson and John Rutledge had prepared drafts which embodied the faults common to Southern gentlemen. "Much fault-finding and declamation, with little sense or dignity. They seem to think a reiteration of tyranny, despotism, bloody, etc. all that is needed to unite us at home and convince the bribed voters of the North of the justice of our cause."[65] The final product was the result of collaboration between Dickinson and Jefferson. The latter's draft was bold, but Dickinson's in some respects proved even more daring. Both kept the door open to a restoration of harmony, but both conveyed an ominous warning.[66] In short, the last draft revealed a basic accord between the two principal authors, even though Jefferson, like other radical delegates, signed without enthusiasm. Dickinson's Olive Branch Petition, adopted by Congress only a few days later, professing as it did a fervent loyalty to the Crown and affection for the ties to Great Britain, was a much harder pill for the radicals to swallow, but gulp it down they did. Henceforth, Jefferson would have no truck with conciliation. He drafted the resolution of Congress rejecting out of hand Lord North's proposals to have Parliament forbear to tax the colonies should they raise a revenue themselves subject to approval by King and Parliament.[67]

After a bare two months in Philadelphia Jefferson had had enough of politics, and August of '75 saw him back at Monticello. He had but two wishes now, he wrote John Randolph, in a note sending for the violin he had purchased along with some violin music. First, he wished for a restoration of "our just rights," and second, "a return of the happy period when, consistently with duty, I may withdraw myself totally from the public stage and pass the rest of my days in domestic ease and tranquillity, banishing every desire of afterwards even hearing what passes in the world."[68] Neither wish was to be gratified, and Jefferson was to see the years of the Revolutionary War fairly evenly divided between private anguish and public turmoil. Back in Philadelphia late that fall, he wrote an intimate about his concern for his family, from whom he had not heard: "The suspense under which I am is too terrible to be endured."[69] The ill health of his wife and then of his mother brought him back to Monticello. His mother's death of an apopleptic stroke laid him low with bouts of migraine that lingered for some five weeks. He did not leave for Congress until May of '76. Meantime, he had managed, though absent, to keep abreast of the rapid drift of affairs.

As the tempo of radicalism increased, Jefferson wrote his Tory-minded friend John Randolph:

> Believe me, Dear Sir, there is not in the British Empire a man who more cordially loves a Union with Great Britain than I do. But by the

god that made me I will cease to exist before I yield to a connection on such terms as the British parliament propose, and in this I think I speak the sentiments of America. We want neither inducements nor power to declare and assert a separation. It is will alone which is wanting and that is growing apace under the fostering hand of our king.[70]

Perhaps Jefferson did not realize when he penned them how prophetic his words would prove or that he himself was to be the literary instrument to assert that "separation." The publication of Tom Paine's *Common Sense* helped forge that "will" to independence and set off the popular ground swell to which leaders like Jefferson were peculiarly sensitive. Not long after Paine's electric presentation of the case against the "Royal Brute" of Britain, Jefferson's writings assume a more antimonarchical stripe. Prompted by the King's speech upon the convening of Parliament in October, 1775, in which George III vowed that he would not give up colonies planted and nursed with "great industry" and "tenderness" and defended "at much expense and treasure," Jefferson researched into America's colonial origins, from which he concluded that the King's statements were a "palpable untruth." "A king who can adopt falshood [sic]" and "solemnize it from the throne," he warned, "justifies the revolution of fortune which reduces him to a private station."[71] Meantime his Virginia correspondents kept him abreast of the burgeoning independence movement in his own colony. "For God's sake declare the Colonies independent at once, and save us from ruin," implored John Page.[72] Two weeks later Page wrote, urging a commercial alliance with France, the drawing up of state constitutions, and the adoption of a plan of confederation, all of which steps were being widely discussed and were soon to be initiated.[73] Then the Virginia Convention formally called upon the Continental Congress to declare independence. Read in Congress on May 27, the call prompted Richard Henry Lee's resolve of June 7[74] "that these United Colonies are, and of right ought to be, free and independent states." While the resolution was put off for three weeks to give the assemblies of the middle colonies time to remove the restrictions imposed on their delegates from voting for separation, Congress went ahead and appointed a committee to prepare a declaration of independence on June 11. The committee comprised Jefferson, John Adams, Franklin, Roger Sherman, and Robert R. Livingston.

Years later, in an uncharacteristic mood of self-belittlement, Jefferson noted in his autobiography: "I have sometimes asked myself whether my country is better for my having lived at all? I do not know that it is. I have been the instrument of doing the following things; but they would have been done by others; some of them perhaps better." First on that list of achievements Jefferson put "the declaration of independance." That he was the principal author is no longer a matter of doubt, although in the partisan acrimony that swept the nation in Jefferson's old age, some old-line Federalists attempted to chip away at this contribution. An old enemy, Timothy Pickering, solicited a comment from John Adams in 1822, and the latter, never at any time given to self-deprecation, claimed that he had been on a subcommittee appointed by the five to draft the document, that Jefferson had drafted it alone, and that he had sat down with the author and "conn'd the paper over." This did not accord with Jefferson's own memory, supported by careful notes entered down not very many years after the event.[75] "Mr. Adams's memory has led him into unquestioned error," he remarked. "At the age of 88 and 47 years after the transaction of Independence, this is not wonderful. Nor should I, at the age of 80, in the small advantage of that difference only, venture to oppose my memory to his, were it not supported by written notes, taken by myself at the moment and on the spot." These notes are no longer extant, but seem to have been written before the end of the Revolution, although Jefferson was mistaken about the timing and details of the actual signing.[76]

That Jefferson should have been entrusted with the composition of a document of such historical magnitude was indeed a tribute to his reputation as a writer rather than a speechifier. As Adams later recalled in his autobiography, "during the whole time I satt with him in Congress, I never heard him utter three sentences together."[77] Jefferson was picked out of regard for his reputation for "literature, science, and a happy talent of composition," and, on equally weighty grounds, because a competitor for that honor, Richard Henry Lee, was highly unpopular with the Virginia delegation.

No one can find fault with the choice. In general, emendations or revisions proposed by Adams and Franklin or by Congress made the Declaration a crisper and more eloquent document. No one is likely to prefer "undeniable" to "self-evident," and save for the deletion by Congress of the indictment of the King for his alleged role in the slave trade, a deletion made to conciliate the delegates from the Lower South, the changes were beneficial. Congress inserted in the last sentence the phrase, "with a firm reliance on the protection of divine providence," but, except for capitalization, left untouched Jefferson's final words: "We mutually pledge to each other our Lives, our Fortunes, and our sacred Honor."[78]

Whether or not all the Signers were convinced of the validity of the principles which the Great Declaration asserted, there is no question that its author, with his enthusiasm for the radical Whiggish line, had convinced himself of their correctness. It seems fair enough, then, to take the testimony of his own actions and see whether it squares with the principles he had phrased with such consummate artistry.

To begin, the Declaration expounded the right of revolution, with the simple caveat that "prudence" would "dictate that governments long established should not be changed for light and transient causes." On the same day that the Declaration of Independence was read and John Hancock's large signature affixed thereto, a committee comprising Franklin, Jefferson, and John Adams was appointed to bring in a device for the seal of the United States. From Franklin came the motto, "Rebellion to tyrants is obedience to God." Jefferson was so enamored of the motto that he included it on the seal of Virginia and stamped it on the wax with which he sealed his own letters,[79] even though Congress rejected it, preferring the theme of union now ("E Pluribus Unum") rather than revolution.

Jefferson's consistency in support of this proposition distinguished the gentleman theorist from the practical politician, although he managed to play both roles to the end. Three thousand miles from the whiff of grapeshot that routed the attackers on the Springfield arsenal, Jefferson, like a true ideologue, took a detached and relaxed view of Shays' Rebellion. While his fellow revolutionaries in America believed that the rebellion was moving the Confederacy toward the brink, from Paris Jefferson managed to be cool and collected. "I hold that a little rebellion now and then is a good thing," he commented. "The tree of liberty must be refreshed from time to time with the blood of patriots and tyrants. It is it's natural manure."[80] Although as Washington's Secretary of State he signed the proclamation denouncing the Whiskey Rebellion,[81] and as Vice President and presiding officer of the Senate he signed the warrant of arrest of William Duane for seditious contempt of that body,[82] Jefferson found grounds as Vice President to applaud the little insurgency of John Fries of Pennsylvania against the direct tax. "Pennsylvania, Jersey, and New York are coming majestically round to the true principles," he commented cheerfully.[83] Holding in the Kentucky Resolves that each state as a party to the compact had a right to judge for itself the mode and measure of redress to be adopted when the general government assumed undelegated powers,[84] he turned the concept of the right of revolution into an argument to be exploited by exponents of nullification, the seedbed of secession. Committed to the notion of periodic change and experimentation, Jefferson fondly referred to his own ascendancy to the presidency as the "revolution of 1800."

That Jefferson was more securely captivated by the idea of a continuing revolution than any of his American contemporaries is evidenced by an extraordinary letter apparently written for Lafayette's use in the French National Assembly in 1789, but later transmitted to Madison. Therein Jefferson expressed the view that *"the earth belongs in usufruct to the living,"* the dead having neither rights nor powers over it. The idea and even the language seem to have drawn upon a set of propositions submitted to Jefferson by a radical English physician friend, Richard Gem, some time early in September, 1789.[85] Gem may well have been the intermediary in conveying Jefferson's exposition of the theme to Lafayette. Since its contents exposed him as a party to direct subversion of the internal affairs of a sovereign power to which he was accredited, Jefferson dressed up his communication with an opening and closing paragraph adapting his proposal to America and addressing it ostensibly to James Madison.

Jefferson suggested that his exposition would "furnish matter for a fine preamble to our first law for appropriating the public revenue." He thought that no other nation could make such "a declaration against the validity of long-contracted debts so disinterestedly as we." In fact, Jefferson was by now hopelessly enmeshed in personal indebtedness that came as a principal legacy of his father-in-law's estate,[86] despite the general sequestration bill that Jefferson had drafted in 1778 for wartime Virginia to liquidate debts to British planters in depreciated paper money, a bill which did not achieve the ends hoped for by its author and other debtors.[87] He might well have subconsciously considered the advantages to unfortunates like himself if the law had not saddled them with the obligations of a previous generation. Aside from placing in stark contrast the notions of Thomas Jefferson and Alexander Hamilton on the inviolability of public contracts,[88] Jefferson's view also did violence to the convictions of the Founding Fathers about the distinction between fundamental law and ordinary legislation. In quite casually proposing the enactment by ordinary legislation of what amounted in fact to a profound amendment of the federal Constitution, Jefferson behaved very much as he had done earlier when he drafted the Virginia Act for Establishing Religious Freedom. Conceding therein that representatives "elected by the people for the ordinary purposes of legislation only, have no power to restrain the acts of succeeding Assemblies," he deemed the rights of conscience as "of the natural rights of mankind." Presumably, the doctrine that the earth belongs to the living expressed a similar natural right. But as applied to America, Jefferson, in his communication, would have applied it exclusively to long-term debts and the protection of copyrights and patents for a term of nineteen rather than fourteen years.[89] As Julian Boyd points out, although Jefferson failed to press for the application of the principle when in office, he never wavered in his allegiance to the concept that the earth belongs to the living. When, as President, he came face to face with John Marshall and the doctrine of the sanctity of contracts, he signally failed to press its relevance to that principle.

In the Revolutionary years Jefferson's dedication to this principle had been manifest by his legislation ending entails and primogeniture, legal devices which would perpetuate the past. By these measures Jefferson believed he had laid "the axe to the foot of pseudo-aristocracy."[90] Similarly motivated were Jefferson's efforts to promote more equitable land distribution and prevent the dead hand of the past from establishing land monopoly. Indeed, the slightest trace of the hereditary principle offended his republican instincts and his concern for the living rather than the dead.[91]

Jefferson's stay in France confirmed his profound sympathy for the poor and downtrodden. "Experience declares that man is the only animal which devours his own kind; for I can apply no milder term to the governments of Europe, and to the general prey of the rich on the poor."[92] On its face Jefferson's comment sharply contrasts with John Adams's observation that "the rich have as clear a right to their liberty and property as the poor."[93] Still, one could never accuse

Jefferson of being a leveler or of favoring a "soak-the-rich" tax policy. Such latter-day notions would have violated what Jefferson called "the first principle of association, 'the *guarantee* to everyone a free exercise of his industry and the fruits acquired by it.' "[94]

Jefferson, like Tom Paine, considered the American Revolution both as a revolution completed and as a revolution continuing. To each it constituted a standing example to all the world. In *Common Sense* Paine had declared: "We have it in our power to begin the world anew." In his old age Jefferson was prepared to see "rivers of blood" and "years of desolation" in order to check absolute monarchy and recover the right of self-government abroad.[95] Of that final outcome he remained temperately optimistic. "I shall not die," he remarked to John Adams, "without a hope that light and liberty are on steady advance." He saw the American Revolution as spreading to other continents and, looking ahead into the nineteenth century, as suffering setbacks, such as in the case of Napoleon, but scoring advances, as with the cause of Greek independence. His closing years saw reactionary governments gripping Europe in an iron fist, but he maintained that "the flames kindled on the 4th of July 1776 have spread over too much of the globe to be extinguished by the feeble engines of despotism."[96] In one of his last recorded remarks, Jefferson, replying to a committee of citizens of Washington who had invited him to be present on the fiftieth anniversary of the Declaration, uttered a fervent wish that it might "be to the world, what I believe it will be (to some parts sooner, to others later, but finally to all) the signal of arousing men to burst the chains, under which monkish ignorance and superstition had persuaded them to bind themselves, and to assume the blessings and security of self-government."[97]

Steadfast in his convictions of the virtues of republicanism—in fact, he was inclined to attribute base monarchistic designs to political adversaries—Jefferson had laid down in the Great Declaration the principle that governments derive their "just powers" from "the consent of the governed." In Jefferson's own day the principle of the sovereignty of the people was universally accepted by his countrymen, who through the adoption of state constitutions and ultimately the federal Constitution institutionalized the principles of a government responsible to the people, a government limited to securing the people's rights, safety, and happiness, and one circumscribed by fundamental written law. Indeed, to Jefferson and the other Founding Fathers republicanism meant more than a system in which the chief executive was elective not hereditary, or weak rather than strong; it meant a government in which the people's share in decisionmaking was to be high by any standard of measurement in the eighteenth-century world, and one capable of carrying through moral as well as political reformation.[98] Jefferson professed to be astonished at the rapidity with which the republican system was everywhere instituted in America. Americans, he observed in the summer of '77, "seem to have deposited the monarchical and taken up the republican government with as much ease as would have attended their throwing off an old and putting on a new suit of clothes."[99]

How democratic would a republican government have to be in fact to satisfy Jefferson's criteria of "popular consent"? While he, like most of his Whig contemporaries, assumed that each voter should possess some stake in society—in short, have "a will of his own," he was prepared to have the government procure such a stake for the voter if he did not already have it. In the summer of '76 Jefferson sought to have his liberal views on the suffrage written into the Virginia Constitution. He favored, as proper evidence of attachment to the community, "either the having resided a certain time, or having a family, or having property, any or all of them." He sought to ensure the enfranchisement of still others by incorporating in each of his three drafts of the Virginia Constitution a proposal that fifty acres of unappropriated lands be distributed to "every person . . . not owning nor having ever owned that quantity" of land, "and no other person shall be capable of taking an appropriation."[100] The delegates followed Pendleton instead and restricted the franchise to the traditional freehold suffrage. But Jefferson's proposed democratic reforms had a much wider ambit. He would have eliminated special property qualifications for officeholders, throwing open public office to an electorate virtually identical with the free white male community, and he would have reapportioned the legislature to achieve fair and equal representation geographically.

Neither a Southern populist demagogue nor a city boss of the modern stripe, Jefferson was a Virginia Whig who believed that democracy would work best in an agrarian society. He had no illusions about the people. Opposing the selection of state senators by the people, he remarked: "I have ever observed that a choice by the people themselves is not generally distinguished for its wisdom."[101]

Nor was he an aficionado of majoritarian perfection. The Revolution was fought to save man from the corrupt will of his neighbors, he believed, and a suspicion of man's actions should remain the keystone of government. As his Kentucky Resolutions of 1798 expressed it, "Government is founded in jealousy, not in confidence." On questions of power, "let no more be said of confidence in man, but bind him down from mischief by the chain of the Constitution."[102] These views were a far cry from *vox populi, vox dei*. Jefferson attributed no peculiar virtue or incorruptibility to the people. True, they could be bribed, but the cost of bribing so many was beyond the means of anyone or even of several men.[103] Thus numbers in themselves constituted a check against corruption. Favoring as he did an enlarged male suffrage (his Ordinance of 1784 guaranteed manhood suffrage at the outset, a step not a single state had yet taken), would Jefferson have extended the franchise to paupers, free blacks, and women? He gives us no hint that he would have supported so universal a suffrage as we have now come to associate with "democracy," although broad male suffrage extension was not inconsistent with his oft-reiterated position. "The mass of mankind has not been born with saddles on their backs, nor a favored few booted and spurred, ready to ride them legitimately, by the grace of God."[104] Closing words of the first Jeffersonian that might appropriately inaugurate the new era of the Age of Jackson.

The Declaration of Independence states that men "are endowed by their creator with certain unalienable[105] rights; that among these are life, liberty, and the pursuit of happiness." The notion of fundamental human rights was not original with Jefferson; nor did he go as far as his contemporaries in spelling them out. Already his fellow Virginian George Mason had drafted the Virginia Declaration of Rights, which was to have so enormous an impact on America and the world.[106] With Madison's strengthening, the clause on religious toleration in its final form asserted that "all men are equally entitled to the free exercise of religion, according to the dictates of conscience."[107]

Although Jefferson was less concerned than either Mason or Madison with the need to spell out the unalterable civil rights of man, his ardor for religious liberty burned as an unquenchable flame. In his own drafts for the Virginia Constitution he would have moved faster than Mason, and from drafts of his speeches he appears to have argued that the state had no right "to adopt an opinion on the matter of religion." A believer in strictly limited government, he justified his position on religion in his *Notes on Virginia,* wherein he claimed that the legitimate power of government extended to such acts only as are injurious to others. "But it does no injury for my neighbor to say there are twenty gods or no god. It neither picks my pocket, nor breaks my leg." Since toleration implied an official preference, Jefferson dropped the term and substituted "liberty." The religious freedom that he advocated in 1776 involved freedom of worship, as guaranteed in Mason's Bill of Rights, and freedom *from* the privileges and oppressions of a state church. Jefferson had pressed ahead to secure the latter objective. Partial victory was won in 1779, with the repeal of laws requiring members of the Anglican Church to contribute to its support and the legalizing of marriages performed by non-Anglican clergy.[108]

Second only to his authorship of the Declaration of Independence Jefferson placed his writing of the Statute for Religious Liberty. He drafted the bill in 1777, introduced it two years later as part of the Revision of the Laws, and then, while he was abroad on diplomatic duties, Madison brought forward the bill and saw to its passage in January of 1786. The bill is unique in two respects, both reflecting Jefferson's personal philosophy. The preamble hurls fire and brimstone upon the hypocrisy and tyranny long associated in Jefferson's mind with the alliance of church and state, and the unusual final clause contains a Jeffersonian warning to the legislature that any act hereafter framed repealing or narrowing its operation "will be an infringement of natural right."[109]

Apart from his championship of religious liberty, Jefferson demonstrated far less dedication to such other fundamental rights as fair trial or free speech.[110] As governor he signed into law a bill imposing fines and imprisonment for any person who "by writing, or by printing, or by open preaching, or by express words" should maintain that the United States was dependent upon the British Crown or Parliament.[111] Under the authority of this act Jefferson ordered the imprisonment of all persons in besieged Gloucester and York counties suspected of treason or misprision of treason or "disaffected to the independence of the United States," against whom "legal evidence cannot be obtained."[112] Jefferson, in supporting the loyalty oath program imposed by the Virginia legislature, conceded that the principle was to punish every person who was "a traitor in thought, but not in deed."[113] In supporting thought control, he himself had been active in drafting a law penalizing nonjurors as well as a revised form of the oath.[114] Like other wartime Patriot governors, Jefferson had disaffected Tories jailed without a hearing and held for months without trial. As a member of the legislature Jefferson drafted a bill of attainder convicting the terrorist Tory Josiah Phillips for having levied war against the commonwealth, attainting him and his confederates of high treason, and authorizing "any person" with or without order to pursue and slay Phillips and others among his associates.[115] As late as 1815, more than a quarter-century after the adoption of the Constitution and the Bill of Rights proscribing bills of attainder and establishing safeguards of due process in criminal trials, Jefferson still saw fit to justify legislative outlawry and attainder.[116] In his furious pursuit of Tory subversion Jefferson as governor was prepared to circumvent if not violate long-established principles of double jeopardy. Should a desperado he sought be acquitted on trial in Maryland, Governor Jefferson was prepared to have him tried in Virginia, perhaps, technically, for a different offense.[117] Should evidence not support a treason conviction, then "perhaps it may be sufficient to convict them of a misprision of treason,"[118] he directed in another case. His behavior in the Phillips and Shoemaker cases forecast the relentless prosecution that he instigated and sustained against Aaron Burr for acts which his old adversary John Marshall regarded as falling short of treason.[119] Toward prisoners he considered war criminals Jefferson was implacable. He had former Lieutenant-Governor Henry Hamilton of Detroit, notorious on the frontier as "the scalp-buyer," thrown in a dungeon and loaded with irons, defending his treatment of the captive "on general principles of national retaliation," warning that "iron will be retaliated by iron."[120] Drawing upon his own experiences as wartime governor of Virginia, he had then asked: "Should we have ever gained our Revolution, if we had bound our hands by manacles of the law?"[121]

As one rather severe critic has observed, Jefferson's threshold of tolerance for hateful political ideas was "less than generous."[122] Jefferson never protested against the substantive law of seditious libel; rather he was opposed to national as distinguished from state prosecutions for verbal crimes. In his draft constitution for Virginia in 1783 he proposed that the press "shall be subject to no other restraint than liableness to legal prosecution for false facts printed and published."[123] This would have amended the pertinent section of Mason's Declaration of Rights, which in more generous terms had declared: "That the freedom of the press is one of the great bulwarks of liberty, and can never be restrained but by despotic government." Jefferson even wanted some such restraints included in Madison's free press amendment to the federal Constitution.[124] Furious in his opposition to prosecutions by the Federalist administration for seditious libel under the hated Sedition Act, he remained silent when Jeffersonian Republican governments in the states prosecuted Federalist newspaper editors for the crime of seditiously libeling the President of the United States.

Jefferson's reputation as the foremost egalitarian of the Revolutionary generation rests upon a simple statement, electrifying in its impact: "All men are created equal." In fact, his original draft, before it was neatly pruned by the Committee of Five, more precisely expressed the rationale behind his affirmation: "We hold these truths to be sacred and undeniable; that all men are created equal and independent, that from that equal creation they derive rights inherent and inalienable."[125] This latter, and fortunately discarded,[126] version betrays its author's anthropological conviction that mankind stemmed from a single source, from which man anciently emigrated, a conviction that spurred Jefferson's amazing studies of the American Indian leagues, which he insisted were of greater antiquity than those of Asia.[127]

All his life Jefferson had a profound sympathy and even rapport with the Indians.[128] He felt called upon to defend them against attacks from the French naturalist Buffon, and to deny that they were basically different from the white man, with whom he fervently hoped a physical amalgamation would take place.[129]

It was precisely such amalgamation that Jefferson abhorred where the black man was concerned. Cascades of words have been spewed forth to show that Jefferson did not extend his egalitarianism to the Negro, that he regarded the black man as inferior to the white, both aesthetically and mentally, and that he never deviated from that "aversion to the mixture of colour" in America that he had set forth in his *Notes on Virginia*.[130]

If Jefferson accepted and publicized the white man's prejudices against the black, he cordially detested slavery and did as much as, if not more than, any of the Founding Fathers to curtail the "peculiar institution." The clause he inserted in the Great Declaration was stricken out by Congress, as Jefferson put it in his *Notes,* "in complaisance with South Carolina and Georgia, who had never attempted to restrain the importation of slaves, and who on the contrary still wished to continue it. Our Northern brethren also I believe felt a little tender under those censures, for tho' their people have very few slaves themselves yet they had been pretty considerable carriers of them to others."[181] But even earlier, at his very first session in the Burgesses, he joined forces with a senior colleague, Richard Bland, to have legislation enacted ameliorating the condition of slaves and looking toward their manumission. For his presumption Richard Bland was "denounced as an enemy of his country,"[132] and no doubt the lesson was carried home to the fledgling legislator and not readily forgotten. Still, Jefferson did not quit. He claimed credit for the bill enacted in 1778 slamming the door on the foreign slave trade,[133] but made no headway in his efforts to encourage the private manumission of slaves. Recognizing the temper of his fellow planters, he did not press too hard for his own proposal for the gradual emancipation of slaves, according to which measure all slaves born after the passage of the act would become free at the age of adulthood and be colonized outside the limits of Virginia. "It was thought better that this should be kept back," Jefferson later wrote, "and attempted only by way of amendment, whenever the bill should be brought on." When the bill did come up, Jefferson was abroad, and the amendment was never offered, perhaps, as he observed, because "the public mind would not yet bear the proposition."[134] His critics have noted that while he continued to favor gradual emancipation, neither he nor his Virginia associates were willing to risk their standing and influence by fighting for it, the kind of risks that did not have to be assumed by a John Jay or an Alexander Hamilton in New York.

If his antislavery efforts in Virginia became increasingly timid, Jefferson's vision for the nation at large consistently encompassed a diminished role for slavery. His Ordinance of 1784 contained the unprecedented clause: "That after the year 1800 of the Christian era, there shall be neither slavery nor involuntary servitude." The clause was lost. Jefferson's own delegation from Virginia abandoned him.

A Declaration by the Representatives of the UNITED STATES OF AMERICA, in General Congress assembled.

When in the course of human events it becomes necessary for one people to dissolve the political bands which have connected them with another, and to assume among the powers of the earth the separate and equal station to which the laws of nature & of nature's god entitle them, a decent respect to the opinions of mankind requires that they should declare the causes which impel them to the separation.

We hold these truths to be self-evident, that all men are created equal, that they are endowed by their creator with equal inherent & inalienable rights; that among these are life, & liberty, & the pursuit of happiness; that to secure these rights, governments are instituted among men, deriving their just powers from the consent of the governed; that whenever any form of government becomes destructive of these ends, it is the right of the people to alter or to abolish it, & to institute new government, laying it's foundation on such principles, & organising it's powers in such form, as to them shall seem most likely to effect their safety & happiness. prudence indeed will dictate that governments long established should not be changed for light & transient causes: and accordingly all experience hath shewn that mankind are more disposed to suffer while evils are sufferable, than to right themselves by abolishing the forms to which they are accustomed. but when a long train of abuses & usurpations [begun at a distinguished period, & pursuing invariably the same object, evinces a design to reduce them to arbitrary power] Despotism, it is their right, it is their duty, to throw off such government & to provide new guards for their future security. such has been the patient sufferance of these colonies; & such is now the necessity which constrains them to expunge their former systems of government. the history of the present king of Great Britain is a history of unremitting injuries and usurpations, [among which appears no solitary fact to contradict the uniform tenor of the rest but all have] in direct object the establishment of an absolute tyranny over these states. to prove this let facts be submitted to a candid world, [for the truth of which we pledge a faith yet unsullied by falsehood]

The Declaration of Independence. First page of Jefferson's draft with the corrections of John Adams and Benjamin Franklin. *(Library of Congress)*

A MISMATCHED
PAIR

Deborah Read, whom Franklin took "to wife, September 1st, 1730." Portrait by Benjamin Wilson ca. 1740. *(American Philosophical Society)*

Benjamin Franklin, printer, entrepreneur, philanthropist, and provincial politician. Portrait by Benjamin Wilson ca. 1740. *(White House Historical Association)*

Franklin in London at sixty. For an international celebrity, a turning point.
Painting by David Martin. *(White House Historical Association)*
"Every man in England seems to consider himself a piece of a sovereign
over America; seems to jostle himself into the throne with the King, and talks
of *our subjects in the Colonies.*"—Franklin to Lord Kames, April 11, 1767

George Washington's first life portrait—in the uniform of an officer of the Virginia militia in the French and Indian War. Painted at Mt. Vernon by Charles Willson Peale. (*George Washington Custis Lee Collection, Washington and Lee University*)

TWO WOMEN IN WASHINGTON'S LIFE

Sarah (Sally) Fairfax, the object of a youthful romance that left Washington with imperishable memories. A primitive painting, artist unknown. *(Courtesy, Mrs. Seymour St. John)*

Martha Parke Custis, as a young widow shortly before her marriage to Washington. Painting by John Wollaston the Younger. *(Washington and Lee University)*

Lawrence Washington, George's elder half-brother and early hero. Portrait dubiously attributed to John Wollaston the Younger, painted ca. 1738. (*Mount Vernon Ladies' Association of the Union*)

The stepchildren Washington adored. John Parke Custis and Martha Parke Custis, painted by John Wollaston the Younger in 1757, two years before Washington acquired his ready-made family. (*Washington and Lee University*)

Harvard College in John Adams's undergraduate days. A famous school for
the Puritan ministry, which Franklin once ridiculed as a place where dull
boys "learn little more than how to carry themselves handsomely and enter
a room genteely . . . and from whence they return, after abundance of trouble
and charge, as great blockheads as ever, only more proud and conceited."
John Adams clearly did not fit Franklin's characterization. "The Burgis-Price
View," 1743. (*Library of Congress*)

Abigail Smith Adams, a bride of two years. Pastel by Benjamin Blyth in 1766. *(Massachusetts Historical Society)*

John Adams at thirty-one. Pastel by Benjamin Blyth in 1766. *(Massachusetts Historical Society)*

Thomas Jefferson, as he must have looked to Maria Cosway. Portrait by John Trumbull, a miniature owned by Angelica Church, Alexander Hamilton's favorite sister-in-law. *(Metropolitan Museum of Art, Bequest of Cornelia Cruger, 1923)*

Maria Cosway, through Jefferson's eyes. Miniature (probably a copy) attributed to Richard Cosway. *(Henry E. Huntington Library and Art Gallery)*

John Jay at thirty-eight, spouse and "inestimable friend" (mixed stiple and line engraving by artist "B.B.E.," London, 1783), and Sarah (Sally) Livingston Jay, whom John adored (steel engraving of painting by Lorenzo Chappel). *(Columbiana Collection, Columbia University)*

King's College (Columbia). The old campus, where John Jay, undergraduate rebel, and Alexander Hamilton, pioneer college dropout, successfully resisted the blandishments of High Toryism. *(Columbiana Collection, Columbia University)*

John Jay's draft of the Olive Branch Petition. The first page. This was scrapped for the less conciliatory petition drafted by John Dickinson and adopted by Congress July 5, 1775. (*Courtesy, The Library Company of Philadelphia; now located in Historical Society of Pennsylvania*)

James Madison, Junior. Miniature painted by Charles Willson Peale, 1782. *(Courtesy, the James Madison Papers)*

A ROMANCE THAT FOUNDERED
For Madison, a Traumatic Experience

Catherine Floyd, the teenage beauty, daughter of a Signer, who found Madison's lack of charm less than irresistible. Miniature painted by Charles Willson Peale, 1782. *(Courtesy, the James Madison Papers)*

A North-West Prospect of Nassau-Hall, with a Front View of the President's House, in New-Jersey.

H.Dawkins Sculp

Nassau Hall at the College of New Jersey (Princeton)—where young Madison imbibed his Whiggish notions, along with a tolerance for dissent, where he interrupted his grinding studies to try his hand at lascivious verse, and then suffered a breakdown. Copperplate engraving by Henry Dawkins from the original drawing by W. Tennent, printed by James Parker, 1764. (Courtesy the Princeton University Archives)

Young Alexander Hamilton. Miniature attributed to Charles Willson Peale, painted shortly before Hamilton's marriage in 1780 and before his temporary break with Washington. *(Columbiana Collection, Columbia University)*

Elizabeth Schuyler Hamilton perfectly fitted her husband's description of what he desired in a wife: "sensible (a little learning will do)," well-bred, chaste, and tender, "but as to fortune, the larger of that the better." Portrait by Ralph Earl. *(Museum of the City of New York)*

Hamilton, the mature statesman. Painted, while still in uniform, by Charles Willson Peale. *(Courtesy, The New-York Historical Society, New York City)*

But still it would have been retained had a New Jersey delegate, ill in his lodgings, been present and voting. "Thus we see the fate of millions unborn hanging on the tongue of one man," Jefferson later reflected, "and heaven was silent in that awful moment."[135] The Northwest Ordinance of 1787 restored Jefferson's antislavery clause in modified form, but had it been extended to all the territories instead of merely to those north of the Ohio, it might well have obviated the coming of the Civil War. And, it must be added, it was Jefferson who prodded Congress and took satisfaction in affixing his signature to the act of Congress abolishing the slave trade.[136]

Whether it was a shocked reaction to the black insurrection in Santo Domingo,[137] a concern about the deepening divisions of the nation over this irreconcilable issue, or simply the disillusionment and weariness of old age, the man who once declared, "I tremble for my country when I reflect that God is just,"[138] came to regard the ending of slavery as an enterprise "for the young—for those who can follow it up, and bear it through to its consummation."[139] In his last letter on the subject, written two weeks before his death, Jefferson expressed the hope that "time, which outlives all things, will outlive this evil also." For forty years he had expressed his views. "Had I repeated them forty times, they would only have become the more stale and threadbare. Although I shall not live to see them consummated," he concluded, "they will not die with me; but living or dying, they will ever be in my most fervent prayer."[140]

In the Revolutionary years Jefferson had built an enormous reputation as a flaming radical, a reputation based on his achievements as draftsman, law reformer, and ideologue. His role as wartime governor of Virginia exposed the other side of the coin—his lack of stamina, staying power, and charismatic leadership. With a bankrupt treasury and a desperate shortage of manpower, Jefferson was bombarded at every turn with pleas for aid. Apprehensive news of Congress made it clear that no help could be secured from that body, whose shortcomings were put down by Madison in no small part to "a defect of adequate statesmen."[141] From the Carolinas Nathanael Greene requested men and matériel; George Rogers Clark and other Westerners warned the governor of impending disaster along the border; a strike by the Southern Indians was hourly expected; Washington needed more men to dislodge the British from New York.[142] Lacking a naval force to guard the approaches to the Chesapeake,

Jefferson was powerless to prevent those systematic raids of plunder and devastation which the turncoat Benedict Arnold, the ex-war prisoner Major General William Phillips, and finally Charles Cornwallis undertook against the Old Dominion. It certainly was not to Jefferson's discredit that when Tarleton's men swarmed into Charlottesville he left Monticello to avoid capture.

Shocking, perhaps, but by no means inconsistent with Jefferson's longtime pattern of commitment and withdrawal, was that, when confronted with the likelihood of an investigation into his behavior by the legislature, he resigned the governorship in a pique. "I have taken my final leave of everything . . . have retired to my farm, my family, and books, from which I think nothing will evermore separate me," he wrote Edmund Randolph, then serving in Congress. Stunned, Randolph rejoined, "If you can justify this resolution to yourself, I am confident that you cannot to the world."[143]

Ever afterward Jefferson was taunted with the memories of an ignominious flight and besmirched with an undeserved reputation as a coward. Indubitably this increased his resentment toward his audacious enemy, Hamilton, whose reputation for military bravery rested so largely on his heroics before Yorktown, an event which came hard on the heels of Jefferson's ignominy. When, in the summer of 1793, Hamilton took to bed during the yellow fever epidemic in Philadelphia, Jefferson remarked in a peculiarly uncharitable vein, quite gratuitously, too, considering his own record, "A man as timid as he is on the water, as timid on horseback, as timid in sickness, would be a phenomenon if his courage of which he has the reputation in military occasions were genuine."[144]

Thin-skinned though he was, Jefferson did confront the Virginia legislature in the fall of '81 and was absolved of the charges against him. Exoneration was not enough, however. The experience had inflicted injuries on him, which, he confessed, would be cured only "by the all-healing grave." He flatly declined attendance at the House of Delegates to which his Albemarle constituency had just elected him, ignoring threats of contempt proceedings. Now, in his retreat, the illness and death of his wife left him completely shattered. An appointment to the Peace Commission in Paris arranged by his solicitous friend James Madison rescued him from his morbid seclusion. Jefferson journeyed first to Philadelphia, then to Baltimore, where he waited some three and one-half months for the French frigate on which he was booked to sail. First, winter storms and then the British blockade kept him fretfully cooped up in that desolate spot. Finally came the news from Europe that a preliminary peace had been signed. His presence no longer needed, Congress withdrew his commission.

Ironically, the author of the Great Declaration passed his final moments of the Revolution in a mood of grief, acute depression, and self-flagellation, scarcely lightened by a spell of fretful inactivity which belied his activist record and offered no true augury of the great years that lay ahead for Jefferson himself and for the nation he would continue to serve.

V

JOHN JAY

AND THE RADICAL

CHIC ELITE

Gilbert Stuart first painted him in London in 1783, capturing on canvas that tall, spare frame, the sensitive, proud face, high forehead, penetrating eyes, conspicuously aquiline nose, and lips which formed an almost straight line. A colorless complexion, accentuated by highly powdered hair, set off his black jacket and matching vest, above which white ruffles peered.

John Jay could not have appeared very different ten years earlier, when he had just turned twenty-seven, for he grew up fast and seemed to have skipped adolescence. At this time, in February, 1773, he is seated at his writing desk putting quill pen to paper to compose a stiff note. With icy politeness he informs Robert Randall that as president of the city's Dancing Assembly he must turn down his application for membership on the ground that Randall lacked suitable connections "with the people who frequent the Assembly." Words had passed between the pair. Randall had charged Jay with having given a "stab" to his "honor," and Jay in turn felt "disposed to violence," but "on cool reflection" he commits his rejoinder to writing. "I desire to withhold justice from no man," Jay concludes, "and if any reasonable person will say I have injured you or that you have a right to satisfaction, I will either ask your pardon or fight you." Since Randall had accused Jay of evading the issue of honor, Jay was obligated to inform him that he had been awaiting word from him "respecting the persons we were to consult on the occasion, and the time and place of doing it."[1]

That the very proper Mr. Jay should have been ready to defend his honor by the *code duello* seems as much out of character as his embracing the cause of violent revolution would have appeared to his New York contemporaries in the year 1773. Fortunately, the issue was left neither to pistol nor épée, and a future Chief Justice was spared for service on the United States Supreme Court.

The Dancing Assembly over which Jay stood guard like a mother hen protecting her brood comprised the best families of New York. Some of its members not too far off would join him in waging a long war against King and Empire, friends like Robert R. Livingston, Jr., Gouverneur Morris, Egbert Benson, and Gulian Verplanck. But at this time scarcely a shadow was cast over their intimacy with such Tories-to-be as Richard Harrison, Peter Van Schaack, Dr. Samuel Bard, and John Moore. Soon war was to make this social club irrelevant, and an unbreachable gulf was to divide the members along political lines.[2]

Jay's interchange with Randall suggests that some of the vain and even imperious traits associated with the New York lawyer came to him very early. The interchange also raises questions about Jay's preoccupation with social trivia at a time of acute political crisis and his social involvement with Tory-minded members of the New York establishment so late in the day. Behind Jay's early drive to obtain for himself an unassailably secure social position lay a long struggle of an outsider to obtain status and security.

Save for Hamilton, none of the Founding Fathers bore the stamp of origins upon him more visibly than did John Jay. Never would he for a moment forget that he descended from French Huguenot refugees. To make sure that the passage of time would not blur the oral tradition, Jay in later life wrote an account of his ancestry which remained unfinished. His forebears were merchants who removed from Poictou to La Rochelle. His great-grandfather Pierre Jay, like his fellow Huguenots, failed to recognize the portents preceding the revocation of the Edict of Nantes, but stayed on in stubborn optimism. Then the church at La Rochelle was leveled, and troops were dispatched to the city and quartered among the Protestant residents. Dragoons moved into Pierre Jay's home, and as the situation was becoming intolerable, he made his move secretly, dispatching his family aboard a ship which sailed to Plymouth, England. He himself stayed on to salvage what he could of the wreck of his fortune, but the suspicious absence of his family led to his own arrest and imprisonment. Through the offices of friendly Catholics he was released and managed to escape on a vessel for Spain in which he had an interest. Ship and cargo, mostly iron, were all that remained of the estate he could bring along with him to England.

Meantime his second son Augustus, who survived his older brother, had been out of France on a business journey to Africa, only to return to Rochelle without knowing of the fate of his family. Augustus managed to escape on a ship bound for Charleston but, finding the Carolina climate uncongenial, moved north and located in New York. There he shipped out as a supercargo for Hamburg, only to be captured by a French privateer and imprisoned in a fortress near St.-Malo. Taking advantage of dark and stormy weather, he and a companion eluded the guards, climbed the fortress wall, dropped into a ditch, and managed to get to La Rochelle, where relatives arranged for his safe passage to Holland, and at last reunion with his family in England. Business opportunities lured this restless Jay back to America, however, and his fortune advanced rapidly, especially so after his marriage to Anne Marie Bayard, a descendant of a French Huguenot refugee theologian. In New York his relatives, the Bayards and the Stuyvesants, brought him useful business connections, as did his brother-in-law, Stephen Peloquin, a merchant of Bristol, England. Augustus took his only son Peter into a prosperous partnership, and Peter in turn advanced his social and business fortunes by marrying a Van Cortlandt.[3]

Indeed it was noteworthy that this activist against English rule came entirely of non-English ancestry. Through his paternal grandmother Jay was related to the French Bayards; his mother was a Dutch Van Cortlandt, and his cousins included De Peysters, De Lanceys, and Stuyvesants. Of his great-grandparents, three were French and five were Dutch. Jay was one of the very few Founding Fathers of whom it could be said, as he asserted in 1796, "Not being of British descent, I cannot be influenced by that delicacy towards their national character, nor that partiality for it, which might otherwise be supposed not to be unnatural."[4]

If Jay had no blood ties to England, there was nothing in his family history which would dispose him cordially toward France either. In Jay's veins ran the blood of martyrs, and he was time and again to remind his children and grandchildren that France had been the enemy and that things Catholic must be viewed with suspicion. This coolness toward France and the Church governed his attitude

toward French Canadians and warped his relations with the government at Versailles, with whom he was to carry on long and delicate
negotiations.[5]

By birth a New Yorker, Jay was taken in infancy to the country
village of Rye, where his family settled down after the early retirement of his father from business. At his mother's lap he learned the
rudiments of English and Latin grammar. "Johnny is of a very grave
disposition and takes to learning exceeding[ly] well," wrote his
father, when the boy was seven. "He will be soon fit to go to a
grammar school."[6] The following year the father could write pride-
fully of his son's talents for book learning,[7] which John demonstrated at the French Huguenot school at New Rochelle, where he
stayed for three years. Thence he returned home for a spell of private
tutoring, entering King's College in 1760, just a little over fourteen
years of age. There at first he benefited by the family friendship with
the college president, Dr. Samuel Johnson, who at his parsonage in
Stratford, Connecticut, had struggled to teach John's older brother
Augustus the elements of reading and writing. Dr. Johnson found
Augustus "bird-witted,"[8] but John a born scholar.

Jay's first recorded rebellion against authority took place during
the presidency of the High Tory Myles Cooper, who succeeded
Johnson. When, in April, 1763, Peter Jay spoke of John's being "a
youth remarkably sedate" and "well-disposed,"[9] he could hardly
have anticipated the difficulty that Jay would be involved in as a
King's College senior. What happened was preserved in the Jay
family traditions, but the official record of the college is conspicuously
silent. It seems that a crowd of students smashed a table in College
Hall. Dr. Cooper rushed in and proceeded to interrogate the students
one by one. None admitted knowing the culprit. When Jay's turn
came, he confessed that he did know who did it, but refused to
inform against a fellow student. Hailed before a faculty committee,
Jay looked up his copy of the college statutes, which he later preserved among his papers. Nowhere did the statutes oblige students to
inform on one another; on the other hand, they did enjoin obedience
and proper deportment.[10]

The long and short of it was that Jay was suspended, but an
indulgent faculty permitted him to return to college in time for
commencement. Jay's name appeared first on the list of graduates,
but since only one other member of the original entering class of

1760 managed to secure his degree at that time, it is straining the evidence to draw conclusions from that, particularly since Jay had the less onerous chore of delivering the valedictory in English on "The Happiness and Advantages Arising from a State of Peace" while his classmate Richard Harrison rendered the salutatory in Latin. After this, the pair debated in English the advantages of national poverty as opposed to national riches.[11] Perhaps of greater relevance to our own time was the debate Jay and Harison engaged in three years later on the occasion of their being awarded master's degrees. The topic: "Whether a Man Ought to Engage in War without being persuaded of the justice of his Cause?"[12]

The incident of the smashed table reveals that the John Jay of King's College days already had achieved a reputation as a principled and unbending young man who would stick by the letter of the law regardless of consequences—a trait which stamped his behavior thereafter whether in law, politics, or diplomacy. Other factors of his formative years left a lasting imprint on his personality. Aside from his oldest brother, James, John, second youngest of seven children who lived to adulthood, was the only member of the family to have any semblance of intellectual capacity. Frederick ("Fady") may have been brighter than the retarded Augustus, but was not cut out to be an intellectual. Smallpox in infancy had left Jay's brother Peter and his sister Anna Maricka totally blind, and he always considered them a personal charge. In addition, Jay's parents were aged and ailing. With James, the senior member of the household, addicted to wanderlust and irresponsibility in equal amounts, the heavy burdens of family obligations were borne by John from almost the moment he left college, and he was never to forsake them. When war broke out, the physical security of the family was a constant concern to him. For these reasons, if for no others, Jay grew up very fast, and despite his junior position in the family in years, he assumed paternal responsibilities at an early age.

Between John and his brother James, thirteen years his senior, a strange sibling rivalry and competition persisted until it turned to mortal antipathy. Talented, vain, and emotionally unstable, James had secured a medical degree at Edinburgh, then returned to practice in New York. Bored, restless, and a bachelor, James jumped at the chance to go abroad to raise funds for King's College. Joining forces with the Reverend William Smith, overseas on a similar errand for the College of Philadelphia, Jay raised some £10,000 for each of the colleges and, for his accomplishment, was knighted by George III in 1763. Then, to the surprise of the governors of the college, Sir James refused to turn over the money, insisting on deducting his expenses first. A public blow-up ensued, in which the embattled James used the printing press interminably to present his case.[13]

One can hardly minimize the effect of this scandal upon the Jay family, whose relations with King's College's first president had been on a footing of great intimacy. Nor can one discount the acute embarrassment the affair caused John, a sensitive, proud, and ambitious youngster, just one year out of college himself. In a revealing letter to a King's College chum, Robert R. Livingston, Jr., Jay described the sort of person he saw himself as being in 1765 at the time the scandal broke. Even then he recognized himself as ambitious, "pertinaceous," "sensible of indignities," and "prone to sudden resentment," even then something of a prude and an introvert, not easily approached.[14]

Not only was John mortified by his brother's instinct for adverse publicity, but he was called upon by his father to "make yourself master of the affair, in order to vindicate your brother's character which I expect is now undeservedly pretty roughly handled."[15] After a controversy dragging over a full decade, the issues between Sir James and the governors were finally compromised, but not before protracted proceedings in Chancery and the intercession of Jay's family.[16] Jay was not one to forget the indignity to which his brother's conduct had exposed him.

The thorn in John Jay's side was not easily plucked out. On the eve of the Revolution Sir James showed up on this side of the Atlantic to the dismay of his relatives. "The black sheep is still in the neighbourhood," brother Frederick wrote John in March, 1776, "but I have full liberty from the master of the flock to sett the dogs at him."[17] James's presence in New York during the early years of the Revolution was not without exasperating moments for the family. True, he had turned over to his brother for the use of the Patriots an invisible ink which was to be used extensively in confidential diplomatic dispatches.[18] For a while Sir James was even a conspicuous rebel, serving in the New York Senate during the years 1778–82. There Sir James made a point of taking stands directly opposed to his now famous brother John. Thus, he sided with John's antagonists in Congress, the Lee faction, hoping to secure thereby a diplomatic assignment abroad, a selection which might have been a national disaster.[19] James then joined forces with John Morin Scott, one of his brother's leading opponents, in securing passage in 1779 of an act of attainder which confiscated the property of conspicuous Loyalists.[20] News of this harsh measure of reprisal came to John Jay at the start of his mission in Spain. Indignantly, he wrote Governor George Clinton that the act "is disgraced by injustice too palpable to admit even of palliation."[21] Consistently, the younger Jay would oppose the confiscation of property because of the opinions held by the owners. So extreme a measure he would have reserved for those who had been either perfidious or cruel.[22] Scornfully, Jay referred to his brother as "our Knight of the Order of Sisiphus," whom he presumed to be "labouring hard to roll some new stone uphill."[23]

Consistency was scarcely an attribute of Jay's oldest brother, but in the art of upstaging John, James displayed a veritable genius. Unable to secure the recognition from the Patriots that he merited according to his own inflated opinion, James vented his spleen against them in a series of indiscreet newspaper attacks.[24] In April, 1782, just as his brother was readying his departure from Spain to join the American Peace Commission in Paris, Sir James by prearrangement was captured in New Jersey and brought into the King's lines. There he had talks with royal officials about his personal project for reuniting the colonies with Great Britain. Although both the British and the Tories were suspicious of him, they allowed him to go to England.[25] In wartime England Sir James carefully abstained from making his presence known to his brother, the peace commissioner in Paris. To the embarrassing gossip about a brother who had gone over to the enemy Jay reacted with a withering blast. "You mention my brother," he wrote to an old friend in England. "If after having made so much bustle in and for America, he has (as I surmised) improperly made his peace with Britain, I shall endeavour to forget that my father had such a son."[26] John Jay's surmise was correct. The frustrated eccentric, determined to score a triumph over his brother in the role of a rival peacemaker, was supported by the British government during the period he spent drafting a bill denying Parliament's jurisdiction over America and authorizing the King to make a peace or truce with America and form a union incorporating the colonies "into one body politic on the solid basis of affection and common interest."[27] Shelburne found that the crafty knight errant was quite evasive when it came to furnishing intelligence of events overseas. As a precondition to Sir James's talking freely, his interrogator was expected first to listen to an "idle story about a naval invention" that James was trying to peddle to the British government. Let's ship him back to Carleton in New York, Shelburne advised, and if he refuses to go, cut off his stipend.[28]

If America could never cope with Sir James, neither could England. Moving one step ahead of the ministry, he made his way to the Continent, where as an unaccredited, self-appointed emissary he saw no impropriety in conducting trade negotiations with the French, presumably on behalf of the United States, and timing his activities to coincide with his brother's authorized trade negotiations with Great Britain. Sir James would have encouraged luxury imports into the United States from France, a course directly opposed to his brother's plans.[29] With mounting irritation and enormous embarrassment, the very proper John Jay watched his older brother follow up his flirtation with treason by making an international spectacle of himself—and not for the first time. To John his brother seemed bent on undermining his own delicate negotiations. When it did finally come, the confrontation between the pair was explosive. Sir James slunk away, and never saw his brother thereafter. Even in his last days the older brother worked hard to disgrace the family name, and in the opinion of his relatives accomplished the feat by living openly in Springfield, New Jersey, with a woman of lower-class origin, something no Jay had ever done before.

Jay's jousts with his oldest brother also marked his relationships with others with whom he worked. He got along swimmingly with his peers—with Franklin, Washington, and John Adams—but his subordinates could find him authoritarian, vain, and stuffy, a man who stiffened at slights deliberate or unintended. Jay's Spanish mission immediately comes to mind. Accompanying him to Spain in 1779 was his personal secretary and brother-in-law Henry Brockholst Livingston. Twenty-two years old when he joined Jay's official family, Brockholst had, as a young army officer, shown himself adept at positioning himself wherever the action might be. In Spain he was captious, sulky, ill-mannered, and spoiled. He constantly baited John Jay by passing indiscreet and improper remarks highly critical of the Americans and their government. His provocative rudeness led to his dismissal, and Jay breathed a sigh of relief when Brockholst took passage for home in the spring of '82.[30] Back in New York, after being captured by the British on the high seas, imprisoned, and then released on parole, Brockholst joined the small group of John Jay haters. With Jay a leading Federalist, he wasted little time in joining the antis. When in 1794 John Jay put his signature to a treaty with England that bears his name, Brockholst stood in the forefront of demonstrations denouncing it. Surely his presence was not fortuitous at the riot at which Hamilton was hit by a flying stone as well as on the occasion in New York when John Jay was burned in effigy. His disaffection for Jay endeared him to the Jeffersonian camp, and President Jefferson put him on the Supreme Court, the first riot provocateur in American history to reach so exalted a station.

Since Congress, not Jay, appointed William Carmichael to the post of secretary to the Spanish Mission, he never felt any loyalty to its head. Jay felt, from the beginning of their trip abroad, that Carmichael had launched upon a systematic intrigue to undermine the authority which the American minister plenipotentiary jealously guarded.[31] Convivial where Jay was stand-offish, a Spanish linguist which Jay was not, Carmichael proved an acute observer of Spanish affairs. From the start he hit it off with the Spaniards as well as with the French ambassador, the Comte de Montmorin, an accomplishment which indubitably earned him black marks in Jay's book. Jay was annoyed by the intimacy between Carmichael and Brockholst Livingston, distrusted his secretary's discretion, questioned his handling of accounts, and took a strict view of his powers. He felt that Carmichael was jealous of him, which was no doubt true, but for his own part he was envious of his subordinate's little successes and recognized the "cloven foot" which his secretary at first took pains to conceal.[32] Jay's antipathy to Carmichael was, if anything, sharpened by the latter's success in Madrid after Jay went on to Paris, leaving his secretary to act as chargé d'affaires. Through Lafayette's intercession, Carmichael was formally received by the Spanish king and royal family in 1783, ten days before the signing of the Definitive Peace, an honor not customarily accorded to any but those holding the rank of minister.[33] It is indeed a pity that, in view of Carmichael's good standing and influence at the Spanish court,[34] Jay could not have been more forbearing of his subordinate. To the last, however, Jay was irreconcilable. When, years after the events, Jay arranged his papers, he made the following notation in the bundle of Carmichael correspondence: "Care should be taken of these Papers. They include Letters to and from William Carmichael—a man who mistook cunning for wisdom; and who in pursuing his Purposes, preferred the guidance of artifice and Simulation, to that of Truth and Rectitude. He finally yielded to Intemperance, and died a Bankrupt."[35]

That the self-righteous Jay would, where his self-esteem was involved, stoop at times to petty and undignified controversy is abundantly illustrated by the contretemps with young Lewis Littlepage. Joining the ill-assorted ménage on San Mateo Street in Madrid was a handsome, foppish, eighteen-year-old Virginian named Lewis Littlepage, whom Jay in a generous moment had agreed with his sponsor Colonel Benjamin Lewis to place under his tutelage in Spain. Littlepage was entirely dependent upon Jay for funds, but preferred señoritas to books and possessed a streak of "military Quixoticism" which sorely tried his mentor. With colossal insolence, Littlepage made extraordinary demands upon Jay and, when the latter attempted to curb his reckless course, turned upon his benefactor with a public display of ingratitude.[36] Having participated in the siege of Gibraltar against the advice of Jay and having escaped unharmed from a floating battery which was blown up, Littlepage turned up in Paris and requested Jay to name him to carry the Definitive Treaty of Peace to Congress. Jay could hardly imagine anyone less entitled to that honor, and declined to do so. But Littlepage still felt that his benefactor owed him a debt, and in the postwar period sought from Jay, then secretary for Foreign Affairs, a letter of recommendation to the King of Poland, in whose service he intended to enter. Instead, Jay brought suit to collect the moneys he had advanced for Littlepage in Spain. The French chargé to the United States, with the connivance of his government, which had no special fondness for Jay, encouraged Littlepage to launch a public attack on Jay, and the secretary ill-advisedly exploited newspaper and pamphlet by way of rebuttal. Jay could not forgive one who had left his home "with my money in his pocket, and my meat still sticking in his teeth," and then traduced him. Littlepage left the country in a French packet, but not before having first deposited with his bail a sum to discharge his debt. This time Jay did get his pound of flesh.[37]

The very qualities that Jay possessed in generous measure—his scrupulous integrity, his finicky attention to detail, his well-known discretion, his oratorical gifts, the result of assiduous efforts in debate to overcome an initial speech hesitancy, and the combative side of his nature—all seemed to point to the law as the right career for him. He himself had no doubts, nor did his father, who paid a stiff fee for his clerkship. Although one usually thinks of the first Chief Justice as above all a lawyer, it is seldom remembered that Jay devoted less than seven years to the private practice of the law out of a lifetime of fourscore and four years. In Jay's case, as in John Adams's, the demands of the state proved more compelling than the call of his profession. Fortunately for the New Yorker and his country, too, he possessed private means adequate to permit him to retire from practice at an incredibly early age. Brief as was his legal career, it was sufficiently varied to permit him to draw upon it for guidelines on numberless occasions in later life.

Take, for example, Jay's earliest public service. Completing a clerkship of somewhat over four years with Benjamin Kissam, a prominent New York attorney, and gaining admission to the bar in 1768,[38] Jay like most young lawyers found that at first he was not harassed by clients. For a brief period he entered into partnership with his friend of King's College days, Robert R. Livingston, Jr., but his really active practice followed the dissolution of that partnership in 1771. At the start, Jay's most enriching experience was derived from his services in the summer and fall of '69 as clerk to the boundary commission created to fix the location of the disputed New York–New Jersey boundary. Here he first displayed that rigid insistence on technicalities which was to mark his entire career. Working round the clock, Jay took down interrogatories and hired six "writers" to make copies of the record for review in England, made a tedious journey to Hartford, only to find that the commission, lacking a quorum, never convened there, and was out of pocket for heat, candlelight, and miscellaneous costs. To compound his frustrations, neither New York nor New Jersey bothered to file an appeal or deigned to indicate that it would accept the commission's findings. As a result, Jay had the mortifying experience of not getting his salary. He finally hit upon the expedient of charging one-half his salary and expense to the agents for New Jersey and presumably the other half to the agents for New York.[39] Finally, both parties abandoned the notion of appealing the decision, and as late as 1773 the New York Assembly directed Jay to release a copy of the proceedings to be transmitted by Governor Tryon to Whitehall. Jay stalled on the ground that the formal requirement of the law had not been met and that as an employee of the commission he had not been so directed by a quorum of its members. For Jay to have turned over the product of his labors before his own claims for back pay and other outlays were settled probably would have foreclosed his chance of recovery. Standing out against the governor, the assembly, and even the Earl of Hillsborough, the British colonial secretary, Jay, by his insistence on complying only after an order in council or an act of the New York Assembly so instructed him, revealed thus early that tenacity with regard to following established procedures which was to mark his entire career. At twenty-eight he was quite prepared to court the ire of top royal officials if he felt his course right, just as a few years later he was ready to defy the principal minister of Spain, the foreign minister of France, and even his own Congress when convinced of the rectitude of his course. Above all, Jay's service as clerk of the boundary commission gave him good grounding in the operation of a mixed commission, a device that he himself was to innovate in the adjustment of international disputes.

As a law clerk and practitioner Jay showed himself completely at ease with social equals, even those quite senior to him in years, but rather prickly and combative toward those he fancied his social inferiors. Thus, his relationship with Benjamin Kissam approached that of law partners or close friends rather than of attorney and clerk. In the summer of 1766, while Kissam was upstate involved in the trial of a group of tenant rioters against big landed proprietors, he instructed Jay to report on his practice back in town. In his reply the twenty-one-year-old law clerk adopted a facetious tone which from anyone of lesser social standing would have been considered impudent by an employer. "You desire me 'to give some account of the business of the office,' " Jay observed, but conceded that his wits seemed too dull to get the point of the inquiry. "You surely do not mean that I should send you a list of *new* causes on your docket; for I imagine 'tis perfectly indifferent whether you receive a fee in the cause of A. *vs*. B., or B. *vs*. A.: the number of them, indeed, may (as the New-England lawyers' phrase is) be a matter of *some speculation*." Jay said that he could hardly have expected to tell Kissam how often the clerks showed up, reminding his master "of the old law maxim, that a man's own evidence is not to be admitted in his own cause." Having read over the uninformative froth that he had spewed out, Jay conceded, "Some folks, I know, would think it too free, considering the relation we stand in to each other." With some folks he would be more prudent, but with Kissam he knew the grounds on which he stood, "and professional pride shall give me no uneasiness, while you continue to turn it, with Satan behind your back."[40]

Jay knew his employer and was confident that he would not take offense. "It would give me pain," Kissam replied, "if I thought you could even suspect me capable of wishing to impose any restraint upon you, in this high and inestimable privilege of friendship." All he wanted to know was whether in his absence his business had fallen off, how well he had fared at the last term, "and whether care has been taken to put that business forward as much as possible."[41] Indeed, Kissam knew that young Jay could be counted on to handle his affairs with competence, and after Jay had been admitted to the bar called upon him to litigate suits in the Westchester court to which, owing to lameness, he was unable to repair. He gave Jay only the briefest directions.

> All I can tell you about the causes, is little more than to give you a list of their titles. But this is quite enough for you. One is about a horse-race, in which I suppose there is some cheat; another is about an eloped wife; another of them also appertains unto horseflesh. . . . I ask these favours from you, John, with great freedom. I wish you good success with my consignments, and hope they'll come to a good market. If they don't, I am sure it will not be the *factor's* fault; and if my clients' *wares* are bad, let them bear the loss.[42]

In such casual fashion were the concerns of litigants dismissed.

Jay accepted the friendship and confidence of this senior member of the bar as merited by ability and social rank. Conversely, he would not tolerate a snub by a social inferior even if the author happened to be the attorney general of the province. For some years there appears to have been bad blood between John Tabor Kempe and young Mr. Jay. Back in 1762 Kempe chaired the committee appointed by King's College to supervise the collection of funds in England, and the dealings of that committee with the willful James Jay still rankled on both sides. Kempe had started his career burdened with family debts while managing to capitalize on favors of the royal government to achieve a position and income which some colleagues at the bar may have considered unwarranted by his low social standing and mediocre abilities.[43]

The contretemps occurred because an Anglican parish in Jamaica sought to install a Presbyterian divine in place of the Reverend Joshua Bloomer, an Anglican and a King's College graduate who had been appointed to the post by the governor. When the parish withheld Bloomer's salary he brought suit and hired a battery of attorneys, including, somewhere along the line, John Tabor Kempe, who as the province's attorney general was of counsel to uphold the authority of the governor, and John Jay. In December, 1771, Jay discovered that Kempe was engaged in Chancery in arguing against the vestryman's demurrer.[44] The interests of his client as well as common courtesy dictated consultation with all the attorneys retained by Bloomer. Jay reacted like a coiled snake that had inadvertently been trod upon. Complaining to Kempe that he had not been "consulted in any one stage of the suit," he observed that, "had it been a mere matter of usual compliment, I should have expected it from the Attorney General's politeness," but as the complainant's "solicitor" Jay "expected some little attention, not from the Attorney General's acquaintance with the rules of politeness, but the rules of business." He demanded an "explanation." "Your conduct at least represents me in an insignificant point of view," Jay noted, a course which one took toward Jay at the actor's peril.

The attorney general was astonished at the presumption of this young lawyer, in practice a bare three years. "This is the first instance I ever met with of such an address," Kempe remonstrated, and since it was without provocation he was "the more astonished." Jay was ready with a chilling rebuttal. If the attorney general had never met with such an address before, he would, had he reflected "another hour," have remembered "that whenever a gentleman's conduct is misunderstood, it is his duty to explain it" and to do so "as a piece of justice to his own reputation." Recounting the studied neglect of Jay by Kempe in this entire litigation, transpiring as it did at a time when Jay "was but just stepping into the world, a season critical to a young man," he insisted that such conduct lowered Jay's estimation in the eyes of his clients. Then came the haughty conclusion: "A rupture with you Sir! would be very disagreeable to me; but I had rather reject the friendship of the world than purchase it by patience under indignities offered by any man in it."[45]

Jay's overreacting to this incident speaks volumes for his concern about his reputation, just as his readiness to court the permanent enmity of the province's attorney general rather than suffer a slight to his self-esteem is evidence of his secure social standing. As for the Reverend Mr. Bloomer, he was successful in Chancery, whether with or without Jay's help at the end is not clear from the record, but although the governor as chancellor entered a decree in his favor, he did not receive his salary for another nine years.

From this extraordinary exchange one must not rashly assume that Jay was also prepared to break with the royal government and rush headlong into the cause of the Whig opposition. He was caution personified. In the first place, he shared the normal interests of the well-to-do and well-connected in securing chunks of unoccupied lands. He was part of a company of distinguished New Yorkers who had received New York grants to land in Vermont which the former colony disputed with New Hampshire. In June of 1771, the same year as Jay's altercation with Kempe, he petitioned for a grant of land in Albany County on behalf of himself and twenty-five others.[46] Alas for the New Yorkers' expectations, the governor at this time received instructions from England to suspend all grants in the disputed tract. The New York speculators in the Vermont lands were beside themselves. Jay, his petition to the governor for confirmation of the grants having been tabled, addressed an impassioned appeal to the Earl of Dartmouth, the colonial secretary, protesting that the existing "monopoly of lands" in the colony constituted "a grievance to the lower class of people in it," and warning that as a result, the only recipients of the royal bounty were "mercenary land-jobbers, and gentlemen who have already shared very largely in the royal munificence."[47] Jay's touching concern about the common man and his own affairs may have been exacerbated when Chief Justice William Smith managed to obtain a huge grant in the same tract for which Jay was contending. He laid his success to the fact that he gave Governor Tryon the impression that he was writing a book on the governor's heroic deeds when as North Carolina's governor he had led a military force to put down the uprising of the upcountry Regulators.[48]

Like other New Yorkers, Jay clung tenaciously to the Vermont claims, even when it seemed clear as the Revolution progressed that Vermonters would go to any lengths, even to entertaining treasonable proposals, in order to secure recognition of their ambiguous titles which only separate statehood or incorporation into the British Empire could confirm. In a rare moment when he lapsed into coarseness, Jay, on receiving bad news about the progress of New York's claims against Vermont, remonstrated to New York's Attorney General Egbert Benson, in a letter written in 1782 from Paris: "From your account of the Vermont Business, it appears to me a vulgar Expression, to have been *bitched* in its last as well as first Stages."[49] The Vermont claims touched the jugular.

Jay's unsuccessful solicitation of Governor Tryon did not preclude at least one more try. Some time in 1772 Jay and his former law partner, Robert R. Livingston, came up with a proposal to add legally trained judges to the common pleas bench, which was manned largely by rustics. He concurred with William Smith, who at this time observed, "How dangerous it is to trust life and property to judges who are not bred to the profession they are called to execute."[50] The solution was to appoint two skilled lawyers who would serve as itinerant judges traveling to various sessions of the common pleas courts at the county seats. Jay and Livingston knew the two best qualified for such posts. Themselves, to be sure. Jay was prepared to serve in Orange, Westchester, and Richmond counties, while Robert Livingston was willing to sit in faraway Tryon, and in upstate Albany, Ulster, and Dutchess. The issue raised a storm in the Council, and Oliver De Lancey, fearing the influence of an opposition party in courthouse politics regarded as a De Lancey preserve, saw that the proposition was turned down, even though the two candidates offered to serve without pay.[51]

That was not the end of the matter, however. Tension with England was rising to fever pitch. Jay himself, after serving on one pro-Revolutionary committee after another, was sent as a New York delegate to the First Continental Congress. At that very time he was in correspondence with two Tory friends, William Laight in New York and the Reverend John Vardill in London, both cronies of King's College days, and both seeking to pull such strings as they could in England to win Jay over to the royalist cause. Jay had not yet closed the door to a royal judgeship if it could be had on his terms. Writing from New York in May, 1774, the New York delegate informed Vardill that he would not accept such a post unless it carried a salary, apparently regretting his momentary enthusiasm of some years earlier when he had offered to serve without pay. Should such a post be proffered to him he "would chearfully resign the toil of my profession for *Otium cum Dignitate*." Again, from Philadelphia on September 24, just four days before the conservative plan of union was proposed to Congress by Tory-to-be Joseph Galloway and supported by Jay, the New York delegate thanked Vardill for his attention to "certain other matters," apparently referring to the judgeship project. However, bound by the injunction of secrecy laid upon the members of Congress, Jay could say nothing about what had transpired to date in Philadelphia. "God knows how the contest will end," he declared. "I sincerely wish it may terminate in a lasting Union with Great Britain."[52]

This was 1774, not 1776. Loyalty oaths were not yet in style. People could straddle, and many in Congress like John Jay did. But the spectacle he offered to Vardill, unbeknown to Jay a hireling of the British secret service, was less than heroic. Jay's letters served as an exhibit offered by Vardill to the Loyalist Commission in November, 1783, to support his claim for compensation for valuable services in fighting the rebellion. Summarizing his contacts with Patriot leaders, Vardill stated therein: "One effect of this correspondence, was to secure to government the interest of two members of the Congress by the promise of the office of judges in America. But the negotiation was quashed by the unexpected fray at Lexington in April, 1775."[53] The matter could hardly have been put more succinctly.

Jay had one more contact with Vardill. On vacation in England after his arduous and successful task of negotiating the peace in Paris, Jay was visited by Vardill in London. Jay never returned the call, nor would he fraternize with other diehard Loyalists connected "with the abominable Tory Club in London (which filled the public papers with the most infamous lies against us)."[54]

It would be doing Jay an injustice to attribute the ultimate attachment to the Patriot cause to his disappointments in land speculation and office seeking and his talent for ruffling the feathers of royal officials. His father and brothers already were pronounced Whigs and, like other merchants concerned with overseas trade, indignant at the new revenue measures launched back in 1764, when young John had just begun his clerkship.[55] Nor could his clientele have nudged him one way or the other. Aside from the usual batch of relatives that most beginning lawyers lean upon—and in Jay's case they always were among his most valued clients—Jay's clientele constituted a mixed bag of Tories and Whigs. In some thousand cases that he litigated during the seven or eight years of his practice, he had shown equal diligence in defending the causes of his Tory and Whig clients.[56]

A few cases brought him a certain éclat in Whig circles and stamped him as an antiadministration man. In April, 1773, he defended Mayor Underhill of the Borough Town of Westchester in a contested election case brought against him by Attorney General Kempe, a foeman of earlier wars. The government contended that unqualified voters had been permitted to vote in the election. By various procedural maneuvers resting largely on the absence of a material witness for the defense, Jay managed to have the case postponed, in effect giving his client another three months of his term. Hard on the heels of the Underhill case was a mandamus issued against the officials of the town ordering them to admit Gilial Honeywell and Isaac Legget to the offices of aldermen to which, the government contended, they had been duly elected. Jay, by dilatory tactics, succeeded in keeping them out of their posts from July, 1773, to April, 1774.[57] Although in the end Jay had not kept the Crown from prevailing, his support of the local authorities against the royal government and of the broader suffrage in effect in the borough and town of Westchester elections increased his popularity throughout the province and marked him as a potential leader of the antiadministration forces.[58]

Jay forged a bond to the Whig cause by marrying the daughter of the Whig lawyer-intellectual William Livingston, who not only was among the most prominent of the Whiggish-leaning Livingstons but was soon to supplant Tory governor William Franklin as the Revolutionary chief executive of New Jersey. But before that marriage transpired, current gossip had Jay courting two different daughters of Peter De Lancey, and marrying Sarah Livingston on the rebound in April, 1774. The acidulous Judge Thomas Jones, a diehard Royalist, put it this way: "Mr. Jay . . . took a wife . . . in that of the Livingstons, a family ever opposed in politics to the De Lanceys, turned republican, espoused the Livingstons interest, and ever after opposed all legal government."[59] Jones himself had married into the De Lancey family and seemed to speak from first hand, but a Freudian explanation of Jay's political motivations, so oversimplified as Jones's, seems to warrant some modification. In any event, Jay never held his early failures as a suitor against the De Lanceys. When they became Tories and James De Lancey was captured and jailed at Hartford, Jay advanced him one hundred dollars along with the assurance that never would "the good offices formerly done me by yourself and family cease to excite my gratitude."[60]

Jay's Sally, a beautiful and gracious, if somewhat shallow, young woman, eleven years Jay's junior, inherited her good looks from her mother, for her father, the governor-to-be, liked to describe himself as "a long-nosed, long-chinned, ugly-looking fellow," but she did not inherit the latter's brains. Bearing a striking resemblance to Marie Antoinette, although less sharp-featured, she was frequently mistaken for the Queen when in the war years she would enter a box at the Paris Opéra.[61] Sweet-tempered and kindly at least to her intimates, but somewhat gushy and light-headed, Sally was considered by some people to be a haughty social climber, but in Whig circles she was in truth born at the top.

That the relationship between the couple might be mistaken for father and daughter should not obscure the true passion that bound them together. Sally considered John a paragon. To her he was ever "Mr. Jay." She found him "composed in danger, resigned in affliction, and even possessing a chearful disposition in every circumstance," in short, "virtue's own self."[62] To John she was "my dear" or "beloved" Sally. Like a parent he would write her to take exercise and get some fresh air. "Have you played battledore and shuttlecock since I left you?" he inquired solicitously less than two years after their marriage.[63] Away from home on a military mission in the summer of 1776 Jay wrote Sally that if she had received half the letters he had written, "I dare say you will at least set me down an attentive Husband and (what is not always the case in Matrimony) a constant Lover."[64] Constancy was indeed the key word in this marriage.

John was always miserable when separated from Sally, as events conspired to keep them apart in the early years of the war, and it was only natural that he should take her to Spain with him. This was indeed noteworthy, for Sally, alone of all the wives of foreign diplomats, accompanied her husband to Spain and France. John Adams was unwilling to have Abigail risk the dangers of a sea voyage and capture by the British, and Benjamin Franklin knew that his dowdy Deborah would have cut a ridiculous figure abroad. Jay was irked at the unnatural separation from Sally enforced by his arduous circuit-riding duties while on the United States Supreme Court, and in leaving the High Court and declining reappointment, he put domestic bliss above these uncongenial duties. Sally died just as he had completed his second term in the governorship of New York, and he remained an inconsolable widower, outliving her by some twenty-seven years.

In fact, Jay's widely known attachment to Sally was considered by some to be his Achilles heel. When Don Diego de Gardoqui arrived in New York in May, 1785, to negotiate a treaty with the United States on behalf of Spain, he prided himself that he knew Jay and his wife perfectly, counting on an acquaintance that reached back to the Jays' stay in Spain. In a report back home he made this observation about the secretary for Foreign Affairs:

> The American, Jay, who is generally considered to possess talent and capacity enough to cover in great part a weakness natural to him, appears (by a consistent behaviour) to be a very self-centered man, which passion his wife augments, because, in addition to considering herself meritoriously and being rather vain, she likes to be catered to and even more to receive presents. This woman, whom he loves blindly, dominates him and nothing is done without her consent, so that her opinion prevails, though her husband at first may disagree; from which I infer that a little management in dealing with her and a few timely gifts will secure the friendship of both, because I have reason to believe that they proceed resolved to make a fortune. . . .[65]

Jay with considerable reluctance accepted a stallion from the Spanish King, and although he relaxed his rigid stand on the navigation of the Mississippi, he viewed his proposal as a stopgap measure supported by most Northerners and even by Washington. It was hardly the result of bribery. Nor could Gardoqui really have believed that the Jays were fortune hunters. Entering on the public service in 1774, before he was thirty years of age, Jay never practiced law again or concerned himself to any great extent in private business affairs. Gardoqui's report came from a gentleman with an eye to an increased expense account, not from a profound judge of character.

A combination of newly formed ties to the politically activist Livingston clan and an upsurge of civil unrest nudged Jay ever so gently into the opposition camp. Happily married, looking forward

to a judicial post, the court dockets bulging with his cases, Jay, hob-
nobbing with New York's elite at the Dancing Assembly, the Debating Society, and the Moot, where bright legal minds argued legal
propositions of an evening, was hardly a frustrated revolutionary. In
his case events took a hand. A few days before his wedding a group
of radicals calling themselves "the Mohawks" dumped a cargo of tea
in New York harbor as a protest against the closing of the port of
Boston by act of Parliament.[66] This disciplined demonstration provided proof of the reemergence of the old Sons of Liberty with
working-class support, and it touched off a renewed battle between
radicals and conservatives for control of the protest movement. The
movement came to a head when on May 12 news reached New York
of the enactment by Parliament of the bill closing the port of Boston.
The conservatives showed themselves adept at political maneuvering
by bringing about the election of a Committee of Fifty-One, in which
they had a slight majority. It is on this committee that John Jay,
along with some nineteen future Tories, including such friends as
Edward Laight, made his initial bow in provincial politics.[67]

Conservative or no, Jay's role as a political activist propelled him
by almost imperceptible stages into a role of leadership of the revolutionary movement in New York. At the start it was as a penman that
his talents were enlisted. The Committee collectively drafted a diplomatic reply to the Bostonians who had demanded complete nonintercourse with England. This reply carefully sidestepped the boycott that
New York merchants would have found so painful, while stressing
the necessity of immediately assembling a general congress. That
latter step ultimately proved the more radical course. Characterized by
that judicial temper that came to be the hallmark of a John Jay paper,
it, first of all, struck a note of caution. "What ought to be done in a
situation so truly critical, while it employs the anxious thoughts of
every generous mind, is very hard to be determined." Certainly a general congress must be assembled "without delay," but pending such
action, it would be "premature" to make a commitment on the "expedient" proposed by the Bostonians.[68] Caution was still the watch-
word of Jay and his associates. Did sponsorship of a call for the
convening of a Continental Congress mean that Jay had crossed his
Rubicon? Clearly not, for the very day the Committee endorsed this
letter he wrote to Vardill in London reporting what had happened
and indicating that he would accept a judicial post.[69]

With conservatives maintaining a checkrein on the contagious "levelling trend" which might be picked up from New England, and after much jockeying for control between radical and moderate factions, a delegation to the First Continental Congress was elected on July 28, a delegation that included Mr. Jay. Jay's election was a victory over the radicals, who had made what Lieutenant Governor Colden described as a "Violent effort" to substitute for the moderate Jay and John Alsop the radical John Morin Scott and that "Wilkes of New York," Alexander McDougall.[70] That so touchy a person as Jay, one so sensitive to his own reputation, could survive the factional brawling of those weeks attests his tenacity and iron will. Along the way he did manage to pay off a score or two. He called upon John Morin Scott to justify or repudiate accusations "so black and so false" against Jay and his fellow committeemen. "It cannot be presumed you would wantonly sport with the reputation of persons whose attachment to the interest of their country has never been questioned," Jay scolded. Scott must have his reasons, and in justice to Jay's character, he insisted on hearing them. This was the same Jay of the Randall correspondence and the Kempe exchange. Always must his reputation be fiercely guarded.[71]

In that memorable session at Philadelphia's Carpenter Hall, which first convened on September 5, 1774, battle lines were quickly drawn between radicals and conservatives, with which latter bloc Jay was quickly identified. His forces were defeated on the choice of a hall, defeated in their picking a secretary, preferring Silas Deane to the more openly acknowledged radical Charles Thomson of Pennsylvania, but proved their tough fiber in contesting Patrick Henry's proposal that the votes of each colony be apportioned on the basis of population. With characteristic impetuosity Henry declared: "Government is dissolved. . . . We are in a state of nature, sir." In a calm rejoinder Jay reminded the delegates that "the measure of arbitrary power is not full, and I think it must run over, before we undertake to frame a new constitution." Rather, the task was to endeavor "to correct faults in an old one." Jay gave a glimmer of the future revolutionary in conceding that the British Constitution which derived its authority "from compact" could impliedly be renounced by compact, but he still steered a cautious middle course, epitomized in a quotation John Adams attributed to him: "Negociation, suspension of commerce, and war." War, he is reported to have said, was "by general consent to be waived at present." "I am for negociation and suspension of commerce."[72] While by no means agreeing with Jay, Adams in a retrospective comment on Jay's performance in the Congress conceded that he, along with Dickinson, had "eloquence," but lacked the "chaste," "pure," "nervous" style of Samuel Adams. To Adams, Jay would show himself to be "a Man of Wit, well-informed, a good Speaker and an elegant Writer."[73] These latter talents Jay would speedily demonstrate, although the conciliatory cause that he had initially pursued earned him "a horrid Opinion" in Patrick Henry's judgment,[74] one which the Virginia Lees fully shared. Jay's arguments against proportionate voting prevailed, and the delegates decided to vote by provincial units, each province having one vote (a rule that governed throughout the history of the Continental Congress).[75]

For the radicals the setback was at most a temporary one. On September 17 they succeeded in winning Congress's endorsement of the Suffolk Resolves, declaring the Intolerable Acts unconstitutional, advising the people to arm and form their own militia, and recommending stringent economic sanctions against Britain.[76] Rebounding from this stunning defeat, Jay, Duane, and Edward Rutledge of South Carolina, along with other conciliationists, rallied behind Joseph Galloway's plan of union, levying as it did so heavily upon Franklin's Albany Plan of 1754. By the margin of a single vote that plan was defeated, and the radical forces gathered enough momentum to have the vote expunged from the record.[77]

For the propaganda battle which Congress now proceeded to wage against Britain the most talented penmen among the moderates were enlisted. John Dickinson drew the petition to the King, when Patrick Henry's draft proved inept, and John Jay, who had, perhaps grudgingly, signed the Continental Association,[78] won the acclaim of both factions for his draft of an Address to the People of Great Britain. The story of that address comes to us from Jefferson secondhand. Richard Henry Lee prepared a first draft, which, when it was read, "every countenance fell and a dead silence ensued for many minutes." Then on the following day, October 19, Jay's father-in-law, William Livingston, read Jay's draft. When it was read, as Jefferson reported it, "there was but one sentiment of admiration."[79] Borrowing the republican rhetoric that Whig radicals had been using for some years, Jay charged the British government with establishing "a system of slavery" at the restoration of the peace in 1763. He reminded his fellow Englishmen that the colonists also claimed the rights of Englishmen, and he branded as "heresies" the claim that Parliament could bind the colonists "in all cases without exception," and dispose of their property without their consent. He indicted the administration for taking over the problems of the East India Company as its "own," and expressed shock that "the great council of the nation descended to intermeddle with a dispute about private property." Stressing fair trial concepts, lawyer Jay made the point that the proceedings against the Bostonians were ex parte. "Neither the persons who destroyed the tea, nor the people of Boston, were called upon to answer the complaint." What was done was to punish men "for imputed crimes, unheard, unquestioned, and without even the specious formality of a trial." Jay joined his complaint against the Intolerable Acts with a citation of the Quebec Act for its encouragement of emigrating Catholics, a people who could be inimical to the "ancient, free Protestant colonies." Remember, he warned the people of England, that the levies upon the wealth of America, including the power of taxation, might render the Crown independent of the people at home. "Take care that you do not fall into the pit that is preparing for us." Jay coupled his appeal to the sense of justice of the English nation with a final warning that, should they back their ministry, "we will never submit to be hewers of wood or drawers of water for any ministry or nation in the world."[80]

Jay's "Address to the People of Great Britain" propelled him at once into the front line of Whig propagandists and survives as proof of the fact that if you associate with radicals long enough some of the radical rhetoric is bound to rub off on you. So indeed the Tories felt, and though Jay's role in the Continental Congress had been that of a moderate, his authorship of the "Address" and his signature on the Continental Association caused raised eyebrows among bitter-end partisans of the Ministry.

The Tories were now ready to write him off, quite prematurely in fact. "You will be surpriz'd, my dear Vardill, as well as affected," wrote William Laight to his London correspondent toward the end of March, 1775, "when I tell you of the loss of, that once steady, honest Protestant *Jay*. He is, in the opinion of almost all of our friends, turned, in politics, a rigid *Blue Skin*." The only way that Laight could account for the switch was Jay's "too sudden elevation to a popular character." To Laight, Jay was obviously courting popularity, "and to please the populace he must have thrown aside his *old principles,*" presumably those of a moderate conservative. Imagine, only a few nights back he presided over a meeting where Lamb, Sears, Garret Roorback, and other activists were the principal speakers! As further evidence of Jay's "defection," Laight cited the fact that "the Blues trumpet his merits and patriotism at every corner of the streets." Whereas once Jay charged McDougall with demagoguery, he now applauded his zeal and supported his measures. Don't let him know how we feel, Laight counseled. Rather, congratulate him on his re-election and tell him how pleased we are to "have a writer and speaker of his abilities among us, who heretofore has, and doubtless continues to counteract the views of our ambitious, Republican demagogues. He may, *and 'tis the prayer of his friends* that he should, see his error."[81] By this date there is no evidence that Jay and Vardill were any longer in communication with each other, although as late as October, 1775, William Laight, from the security of London, was writing an unsolicited letter, admonishing Jay about the prudence of being contented with "a moderate share of civil liberty" rather than "aiming at visionary schemes of perfect freedom" which the British army, preparing to descend upon the colonies in the spring and to "cover the face of the *whole* country," would most certainly crush.[82]

Moderate though he had been in the First Congress, Jay found that his prestige had risen among the Whig activists, and they in turn, as the Tories found to their chagrin, embraced him as one of their own. On his return to New York he, along with his brother Frederick, was elected to the newest extralegal governing body, the Committee of Sixty,[83] as well as to the Committee of Inspection appointed to police compliance with the Continental Association. A stickler for the rules, Jay quickly won a reputation as a zealous inspector. Tories whispered that he informed the Sons of Liberty of the names of ladies and gentlemen who drank tea at the dancing assembly over which he presided.[84] Various signs indicated that Jay was more and more being propelled to a position of leadership of the moderate wing of the protest movement. It was he who drafted the letter from the New York Committee of Sixty to the Committee of New Haven, assuring the latter that they should have no cause for fearing "a defection" on the part of "the bulk of the people."[85] As a moderate he still sought to have some control over citywide elections. Rather than have the election of delegates to the Provincial Convention conducted at an unsupervised mass meeting, Jay proposed that the elections be held in the wards under the inspection of the vestrymen and subcommittees of the Sixty, the voting to be confined to free-holders and freemen.[86] The radicals conceded this point, and with their support, the slate, including John Jay, was declared duly elected.

Aside from his lawyerlike repugnance to unsupervised elections at large mass meetings, Jay made it clear that he preferred to have the delegates to the Continental Congress elected by the Provincial Convention rather than by the voters directly, a preference which he asserted again at election time the following year.[87] That is precisely what was done. The Provincial Convention, assembling in New York City on April 20, elected a slate of delegates to the Second Continental Congress which included Jay but substituted for two conservatives men of more radical complexion. In the wild demonstration that broke out upon news of Lexington and Concord, the Committee of Sixty recommended that a Committee of One Hundred be elected with enlarged powers and that a Provincial Congress be summoned, as the Tory Assembly had already adjourned. In the enthusiasm of the moment it seemed an effortless task to secure a thousand signatures to a new Association, in whose drafting Jay was prominent, pledging obedience to all acts of the Continental and Provincial congresses. Before Jay left for Philadelphia in early May the new governing committee commanded most of his time.

In the Second Continental Congress Jay, along with John Dickinson and Edward Rutledge, quickly assumed the leadership of the moderate wing. Still he allowed himself to be drafted to prepare a "Letter to the Oppressed Inhabitants of Canada," in the course of which he turned a complete ideological somersault. In his Address Jay had charged the British government with backing "our Roman Catholic neighbours" against the English Protestant colonists to reduce them to a form of slavery by unconstitutional taxation. Now, in seeking support from Catholic Quebec, Jay, perhaps with tongue in cheek, reminded the people of Canada that "the fate of the Protestant and Catholick Colonies" was "strongly linked together," and invited their support in breaking "the fetters of slavery."[88]

Throughout the spring and summer of '75 Jay continued to perform a neat balancing act, skimming along the narrow wire of conciliation while allowing himself to be utilized by the forces that were prepared for direct confrontation. The spring of '75 marked the climax of the final conciliation effort. The hour was late. Congress, upon convening in May, learned that its petition of October, 1774, had been virtually ignored by Parliament, that the Ministry intended to use troops, and that in fact a shooting war had already broken out in New England. Against the burgeoning opinion that any further conciliatory moves were fruitless, the conciliatory party in Congress, centering on Jay, Duane, and John Dickinson, made one last desperate stand. The opportunity arose on May 15, when Congress adopted a resolution instructing the inhabitants of New York to "defend themselves and their property and repel force by force."[89] It was at this time, with a view to obviating any decision that might invite attack or close the door to reconciliation, that Jay made a motion for a second petition to the King, which Dickinson seconded. To win over the war hawks the two moderates pointed out that any delay would give the colonists needed time for military preparations, while a rejection of the appeal by the home government would serve only to unite the colonies. Congress, despite the diehards, saw the force of their argument and authorized such a petition, naming Jay, along with Dickinson, Franklin, Thomas Johnson, and John Rutledge as a committee to draft it.

The petition as finally adopted is indisputably from the pen of John Dickinson, but Jay's original draft suggests how much more conciliatory he was prepared to be than his fellow committeemen. Jay asked that "every irritating measure be suspended," while Dickinson proposed the repeal of distasteful statutes. With his fondness for commissions, Jay proposed that George III "commission some good and great men to enquire into the grievances of her faithful subjects," while Dickinson contented himself with leaving it to His Majesty to "direct some mode" by which reconciliation could be achieved. Jay explicitly disavowed independence as an end, a commitment which Dickinson shrewdly sidestepped. Jay suggested that, should the royal government prefer not to deal with Congress, negotiations might be conducted with the colonial assemblies. Dickinson realized that Congress could not be expected to adopt a self-denying ordinance and avoided including the proposal, while at the same time arranging that the petition be signed by individuals to offset the fact that it was adopted in a general congress, a body so unpalatable to George III. In short, Dickinson's final draft scrupulously avoided ruffling the sensibilities of Congress by making injudicious and even unnecessary admissions or concessions. In view of the heated opposition in Congress to so watered-down a version as the final Olive Branch Petition, it is obvious that the Jay draft never had the slightest chance of adoption.[90]

Still an empire man, still loyal to the King, Jay throughout the greater part of the summer and fall of '75 was hopeful of the petition's favorable reception. As late as October 17 he wrote Alexander McDougall, "No news yet as to the effect of our petition. God grant it may be a means of restoring the peace and I may add the prosperity of the Empire now rent by unnatural convulsions. But we ought not to rely wholly on it, lest it prove a broken reed and pierce us."[91] Jay's sober conclusion proved amply justified, for on November 9 Congress learned of its rejection by the King.

The Lee faction in Congress had long distrusted Jay's conciliation stance and had begun circulating stories reflecting on his talents and loyalty. Arthur Lee, the more paranoid member of the family, had heard some insinuations against Jay which he dutifully spread from London, unsubstantiated gossip implicating Jay, Duane, and Robert R. Livingston, Jr., in leaking intelligence to the enemy.[92] In Philadelphia Richard Henry Lee, still fuming over the frigid reception accorded his draft of the Address to Great Britain so summarily discarded to make room for Jay's, and still bearing scars from numerous debating jousts with the New Yorker, now went around ascribing the authorship of Jay's Address to his father-in-law William Livingston. Whenever his prestige was involved, Jay never ducked a direct confrontation. Just as his propensity for squaring off with adversaries had already been demonstrated in his contretemps with Randall, Kempe, and John Morin Scott, now he sought to scotch this piece of silly gossip at its source. One morning late in June of '75, when the Olive Branch Petition was overhanging the Congress, Jay encountered a new member from Virginia, Thomas Jefferson, engaged in conversation with Lee outside the assembly rooms of Congress. Marching up to Lee, he grabbed hold of one of the buttons of his jacket and accused him of spreading the canard. Before Lee could answer, Jefferson, by instinct a conciliator, intervened to say that he had been so informed but not by Lee. Jay appeared content and strode off.[93]

Meantime, Jay, indubitably expressing the views of New York's merchants, put up a vigorous stand against Richard Henry Lee's motion that all customs houses be shut down. To the New Yorker this seemed as foolhardy as making the right arm sore because the left arm was. Just because a man had lost his teeth on one side of his face, must he pull out those on the other so "that both sides may be upon a footing?" he asked. And just "because the Enemy have burned Charlestown, would Gentlemen have Us burn New York?"[94] His sarcastic tone was not lost on Lee.

In the weeks and months following the adoption of the Olive Branch Petition, Jay found himself in an increasingly ambivalent position, very much as Congress itself, in John Adams's impatient view, was suspended "between hawk and buzzard." Even after the rejection of the Petition Jay continued to hope, vainly as it proved, for a conciliatory gesture from the Crown, and in a speech in March of '76 criticized the wording of a privateering bill because it indicted the King as the author of colonial miseries instead of putting the onus on the Ministry.[95]

A do-nothing policy would in the longer run be insupportable to Jay, who was by temperament an activist, a believer that government must be infused with energy. He was coming to take a continental approach to the distribution of war powers, an approach which would not too long thereafter stamp him as a leading nationalist. Thus, he no longer believed that the states should retain the initiative in making separate proposals for conciliation, but that such matters be left to the Congress. He and his fellow delegates from New York realistically abstained from presenting to Congress a plan of accommodation adopted earlier by his own colony's Provincial Congress. It was altogether fitting that he, along with such other legal lights as John Dickinson and George Wythe of Virginia, should be dispatched to Trenton by Congress to talk the New Jersey Assembly out of their plan to send their own petition to the King.[96] He told the Jerseymen that "we had nothing to expect from *the Mercy* or *Justice* of Britain," that petitions were no longer the means, rather vigor and unanimity were "the only Means." Only the "Petition of *United America* presented by Congress, ought to be relied on," he insisted; all else was "unnecessary."[97]

Whether Jay willed it or no, there was a war on, one being waged on several fronts, and it was up to the states and the Congress to carry it on effectively. Jay served on such crucial Congressional committees as the Committee of Secret Correspondence to secure aid from abroad, an assignment which provided him with a cloak-and-dagger encounter with the French secret agent Bônvouloir[98] and an active correspondence with the American agent to France, Silas Deane, using an invisible ink according to a formula provided by Jay's brother Sir James. On a committee of Congress to deal with disaffection in Queens County, New York, he participated in drafting a report which urged that all persons who voted against sending deputies to the provincial convention "be put out of the protection of the United Colonies," that such persons may not leave the county without a certificate from the New York convention, that they be debarred from courts of law, that their names be published in county newspapers for one month, and that they be disarmed—in all, strong medicine for a moderate.[99] Constantly now he prodded Patriots back in New York to begin exercising essential governmental functions. To Alexander McDougall he wrote on December 23, 1775, "It appears to me prudent that you should begin to impose light taxes, rather with a view to *precedent* than profit." He went on to suggest that saltpeter and wool might be accepted in payment, a step which would "encourage manufacture." Then, pointing out that such measures were essential "to the support of the poor," he added this revelatory comment: "It keeps people easy and quiet. By being employed they gain bread. And when our Fellow Mortals are busy and well fed, they forget to complain."[100] Learning that the Provincial Congress had emitted more paper money, Jay admonished, "Will you never think of taxes? The ice must be broken, the sooner it is begun and more insensibly performed the better. I tremble for this delay."[101] McDougall soon persuaded Jay that New York City under its existing stresses and strains should not have to bear a disproportionate share of the state's tax burdens.[102]

A reluctance on the part of Jay to move toward independence combined with an enthusiasm for the assertion by the Thirteen Colonies of the governmental powers of autonomous states epitomizes his ambivalent frame of mind throughout the spring of '76. As the ground swell for independence seemed to be carrying all before it, Jay inched toward overt resistance. At McDougall's suggestion he applied for a military commission and was duly appointed colonel of the Second Regiment, New York City militia.[103]

With the spring of '76 Jay's own province had first call upon his time. Elected a delegate to the New York Provincial Congress in April, Jay was not present in the Continental Congress when some of the crucial decisions of the spring and summer of '76 were made. Thus, on May 11 James Duane wrote to apprise him that the day before Congress had adopted a momentous resolution recommending the colonies "to adopt such government as shall, in the opinion of the representatives of the people, best conduce to the happiness and safety of their constituents in particular, and Americans in general."[104] Jay took his seat in the new Provincial Congress on May 25, and was at once placed on one committee to draft a law relating to the perils to which the colony was exposed by "its intestine enemies" and on another to act on the congressional mandate to form a new government.[105] On the one hand, Jay was convinced that a new government must be formed, as the old colonial one would "no longer work any thing but mischief."[106] On the other, he was opposed to a precipitate move toward independence. On June 11, four days after Richard Henry Lee had offered in Congress a resolution affirming that the United Colonies "are, and of right ought to be, free and independent states," Jay moved that it was the sense of the Provincial Congress "that the good people of this colony have not, in the opinion of this congress, authorized this congress, or the delegates of this colony, in the Continental Congress, to declare this colony to be and continue independent of the crown of Great Britain."[107] Jay might well have made this proposal on his own initiative, but he had been prodded by James Duane in Congress to see that New York did not follow the precipitate action urged by "the orators from Virginia."[108] Jay was prepared to "take a solitary ride to Philadelphia" when he was so charged by the Provincial Congress, but since his presence was urgently needed in New York he was, perhaps conveniently, absent on July 2 when the decisive vote on independence took place in Congress. Since he did not find an opportunity to return to Congress for the rest of the year, his signature was never affixed to the Declaration of Independence.

Would Jay have signed the Great Declaration had he been present in Philadelphia that summer? The signs are none too clear. Bear in mind that it was his resolution of June 11 which withheld from the New York delegates the power of voting for independence. Remember that Jay had long hoped for a conciliatory resolution of the issues between colonies and empire. Even as late as April, 1778, Jay confided to his friend Gouverneur Morris, a man of like views on many political subjects though lacking Jay's balanced judgment and prudence, "The destruction of old England would hurt me. I wish it well. It afforded my ancestors an asylum from persecution." Even at that date Jay, aside from independence, would have been content with a treaty affording the new United States commercial advantages—in other words, a negotiated peace that would let England withdraw from the war with honor.[109] Evidently his friend Edward Rutledge felt that Jay's vote, had he been in Congress, would have been cast with "the sensible part of the house," opposing Lee's motion for independence. "I wish you had been here," he wrote on June 8 disconsolately.[110] On June 29 he wrote again to urge that Jay attend the Congress "on Monday next" when the Declaration of Independence, a draft of the Articles of Confederation, and a scheme for a treaty with foreign powers were to be laid before the house. "Whether we shall be able effectually to oppose the first, and infuse Wisdom into the others will depend in a great Measure upon the Exertions of" what Rutledge called the "Honest and sensible part of the members."[111] Alas, Jay could not come, as he explained in a letter of July 6. He was engaged "by plots, conspiracies, and chimeras dire." State business came first. "We have a government, you know, to form; and God only knows what it will resemble."[112]

Many years later, in a retrospective comment, Jay denied ever having heard "any American of any Class, or of any Description, express a Wish for the Independence of the Colonies" until after the rejection of the Olive Branch Petition. He affirmed that "It has always been, and still is my opinion and Belief that our Country was prompted and impelled to Independence by *necessity* and not by choice."[113] Now the dread necessity had arrived, and even though Jay's ideas "of men and things" ran "for the most part" parallel with Rutledge's, he would not be found wanting when the die was cast. The Convention to which Jay was a member had not been authorized to commit itself on the subject of independence. Accordingly, some facile name-changing took place. The assembly became the "Convention of the Representatives of the State of New York." Meeting at White Plains on July 9, the Convention at once referred to a committee a copy of the Declaration of Independence just received from Philadelphia. That same afternoon, Jay, as committee chairman, reported a resolution of his own drafting, which was unanimously adopted. "While we lament the cruel necessity which has rendered that measure unavoidable, we approve the same, and will, at the risk of our lives and fortunes, join with the other colonies in supporting it."[114] Jay no longer had any doubts. "I am rather inclined to think that our declaring Independence in the face of so powerful a fleet and army will impress" foreign nations with "an opinion of our strength and spirit; and when they are informed how little our country is in the enemy's possession, they will unite in declaring us invincible by the arms of Britain."[115]

Jay was not only a convert to independence, but one imbued with perhaps false optimism about the cause. By July of '76 he had assumed leadership in two areas which would irrevocably stamp him as a rebel—that of organizing the military defenses of his state and that of constitution maker. On July 2 the British launched their conquest of New York, with Sir William Howe's unopposed landing of some ten thousand troops, followed ten days later by the arrival of brother Lord Richard Howe's powerful fleet and transports, along with huge reinforcements. On July 16 the New York Convention appointed Jay to a secret committee charged with obstructing the channel of the Hudson River and harassing the enemy's shipping. They were authorized "to impress carriages, teams, sloops, and horses, and to call out detachments of the militia." Specifically, Jay was commissioned to secure cannon at a foundry in Salisbury, Connecticut, for Fort Montgomery in the Highlands. Jay sped over to Salisbury, learned from the proprietors that the cannon and shot could be released only by authorization of Governor Trumbull, then dashed across the mountains to Lebanon, where the governor summoned his council to act upon Jay's request. With the authorization in his pocket, Jay turned back to the Furnace, managed to round up teams to carry four twelve-pounders which were quickly made ready, then pushed across the state boundary to Livingston Manor to secure trucks and shot from Colonel Gilbert Livingston. On his return journey he overtook the convoy of cannon and shot moving toward Colonel Hoffman's Landing, and was able to oversee the cargo being put aboard ship for transport across the river to Fort Montgomery. A triumphantly breathless journey, and Jay managed to record it all in a diary fragment that has survived.[116]

Thus the Revolution came to Jay rather than vice versa. When his commitment was made he entered into the cause with all the zealotry of a recent convert. No appeasement for him even when the hour seemed darkest. Howe's forces were readying for the amphibious landing on Long Island, and the Battle of New York was soon to follow. The British threat to Westchester forced Jay's elderly parents from their home at Rye to find a retreat in Fishkill, where Jay joined them when the New York Convention was forced to find safety, one step ahead of the Redcoats, first in White Plains, then in Poughkeepsie, and then across the Hudson at Kingston.

Reasonable men are not the slaves of rigid ideologies, and Jay was above all a reasonable man. He had taken sides even though this involved repudiating his own past public positions. In October of '75 he had opposed the passage in Congress of a total nonimportation resolution, sarcastically demanding to know why, just because Charlestown was burned, New York would have to be put to the torch. Now, after the disaster on Long Island and the occupation of New York City, Jay wrote Robert Morris, from his refuge in Fishkill, revealing that for some time he had been converted to a scorched-earth policy. "Had I been vested with absolute power in the state," he commented, "I have often said and still think that I would last Spring have desolated all Long Island, Staten Island, the City and County of New York and all that part of the County of West Chester which lies below the mountains. I could then have stationed the main body of the army on the mountains of the East, and eight or ten thousand men in the Highlands on the West Side of the River. I would have directed the rivers at Fort Montgomery, which is nearly at the Southern extremity of the mountains, to be so shallow as to afford only depth sufficient for an Albany sloop, and all Southern passes and defiles in the mountains to be strongly fortified." Had this defense plan been adhered to, Jay argued, the state "would be absolutely impregnable against all the world on the sea side." There would be "nothing to fear except from the way of the lakes."[117]

In short, from a wishy-washy appeaser Jay had been transformed into a hard-line insurgent. As early as the spring of '76 he had counseled McDougall as to the expediency of removing to less sensitive places "such as are notoriously disaffected."[118] Already on July 16, prior to Howe's appearance, the Convention on motion of Jay had prescribed the death penalty of treason for those giving aid or comfort to the enemy.[119] Jay was made chairman of a Committee to

Detect Conspiracies, with power to seize, try, and sentence disaffected persons. The committee, which held daily sittings until the arrival of the British fleet sent them scurrying, investigated an alleged plot against the life of Washington, sentenced Thomas Hickey, one of Washington's soldiers, to be hanged, and threw Mayor David Matthews into jail, along with some thirteen other disaffected persons, aside from a sizable number who were banished.[120]

Late in September Jay was put on a reorganized committee which operated out of Fishkill. This committee was authorized not only to stamp out disaffection but to call out the militia to suppress counterrevolutionary activities, to make drafts on the state treasury, and to raise and officer two hundred and twenty men to use as they saw fit. Sitting at Conner's tavern in Fishkill, the committee day after day examined prisoners under guard. Minutes of the hearings were kept by Jay, who, besides acting as secretary, assumed the permanent chairmanship after a few meetings. The suspects were interrogated and then asked to take the oath of allegiance to Congress. When they refused, Jay, with that stern sense of duty of a Roman patriot, sentenced them to be jailed, transported to New Hampshire, or allowed to remain at home under parole. Some of those sentenced were good friends like Jay's classmate Peter Van Schaack, whom he sent to Boston on parole. Jay's inexorable performance of unpleasant duties earned him the vituperation of the enemy. Major John André attacked him in James Rivington's *Royal Gazette* as "remarkable for a mixture of the lowest cunning and the most unfeeling barbarity" and for enforcing statutes "that destroyed every species of private property and repose."[121]

By recent criteria André's censure was far off the mark. Jay was no Saint-Just. A sense of fairness, a strong humanitarian impulse, and a vigilant concern for civil liberties and due process tempered his rulings toward the disaffected. In defending his treatment of Van Schaack, Jay asserted toward the end of the war: "I have adhered to certain fixed Principles, and faithfully obeyed their Dictates, without regarding the Consequence of such Conduct to my Friends, my Family, or myself," and Van Schaack chivalrously conceded that he had been treated justly. Jay distinguished between Tories who had acted an honorable part and those whom he deemed despicable. To Van Schaack, a refugee in England in 1782, he confessed, "I considered all who were not for us, and You among the Rest, as against us; yet be assured that John Jay did not cease to be a friend to Peter Van Schaack."[122] To Colonel James De Lancey, a prisoner of war in Hartford jail, he sent one hundred dollars so that his situation might "be comfortable and easy," but when in postwar London he encountered Colonel Peter De Lancey, who commanded the lawless Tory cowboys of Cooper's *Spy,* he cut him dead.

To ferret out hidden enemies Jay organized an intelligence operation, and one of his most trusted agents who reported to Jay's secret committee was reputedly Enoch Crosby, the self-confessed original for Harvey Birch, hero of James Fenimore Cooper's *The Spy.* As Cooper acknowledged, Jay supplied the main outlines of that story.[123]

Jay, like Hamilton, was deeply concerned that the administration of the loyalty oath program should remain in the hands of civilians and not be assumed by the military. "To impose a Test is a sovereign act of Legislation," he remonstrated to McDougall, "and when the army become our Legislators, the People that Moment become Slaves."[124] Along like lines he deplored such acts of mobbism as Isaac Sears's "valorous Expedition" against Rivington's printing establishment. Such actions Jay considered an affront to the "Honor of the Colony," not to speak of the liberty of the press, one which should not for an instant be tolerated. "The Tenderness shewn to some wild People on Account of their supposed attachment to the Cause has been of Disservice," he admonished. "Their eccentric Behaviour, has by passing unreproved, gained Countenance, lessened your Authority and diminished that Dignity so Essential to give weight and Respect to your ordinances."[125]

When the revolutionary legislature turned to the adoption of a constitution for the new state, the naming of Jay to a select drafting committee seemed an obvious choice. Work on it was interrupted by Jay's more compelling duties in fortifying the Hudson, checking subversion, and running an intelligence service, but by March of 1777 a draft in Jay's hand was submitted to the Provincial Congress. Jay's draft underwent minor amendments and alterations, mainly introduced by Jay himself, along with Duane, Gouverneur Morris, and Robert R. Livingston.[126]

Edward Rutledge had cautioned Jay about the need for strong government. "A pure democracy may possibly do when patriotism is the ruling passion," he had written in November, 1776, "but when a State abounds in Rascals (as is the case with too many at this day) you must suppress a little of that Popular Spirit, vest the executive Powers of Government in an individual that they may have Vigor, and let them be as ample as is consistent with the great Outlines of Freedom."[127]

Rutledge must have been astonished at the results of Jay's labors and those of his aristocratic associates, for the New York Constitution contained some extraordinary innovations in government, most of which the South Carolinian must surely have disapproved. First of all, contrary to Rutledge's advice, Jay's constitution provided for a relatively weak governor, who shared appointing power with a council of appointment and veto power with a council of revision, while a court of impeachment and correction of errors assumed some functions that had traditionally belonged to the legislature. Jay's thinking on the executive power reflected the unfavorable view he shared with most patriots of the almost uninhibited powers of the old royal governor. Jay was determined that such executive tyranny should not occur under a republican government. It was Jay who proposed the section of the constitution guaranteeing complete religious toleration "without discrimination or preference" and "to all mankind," the broadest enunciation of the principles of religious liberty that had as yet been granted by any state of the modern world. Yet, with that deep-seated anti-Catholic prejudice of a line of Huguenot refugees, Jay would have barred officeholders who would not publicly abjure the authority of the pope. In this he was unsuccessful, but he did manage to keep ministers and priests from holding civil or military office and to persuade his colleagues to withhold naturalization from persons who would not renounce "all allegiance" to "every foreign king, prince, potentate, and state, in all matters, ecclesiastical as well as civil."

Elitist though he was, Jay recognized how essential popular participation was to the stability of republican government. He would have extended the franchise to all who had paid both state and county taxes—a proposal very close to universal manhood suffrage. During the debates over the draft he succeeded in having voting by ballot substituted for the viva-voce method of electing representatives, and provided a means whereby illiterate voters could indicate their choices. All in all, his constitutional innovations, motions, and amendments hardly support the antidemocratic label that historians have attached to his name.[128]

Significantly, Jay supported the insertion into the Constitution of 1777 of a clause forbidding the continuation of slavery, an institution which he held in deep abhorrence. He was to become president of the New York Manumission Society in the postwar period, and his sons were later renowned leaders of the antislavery movement. In light of his lifetime aversion to slavery, it was fitting and proper that during Jay's term as governor of New York he was to affix his signature to a bill providing for the end of slavery in the state.[129]

Appropriately, the Convention rewarded Jay for his heroic labors on the new constitution by electing him the state's chief justice, a post far more elevated than the one he had sought from the Crown scarce three years before. Finding judicial duties more congenial than executive ones, Jay accepted, declining to have his name advanced for the governorship.[130] Although the cases before him did not concern large constitutional questions, Jay went out of his way to criticize the impressment of horses, teams, and carriages "by the military, without the Intervention of a civil magistrate" as violative of due process of law, and urged the legislature to curb this "extraordinary power."[131] Again, as a member of the Council of Revision, he wrote the veto of an excess profits tax levied upon war profiteers on the ground that it was violative of the equal protection of the law to which all citizens were entitled.[132]

In short, Jay brought to his revolutionary commitment a deep concern for civil liberty, property rights, and a sense of justice rooted in the English constitutional system. An empire man and a moderate, he had traveled the long road by the winter of 1776–77. At the nadir of the Patriots' military hopes he stirred the delegates to the New York Convention with an address "to their constituents" which they enthusiastically adopted before the heartening news of the Trenton victory and which the Continental Congress ordered translated into German. In words that might have come out of Tom Paine's contemporary *American Crisis* pamphlet, Jay declared, "We do not fight for a few acres of land, but for freedom—for the freedom and happiness of millions yet unborn."[133] To Jay and to the other Founding Fathers these words were no mere rhetorical outpouring. Now embattled in a struggle not of his choosing, Jay felt that the fight must go on until independence was achieved. "War must make peace for us," he was to tell John Adams, "and we shall always find well-appointed armies to be our ablest Negotiators."[134]

Gone were the ambiguities, the hesitancies, the political trimming. Jay now stood at the center of the great events of the Revolutionary and early national years, a committed nationalist, an agitator for energetic government, whose career exemplifies that very special kind of revolutionary mentality that was the stamp of men of wealth and talent in New York who shared a common dream while declining to stoop to demagoguery or extremism to achieve its fulfillment.

VI

JAMES MADISON:

THE REVOLUTIONARY AS

A MAN OF CONSCIENCE

In his youth Madison expected death momentarily and made his poor health an excuse for not settling down to a career. Like so many hypochondriacs, he outlasted all his contemporaries, dying at the ripe old age of eighty-four. He repeatedly complained of being "feeble" and "sickly," but never, except in old age, suffered a clearly identifiable disease. What was important, however, was not the diseases that Madison had but what he thought he had. He was terrified that he was afflicted with epilepsy.

Madison may have been right in his self-diagnosis, but his magisterial biographer suggests that the spells he suffered could be interpreted as "epileptoid hysteria" rather than the disease itself.[1] Madison described his disease as "a constitutional liability to sudden attacks, somewhat resembling Epilepsy, and suspending the intellectual functions." He stated that these attacks continued throughout his life, "with prolonged intervals."[2] While epilepsy is not inherited, a predisposition to it is, and we know that Madison's father had among his papers, dated October 11, 1753, a list of drugs "for an Epilepsy." Since electroencephalograms were never taken either of Madison's family or of Madison himself, we will never know the answer. But if these symptoms developed in the younger Madison at two and one-half years of age, and if the attacks, though most serious in his postcollege years, continued, as Madison states, throughout his life, one would be inclined to rule out epileptoid hysteria, associated with years immediately following puberty, and to suggest some nervous or physical disorder which, without records of the symptoms, cannot be diagnosed at this distance from the events.

That Madison suffered nervous indigestion—"a bilious indisposition," he called it—and perhaps dizzy spells might be a fair inference from his remarks to Jefferson in 1785, excusing himself from taking a trip to Europe because "I have some reason to suspect crossing the sea would be unfriendly to a singular disease of my constitution." Whatever was bothering Madison was singular enough to keep him from carrying a gun when he first lined up with the Minute Men in his county,[3] and to dictate a life bereft of strenuous physical activity. How Madison would have campaigned in an age of air travel must remain a matter of speculation, and just how the voters of today might react to a candidate with a suspicious background of nervous disorder is equally a matter of speculation, especially since the cavalier removal of one vice-presidential nominee during the presidential election of 1972 for such reasons has left the issue moot.

The mystery surrounding Madison's early breakdown which occurred around the time of his graduation from Princeton is of a piece with the larger mystery of his intimate life. A very private man, Madison made sure that posterity would know what he had contributed and be able to appraise the record fairly. What he had done in a public way he spread out on the record and carefully preserved, but he drew a curtain across his personal life.

No one among the Founding Fathers was more assiduous in arranging for the publication of his public papers, and no one was more careful to exclude private correspondence. Much of a private nature he himself destroyed; other personal items were scattered among kinsfolk, friends, and autograph collectors. He made a point of going over letters written more than fifty years earlier and striking out embarrassing personal references to events he could not bear to recall, and he authorized his wife Dolley to withhold letters likely to "injure the feelings of any one or wrong in themselves." Before his papers were turned over to the United States government, his stepson John Payne Todd rifled the collection of some of its choicest items to pay his gambling and liquor debts. Then Madison's biographer, Senator Cabell Rives, persuaded the government to entrust the records to his custody, and they remained in the Confederacy during the Civil War, only part being returned at war's end. It took another seventy-five years before some additional nine hundred items were recovered by the federal government.[4]

Whatever inner tension or even hysteria may have rendered young

Madison ineffectual for varying spells, we know enough about his early life to explain some of his neuroses. As a child he was overly protected, and maturity came to him much later than with most of his peers. For fifty years he signed his name "James Madison Junr," testifying thereby that he was under the shadow of a father who was a big landowner and important public figure on his own. His rearing seems to have been largely the responsibility of a strong-minded grandmother, Frances Madison, whose early widowhood had entailed the management of both a large plantation and a large family. Living with her oldest son's family, she gave Madison his first lessons.

Physically frail, his adult height a bare five feet six inches in stature, making him almost dwarflike in a region where six-footers were commonplace, so feeble in voice that some of his remarks at the Constitutional Convention were inaudible,[5] unable to boast of conquests of the opposite sex, withdrawn with strangers and to many (and there were notable exceptions) devoid of charm, it is understandable why Madison, endowed with a formidable mind, tackled his studies and his books with furious intensity, finding therein a substitute for competitive physical activities.

Some great men have managed to survive exposure to formal education. In young Madison's case the rigorous instruction that he received sharpened his logical powers, shaped his lucid style, and slanted his political thinking. By the time he was eleven years old he had devoured every book in his father's house. At that point he was ready for a private tutor, the learned Donald Robertson, who had established a school a few years earlier down in Tidewater country. There young James rubbed elbows with such fellow students as George Rogers Clark, later renowned for his Northwest campaign, John Taylor of Caroline, a distant relative of James's, and destined to become a political foe, and John Tyler, whose constitutional views were to differ sharply from Madison's, as did those of his son President Tyler.[6] Robertson drilled Madison well in his Latin lessons and seems to have started him in his studies of Greek. What else Robertson taught must have added up to a great deal, for Madison was reported to have remarked in later life, "All that I have been in life I owe largely to that man."[7]

Madison had two more years of tutoring, this time at home under the Reverend Thomas Martin, the newly appointed rector of the nearby church who lived with the Madisons. A graduate of the College of New Jersey at Princeton in 1762, Martin had been touched by the "New Light" zeal which charged the early atmosphere of the college. When the time came for young Madison to go to college, he was advised to steer clear of William and Mary, notorious at that time for poor teaching and all-night student carousing. If that were not enough, concern over his health made it prudent for him to avoid the Tidewater during the hot or "sickly" season. Madison, surely at Martin's prompting, picked Princeton instead, entering in his nineteenth year, rather old to start college in those days, but equally anxious to make up the lost time. That he was very much the grind was evidenced by his ability to compress three years of college work in two, enabling him to graduate in September, 1771.

No Founding Father was more profoundly influenced by his undergraduate experience than was James Madison. First of all, he partook of the "New Light" Presbyterian atmosphere, with its hostility to religious establishments, whether that of the New England Congregationalists or the Virginia Anglicans. Taught by a faculty of religious dissenters, he quickly imbibed a profound respect for the newly emerging dissenting tradition. By the standards of the day Princeton was ultraliberal, and its liberalism rubbed off on its students. Its stated goal: "In the instruction of the Youth, care is taken to cherish the spirit of liberty, and free enquiry; and not only to permit, but even to encourage their right of private judgment, without presuming to dictate with an air of infallibility, or demanding an implicit assent to the decisions of the preceptor."[8] One might imagine that these objectives had been dictated by rebellious American college students of our own age, not by the college establishment itself!

Madison was favored with exceptional tutors, the contagion of whose Whiggish inclinations infected their pupil. One of his teachers, William Churchill Houston, plunged into local Revolutionary politics in 1776, served in the Continental Congress, and was associated with Madison at both the Annapolis and the Constitutional conventions. Most influential in shaping Madison's Whiggish outlook was Princeton's president, John Witherspoon, a leading empiricist of his day, whose thinking was permeated by the philosophy of "common sense," and whose expositions of the doctrines of resistance and liberty quickly established him throughout the Continent as an imposing Whig intellectual. An activist who had talked "war" as early as the summer of 1775,[9] he saw to it that New Jersey's royal governor, William Franklin (Benjamin Franklin's illegitimate son), was imprisoned, then went to the Second Continental Congress, where he had the distinction of being a Signer of the Declaration of Independence, whose advocacy he eloquently pressed.[10] He also buttressed Madison's earlier work with Donald Robertson in logic.[11]

During his student years Madison kept a notebook, wherein he summarized his readings, excerpting or encapsulating ideas deemed worthy of record. Some of these he may well have taken to heart. For example, from the *Memoirs* of Cardinal de Retz, he abstracted the following:

> Strength of Mind or Resolution is much more necessary for great actions than stoutness of Heart.
>
> A grave air hides many defects.

If these adages buttressed Madison's self-esteem, he might also have taken comfort from one of the Abbé de Bos's *Critical Reflections:* "The strongest and soundest minds often possess the weakest and most sickly bodies."

Pigeonholed for future reference as a statesman was de Retz's observation: "A Blind Rashness and an excessive timorousness cause the same Effects when the Danger is not known. For both endeavour to persuade themselves that the Danger is not real." Madison seems to have given further thought at this time to the problem of whether to temporize or to strike swiftly. In his notes on logic he cited the case of King Rehoboam who, faced with tumultuous popular demonstrations, preferred the advice of the "young men" to be a harsh ruler to the example of his father, King Solomon, who had followed the prudent counsel of the elders for "mildness and complyance." As a result, ten of the twelve tribes of Israel seceded.[12] Madison might well have remembered Rehoboam's fate when he himself gave counsel during times of tumult and dissension.

To President Witherspoon, Madison's personal mentor, the young man was the perfect model of a serious-minded grind. Witherspoon was wont to reminisce that during the "whole time" Madison was under his tuition he "never knew him to do, or to say, one improper thing." Could Madison really have been that prissy and inhibited? Certainly his intimates doubted it, and Jefferson relished embarrassing Madison with the anecdote on any and all occasions.[13] But perhaps Madison carefully withheld from his revered president some of the scatological verse that he wrote at the time of his graduation. One bit of doggerel, "The aerial journey of the poet Laureat of the Cliosophic Society," was typical of the literary ammunition fired off by his radical Whig Society against the more Toryish Cliosophic rivals. In one piece of wretched doggerel he has the poet laureate of the hated rivals beaten up on a journey, struck about eyes, ears, and nose with a chamber pot Urania brought from beneath her bed, and healed by Clio, who took the victim to her private rooms whence

> Straight an eunuch out I come
> My voice to render more melodious.

In another, Clio issues a proclamation, condemning a fellow Princetonian, Moses Allen, soon to be a Congregational pastor, in these words:

> Great Allen founder of the crew
> If right I guess must keep a stew
> The lecherous rascal there will find
> A place just suited to his mind
> May whore and pimp and drink and swear
> Nor more the garb of christians wear
> And free Nassau from such a pest
> A dunce a fool an ass at best.[14]

Still another, unsigned and in the Hudibrastic style affected at the time, attributed venereal disease to the less than Platonic relations engaged in by one of the Clios with the stagecoachman's daughter. The piece could have been written by either Madison or Hugh Henry Brackenridge. The latter attained greater heights in other poetic effusions, as he did in the drama and in his picaresque novels. One of Madison's biographers credits this creation to the future President, however.[15]

Now, it was not unusual for young men of Madison's age to be preoccupied with lechery, lust, and ribaldry, but in Madison's case it does suggest depths hidden beneath a sedate, prim, and humorless exterior (smiles always came hard to Madison), a sublimation of ungratified sexual urges. Whether coincident or no, it is around this time, too, that Madison suffered what seems to have been a physical or nervous breakdown, traditionally attributed to overstudy and possibly triggered by extreme anxiety about his own fate after learning of the sudden death of a close classmate, Joseph Ross.[16] Back at the family plantation, Montpelier, after a year of postgraduate study at Princeton, he wrote of himself as "too dull and infirm now to look out for any extraordinary things in this world for I think my sensations for many months past have intimated to me not to expect a long or healthy life."[17]

Still without forming any career pattern, Madison assumed the role of oldest brother, passing his time tutoring his brothers and sisters, of whom there were seven in all, ranging from nineteen to age one, but probably concentrating on the teenagers. Occasionally he was diverted by gossipy letters from Princeton friends. The scapegrace Philip Freneau recounted his obstreperous career as a teacher on Long Island, whence he headed for the safety of Maryland ("Long Island I have bid adieu/ With all its brutish brainless crew"). There he was equally disenchanted ("When shall I quit this whimp'ring pack,/ and hide my head in Acomack!"). Another Princetonian, William Bradford, enlivened Madison's staid moments by relaying a tale of a fellow Princetonian, newly admitted to the bar, who married but kept the relationship a secret "till the fruit of it appeared in a fine daughter." Madison, who felt that the unfortunate chap "has been long intoxicating his brain with Idleness and disapation," hoped "this larger draught of folly he has now taken" would prove a sobering experience.[18]

When he learned a couple of years later that a theology student named Thaddeus Dod had, in Bradford's homely language, "put the cart before the horse," becoming "a father before he was an husband," with every indication that the girl's friends had "forced the old fellow's head in the noose," Madison, in one of his more priggish moods, remarked: "I agree with you that the world needs to be peopled but I should be sorry it should be peopled with bastards as my old friend Dod" and his lady "seem to incline." His lack of charity did not inhibit one chuckle. "Who could have thought the old monk had been so lecherous," he commented, speculating "whether he had perhaps merited his religious enthusiasms to fan the amorous fire."[19]

Perhaps by observing his doctor's regimen to take more physical exercise and cut down on his studies, Madison slowly recovered his health, while managing during these years of tense political activity to remain aloof from political involvements and to put off a decision on a career. When Bradford asked "Jemmy" for advice, "J. M. Junr" considered the choices open to his friend: the ministry, law, medicine, business. Madison felt that if Bradford chose the law, the church would lose "a fine Genius and persuasive Orator." "Always keep the Ministry obliquely in view," he counseled, while agreeing with his friend that the law was "the most eligible" profession, the one to which he himself was leaning.[20]

This was indeed a significant admission, for if Madison was beginning to take up the study of the law, it was already evident that he was much too principled a young man to confront the grubby realities of ordinary practice. From the way he approached his studies, and his dilettantish attitude toward the legal profession ("I intend myself to read law occasionally"[21]), it became clear that Madison's interest was spurred by a scholar's desire to know more about constitutional systems and the problems of church establishments, subjects at that time very much on his mind. There is no evidence that he ever intended to practice, and though widely read, he never sought or gained admission to the bar. Counting on support from his family and the income that he could expect from the family properties, Madison had no intention of working for a living. Even a gentleman scholar like Jefferson had, despite certain disinclinations, assumed an active law practice, while Washington and John Adams at Madison's age were knee deep in their careers. But such decisions suggested a degree of maturity and self-assurance that Madison at that age did not possess.

Save for participating in the literary exercises and debates of the Whig Club at Princeton, with their radical overtones, Madison managed as late as the summer of 1773 to maintain an astonishing detachment from the revolutionary ferment swirling about him, even in upland Orange County, Virginia. In a letter to Bradford in late September of '73 he did add a comment on the scarcity of circulating cash in Virginia and its deflationary effect on prices, but coupled the observation with an apology for introducing so mundane a subject. "I do not meddle with politics," he added, "but this calamity lies so near the heart of every friend of the country that I could not but mention it."

What first stirred Madison was not the controversy between the mother country and the colonies, which was fast moving toward a climax, but the issues of religious toleration and establishment. By this time he was moving toward the position that the Anglican establishment in Virginia encroached upon the liberties of its citizens, but he was not yet prepared to sympathize with critics of religion itself or to endorse free thinking. Witherspoon had warned his students against reading ephemeral works dangerous to sound religion and morality, and at this time, contrary to his later attachment to freedom of religion, speech, and the press, Madison sought to be scrupulously sound.[22]

It was the Boston Tea Party that roused Madison out of his political apathy.[23] But his reaction could scarcely be considered a salvo fired off in support of mobbism. "I wish Boston may conduct matters with as much discretion as they seem to do with boldness," was his reaction. He quickly changed the subject, focusing on an issue of increasingly current concern to himself, his speculations about what would have happened if the Church of England had been uniformly established throughout the colonies. Then "slavery and Subjection might and would have been gradually insinuated among us."[24] Thus, while Boston might have been too rash, Virginia was too submissive, and he could find nothing to brag about concerning "the State and Liberty of my Country." Significantly, Madison, as a foremost nationalist in the years ahead, spoke of Virginia in 1774 as "my country." "Poverty and Luxury prevail among all sorts: Pride, ignorance and Knavery among the Priesthood and Vice and Wickedness among the Laity." Worst of all was the prevalence of religious persecution. Close by Montpelier he had seen "five or six well meaning men" put "in close Gaol for publishing their religious Sentiments which in the main are very orthodox." He was, of course, alluding to the flare-up of religious intolerance in Culpeper County, with the imprisonment of a half-dozen Baptist preachers. Madison had not been quiet. "I have squabbled and scolded, abused and ridiculed so long about it," and to so little purpose that he confessed to being "without common patience."

Thus, it was the religious issue rather than the taxation and constitutional disputes with England which inspired Madison's first extant emotionally charged letter; it was his concern over the persecuted dissenters in his environs, not over the aggrieved Bostonians, which wrenched him from his studies and thrust him into the embattled field of politics.

If Madison counted on the "people of fortune and fashion" of "his country" to support the petition of the Presbyterians and Baptists to the colonial legislature for religious liberty, he was quickly disillusioned. He discovered the Anglican Church both too powerful and too fearful to permit toleration for dissenters. Madison's involvement in the case of the persecuted clergy led to his enunciating what was to become a first principle: "Religious bondage shackles and debilitates the mind and unfits it for every noble enterprize, every expanded prospect."[25] It was two more long years before the dissenters would achieve their primary objective, religious toleration, and then not without the active intercession of Madison himself.

As the frontier flared up with the launching of Lord Dunmore's Indian War and imperial tensions mounted across America, it seemed only a matter of time before even so retiring and introspective a person as Madison would be drawn into the fray. Privately Madison observed the near-unanimous support for a boycott on trade with England, the Scottish merchants the chief dissenters, and one can infer from his correspondence that he had moved to a position of denying to Parliament any rightful authority over the colonies—a position the great Whig leaders like Jefferson and John Adams were also approaching.[26] But unlike these relatively elder statesmen, or even young Hamilton, four years his junior, he confined his Whiggish views to private correspondence. Now his health had improved sufficiently for him to take a trip during May and June to New York and Pennsylvania, timing his return to Virginia too soon to have been in Philadelphia when the First Continental Congress opened its sessions.[27] Certainly, with Bradford's father and brother acting as official printers of the Congress, he would have been in an enviable position to getting a line on what was going on behind closed doors had he stayed on in Philadelphia until the end of summer.

For four years since returning to Montpelier from Princeton, Madison had avoided either embarking on a career or plunging into politics. Even a recluse like Madison could no longer resist the pressures of the spirited upcountry in which he dwelt or the prominent stand that the senior Madison took as chairman of the Orange County Committee of Safety. The Madisons and their friends were committed, and he himself was at last torn from his law books and thrust into political action.

Along with his father, who signed as chairman, Madison, Jr., affixed his own signature to an address transmitted directly to Patrick Henry praising the fiery radical spokesman of the Piedmont for pressing for compensation for the powder which Lord Dunmore had removed from the county magazine. The address concluded with the sweeping observation: "We take this occasion also to give it as our opinion, that the blow struck in the Massachusetts government is a hostile attack on this and every other colony, and a sufficient warrant to use violence and reprisal, in all cases where it may be expedient for our security and welfare."[28] Young Madison was reputedly among the party that personally conveyed the address to Henry at Port Royal, Virginia, en route to the Second Continental Congress, and authorized Henry to publish their declaration of support.[29] It was not until April of '76, however, a full year after Lexington and Concord, that Madison assumed a public role in the Revolutionary cause by running successfully for election as a delegate from Orange County to the Virginia Convention, a brief but important chapter in Madison's political biography.

In short, Madison by environment, education, and associations was readily persuaded of the validity of the Revolutionary cause. What impeded his early participation was a preoccupation with personal concerns, physical or psychological barriers to activism. Even when these barriers were removed, there remained an indecisive quality about Madison as activist that critics were wont to pounce upon at some of the less fortunate moments of his public career. By the spring of '76, with independence in the air, with Virginia planning to set up its own government, and about to press the rest of the continent to formalize its separation from the empire, Madison quickly won a position of influence among a leadership distinguished for maturity, experience, and eloquence, none of which qualities he then possessed. What he did have was intellectual power, and what he was prepared to give to the cause was an assiduous dedication to his duties as a legislator, qualities which in combination would prove increasingly rare among later generations of American politicians.

Madison's initiation into legislative committees was as a member of the Committee on Privileges and Elections. Apart from its concern with the validity of the election of delegates, that Committee also dealt with individual Virginians manifestly disloyal to the Patriot cause. There is no evidence that Madison felt the same concern for political dissenters as he did for religious ones, and for the latter he reserved his truly creative efforts.

The chief architect of Virginia's Declaration of Rights as well as that state's Constitution of 1776 was George Mason, whose cogitations about both great projects went back for at least a decade. Mason's first draft of the Declaration of Rights upset all the conservatives and at least one liberal. Robert Carter Nicholas, for example, caviled over the first line, with its revolutionary assertion "that all men are born equally free and independent." Was not this an open invitation to a slave insurrection? The liberals reassured Nicholas that the slaves were not constituent members of their society and hence "could never pretend to any benefit from such a maxim,"[30] and Mason's clause was permitted to stand. Patrick Henry objected, warning that the expressed ban on ex post facto laws might allow a public enemy to escape justice. Accordingly, that provision was dropped.

Then came Madison's turn. Mason had expressed his views on religious toleration in a way befitting an enlightened Anglican vestryman and county justice of the peace who had been exposed to Locke's *Essay on Toleration*. As Mason first phrased it:

> That as Religion, or the Duty which we owe to our divine and omnipotent Creator, and the Manner of discharging it can be governed only by Reason and Conviction, not by Force or Violence; and therefore that all Men should enjoy the fullest Toleration in the Exercise of Religion, according to the Dictates of Conscience, unpunished and unrestrained by the Magistrate, unless, under Colour of Religion, any Man disturb the Peace, the Happiness, or Safety of Society, or of Individuals. And that it is the mutual Duty of all, to practice Christian Forbearance, Love and Charity towards Each other.[31]

That did not go far enough for Madison. He proposed an amendment designed to establish absolute religious freedom in Virginia rather than the toleration within the limits Mason had drawn. Madison shrank from speaking in public, as was to be his wont, and turned to Patrick Henry to plead his case. Henry took a look at the draft and begged off on the ground that it was the apparent intent of the amendment to disestablish the church.[32] Lacking a sponsor, Madison substituted a new amendment providing for a degree of religious freedom without actually disestablishing the church. The key words of this proposal were written into the last article of the Virginia Declaration of Rights, adopted in its entirety by the Convention on June 12, 1776. Madison had already learned the first lesson of a successful politician, to work for the possible.

Madison had persuaded the Convention to replace Mason's words "fullest toleration in the exercise of religion" with "free exercise of religion," a more sweeping phrase, implying an inherent personal right rather than a limit upon state action. Not only did his amendment provide for "free exercise" but it also deleted the Masonian exception, "unpunished and unrestrained by the magistrate, unless, under colour of religion, any man disturb the peace, the happiness, or safety of society, or of individuals." In its final form the clause read:

> That religion, or the duty which we owe to our Creator, and the manner of discharging it, can be directed only by reason and conviction, not by force or violence; and, therefore, all men (are equally entitled to the free) exercise of religion, according to the dictates of conscience; and that it is the mutual duty of all to practise Christian forbearance, love, and charity, towards each other.[33]

Atheists and non-Christians might still feel uncomfortable even with these protections, and while adherents of the church establishment might have seen the handwriting on the wall, they were prepared to fight every inch of the way. Nor was Madison content with his victory. He resumed the fight in October, and this time he fought by the side of one of Virginia's rising giants, Thomas Jefferson. Already in the spring of '76 Jefferson, in sketching a draft constitution for his state, had included a guarantee of "full and free liberty of religious opinion," but with exceptions that watered down its effectiveness.[34] Now, as a member of the Committee on Religion, Madison scrutinized a bushel of petitions from dissenting areas to end religious establishment in Virginia. It has been suggested that Madison had his hand in one of the petitions drawn up by his close friend Samuel Stanhope Smith, then engaged in plans for the founding of Hampden-Sydney Academy, of which Madison served as a trustee.[35] The allegedly Smith-Madison petition besought "without delay" the ending of "all Church establishments" and the abolition of "every tax upon conscience and private judgment."

The church establishment issue triggered a battle of giants, with

Jefferson pressing for disestablishment and Edmund Pendleton vigorously refuting him. Pendleton, using delaying tactics, put off positive
action, and the matter was referred to another committee, of which
Madison was a member. That committee reported a bill substantially
disestablishing the church. Pendleton managed to modify the with-
drawing of state pay to the clergy to a mere year's suspension of pay.
The fact of the matter is that, once suspended, the pay was never
reinstated, and in effect the church was disestablished.[36]

It was not by one stroke that church and state were divorced and
absolute religious liberty established in Virginia, but by piecemeal
steps in which Madison's collaboration with Jefferson proved a fore-
runner of the most fruitful political partnership in American history.
Jefferson took off the shelves his longtime draft of a Statute for
Religious Liberty, introducing it in 1779 as a part of his Revision of
the Laws.[37] With Jefferson involved in his administrative duties as
governor, then in voluntary retirement, followed by his brief spell in
Congress and a longer period abroad as minister to France, the
burden of securing the passage of this major piece of legislation fell
to Madison. Now a national figure after distinguished service in the
Continental Congress, Madison, back in the state assembly, threw all
his newly won prestige against an effort by the Protestant Episcopal
Church, the successor in Virginia to the Church of England, to have a
general assessment levied for the support of religion and to incorporate the clergy of their denomination. It was clear to Madison that the
first proposal would undo the abolition of the tithe system which
Jefferson had already secured and that incorporating the clergy would
in effect make it impossible for the lay vestries to remove Episcopal
clergymen. Madison now found himself arrayed against the quondam
radical Patrick Henry, who used every trick in the book to lay the bills
over for another session when it was unclear that he had the votes to
pass the measures at that time.[38]

What made the new proposals so insidiously clever is that they
might draw upon other Christian denominations for support. That
was just what happened. The Presbyterians, lured by the prospect of
securing state funds, backed Henry's resolution requiring the people
to "pay a moderate tax or contribution annually for the support of the
Christian religion or of some Christian church, denomination or
communion of Christians or of some form of Christian worship."
Henry spoke in behalf of religious assessments with his customary

eloquence. Madison in reply demolished Henry's arguments. As he construed the bill, it violated Virginia's Declaration of Rights. Refuting Henry's arguments that the decline of religion went hand in hand with the decline of states, Madison parried Henry's thrust that religion was necessary to the state, while questioning whether religious establishments were necessary for religion. This Madison stoutly denied; maintaining that religion is corrupted when established by law. In every state that Henry cited which had undergone deterioration, Madison showed that there had been a religious establishment, whereas the most flourishing periods of Christianity he found in the primitive years and in the Reformation, in both of which religion flourished among dissenters and in opposition to the state establishment. If one wishes to improve morals, Madison retorted, then improve the administration of justice; set a personal example by proper morality and by suitable provisions for the education of young people.

It is noteworthy that the entire debate centered on the issue of what kind of Christian society the state needed or should support. Madison, while pointing out the inherent dangers of leaving it to the courts to decide what Christianity really was, what parts of the Scriptures were canonical or apocryphal, and whether one should obtain salvation alone or in conjunction with good works, avoided a frontal attack on Christianity itself. His notes, scribbled in his characteristically crabbed and minuscule handwriting on the back of a letter,[39] indicate that he concluded his discussion with "panegyric on it, on our side."

So powerful did Madison's argument prove to be on the inherent dangers of having the courts construe Christian doctrine that the delegates in committee of the whole voted to include all religions, non-Christian as well as Christian, in the assessment plan, and also to permit the incorporation of all Christian societies desiring it. As a result of the latter vote a committee brought in a bill to incorporate the Episcopal Church, while taking no action on the Presbyterian petition for like treatment.

What to do? Patrick Henry and his tight-minded following seemed in complete control. From Paris, Jefferson around this time commented to Madison: "What we have to do I think is *devoutly to pray for his death*."[40] Much as Madison may have shared Jefferson's homicidal instincts on the subject of their common adversary, neither could count on the Lord to act quickly enough. Instead Madison joined, if he did not promote, the move to elect Henry governor. Thus, for mixed reasons, Henry was elected to the post "without competition or opposition."[41] Henry's exalted elevation left him only ten days in the legislature to get his assessment project through, and as Madison saw it, the circumstances were "very inauspicious to his offspring."[42] Hoping to stem a rising tide of opposition to the bill, its proponents now camouflaged it by including a clause providing that money not allocated for any particular sect by the taxpayers should be disposed of "for the encouragement of seminaries of learning within the counties whence such sums shall arise." Since most education was in the hands of parish schools, the proposition was in diametrical opposition to Jefferson's free public school system proposed back in 1779.

Once more Madison exhibited his political adroitness by conceding a little in order to gain a great deal. This time he yielded on the issue of the Episcopal incorporation bill, now revised to include both clergy and vestries. Madison's tactics appear to have won over nine supporters of incorporation who now voted against the assessment and another eight who abstained. By forty-five to thirty-eight the House of Delegates voted to postpone reading the bill for almost a year.[43] Meantime a new election reflected a growing sentiment in opposition to the measure, including the Episcopal laity who, on careful scrutiny of the incorporation bill, found it seriously defective from the point of view of their control. Indeed, it was they who initiated a move for its repeal, which was accomplished in 1787.

The defeat of church incorporation left Madison free to rally opinion in the Piedmont and back counties against the assessment measure. Back in June of 1785 he had scored a great propaganda coup by drafting a "Memorial and Remonstrance against Religious Assessments." Printed by George Mason in Alexandria and circulated throughout the state, the "Memorial and Remonstrance" elicited so extraordinary a popular response that the assessment bill never even came up for a vote.[44] This nonaction must have pleased George Washington, who feared that agitation over the bill might "convulse the State," and expressed the hope that "the bill could die an easy death."[45]

It would be fair to say that few state papers framed in the Revolutionary era had so momentous an impact on American constitutional law as did Madison's "Memorial and Remonstrance." It was the principal authority for the scholarly dissenting opinion of Mr. Justice Rutledge in a 1947 decision of the Supreme Court in which a five-to-four majority upheld reimbursing parents with public funds for costs of transportation to parochial schools.[46] It is the great omnipresence overhanging every court which is confronted with the variety of subterfuges that have been proposed and enacted during the last generation to provide tax support for church or private schools. Indeed, Madison's "Memorial and Remonstrance," along with his First Amendment to the Constitution, raised at that time and has continued to raise questions in our own day as to whether it was the intention of the Founding Fathers to forbid completely all government aid to religion whatsoever.[47]

In his "Memorial and Remonstrance" Madison declared that the right of every man to exercise religion according to his own conviction and conscience, a right guaranteed by the Virginia Declaration of Rights, was by nature unalienable. Arguing that religion was wholly exempt from the authority of society at large, and *a fortiori* from a legislative body, he denounced as "tyrants" those rulers who would encroach on the right of the people, and denigrated as "slaves" the people who would submit to it. Strong language, indeed, but Madison regarded the moves toward establishment and assessments as constituting the first serious challenge to America's liberties. Citing the American Revolution as an example, he declared, "The freemen of America did not wait till usurped power had strengthened itself by exercise, and entangled the question in precedents." Who does not see, he asked, that "the same authority which can force a citizen to contribute three pence only of his property for the support of any one establishment, may force him to conform to any other establishment in all cases whatsoever?" Thus, as in the case of the popular resistance to the Tea Tax, Madison, a true revolutionary, looked beyond the trivial levy that was contemplated to aid religious teachers and saw as its logical consequence the imposition of church control upon the state. To Madison the issue posed by assessment constituted a test of the fundamental rights guaranteed by Virginia's Declaration of Rights. If the legislature could demolish this right, then they could control freedom of the press, abolish trial by jury, and, indeed, deprive the people of the suffrage and even establish "an independent and hereditary assembly." No, Madison concluded, "the General Assembly of this Commonwealth have no such authority."

Madison had grounds for rejoicing when, just a few months before he drew up the "Memorial and Remonstrance," Congress, in voting a plan for the government of the Western territories, retained a clause setting aside one section in each township for the support of public schools, while striking out the provision reserving a section for the support of religion.[48] Commented Madison: "How a regulation so unjust in itself, so foreign to the authority of Congress, and so hurtful to the sale of public land, and smelling so strongly of an antiquated bigotry, could have received the countenance of a committee is truly a matter of astonishment."[49]

The capstone of Madison's great revolutionary achievement was the all-inclusive injunction of the First Amendment: "Congress shall make no law respecting the establishment of religion, or prohibiting the free exercise thereof." Had Madison achieved no more he would be entitled to rank among America's foremost libertarians, whose sustained efforts propelled the American Revolution in a distinctive channel, anticipating thereby the worldwide trend toward separation of church and state, with consequences so pregnant for American education and culture and for the perpetuation and enhancement of religious diversity. But the fact of the matter is that Americans in the years ahead were to be indebted to him for a great deal more, for legislation and policies embodying his wisdom and sound judgment.

To Madison the complete separation of church and state formed "the great barrier against usurpations on the rights of conscience. So long as it is respected and no longer, these will be safe. Every provision for them short of this principle, will be found to leave crevices at least through which bigotry may introduce persecution; a monster, that feeding and thriving on its own venom, gradually swells to a size and strength overwhelming all laws divine and human."[50] How astonishing that Madison, looking back on the persecutions of earlier times and his own day, could forecast the shape of things to come— that monster genocide, which our own century has spawned.

The great church-state struggle takes us ahead of the story, but one cannot leave in midair Madison's first distinctive contribution to the ideology of the American Revolution and his first collaboration with Jefferson in what proved to be an epochal partnership.

Alas for young Madison, he brought to his campaign for reelection to the lower house in 1777 a set of lofty ethical values untainted by maturity. In combination with a characteristic priggishness and an innately introvert manner he hardly cut the ideal figure on the hustings. In Virginia, as Washington soon found out, one treated the voters to drinks on election day. "Swilling the planters with bumbo," as Theodorick Bland, Jr., indelicately described the rum punch ladled out in generous quantities, was the customary way of winning votes. During a July election day in Frederick County in the year 1758, George Washington's agents, it has been estimated, supplied 160 gallons of rum, beer, and cider royal to 391 voters and unnumbered hangers-on, more than a quart and a half to a voter.[51] What was considered protocol in Washington's county was also the practice in Jefferson's and in John Marshall's.[52]

This was the custom of the country, but it was a custom repulsive to the junior Madison. He denounced it "as equally inconsistent with the purity of moral and of republican principles." Instead of applauding him for his reformist and republican zeal, the voters regarded his stand as prideful and stingy, choosing in his place an ex-tavernkeeper named Charles Porter, whose conscience did not interpose bars between the voters and "the corrupting influence of spirituous liquors, and other treats, having a like tendency," so distasteful to Madison.[53] As a result, Madison was unseated in the assembly. The fact is that for a man who was so politically minded and ultimately so successful as a party organizer and leader Madison had a positive distaste for electioneering, for rubbing elbows with the voters, in which respect he was very much like some of the later Federalists who regarded active campaigning as unseemly.[54]

Fortunately for Madison, under the Constitution of 1776 the lower house elected the members of the Council of State. Where he had failed with the people he now succeeded with the professionals, who recognized young talent when they saw it and brought young men into politics without unseemly delay. Accordingly, in November of '77 he was elected by the House of Delegates to the Virginia Council of State.[55] Madison faithfully attended every session of the Council from January to June of '78, absenting himself as was to be his custom during the "sickly season," but returning in November of that year. He continued on the Council until December of '79, when the legislature chose him as a delegate to the Continental Congress. Thus, while he served the war effort with commendable diligence but in a civilian capacity, his father was finding his military duties as lieutenant of the county increasingly irksome. Not that Junior was prepared to assume them. Quite the contrary, in a letter in which he addressed his father, as customary, as "Honored Sir," he warned that the latter's resignation as a militia officer would "have a very unfriendly aspect on the execution of the draught" and would be construed as evidence of "a want of patriotism and perseverance."[56] Since the twenty-seven-year-old Madison never shouldered a gun throughout the war, his gratuitous advice to his fifty-five-year-old parent seems self-serving, granted its political perspicacity.

It has not been possible to disentangle Madison's contributions to the Council from those of his associates. Tradition attributed to Jefferson had Madison serving as amanuensis of Governor Patrick Henry, but none of Henry's communications published in the *Madison Papers* bear this out. What he did acquire was experience at first hand in exercising the emergency war powers of the Council in dealing with such problems as recruiting, disciplining a refractory militia, dispatching expeditions to the western frontier, along with other military matters, tracking down and punishing enemies of the state, and the perplexing fiscal problems of wartime government, the last of which were to prove an increasing concern of Madison's.[57] Most important of all from the point of view of Madison's political education was the election of Thomas Jefferson in June, 1779, as governor of Virginia. Previously they had met briefly. Now they worked together daily and, despite a disparity of eight years in their respective ages, quickly found a commonality of interests and attitudes that served to cement a lifetime of friendship and collaboration.

Madison's growing expertise in statecraft contributed to a political maturity which his shy and youthful exterior belied. It seemed all work and little play, at least from the record. His twelve-year-old sorrel was stolen or strayed away. Somebody put a hand through a window at a residence at which he was staying and stole his hat. As Madison told it to a friend many years later, "It was about a mile from the house to the palace, and I was kept from going to the latter for two days, by the impossibility of getting a hat of any kind. At last, however, I obtained one from a little Frenchman who sold snuff—very coarse—an extremely small crown and broad brim, and it was a subject of great merriment to my friends."[58] Whether they found the new hat ridiculous or were amazed that he would not dare venture onto the streets of Williamsburg uncovered is a matter of speculation, but probably both elements contributed to the hilarity.

It was Madison's election as a delegate to the Continental Congress in December of 1779[59] which converted him from a precocious state politician, whose reputation had rested on one major issue, into a continentalist whose nationalist views were to be shaped in the forge of his new experiences and enlarged outlook. He did not attend Congress until March 20, 1780,[60] but meantime he had turned his attention to the great issues of money and prices which were proving so critical to nation and state. Two days before Madison appeared on the floor of Congress that body had declared that the old continental issues of paper money would be redeemed at only one-fortieth of their face value.[61] The states had been warned that a fiscal crisis was impending. In September, 1779, John Jay, as president of the Congress, had drafted a "Circular Address" to the states exhorting them to supply enough soldiers, money, and matériel to restore public credit and advance the common cause. For some time Madison had been disturbed about the alarming inflationary trends and let his friend Bradford know how much he approved the exertions by Philadelphians and the people of Williamsburg to go after the monopolizers, then the popular scapegoats for rampant currency depreciation.[62] Now, President Jay's circular letter, with its pledge that Congress would not increase its outstanding bills of credit, a pledge made to boost the public's fast-eroding faith in the government's ability to redeem their bills, set Madison to cogitating. He not only read Jay's Address, but examined Montesquieu and Hume as well, and he came to the conclusion that the depreciation of the continental paper had been ascribed to the wrong cause. He disagreed with Hume's proposition that the price of goods bore a direct relationship to the quantity of money in circulation. What made the paper of the United States inferior to specie, Madison argued, was the fact that it was not redeemable on demand but at some future date. Thus, as he saw it, the crux of the matter was the *intention to redeem* and not the *quantity of paper* issued. That the government's intentions, however explicitly professed, could become increasingly suspect as the printing presses ground out paper without limitation of amount, did not seem to Madison to offer a formidable objection to his views. As he put it succinctly, "the situation of the United States resembled that of an individual engaged in an expensive undertaking, carried on, for want of cash, with bonds and notes secured on an estate to which his title was disputed; and who had besides, a combination of enemies employing every artifice to disparage that security." In short, in Madison's view, "Instead of paying off the capital to the public creditors, we give them an enormous interest to change the name of the bit of paper which expresses the sum due to them; and think it a piece of dexterity in finance, by emitting *loan-office certificates,* to elude the necessity of emitting *bills of credit.*"[63]

Since Madison's essay was not published until 1791,[64] it is by no means clear how widely it was read at the time it was written. What is extraordinary is that Madison should have had the presumption to challenge such preeminent authorities as Montesquieu and Hume. What was of larger significance is that Madison's essay set him on a path toward enlarging the powers of the Confederation government as well as investing it with energy. To Madison, this meant, first of all, that the national government must be empowered to issue money and to tax, a view consistent with his conviction that Congress had erred in abdicating its power to issue money, for Congress alone could command the resources of the Continent.[65] At this very time a brilliant young aide of Washington's was to express almost identical views, and two years later he would join forces with Madison in the Congress, notably in supporting Madison's Address to the States of April 25, 1783, supporting a federal impost.[66] The alliance of Madison and Hamilton was to have extraordinary consequences for the nation in the Confederation years, even though, ironically, the historic break between the pair would be precipitated by their subsequently divergent views on fiscal matters.

If Madison's firsthand knowledge of the fiscal impotence of the central government quickly converted him into an ardent nationalist, that continentalist point of view was enhanced by insights gained from his outstanding service on congressional committees dealing with foreign affairs. It was he who drafted the instructions to John Jay in Spain in 1780, insisting that the United States succeeded to the rights of the British Crown in the western lands. Inferentially, Madison weakened the individual state's titles he was upholding by laying the greatest weight on the Crown's rights secured by the Treaty of Paris made with France in 1763 rather than on the claims of the states derived from their respective ancient charters. Surely he realized this, because, although a Virginian and devoted to the interests of his state, he took a prominent part in persuading the claimant states to relinquish to Congress the territory of the Old Northwest, a cession which, by meeting the conditions laid down by Maryland, the last holdout, put the Articles of Confederation into force and effect.

In addition to his own state's huge western claims, Congress had to consider the pretensions of the speculative land companies. Madison, with his built-in distaste for speculators (Robert Morris excepted), felt that one virtue of turning the territory over to Congress would be that it would keep it out of the reach of speculators. In short, there would be less chance that Congress would "gratify the avidity of land mongers" than that the states would.[67] Unlike many of his compatriots from Virginia among other states, Madison had no interest in western land speculation, having already put into effect the rule of conduct laid down in his autobiography, "never to deal in public property, land, debts or money, whilst a member of the body whose proceedings might influence these transactions."[68] To say that Madison's notions of conflict of interest were more virtuous than the standards then prevailing would be a gross understatement.

By favoring the relinquishments on the part of all states claiming western lands, Madison did not indicate any lack of sympathy for the interests of frontier settlers. Quite the contrary. He strongly supported America's claims to the navigation of the Mississippi on the basis of international law as he construed it, and only with reluctance yielded to the instructions from the Virginia legislature to agree to cede such a right. When Jay interpreted the instructions as being contingent upon Spain's making a prompt treaty with the United States, and as lapsing if Spain did not move fast, Congress, including Madison, applauded Jay for his sound judgment.[69]

Suddenly, and to everyone's amazement, the prudent and judicious bachelor was smitten by a teenage charmer, junior to him by sixteen years. The scene of the romance was Mrs. Mary House's lodgings, located a block from what is now Independence Hall. Mrs. House's was a favorite rooming house for delegates from New York and Virginia. There Madison had found board and lodging since first coming to Congress in 1780, and it was around the dining table and the drawing room that he became acquainted with the family of William Floyd, a New York delegate, whose chief distinction came from his being a Signer of the Declaration of Independence, but who managed to maintain a low profile during his long years of service in the Congress. Catherine, his youngest daughter, was fifteen years old when Madison seems to have first taken notice of her. A charmer and coquette, who captivated her listeners by renditions on the harpsichord, she quickly won Madison's heart. Judging from Madison's letters to Jefferson, the suitor finally succeeded in his quest. Kitty agreed to marry him. The pair then posed for Charles Willson Peale, whose miniature portraits show Madison looking even younger than his pretty fiancée.[70]

Whether because of Kitty's growing doubts or Madison's heavy involvements in congressional affairs, the parties agreed to postpone the announcement of the engagement until the end of Madison's term in Congress in November, 1783. In April of that year Madison set out with the Floyd family for New Brunswick, New Jersey, Madison's first trip away from Philadelphia in three years. He spent a day or two with the Floyds in New Brunswick, and returned to Philadelphia.

Perhaps his departure was a mistake, for Kitty had second thoughts, and they revolved mostly around another suitor, William Clarkson, a nineteen-year-old medical student and fellow lodger of Madison's at Mrs. House's. Clarkson's youth and ardor, along with that inscrutable feminine intuition, won the day. For weeks Madison did not hear from Kitty. Even as late as July 17, when Congress was forced by mutinous soldiers to flee from Philadelphia to Princeton, he had had no word from her. Eleven days later the letter came. As Madison reported to Jefferson, the letter contained a "profession of indifference," and it was sealed, according to Floyd family tradition, with a piece of rye dough.

Broken-hearted, Madison wrote Edmund Randolph that "contrary to my intentions I shall be detained here several weeks yet, by a disappointment in some circumstances which must precede my setting out for Virginia." By August he had given up the cause, and in a letter (only partially legible, as Madison in his old age endeavored to strike out all reference in any of his letters to Kitty Floyd) he advised Jefferson of the shattered romance.[71] What had seemed a heady courtship for Madison had proved a bore to Kitty. Madison's graceless figure, unstylish clothes, and intellectual conversation did not provide the right bill of fare for a romantic repast with a "capricious" young girl, to use an adjective that Madison himself may have employed in describing her.[72] Evidently the fervent Clarkson had what Kitty wanted, and Madison did not.

Madison had suffered a shattering personal experience, and there would be no other woman in his life for more than a decade until he met and married Dolley Payne Todd, a buxom and engaging widow, who proved the ideal partner for his public career. How compatible they were sexually is a matter of surmise. Dolley had had two children by her first husband; she had none by Madison. The barrenness of the new marriage proved a matter of some comment. Some eighteen months after the marriage Aaron Burr, who seems to have played a key role in bringing the pair together, remarked to James Monroe, "Madison still childless, and I fear like to continue so."[73] Whether Madison's failure to prove his manhood in a tangible way turned him inward and even irascible is purely speculative. One scholar has even ventured to suggest that, alongside Alexander Hamilton's established fecundity and sexual attractiveness, Madison's sense of his own impotence played a major role in that hostility and feeling of inferiority he manifested toward his political foe.[74]

Like all complex statesmen, Madison, in his life and views, embodied abundant paradoxes. His notorious dislike of speculators and speculative activities in land must be set against his own fling in land speculation. Even during the war Madison was involved with his family in the acquisition of extensive tracts in Kentucky, and he himself held some acreage there as long as he lived.[75] Shortly after the war ended, Madison, having definitely decided against the practice of the law, set his mind toward land speculation on his own. His judgment buttressed by Washington's advice, he made a purchase contract with James Monroe as a partner of a thousand acres in the fertile Mohawk Valley of New York State. His initial investment was barely over $300, but he tried to persuade Jefferson, then America's minister to France, that he use his "credit" in his "private capacity" to borrow up to $20,000 abroad, for further purchases to be made on behalf of Madison, Monroe, and Jefferson. Confident that he could buy the land from speculators at bargain rates because of the shortage of specie, he himself figured that his own profit would run to as much as $40,000. Jefferson's reply was discouraging. French bankers would not be tempted except for a higher rate of interest than Madison was prepared to pay. That ended Madison's dreams of a quick killing, although when he eventually sold his original Mohawk acreage he netted a profit of nearly 200 percent. The original investment, however, was not calculated to make him rich from the venture.[76] Lack of cash, rather than conscience, compelled him to drop out of another scheme proposed to him around the same time to take a one-third share in a tract through which the Potomac Canal would be built— the kind of insiders' deal which has become commonplace among politicians of more recent vintage.[77]

Throughout his life Madison derived his chief source of income from his ownership and operation of his plantation, Montpelier, like Jefferson's Monticello after which it was modeled, and it nearly ruined its owner financially. It was the unhappy fate of this civil libertarian to be dependent upon a system of labor which he abhorred. His distaste for the institution was founded on moral grounds, but one can detect an element of insecurity, shared by all slaveowners, stemming from its destructive potential. Indeed, his earliest recorded comments on the "peculiar system" dealt directly with the latter element. On the outbreak of the war between England and the colonies he expressed the hope that any attempts at slave insurrections, which he thought not unlikely, would be "concealed as well as suppressed," and considered the possibility as being the Achilles heel of Virginia's defense against the British.[78]

Like Henry Laurens, George Mason, and a few other Southern slaveowners, Madison frankly recognized the incompatibility of slavery with the ideals professed in Jefferson's immortal Declaration. To a proposal to give slaves as a bounty to army recruits, Madison countered with a proposition to enlist and liberate the slaves, a move which, in his mind, would "be more consonant to the principles of liberty which ought never to be lost sight of in a contest for liberty."[79] Herein, perhaps unknowingly at this time, he advocated a policy which Hamilton and John Laurens also supported. Madison was breathing the free air of Philadelphia when he made the proposal to a member of the Virginia Assembly. He was promptly rebuked. "The Negro scheme," he was informed, "is laid aside upon a doubt of its practicability" and was considered "as unjust, sacrificing the property of a part of the Community to the exoneration of the rest." Besides, if we did, the British would follow suit and draw off the field hands in such numbers as would bring widespread ruin.[80]

A long stay in Philadelphia could play hob with a slaveowner's convictions, and such was the case with Madison, who, to begin with, was no diehard Southerner. Short of funds, he was faced with "the necessity of selling a negro," as he confided to his father.[81] At the end of his stay in Congress he realized that it would be risky, to say the least, to send back Billy, his manservant, to Montpelier, after four years in the Quaker citadel in the company of free servants. He was now "too thoroughly tainted to be a fit companion for fellow slaves in Virginia." Instead, he sold him in Philadelphia, where under the prevailing laws he would be free in seven years. Madison thought he had to explain his action to his father. There is no reason, he told Madison, Sr., why Billy should be punished "merely for coveting that liberty for which we have paid the price of so much blood, and have proclaimed so often to be the right, and worthy the pursuit of every human being."[82]

Madison was not long settled at Montpelier when he expressed the wish "to depend as little as possible on the labour of slaves." In 1785 Madison perceived that the climate of opinion was not favorable to any legislation providing for a gradual emancipation of slaves, but he helped defeat a reactionary bill which would have outlawed the manumission of individual slaves.[83] Having exposed himself on the most sensitive of all issues in his region, he, like Jefferson, an astute politician who learned his lessons quickly, was not likely to forget the bruises of the battle. No longer did he undertake a frontal attack on the slave system, but temporized and compromised. Take, for example, his backing for the three-fifths compromise of the Constitution at the Federal Convention. This he deemed to be a realistic acknowledgment that "the real difference of interests lay not between the large and small" states but "between the Northern and Southern states" over "the institution of slavery."[84] He followed up this observation with an analysis of the compromise in *The Federalist* No. 54, where he defended that result as appropriate to the condition of slaves, possessing as they did a mixed character of being both persons and property, "in fact, their true character."[85] Granted, at the Convention he vigorously opposed the extension for twenty years of the foreign slave trade as "dishonourable to the American character,"[86] and both as Secretary of State and as President was concerned with the enforcement of the prohibition of that trade, but his public position on the domestic slave trade and internal migration was increasingly timid, if not mute. When in Congress, he declined to present a petition of the Pennsylvania Abolition Society, one of the first of a flood of such petitions to inundate that body, reminding his correspondent that "those from whom I derive my public station are known by me to be greatly interested in that species of property" and could properly charge him with "want of candour, if not of fidelity," were he "to become a volunteer in giving a public wound, as they would deem it, to an interest on which they set so great a value." Why not, Madison countered, withdraw the privilege of manumitting slaves, or at least require "that the persons freed should be removed from the Country?" Such a position, he felt, might remove the sting from the objections of the slave interest.[87]

In short, Madison's original objection to slavery was transmuted into active support for the African colonization movement. He enthusiastically endorsed this program, even accepting the presidency of the Colonization Society at the advanced age of eighty-two. This activity bespoke less a personal involvement in the black man's plight than a growing conviction that it would be impossible to integrate the free Negro in America. Because of "the difference of colour," he felt that racial divisions in America would be "permanent and insuperable."[88]

As time went on, Madison was much more provoked at the persistence of the slavery issue and its threat to the union than concerned about the human condition of the blacks themselves. At the time of the Missouri Compromise he expressed the opinion that under the Constitution Congress could not prevent a state, once admitted into the union, from permitting slavery, insisting that the authority conferred upon the federal government by the Constitution was limited to the migration and importation of slaves *into* the United States, not to internal migration.[89]

If Madison in his old age was in despair over slavery, it was, again, not because of any specially warm feeling toward the black people. The quantity of warmth that Madison could feel to other human beings was to the end carefully rationed. He died without making any provision for freeing his slaves, his will merely providing that none should be sold without the slave's consent as well as Dolley Madison's. Nothing could have been more ineffectual. Litigation, the sale of Montpelier, and the deaths of his widow and her children left his slaves subject to all the insecurities and insensitivities stemming from their status as chattels.[90]

It may come as something of a shock to know that America's

foremost civil libertarian, not even Thomas Jefferson excepted, manifested barely the slightest concern for due process insofar as Tories and enemies of the state were concerned during the Revolution. In early '75 he applauded the tarring and feathering of one Virginian who ventured to treat a county committeeman with "disrespect." So far as the free press was concerned, Madison only wished that he could get his hands on New York's notorious Tory printer James Rivington "for 24 hours in this place." Here in Virginia he could be sure of being adequately punished, unlike New York, where Tories were permitted to "insult the whole Colony and Continent with impunity."[91]

Here is how young Madison felt about a Scotch parson in an adjoining county who refused to observe the fast designated for July 20, 1775, by the Continental Congress or preach on fast day on the ground of conscience. Madison applauded the committee's ordering his church doors closed and his salary stopped. Should the Virginia Convention endorse the action of the local committee, Madison gleefully anticipated that the parson would "get ducked in a coat of tar and surplice of feathers," assuming his insolence would not abate. "In his new Canonicals" the parson would be free to "act under the lawful Authority of General Gage if he pleases." Madison added that in his parish they had "one of the same Kidney," but after being "published in the Gazette for his insolence," he narrowly missed receiving the like treatment. "Finding his protection to be not so much in the Law as the favour of the people he is grown very Supple and obsequious."[92]

The '76 legislature, of which Madison was a member, had set penalties up to £20,000 and five years in jail for persons convicted after a jury trial of maintaining and defending the authority of the King or Parliament.[93] Some time thereafter Madison informed his father of a hot-headed, obstreperous Tory named Benjamin Haley who had the presumption to debate the issues of the war with a French officer in the Continental army. He was committed to close gaol, then allowed to post bail the next day and go home. This information was passed on to Madison, Sr., so that "if an opportunity occurs," he could "take the advice of some Gentleman skilled in the Law, on the most proper and legal mode of proceeding against him." When he was brought to trial, the Orange County Court merely sentenced Haley to a fine of 12 shillings and one hour's imprisonment, showing a lot more common sense in the matter than Madison would have, quick as he was on the basis of conversation to label the accused "a dangerous Enemy to the State."[94]

When his friend Bradford passed on to Madison certain suspicions, spread presumably by the Lees, of Benjamin Franklin's allegedly "wicked" character, Madison, who one day would give Franklin the stoutest kind of support and become an inveterate foe of the Lees, reacted quite extraordinarily to this idle gossip. "It appears to me," he replied, "that the *bare suspicion* of" Franklin's "guilt amounts very nearly to a proof of its reality."[95] In this period young Madison seemed not only infected with notions of guilt by association, but, worse, of guilt by gossip.

With Madison, this vindictive spirit toward the internal foes of the Revolution passed, as it did in the case of Jefferson, John Jay, and other fair-minded men of that generation. The champion of liberty of conscience, and the Bill of Rights, and a principal rallier of public opinion against the hated Alien and Sedition Laws, Madison found out in time that without civil rights and due process no republican system can survive.

Like his longtime senior partner, Thomas Jefferson, Madison exhibited ambivalent feelings toward a number of notions which today's generation associates, rightly or wrongly, with the republican system, to whose dedication the Founding Fathers gave their best years. Madison believed in government resting upon the consent of the people, but in the Revolutionary years he took it for granted that "the Common people" would support the radical measures urged by the leadership.[96] Thus he was a Revolutionary elitist like most of the Founding Fathers who constituted the Establishment. Believing that power could corrupt, he held no illusions about the virtuousness of the masses. His pessimism was buttressed by the excesses committed by state legislatures in the Confederation period. To Madison such irresponsible legislation proved that the people possessed as great a potential for despotism as any prince, and their "licentious" behavior was quickly turning his thoughts to strengthening the national government.[97] To protect the government against the dangers of an "overbearing" majority while at the same time preserving the spirit and form of popular government was, to Madison, "the great *desideratum* of republican wisdom." Regular elections, the separation of powers, a bill of rights, among other safeguards, were political mechanisms calculated to accomplish that great objective, along with moral goals, which Madison never ignored. Never would he forget the twin evil potentialities of unrestrained popular rule and unrestrained government itself. As he brilliantly analyzed the problem in *The Federalist* No. 51, "In framing a government which is to be administered by men over men, the great difficulty lies in this: you must first enable the government to control the governed; and in the next place oblige it to control itself."

Nor did Madison look forward to the development in America of a classless society. He feared that in time the gap between rich and poor would widen, and instead of homogeneity within the Thirteen States saw groupings of interests and factions made up of rich and poor, creditors and debtors, a landed interest, a monied interest, and a manufacturing interest, views he expounded in his celebrated *Federalist* No. 10.[98]

In the closing years of the American Revolution Madison had taken his stance in Congress as an outstanding continentalist. Within a few years he had, in his role both as activist at the Federal Convention and as expositor of the Constitution, become a thoroughgoing nationalist intent on subordinating the states to the sovereignty of the central government. Indubitably, his notions of Federalism exhibited a greater sensitivity than did those of Jay or Hamilton to the power mix of states' reserved rights and the national government's express and implied powers. Nonetheless, it seems extraordinarily paradoxical and completely inconsistent with his previously held constitutional views that he, along with Jefferson, should have been associated with the initiation of the compact and strict construction theories at the time of the Alien and Sedition Acts, with their enunciation of the mischievous doctrine of interposition, a spurious theory from whose seed the even more mischievous notion of nullification proved the logical offshoot. Indubitably Madison's connection with this doctrine seemed to him in retrospect one of the embarrassing literary efforts of his long career. With doctrines of nullification and secession on the rise, Madison's deathbed counsel was in effect a repudiation of the implications of his earlier views: "The advice nearest to my heart and deepest in my convictions is that the Union of the States be cherished and perpetuated."[99]

Lastly, Madison had rather decided reservations about Jefferson's notions that "the earth belongs to the living,"[100] with its concomitant idea that "a little rebellion now and then is a good thing." Madison usually kept his feet on the ground. Dedicated as he was, however, to setting on a firm base the republican ideals for which the American Revolution was fought, he rejected any notion that the Revolution had been completed and its reformist aims frozen in a mold by 1783. Convinced that the Revolution had set a standard to which the peoples of the world should and would repair, he anticipated its continuing impact on the world of revolutions which was emerging during his more mature years. Near the close of his life he observed: "Our Country, if it does justice to itself, will be the workshop of liberty to the Civilized World, and do more than any other for the uncivilized."[101]

That Americans still feel his benign presence two hundred years later may provide reassurance to those who believe that this nation, as a workshop dedicated to liberty, can once more command the admiration of nations, those long established and others just emerging, and will once again resume the leadership in a worldwide war against tyranny, poverty, and ignorance.

VII

ALEXANDER HAMILTON

AND THE GLORY ROAD

John Adams called him "the bastard brat of a Scots pedlar." Unchari-table as one might expect of an Adams, but a characterization aimed right at the jugular. Alexander Hamilton's illegitimacy was not a matter of spurious conjecture; its ugly truth was embalmed in the court record. The humiliating circumstances of his origins, childhood, and early poverty left galling memories, memories effaced only by romanticizing the past, establishing respectable credentials in the present, and feeding one's cyclonic ambitions for the future.

The first time Alexander Hamilton's name appears in any extant record is February 22, 1768, when the probate court of Christiansted, on the Danish West Indian island of St. Croix, sealed up the effects of the deceased "Madame Rachel Lewine" for distribution among her three sons, Peter Lewine, James Hamilton, and Alexander Hamilton, the last two designated as fifteen and thirteen years old respectively, and denominated "illegitimate children, born after the decedent's separation from the aforesaid Lewine."[1]

Behind the lines of the terse probate court transaction in Danish lies the story of a wildly tragic marriage and a romantic if troubled and frustrating liaison. Had Rachel Faucett of the British island of Nevis stayed married to John Michael Levine,[2] as Hamilton and his descendants spelled it, Alexander would have been born legitimate but half-Jewish, the latter indubitably a far greater handicap than bastardy to one with soaring ambitions in that day and age. Rachel was the daughter of British parents whose marriage went on the rocks. Her mother legally separated from her father, and upon his death removed with her daughter to St. Croix, where they had pros-perous relatives. There Rachel met Levine, married him in 1745, and seems not to have known a moment of happiness with her husband. Hamilton's grandson asserted that Levine was "a rich Danish Jew,"[3] but he was probably of German origin, wrote in German rather than Danish, kept his accounts in English, and apparently understood Dutch. Beautiful Rachel was, but hardly the submissive type. After five years of marital incompatibility, she left Levine, only to be jailed in the fort in Christiansted on her husband's orders under the curious laws of the island. Refusing a reconciliation on being discharged, she abandoned her four-year-old son, Peter, returned to Nevis, and took up with the thirty-three-year-old Scottish merchant James Hamilton, a younger son of the Laird of Cambuskeith, but something of a drifter and ne'er-do-well, albeit a charming one. James, Jr., and Alexander were the two sons born of this union, both probably on Nevis.

With his wife living in flagrant adultery, Levine brought suit for divorce in 1759 in the matrimonial court of St. Croix, winning a dissolution of the marriage in a decree which denied to Rachel Levine's illegitimate children "all rights or pretensions to the plaintiff's possessions" and forbade her remarrying.[4] Rachel and Hamilton moved around the islands, finally to St. Croix, whence the bankrupt Hamilton shoved off and abandoned his brood.

If Levine was the villain of the piece, Hamilton shows up as a pretty shabby character, too. He deserted Rachel, even in her last illness, nor did he evidence the least concern for his two young sons. He could be called a "father" only by biological accident. It was Rachel who shouldered the responsibilities of father and mother down to the end. It was she who seems to have tutored Alexander and then sent him to a Jewish school in Nevis, where he was so tiny that his teacher had to stand him on a table to have him recite the Ten Commandments in Hebrew. Deserted by her paramour, Rachel Levine, as she called herself,[5] ran a general store in St. Croix and probably taught her younger son to keep the accounts for her. Taken ill of a fever in February, 1768, she died, leaving her two sons five women slaves, three Negro boys, and a stock of salt, pork, butter, and flour. Just as the estate was being settled, John Michael Levine, with fiendish vindictiveness, showed up in court and successfully laid claim to all of the paltry remnants for Peter, Rachel's legitimate child, cutting off the Hamilton boys without a stiver.[6]

The facts of paternal neglect notwithstanding, young Alexander never bore any outward animosity toward his father but disdained from putting on the record any testimony of affection for his devoted if wayward mother. If the son was ashamed of the mother, he stood in need of a father whose respectable Scottish lineage served as important credentials for a poor immigrant. "My blood," he once said, "is as good as that of those who plume themselves upon their ancestry." Toward the Levines, on the other hand, he remained unreconciled. When he learned that his half-brother Peter had died in South Carolina, he was concerned about securing "the rights of a brother," confessing to his wife that "the circumstances" abated his "distress." "My brother Levine," he added, "dies rich, but has disposed of the bulk of his fortune to strangers. I am told he has left me a legacy. I did not inquire how much."[7]

In later life Alexander spoke of James Hamilton with filial respect, never once reproaching him for his irresponsible behavior. In fact, however, he had cut his ties with his family pretty completely. Some dozen years after coming to America he revealed in a letter to his brother James that he did not even know whether or not he had ever married. He did, however, accept a draft on him for £50 sterling, coupling it with an admonition "to avoid if possible getting in debt." With pious hypocrisy he added, "But what has become of our dear father? It is an age since I have heard from him or of him, though I have written him several letters. Perhaps, alas! he is no more, and I shall not have the pleasing opportunity of contributing to render the close of his life more happy than the progress of it. My heart bleeds at the recollection of his misfortunes and embarrassments." His older brother died in obscurity the following year, but his father, whom he last heard of as being in sorry straits at St. Vincent's, lived to an impenitent old age, declining to intrude on the privacy of his illustrious son in America.[8] Throughout his life Hamilton kept up the fiction of an endearing father-son relationship, while in fact his quest for both a father and a respectable family connection governed to some extent his relationship with both Washington and Philip Schuyler, whose daughter he was one day to marry.

The real debt Hamilton owed his father he never could have acknowledged. The stain of illegitimacy and poverty that James Hamilton had left on the family name could be effaced only by illustrious achievement, and Hamilton from boyhood was an overachiever, one who found it necessary to more than compensate for his feelings of inadequacy. A dreamer, irked at the unglamorous clerkship that was his lot, he became competitive, audacious, and exceedingly ambitious. Anxiety over family and money, combined with resentment over the stigma of bastardy that he was forced to bear, made him enormously concerned about his reputation above all else, a concern which was to prove his ultimate undoing.

Young Hamilton was quickly acknowledged to be a prodigy. Although he stated his age variously, the probate record of 1768 established the year of his birth as 1755, not 1757 as he would have had his acquaintances in America believe, but closer to that which he publicly acknowledged in 1771.[9] Adding two years to his age scarcely detracts from his precocity. Alexander's intellectual superiority over James was implicitly acknowledged by his mother in apprenticing the older brother to a carpenter while arranging to have the younger son serve a clerkship with a friend of the family, the merchant Nicholas Cruger. As a merchant's clerk, Alexander revealed a precocious aptitude for business and management.

All of this would serve him in good stead when going over the ledgers of the United States Treasury, but that was not the career for which young Alexander yearned. Writing to his friend Ned Stevens in New York, the fourteen-year-old confessed his weakness. "Ned, my Ambition is [so] prevalent that I contemn the groveling condition of a Clerk or the like, to which my Fortune, etc. condemns me and would willingly risk my life though not my Character, to exalt my Station." Without hopes of immediate preferment, he was preparing the way "for futurity." Though these were perhaps "Castles in the Air," he reminded his correspondent that "we have seen such Schemes successful when the Projector is Constant." Then the last, almost ominous words, "I shall Conclude saying I wish there was a War."[10]

Hamilton was to get his war sooner than he anticipated, but, save in its closing moments, he was not to ride the glory road of battle command to which he had aspired from boyhood. It was characteristic of Hamilton that throughout his life he was wont to prefer military solutions to political ones in times of emergency, whether it was to satisfy the officers and public creditors in 1783, or to put down the wretched whiskey insurrectionaries a decade later, or to settle differences with France arising during President Adams's administration. In fact, his admiration for Julius Caesar continued throughout his life, giving credence to Jefferson's account of a visit Hamilton paid to the home of the Secretary of State in Philadelphia probably in the spring of 1791. Hamilton inquired about three portraits hanging on the wall. Jefferson identified the subjects as Sir Francis Bacon, Sir Isaac Newton, and John Locke, claiming them to be his "trinity of the three greatest men the world has ever produced." Hamilton was unimpressed. "The greatest man that ever lived," he remarked, "was Julius Caesar."[11]

Fortunately for young Hamilton, his talents were not fated to wither away in the languid climate of a semitropical paradise. Fate, connections, and Hamilton himself took a hand. It was in the disparate roles of businessman and writer, rather than warrior, that Hamilton's precocity was first recognized. In the five-month period in 1771 during which Nicholas Cruger was away in New York on a trip for his health, his sixteen-year-old clerk conducted the business affairs of the firm with a sure hand. He took risks and made decisions. He lowered the price of some barrels of worm-eaten flour and a cargo of water-logged mahogany and sent out to pasture a shipment of mules that had arrived as "skeletons" and needed to be fattened up to secure a fair price. With something of the imperious manner of later days he issued orders to ship captains and kept the firm afloat.[12]

Keeping accounts and writing business letters did not satisfy Hamilton's itch for authorship. In his spare time he composed bad sentimental poems for the local newspaper[13] and a set of "Rules for Statesmen" wherein praise was bestowed on the British system which sets over all departments "a Prime Minister like a Commander in Chief,"[14] a notion he was one day to put into practice when as Secretary of the Treasury he assumed the powers of first minister in Washington's cabinet, and in which he early reveals a debt to Machiavelli, that Renaissance expert on the depravity of man.

It took a hurricane to shake Hamilton loose from his moorings in the West Indies and sweep him to the main of America. The tempest, the worst in the memory of men, hit St. Croix and the neighboring islands on the last night of August, 1772, with tragic loss of life and property. In a letter ostensibly to his father ("Honoured Sir") and dated September 6, Hamilton reported the event, which the local paper published the following month.[15] Florid, self-conscious, and pious, but withal compassionate ("see tender infancy pinched with hunger and hanging on the mother's knee for food!"), it appealed to the religiosity of Hugh Knox, Christiansted's Presbyterian minister, a talent scout who at last had found a subject worthy of his enthusiasm. It was Knox who appears to have raised among friends and acquaintances of Hamilton a fund to send the budding poet and journalist to America and support him while he was pursuing his studies.[16]

How much these and other effusions[17] reflected a deep-felt piety or rhetoric calculated to win Knox's favor remains one of the numerous enigmas which enshroud Hamilton's early days. If young Hamilton "got religion," it wore off rather fast after his coming to America. He never shared the lifelong religious orthodoxy of his New York associate John Jay. Indeed, during the Constitutional Convention in Philadelphia, as a result of intensified debates and rising tempers over the issue of the suffrage for the lower house, the Deistic-minded Franklin urged that henceforth clergymen be invited to offer prayers at each session. Hamilton opposed the motion as likely "to bring on" the Convention "some disagreeable animadversions," or, according to a later version, expressed confidence that the Convention could transact the business entrusted to its care without "the necessity of calling in foreign aid!"[18] What roused Hamilton to the formal piety of his youth was the threat posed by the radical ideology of the French Revolutionary period. Then, in imitation of the Jefferson-controlled Democratic-Republican Societies of the 1790's, he proposed a Christian Constitutional Society,[19] to support the Christian religion and the Constitution. This increasing devotion to Christian doctrine in his last years was dramatically borne out when, having accepted Aaron Burr's challenge to a duel, he also obeyed the injunction of Christianity by throwing away his shot.[20]

It would be idle to speculate on what Hamilton's politics might have been had he not secured the sponsorship of so stout a Whig Presbyterian as Hugh Knox, for as he later acknowledged, he came to America with a broad bias toward monarchy, a bias which eroded under the spell of powerful republican ideologists but was never completely eradicated. It was Hamilton's and the nation's good fortune that the republican faction took him up at once and gave him both hospitality and tutelage. With his looks, charm, and talents Hamilton might have won a hearing anywhere, but it speaks well for the perception and open-mindedness of the government's critics that an obscure pauper could win access to the highest Whig circles within weeks of being cast upon an alien shore.

Hamilton, who disembarked in Boston sometime in the late fall or winter of 1772–73, tarried there too short a time to be infected with the radical virus that held the tense, mutinous town in its grip. Arriving in New York, he presented himself at the counting house of Kortright & Company, the firm that was to handle a trading account set up for young Hamilton's support. Kortright's partner, Hugh Mulligan, turned him over to his bachelor brother Hercules, with whom Hamilton stayed. It is to the recollections of this Irish radical activist and Liberty Boy, later to serve in Washington's espionage service, recorded some forty years after the facts, that we are indebted for scraps of information about Hamilton that help fill in some of those exasperating gaps in Hamilton's early life.[21] Along with Mulligan, Hamilton's sponsors in the city were two leading Presbyterian clergymen, Dr. John Rodgers and the Reverend John Mason, and they were concerned that their protégé be given a good Presbyterian education.

The nearest place where such could be obtained was a preparatory school in Elizabethtown, New Jersey, conducted by the republican-minded Princeton-born Francis Barber, who was to fight alongside Hamilton for most of the war ahead. Enrolled at Barber's Academy, Hamilton stayed for a time at the home of the reigning Whig Presbyterian intellect of the middle colonies, William Livingston, soon to be Revolutionary governor of New Jersey, succeeding the deposed Tory William Franklin. At the Livingstons Hamilton met a coterie of staunch Whigs, among them Elias Boudinot, whose Presbyterian piety matched his republican zeal, and John Jay of New York, who was courting Livingston's daughter Sarah. All along Hamilton's sponsors planned to enroll him at Princeton, that citadel of "New Light" Presbyterian doctrine under the strong leadership of the Reverend John Witherspoon, an eloquent Scotsman. Princeton was also Hamilton's own preference. However, with an audacity and assurance that belied his years, he expected to hold to the galloping pace he had set at the academy and accordingly insisted that he be advanced from class to class as rapidly as his achievements warranted. Witherspoon was impressed by Hamilton's scholarship, but the trustees would have no truck with such unconventional notions.

Hamilton then turned to his second choice, King's College in New York City, where the authorities accepted him as a special student who did not formally matriculate with a class until 1774, by which time he seems to have been a sophomore.[22] Hamilton's admission to

King's was indubitably a blow to William Livingston, who had scathingly attacked the original chartering of the institution back in 1754 under the auspices of the Church of England.[23] Livingston's attack both hurt and helped. Half of the funds intended for the college were diverted to a jail and pesthouse,[24] but to placate dissenting groups, the college, although nominally Anglican, became in fact nondenominational, with its trustees picked from a variety of creeds and boasting a thoroughly secular curriculum, extremely liberal by the traditional academic standards of that age. For a time Hamilton pursued medical studies which had been initiated at the college in 1767, but the lure of New York politics proved a jealous mistress, with Dr. Clossy's anatomical lectures a first casualty. Having shown a good head for figures during the time of his West Indian clerkship, Hamilton was especially attracted to mathematics, and to catch up with his group secured private tutoring from Professor Robert Harpur,[25] a Presbyterian and a Whig whose presence on the faculty gave a slightly nonpartisan tinge to that heavily Loyalist stronghold. Those mathematics lessons proved the most immediately useful activity that a future artillery officer could undertake. Hamilton used the college library to good account, devouring Grotius, Pufendorf, Burlamaqui, familiarizing himself with Locke, Hobbes, and Montesquieu, as well as Blackstone, the then prevailing rage in England and the colonies, and, above all, imbibing heavy drafts of David Hume, upon whose *Essays* he was to levy so conspicuously throughout his life. These and other jurists and philosophers were bandied about in the weekly sessions of the undergraduate debating club in which Hamilton participated.

In short, despite the Establishment atmosphere prevailing at King's College, and despite the friendship Hamilton quickly struck up with its president, the High Tory Myles Cooper, the college held adequate reserves of liberalism to replenish one's Whiggish religiosity if one were so inclined. It was only a short stroll from the college campus, located between Barclay and Murray streets and running down to the Hudson River, to the Fields, now City Hall Park, where crowds assembled to hear the Liberty Boys assail the tea duties and the Intolerable Acts passed by Parliament to punish Massachusetts for its presumption. Here activists stirred up the crowd to put the fear of God into violators of the boycott of British goods. Amid the political commotion within earshot of the college any red-blooded young man must have found it impossible to concentrate solely on his studies. And Hamilton was even more restless than his peers.

Today the spectacle of a college sophomore exhorting the crowd to overthrow the Establishment has become a rather boring stereotype, whether at Berkeley, Morningside Heights, the Luxembourg Gardens, or Dahlem. In the year 1774 it was still something of a novelty. According to Hamilton family tradition, Alexander made his initial public address at a meeting in the Fields held on July 6, 1774, in which the leader of the Liberty Boys, Alexander McDougall, pushed through the adoption of a nonimportation agreement, one that lacked a single loophole. It is by no means unlikely, but no contemporary found it significant enough to report.[26]

It was not as a flaming orator but rather as a penman that young Hamilton made his dramatic entry onto the stage of politics. The time was December, 1774; the occasion, a public tract whose publication thrust the author into the very front line of Whig publicists. *A Full Vindication of the Measures of the Congress* was framed as an answer to *Free Thoughts,* a Tory pamphlet attacking the Congress, attributed to Samuel Seabury, the Anglican rector at West Chester. Under the pseudonym "A Friend to America," Hamilton's *Vindication,* followed in February of '75 by *The Farmer Refuted,*[27] laid down a body of political thought to which the author, with surprising consistency, adhered for his entire public career. For a youngster of nineteen to have underscored the principles of a longtime ideological commitment revealed a precocity which is the hallmark of genius.

A Full Vindication was written to defend the reputation of the respectable delegates to the First Congress whom Seabury had excoriated, and on matters of reputation Hamilton then and later proved exceptionally alert. It did much more than that, however. It denied to Parliament any authority over the colonies and rested the imperial connection on allegiance to the King alone. If similar arguments had been advanced by Thomas Jefferson in July of '74 in his *Summary View* and by James Wilson in his *Considerations* the following month, and, if, almost coincidentally with Hamilton, John Adams was pursuing the identical line in his series of "Massachusettensis" letters, Hamilton's *Vindication* took him in one grand leap to that advanced position now claimed by American Whigs, senior to him by a good many years.

By February Hamilton had adopted an even more radical posture.

In his *The Farmer Refuted,* a reply to Seabury's *View of the Controversy* (the Anglican rector's refutation of *A Full Vindication*), Hamilton proceeded to justify the right of revolution by resort to first principles. When the principles of civil society are violated, men may betake themselves to the law of nature. Hamilton had respectable authority for his argument—the eminent jurist William Blackstone, who not so long before had spoken of "those extraordinary recourses to first principles, which are necessary when the contracts of society are in danger of dissolution."[28] Indubitably, too, Hamilton's ideas were shaped by the combative pamphlet of his favorite parson, Hugh Knox. Denying the relevance of the argument that New York lacked a charter, unlike the other colonies, and therefore had no constitution, he affirmed in his most eloquent passage: "The sacred rights of mankind are not to be rummaged for, among old parchments, or musty records. They are written, as with a sunbeam, in the whole *volume* of human nature, by the hand of the divinity itself; and can never be erased or obscured by mortal power."[29] It is not unlikely that for this metaphor Hamilton borrowed from Knox's *Discourses,* wherein the latter states: "Our duty is written, as it were, with sun beams."[30] Regardless of Hamilton's ideas and figure of speech, he had, by his writings, attracted wide attention. "I hope Mr. Hamilton continues busy," wrote John Jay to McDougall in December, 1775.[31]

If Hamilton was later embarrassed by the thoroughgoing radicalism implicit in this resort to first principles, he never confessed the fact. Like other revolutionaries before or since—Jefferson was perhaps *sui generis*—he came to feel that a resort to first principles was an "exceptional" and "extraordinary" step and that the constitution of the country, having fulfilled the ends of the revolution, should be treated with "sacred reverence." To allay all doubts about his loyalty to the monarchy, Hamilton, in this pair of pamphlets, took pains to disavow any scheme attributed to "some turbulent men" to establish "a republican government," insisting that the king would be "the great connecting principle."[32] This monarchical predilection would betray Hamilton into one of the greatest indiscretions of his career, his unfortunate speech of June 18, 1787, delivered at the Constitutional Convention, wherein he advocated a "high-toned" government which would be a "republic" only in the technical sense that a life-tenured chief executive would be elected (indirectly), and not be hereditary, while replacing the House of Lords would be a life-tenured elective senate. He was even prepared to have the system characterized as an "elective" monarchy.[33]

In later years Thomas Jefferson was to charge Hamilton with being "not only a monarchist, but for a monarchy bottomed on corruption." Jefferson was guilty of oversimplifying the aims of his foremost political antagonist and putting the worst light on principles which were deeply rooted. In his *Vindication* and *The Farmer Refuted* Hamilton first let the public in on his pessimistic views about human nature. In *The Farmer* he quotes with approval "the ingenious" David Hume to support the political maxim that "every man must be supposed a knave." This was a cynical point of view he never abandoned. If one took mankind in general, he told the Federal Convention twenty-two years later, "they are vicious" and governed by their passions. He hammered the point home at the New York Ratifying Convention, where he confessed that "I rely more on the interest and opinions of men than on any speculative parchment provisions whatever."[34]

Like Hobbes and Locke before him, Hamilton regarded "self preservation" as "the first principle of our nature" and the "most powerful incentive of human actions." And what could one count on men's doing? Being self-centered, they could be expected to take such measures as might be necessary to preserve life and property, measures which Hamilton approved even though they might be "detrimental to others."[35]

Obsessed as he was with the overriding influence of self-interest, Hamilton believed that if one controlled a man's property, one controlled his will,[36] and as a corollary of that observation, that every man had his price, even though, he felt, persons attached to elitist groups might also be influenced by concepts of honor, which Hamilton pulled right out of the age of chivalry. As a young officer anxious to enlist men in his artillery company, he pointed out to the New York Provincial Congress that "men will naturally go to those who paid them best." The Provincial Congress clearly agreed with him, as it promptly granted Hamilton's artillerymen the same scale of pay enjoyed by like companies in the Continental forces.[37]

Erecting as he did his entire politico-economic system on the principle of "self-interest," Hamilton by war's end ridiculed the notion that a republic could be disinterested;[38] he predicted at the Federal Convention that "separate interests" would arise, and, to the extent that wealth accumulated in a few hands, virtue would decline. He struck the same note at the New York Ratifying Convention, where he pessimistically stated that "the tendency of things will be to depart from the republican standard." Perhaps the wish was father to the thought, but he told his hearers that this would be the "common misfortune" which would await New York's own constitution as well as those of the other states.[39] Granted that nobody had a monopoly of either virtue or vice, Hamilton disclosed to his upstate anti-Federalist critics that the rich had "the advantage of character" and therefore "their vices" could be considered "more favorable to the prosperity of the state than those of the indigent," and partaking "less of moral depravity."[40] It was in poor taste for Hamilton to have chosen as the closing note for *The Federalist* a dismissal of the accusations against "the wealthy, the well-born, and the great" as inspiring "the disgust of all sensible men."[41] It was this kind of pseudosophistication, this confessed prejudice in favor of the affluent and the powerful, along with Hamilton's insensitivity as Secretary of the Treasury to consorting with financiers and speculators of unsavory character, that prompted Senator Samuel Maclay, a Jeffersonian Republican, to call him a crook. Needless to say, if Maclay presumed that Hamilton was interested in feathering his own nest, he could not have been further from the mark. Hamilton's personal financial integrity was unimpeachable. Perhaps it would have been more supportable to say that Hamilton was crooked in all matters *save money*.

Hamilton's indiscreet remarks and his constant concern for the creditors, the rich, and the powerful lent credence to Jefferson's charge that his opponent sought a system based upon "corruption." Hamilton was perfectly frank about it. He told the Constitutional Convention that "a reliance on pure patriotism had been a source of many of our errors," and reminded them that so astute a political savant as Hume had approved "all that influence on the side of the Crown which went under the name of corruption," accepting it as "an essential part of the weight which maintained the equilibrium of the Constitution."[42]

What is perhaps astonishing is that so perceptive a nationalist as Hamilton, one so concerned with developing a national consciousness and a national character,[43] so thoroughly alert to the need for shaping public opinion, should have been insensitive to the new ideological fervor which the French Revolution touched off, that feverish nationalism which enlisted men's devotion to abstract causes and when tested, again and again, revealed that in the contest between ideology and self-interest the latter was so often sacrificed. But then Hamilton never really understood the masses and what made them tick.

Hamilton was the sort of revolutionary who detested mobs and mobbism, whether Whig mobs, Shaysites, Whiskey Boys, or French Revolutionary terrorists from afar. Always he insisted that due process be observed and the civil rights of adversaries protected. In this respect he differed no whit from other responsible Revolutionary leaders who eschewed both demagoguery and lynch law and managed to keep a checkrein on mobbism.

Hamilton's first encounter with a menacing mob occurred late on the night of May 10, 1775. An ugly crowd of some four hundred, aroused by rumors that King's College president Myles Cooper was stirring up Tory resistance, made for the college building in which he resided, intending at the least to tar and feather the miscreant. Getting wind of the move, Hamilton, accompanied by his friend Robert Troup, reputedly awakened the sleeping president and, while the mob shook the "groaning" college gates, hustled him out the back way to the banks of the Hudson or harangued the mob to give Cooper a chance to slip away, according to another account. That night Cooper took refuge in the home of the parents of one of his students, Petrus Stuyvesant, grandson of the testy Dutch governor, and then found refuge on the British frigate *Kingfisher*. Governments in those days were more foresighted than present ones in holding frigates in readiness for university officials. Cooper lived to reach England and to memorialize his delivery at a student's hands in stanzas he published in the *Gentleman's Magazine*.[44]

Next, Hamilton rushed to the defense of the Tory printer James Rivington, who had published several of his pieces critical of the government. In October, 1775, Isaac Sears, one of the original New York Sons of Liberty, rode into town at the head of a body of Connecticut horsemen. Finding the printer had fled, they proceeded to wreck his press and remove the type. According to some accounts, Hamilton risked his neck by haranguing the onlookers to defend Rivington's press against the "invaders." Finding the mob out of control, he dashed off a letter to John Jay, whose prudent and legal-minded course he so admired. While conceding that Rivington's paper had been "dangerous and pernicious" and the man's character "detestable," he condemned Sears's action. If the "multitude, who have not a sufficient stock of reason and knowledge to guide them," fail to take a stand against "tyranny and oppression," he warned, they would in the same state of unreason show "a contempt and disregard of all authority." What concerned him was not so much the suppression of a free press, but the behavior of "the unthinking populace" who were growing "giddy" and liable to "run into anarchy." What Hamilton proposed was that Congress station in the city troops from colonies other than New York and New England; the latter's encroachments and arrogance he particularly resented.[45] New Yorkers preferred to handle policing problems with their own troops, however.

Hamilton may have been young, but he was no innocent. He detested the Loyalists and was aware of their political intrigues and the danger they posed to the Revolutionary movement. On the other hand, he shared Jay's conviction that a large portion of them were not beyond redemption and that serious punishment should be reserved for flagrant offenders. "Tenderness to the innocent," caution in dispensing punishments, a stern stand toward "atrocious offenders," guarding against persecuting persons out of "private pique and resentment," and the avoidance of inflicting trivial penalties which would not serve as deterrents—these sensible principles shaped his attitude toward the Tories. "I would either disable them from doing us any injury," he declared, "or I would endeavour to gain their friendship by clemency."[46]

At war's end Hamilton continued his vigilance on behalf of fair treatment for the Tories. What part concern over due process, civil liberties, and the nation's treaty obligations played in his efforts, and what part class bias and a desire to forge an alliance of capitalists and creditors with the central government, would be difficult to apportion. In fairness, however, it must be said that Hamilton was thoroughly consistent on this issue. Like Jay he was prepared to let bygones be bygones, and anxious to hold on to Loyalists possessing capital. Hamilton realized that discriminatory taxation, stemming in part from prejudicial local assessments,[47] as well as other negative policies, were calculated to drive them away. With the imminent evacuation of New York City by the British, Hamilton was alarmed at the great exodus that he foresaw. He charged that "some violent papers sent into the city have determined many to depart." These included "merchants of the second class, characters of no political consequence, each of whom may carry eight or ten thousand guineas."[48]

Once the treaty was ratified, with its clauses protecting Loyalists and British creditors, Hamilton advocated strict and honorable compliance with its terms. With characteristic courage, even imprudence, he risked his political future by insisting that reprisals against the Tories should cease and that lawful debts due to British and Loyalist creditors be paid. One could hardly imagine a more unpopular policy. For seven long years the Redcoats and the Tories had occupied New York City, and when they left, the city was a shambles. Long before the war had ended, the New York legislature had begun confiscating the property of notorious Loyalists, but now, in response to public clamor, the legislature passed a law providing that any citizen whose property, while within British lines, had been occupied by any person other than its lawful owner, might sue such occupant for damages in trespass.[49] Nobody benefited as much from this law as the lawyers. As Hamilton wrote Gouverneur Morris, "legislative folly has afforded so plentiful a harvest to us lawyers that we have scarcely a moment to spare from the substantial business of reaping."[50]

Hamilton knew whereof he spoke, for having taken a crash clerkship program involving three months' intensive study of the law in Albany, he was admitted to practice in July, 1782. A few days after the British evacuated the city of New York he opened law offices at 57 Wall Street, where he also made his home. It was not long before he was involved as defense counsel for an aggrieved British merchant named Joshua Waddington, who happened to be a director of the Bank of New York, in whose founding Hamilton played a central role.[51] His client, who had been so imprudent as to remain behind after the British quit New York, was being sued by Mrs. Elizabeth Rutgers for redress under the Trespass Act. On the eve of the British occupation she had abandoned her brewery and fled the city, and Waddington's firm occupied the premises under an order of the British commissary general and then of the British military authorities. Hamilton's demurrer to the complaint rested on the twin contentions that the British army had a right to license the property under international law and that the Trespass Act, passed after and in violation of the peace treaty with Great Britain, was null and void. It did Waddington no harm that James Duane, the conservative judge and then mayor, who presided over the case, happened to be a good friend of Hamilton's. He carefully straddled the issue of judicial review. He allowed the plaintiff damages merely for the period in which the defendant held the property under the authority of the commissary general and not for the subsequent period when the defendant had occupied the property under license from the British commander in chief. In so ruling, the court followed Hamilton's shrewd line of argument on statutory interpretation, holding that it might assume that it was the intent of the legislature to conform to international law. If the court merely took a roundabout way of annulling a statute as violative of a higher law,[52] Hamilton himself had no doubts on the power of the courts, later of the federal courts, to pass on matters of constitutionality. In the 78th *Federalist* he asserted the Constitution to be the supreme law of the land, that in any conflict between the Constitution and an act of Congress the former should prevail, and that it was the proper function of the courts to interpret the laws.

Hamilton's partial victory evoked a storm of protest. Committees were formed, and a resolve of the state assembly denounced the decision as "subversive of law and good order" and censured the court. Hamilton felt obliged to defend the court and his own course in a vigorous letter to the press under the pseudonym "Phocion," pleading for justice and moderation for the Tories and observance of the terms of the treaty. One of the anti-Federalists, Isaac Ledyard, replying as "Mentor," denied Hamilton's contentions and insisted on the unrestricted sovereignty of the state of New York. In rejoinder Hamilton fired off his second "Phocion" letter. Once more Hamilton laid it down as a first principle that "the safest reliance of every government is on men's interest." "Make it the interest of those citizens who, during the Revolution, were opposed to us, to be friends to the new government, by affording them not only protection, but a participation in its privileges, and they will undoubtedly become its friends," he urged. His argument so infuriated his hot-headed opponents that they actually concocted a plot to challenge him successively to a series of duels, to be continued until this champion of Tory rights was liquidated.[53] For his role on behalf of the Tories, Hamilton was attacked in the spring of 1784 by a "Mechanic" as "the Confidential or ridiculous earwig of our late worthy General . . . the little

pompose, stripling delegate—the Jack-Daw of public affairs . . .
Fox instead of Phocion."[54]

With bulldog tenacity Hamilton clung to the cause of the Tories
and the British creditors. A few years later he managed to push
through the legislature a bill repealing the Trespass Act, and when
the very same issues arose again during the debate over Jay's Treaty,
Hamilton was to insist upon honest compliance with the provisions
of the Treaty of 1783 regarding the property rights of both Loyalists
and British subjects. "No power of language at my command," he
declared, "can express the abhorrence I feel at the idea of violating
the property of individuals" because of "controversies between nation
and nation."[55] With considerable consistency Hamilton fought
against the disenfranchisement of the Tories and objected to making
them take loyalty oaths. The latter he denounced in his second
"Phocion" letter as "retrospective oaths."[56] As a result in no incon-
siderable part of Hamilton's heroic efforts, the Tories by 1787 were
restored to their full rights as citizens. If Hamilton was motivated at
least in some measure by a desire to gain Tory support for his larger
program, he was to be rewarded by their allegiance to the constitutional principles he espoused and the party he was to head.[57]

If Hamilton was gifted with the pen, his temperament was activist
rather than reflective, and his longtime goal, military glory. Fortunately for him a war was brewing where his martial inclinations
could find ready outlet. In the spring of '75 he joined a militia
company known as the "Corsicans," in tribute to the brave stand of
Pasquale Paoli and his fellow Corsicans, first against the colonial rule
of the city-state of Genoa and then against France.[58] Every morning
saw him drilling in St. George's churchyard, and then rushing back to
the college campus close by to rejoin his classes. Hamilton first came
under fire during a successful engagement on August 23 to remove a
score of cannon from under the guns of British warships at the
Battery, dragging these heavy pieces up Broadway to the liberty pole
on the Commons. In the course of the foray the company came under
direct bombardment from the British warship *Asia*.[59]

Young Hamilton had aspirations for command, and he had the
political connections that could fulfill them. With the probable
sponsorship of Alexander McDougall and John Jay, he secured from
the New York Provincial Legislature a commission as captain in
command of the Provincial Company of Artillery. Counting on his

mathematics studies, buttressed by a cram course in artillery science lasting but a few weeks, Hamilton had already passed an examination and obtained a certificate of fitness for his duties.[60] With furious zeal he recruited his own company, some sixty-eight officers and men in all, and used his personal credit to clothe and equip them.[61]

The brief seven months of Hamilton's command of his artillery company were crowded with action, and the captain and his men shared moments of deep frustration and brilliant achievement. In the battle for New York in late August, 1776, Hamilton's artillerymen were stationed for the defense of the city in the main Manhattan works on Bayard's Hill. The British landing at Kip's Bay threatened to cut the company, and by following the advice of a young Princetonian, Major Aaron Burr, Hamilton moved his heavy equipment north on an unobstructed road on Manhattan's west side until he reached the security of the entrenchments at Harlem Heights, losing his baggage and a fieldpiece in the frantic withdrawal.[62] Hamilton's family insisted on placing him on Chatterton Hill during the Battle of White Plains, but it is better for his military reputation that this claim cannot be supported, as the artillery on that occasion made so lamentable a showing. In the retreat to New Jersey, Hamilton's company was somewhat ahead of Washington's main army.

The first action of Hamilton that could not have failed to catch Washington's eye was his key role at New Brunswick. Stationing his battery on the high west bank a few hundred yards from the Raritan River, his guns covered Washington's crossing to the west side of the Delaware and prevented Lord Cornwallis from crossing that river while Washington and his army struck out for Princeton. Then he joined the main forces in their withdrawal. Someone saw him on the spot and was struck by the portrait of "a youth, a mere stripling, small, slender, almost delicate in frame," marching, his "cocked hat pulled down over his eyes, apparently lost in thought, with his hand resting on a cannon, and every now and then patting it, as if it were a favorite horse or a pet plaything."[63] Hamilton's pay book shows him to have participated in the brilliantly successful attack upon the Hessians at Trenton, and at some spot in Princeton his guns went off. Again unverified tradition had Captain Hamilton firing the ball that entered the chapel and pierced a portrait of George II. If he did so, it is doubtful that he nursed any grievance against that long-dead monarch, but he may well have remembered the Princeton trustees who turned down the application of a nonconforming student. In any event, with Nassau Hall under cannon fire, somewhere between sixty and two hundred Britishers holed up in that edifice surrendered.[64]

Save for a well-publicized performance in the last big battle of the war and his role against the Whiskey Boys years later, Hamilton never commanded troops in battle again, although it was not for want of trying. At a critical moment in his military career, with his company down to two officers and thirty men because of casualties, desertion, and the expiration of terms of enlistment, Hamilton was invited to become an aide-de-camp to General Washington with the rank of lieutenant colonel. Indubitably, the General, who was not known to pick his aides from among the rabble in arms, must have been impressed not alone by Hamilton's intellectual gifts and fluency in French, but by his bearing, his manners, and his socially impeccable sponsorship among the Patriots.

March 1, 1777,[65] the date of Hamilton's appointment, marks the turning point in his career. At once he was rocketed to the center of military decision making. At once he was marked by New York's political leaders as the man to turn to if they wished to be posted regularly on the course and conduct of the war. With an aplomb matched by analytical power, Hamilton proceeded to give the New Yorkers an illuminating commentary on the war, along with his own solutions for all the complex domestic and foreign problems which it posed.

Physically and temperamentally Washington and Hamilton were diametrically different. The General, then in his mid-forties, towered over his diminutive subordinate by a good seven inches. Whereas Hamilton was quick, voluble, and excitable, Washington was deliberate in thought and speech and much more forbearing than his aide, who was quick to take offense. One can hardly speak of them as compatible spirits, and yet the addition of Hamilton to Washington's official family marked the start of the most extraordinary partnership in American history, one that continued with only one break, that taking place in the latter part of the war. One could expatiate on father images and father substitutes, but though Washington admired Hamilton, he seemed to have felt more affection for the young Marquis de Lafayette and for Hamilton's close friend, young John Laurens. Writing retrospectively, and in terms of Washington's presidency, some historians have made extravagant claims about Hamilton's influence upon the General and affirmed that Hamilton was intellectually the dominant member of the team even when serving as an aide.

The facts hardly support these preposterous claims of early influence. One cannot decide with finality how much of Washington's thinking was reflected in the letters which were often drafted by Hamilton and other aides, for Hamilton shared his literary duties with a brilliant group of young officers, including, at various times, Richard Meade, Tench Tilghman, Robert Harrison, John Laurens, and others. No one of these men wrote or copied all of Washington's correspondence. That would have been physically impossible. Just take the month of July, 1777, alone. The correspondence and general orders for that month fill 183 pages of the eighth volume of the Fitzpatrick edition of Washington's writings. As late as December, Washington wrote a friend in Congress that at times "the multiplicity of writing, and other business" were "too great" for the aides he had.[66]

These men were buried under a mountain of paper work and were scarcely in a position in the early years of the war to shape much of Washington's thinking. Contrariwise, it is far more likely that this little band of ardent admirers, among whom one must, on the extant literary evidence, include Hamilton, took their line from their chief, who had demonstrated his ardent attachment to radical Whig views almost a decade before young Hamilton embraced the cause. Consider the theme of nationalism and national unity. Long before March 1, 1777, these concepts, which became a cardinal tenet of Hamilton's political creed, were voiced by Washington. In his general orders of August 1, 1776, Washington urged: "Let all distinctions of Nations, Countries, and Provinces . . . be lost in the generous contest."[67] Washington's Fabian tactics of avoiding full-scale engagements with the enemy were clearly articulated in his letter to Congress of September 8, 1776.[68] They are also mirrored in numerous letters of Hamilton written when he was Washington's aide, among them his letter to Robert R. Livingston, penned a few months after joining Washington's staff.[69] Oftentime, and long before he met Hamilton, Washington had pointed out that the army was riddled with plunderers, drifters, and fair-weather soldiers, and proposed as his solution: better pay and more prestige for officers, long-term enlistments for privates, no dependence upon the militia. Rather a standing army than "inevitable ruin," he wrote John Hancock from the Heights of Harlem on September 24, 1776.[70]

On such matters as the urgency of national unity, the need for providing a more secure establishment of the army, and the basic military tactics essential to ultimate victory, Hamilton was in complete agreement with and was indubitably influenced by the well-matured ideas of the older and more seasoned warrior. Many of Hamilton's letters written in these early years seem like an echo of his chief, and a brilliant one. Thus, he argues for the need "to preserve a national character," in a letter to Governor George Clinton written in March, 1778.[71] Indeed, in the years that followed, that alertness to the national interest was to be the most powerful intellectual bond between Hamilton and Washington.

That Washington and Hamilton were in complete accord on the need for reforming the army seems evident from the plan for reorganizing the army which was drafted in January, 1778. Prepared for the Board of War, this document bears the imprint of Washington's thinking at every point, as well as the thought of his leading officers, but it is couched in language which has that indubitable Hamiltonian stamp.[72]

Any speculators or profiteers venturing near Washington's headquarters either at Morristown or at Valley Forge would find the climate frigid. Nothing aroused the General more than the spectacle of monopolizers withholding supplies desperately needed by the army and waxing rich while officers and soldiers were undergoing unparalleled privations. In a letter to Gouverneur Morris of October 4, 1778, Washington advocated the stern enforcement of price and other controls on profiteering and engrossing,[73] and a few months later, urged that profiteers be strung up.[74] It is perhaps significant that Hamilton, who in later life was never accused by his enemies of curbing speculation or of being a foe of the profit system, now wrote two letters denouncing Congressman Samuel Chase for his attempts to corner the market on wheat and thereby obstruct the war effort. These fervent attacks were embodied in his "Publius" letters which appeared in the New York *Journal* on October 19 and 26 of the same year. There can be little doubt that Washington's frequently voiced Spartan views about the need for patriotic sacrifice had struck a responsive chord in Hamilton. To such a person as Chase, Hamilton declared, there is "no punishment the vengeance of the people can inflict, which may not be applied to him with justice." This was virtually an invitation to a lynching party and was almost identical in temper with Washington's subsequent exhortation to hang profiteers.

It would be doing both men a serious injustice, however, to infer that the younger man was merely reflecting the ideas of his chief in these early years of their relationship. Indeed, the period between 1778 and 1782 found Hamilton's thoughts on constitutional and fiscal reform being crystallized and first given brilliant exposition. There comes to mind at once his famous "Liberty Pole" letter of September 3, 1780, to James Duane, in which he expounded his ideas of national sovereignty along with the need for a national bank.[75] One might cite, too, his justly celebrated undated letter to a "Member of Congress," written probably in the winter of 1779–80, in which he stated what was to be a basic maxim of the Hamiltonian system: "The only plan that can preserve the currency is one that will make it the *immediate* interest of the monied men to cooperate with government in its support."[76] He hammered home these thoughts in a letter to Robert Morris of April 30, 1781,[77] and in his published "Continentalist" letters of 1781 and 1782.

Shedding significant light on the Washington-Hamilton relationship at that time is the fact that the "Member of Congress" and "Liberty Pole" letters were written before the temporary break with Washington occurred, and yet the fiscal concepts envisioned therein were never expounded by Hamilton to Washington while he was Washington's aide. This is made clear from the correspondence between Washington and General John Sullivan. The latter had asked the commander what he thought of Hamilton for the post of minister of finance. Washington was evidently taken aback, for he replied on February 4, 1781: "I never entered upon a discussion on this point with him."[78] Washington, who naturally thought of Robert Morris as the logical contender for the post of financier, was quick to point out that he had the highest regard for Hamilton's talents and integrity; and it should be added that both the General and Hamilton enthusiastically supported Morris's efforts when he assumed that arduous responsibility. What is noteworthy then is not the fact that Hamilton was not Washington's first choice for the post of financier, but rather that up to that moment Hamilton had never conferred with Washington on the subjects of banking and fiscal management.

Although Hamilton came to be increasingly critical and disillusioned about the General, he maintained a public posture of unflinching loyalty. It was Hamilton to whom Washington turned to deal with an insubordinate general. So inflated was Horatio Gates by his victory at Saratoga that he did not even deign to send an account to the commander in chief. Confident of New England support and of powerful friends in Congress, Gates behaved as though he held an independent command. Washington dispatched Hamilton to Gates in Albany to secure immediate reinforcements. Hamilton was vested with discretionary powers to decide on the spot whether Gates could use the needed troops more effectively in his theater of operations than could Washington—in short, whether the war could be more decisively waged against Sir Henry Clinton bedded down in New York City or against Sir William Howe on the Delaware. This was an extraordinary responsibility to be thrust upon the shoulders of a twenty-two-year-old aide, but the General knew his man.

After much unpleasant sparring, Gates, always an irresolute antagonist, finally proposed releasing to Washington what Hamilton considered the "weakest" of the three Continental brigades. Hamilton rejected the proffer, insisting on Glover's brigade. Gates sat down and drafted a sizzling letter to Washington, protesting against the latter's delegating "dictatorial powers to one aide de camp sent to an army 300 miles distant." On second thought he crossed the passage out, and yielded without grace to Hamilton. Similarly, Israel ("Old Put") Putnam, whose incompetence as a field commander had long plagued operations, acceded to Hamilton's request for troops grudgingly, and only when the aide-de-camp presented him with "a positive order." There are probably few precedents in military annals of a youthful lieutenant colonel issuing oral commands to a couple of major generals and getting away with it. Washington was pleased, but not surprised. "I approve entirely of all the steps you have taken," he later wrote Hamilton. Worn out by the bitter disputes, Hamilton fell ill with rheumatic fever, which laid him low some five or six weeks.[79]

Time did little to dissipate Hamilton's utter contempt for Gates. After the rout suffered by that general at Cornwallis's hands at

Camden in the summer of 1780, Hamilton relished writing these barbed comments to Congressman James Duane: "Was there ever an instance of a General running away as Gates has done from his whole army? And was there ever so precipitous a flight? One hundred and eighty miles in three days and a half. It does admirable credit to the activity of a man at his time of life. But it disgraces the General and the Soldiers."[80]

Nor did Gates soon forget Hamilton. When that master intriguer, James Wilkinson, indiscreetly babbled the story about the correspondence between General Thomas Conway and Gates derogatory of Washington, the victor of Saratoga tried to crawl out of the cabal, not by disowning the correspondence, but by accusing Hamilton of having purloined his private papers when at Albany. The true source of the "leak" only confounded Gates's embarrassments, and from accusations he turned to blanket denials, which proved him a liar if not a plotter. Henceforth Hamilton regarded Gates as "his enemy personally, for unjust and unprovoked attacks" upon his character, and denounced Conway as "one of the vermin bred in the entrails of this chimera dire," making a point of warning Governor Clinton that "there does not exist a more villainous calumniator and incendiary."[81] Hamilton's splendid gifts of invective would one day prove his undoing.

Hamilton had a good head for military affairs and a courage bordering on the reckless, but his conduct at times could be impulsively romantic, and he was governed by a code shot through with chivalric notions which he believed applied to officers and gentlemen. His impulsiveness was abundantly demonstrated at the Battle of Monmouth, where he had his third recorded altercation with a major general. British-born Charles Lee, whose relations with the enemy were not above suspicion, persuaded a council of war to permit Sir Henry Clinton's army to withdraw from Philadelphia, cross Jersey to New York, and avoid a major engagement. Such a decision, in Hamilton's opinion, "would have done honor to the most honorable society of midwives, and to them only." Dispatched by Washington to obtain intelligence of the enemy's position, Hamilton found Lee in a state bordering on paralysis. Warning Lee that a British troop of cavalry deploying to the left of the American forces would soon be in a position to attack Lee's exposed flank, he advised him to counterattack.

"Do I appear to you to have lost my senses?" Lee asked.

Hamilton reassured him, but privately believed that the general was under a strange "hurry of mind." To bolster Lee's sagging morale and momentary witlessness, Hamilton exclaimed, "That's right, my dear General, and I will stay, and we will all die here on this spot!" On second thought Hamilton decided that he had better report back to Washington and let him know the perilous position of Lee's forces. Washington put spurs to his horse, and soon came upon Lee's troops retreating in wild disorder. After a wrathful outburst against Lee, Washington took command of the situation himself, ordered the soldiers to take cover behind a hedgerow, and placed Anthony Wayne's brigade where it could hold off the enemy. American fire swept back a British cavalry charge, and the next day the enemy was gone. Hamilton never forgot the "childish" behavior of Charles Lee, whom he considered "either a driveler in the business of soldiership or something much worse," and the court-martial in effect terminated Lee's connection with the American army.[82]

Hamilton's chivalric concepts of warfare were fully aroused by the treason of Benedict Arnold. Washington's aide enjoyed a front seat at the foul spectacle. Acting as interpreter, as he usually did with French officers, Hamilton sat in with Washington at the conference with the Comte de Rochambeau held at Hartford on September 23, 1780. The returning party spent the night in Fishkill, New York, setting out on the morrow for West Point, whose defenses Washington wished to inspect. At 10:30 A.M. the party reached the Beverly Robinson house, some two miles southeast of West Point, and Arnold's headquarters. When Washington made his inspection and returned to the Robinson home, Hamilton handed him a packet of papers which had been found in the boot of Major John André by "three simple peasants," as Hamilton described his captors who intercepted him near Tarrytown—documents making clear Arnold's treasonable course. Washington had Hamilton put spurs to his horse to capture the traitor before he could escape to the British man-of-war *Vulture,* anchored in the Hudson River. Not known as the swiftest horseman in the Continental army, Hamilton arrived too late, but he was quick-thinking enough to give out orders on his own to have the guard at West Point reinforced.[83] Up to this point he was sharp, resilient, and realistic, but when he confronted Peggy Shippen Arnold, he was completely taken in by her hysterics, swoons, and professions of innocence. We now know from the British Head-quarters Papers that Peggy was in the plot up to her eyeballs, but Hamilton, always extremely impressionable where women were concerned, found her "an amiable woman, frantic with distress for the loss of a husband she tenderly loved," and to confound his naïveté, confessed to his own wife, "I wished myself her brother, to have a right to become her defender." Then, realizing that a wife would not perhaps share her husband's concern for another woman's afflictions, he added, "I think you may rely I shall never make you blush."[84] Perhaps our hero did protest too much.

For the unfortunate André, a romantic figure even in his misery, Hamilton felt an enormous amount of misdirected sympathy. A man of breeding, who managed playacting and flirtations more skillfully than espionage, André had in fact breached the code of gentlemen and warriors by prostituting a flag of truce to engage in treasonable negotiations, and then compounded his deception by recklessly abandoning his uniform and changing into civilian clothes. Yet André had no more valiant defender than Hamilton. On September 30 a letter was dispatched to General Clinton in New York, signed "AB" (a pseudonym Hamilton also used for his "Continentalist" letters, the first of which was published less than a year later), proposing Arnold's exchange for André. Washington could not with propriety have formally requested the exchange, but there is no question that he was dying to get his hands on the scoundrel. Not only did Clinton endorse the letter as coming from Hamilton, but Lieutenant Colonel John G. Simcoe made the same attribution. More telling corroborative evidence is found in comparing this letter with one that Hamilton wrote John Laurens a few weeks later, wherein almost identical phraseology is found.[85]

Since he could not save André's skin, Hamilton then sought to have the British spy executed as a gentleman should, by being shot, rather than suffering the death of a varlet, by dangling from the gallows. André made a personal appeal to Hamilton, who then interceded with the General. Washington could not agree to modifying the sentence pronounced by the Board of General Officers, and Hamilton, enraged, stomped off, muttering that "some people are only sensible to motives of policy!"[86]

Washington understood the necessity of fighting an all-out war; Hamilton believed that exceptions should be made when the adversary happened to be a gentleman. No better example of Hamilton's double standard comes to mind than the case of Captain Charles Asgill. In March, 1782, a group of Loyalist irregulars captured an American Patriot soldier, Captain Joshua Huddy. Although Huddy was first turned over to General Clinton in New York, the British commander shipped him right back to his Tory captors. They promptly strung him up without a trial as a protest against alleged Patriot atrocities. Washington, supported by a council of war, promptly decided on retaliation, and demanded that Clinton turn over to him for punishment Captain Richard Lippincott, the officer who commanded at Huddy's execution. Clinton disowned the Tory action, but refused to surrender one of his own officers. Washington then determined to retaliate on a British prisoner selected by lot, and the choice fell on Captain Asgill, one of the thousands of prisoners surrendered at Yorktown.

The choice was unfortunate. Young Asgill, not yet twenty, was the son of Sir Charles Asgill, once Lord Mayor of London and a long-time friend to the American cause, and Washington's determination to execute Asgill created an international hubbub. Hamilton, aroused from his law books in Albany, dashed off a note to General Henry Knox, charging the act as being "repugnant to the genius of the age we live in," and encouraging an opinion that America was "in a state of barbarism." He could not end, however, without an analogy to the death of André and a gratuitous slap at Washington. "The death of André could not have been dispensed with; but it must still be viewed at a distance as an act of *rigid justice;* if we wreak our resentment on an innocent person, it will be suspected that we are too fond of executions. I am persuaded it will have an influence peculiarly unfavourable to the General's character."[87] When Isaac Hayne, a prominent South Carolinian and a colonel in the militia, was hanged without formal trial by the British on the technical charge of violating his parole after the surrender of Charleston—the execution being a clear war atrocity—Hamilton never raised his voice. Happily for Hamilton, the French government at the entreaties of Lady Asgill interceded, and Congress instructed Washington "that the life of Captain Asgill should be given as a compliment to the King of France."[88]

Disapprove though Hamilton might of his general's Spartan methods of conducting the war, he himself possessed a streak of military adventurism which betrayed him at times into behaving more like Julius Caesar and less like George Washington. A few examples from the Revolutionary years cast a longer shadow ahead. In the spring of '79 a report spread that Hamilton had remarked in a Philadelphia coffeehouse that "it was high time for the people to rise, join General Washington, and turn Congress out of doors." Francis Dana, a member of Congress from Massachusetts, to whom the report was traced, declared that he heard it from the Reverend William Gordon, a notorious gossip, then engaged in gathering material for his history of the American Revolution. When Gordon, on Hamilton's demand, refused to name his informant unless Hamilton swore that he would not challenge him to a duel, Hamilton called him a liar. Gordon in turn appealed to Washington to have him discipline Hamilton, and the General replied that if Gordon had any evidence he should bring it before a court-martial or else hold his peace. Significantly, Washington did not feel it incumbent upon himself either to defend Hamilton of the charges or to take further steps to clear his aide. In fact, he managed to keep up friendly relations and continued to correspond with Gordon down to the very end of his life.[89] From this it is clear that Washington was well aware of his talented young aide's impulsive streak, his occasional indiscretions that could be such a source of embarrassment to his friends, and his incessant itch to defend his personal honor. Washington put up with these minor flaws, and even with Hamilton's extraordinary rudeness, because he appreciated just what Hamilton could and did contribute as an aide.

Chained to a desk job and not given the chance for combat duty that he craved, Hamilton became increasingly disapproving of the irascible moods and manners of his commander. His reactions show evidence of the "Hate Papa" syndrome. The quarrel with the General that he deliberately provoked revealed him to be an insufferably touchy young man. Had his ego been deflated to more normal dimensions, he might have learned to take the chip off his shoulder and not incessantly seek out controversy. Then, indeed, he would have been a better actuarial risk but a less colorful human being. Hamilton's letter to his father-in-law, General Philip Schuyler, written in February, 1781, is revealing not only for what it tells us about Hamilton's feelings of the moment but also for its insights into the relationship between men who were one day to forge a notable and unbroken collaboration.

"I believe you know the place I held in the General's confidence and counsels," Hamilton wrote Schuyler, "which will make it the more extraordinary to you to learn that for three years past I have felt no friendship for him and have professed none. The truth is our own dispositions are the opposites of each other, and the pride of my temper would not suffer me to profess what I did not feel." Boasting that he had rebuffed conciliatory advances by the General, he added: "You are too good a judge of human nature not to be sensible how this conduct in me must have operated on a man to whom all the world is offering incense." Hamilton's original draft was written in even greater heat. He first put down, "must have operated on the self-love of a man," but then crossed out that characterization, as he had previously made the point that Washington's "self-love would never forgive me what it would regard as a humiliation."[90]

Of the two men, Washington in this incident exhibited the greater forbearance and humility. Hamilton wrote and talked about his break with the General; Washington refrained from the slightest criticism of Hamilton. This was proof of a quality in Washington which contributed to making him a great commander in chief—his ability to handle temperamental subordinates despite a ferocious temper which at times he failed to curb. In the end, overlooking the breach, Washington yielded to Hamilton's importunities and gave him his chance for glory at Yorktown. Though his battalion was to be included in the assault on the Number 10 redoubt, Hamilton craved to lead the whole attacking force. With Lafayette as friend at court, he won that assignment from the General. First over the parapet into the redoubt, Hamilton directed a bayonet attack which was over in minutes.[91]

The so-called Newburgh Conspiracy, in which a hero's role was reserved for Washington, reveals not only Hamilton's inclinations to flirt with military solutions but his very special talents for dissimulation. That Hamilton was one of the chief instigators of the "plot," along with Robert and Gouverneur Morris, can no longer be doubted. Some two years earlier Hamilton had laid down the bases of a nationalist program, central to which would be the power of Congress to collect an impost. "Without certain revenues," Hamilton had then warned, "a government can have no power; that power, which holds the purse strings absolutely, must rule."[92] By the end of 1782 it was clear to such delegates in the Congress as James Madison and Hamilton that the states would continue to block the impost.[93]

Along with a few other nationalists who thought "continentally," Hamilton saw the possibility of exploiting the discontent of the payless army as "a powerful engine" to force Congress to make the necessary moves to restore public credit.

The first move was to bring the army officers in. General Alexander McDougall and Colonel John Brooks were enlisted as the nucleus of an army lobby to impress Congress with the deep discontent of the military. A "grand committee" of Congress considered their memorial, and Hamilton was placed on the subcommittee charged with preparing a report dealing with the army's claims. The heart of his report was a provision for commuting half-pay into an outright grant to be paid by the Confederation government in order to attach the army's interest to those of the other public creditors. Hamilton's proposal touched off a warm debate. Hamilton had a habit of becoming overexcited in debate and of disclosing too much. He indiscreetly proposed making the army claims the basis for forcing a national fund upon the states. Madison notes that the opposition "smiled at the disclosure," declaring "in private conversation, that Mr. Hamilton had let out the secret."[94]

As Congress stalled, army officers became more intransigent. In a secret letter to General Henry Knox, McDougall threatened mutiny.[95] To the nationalists two alternatives seemed likely. Either the army would affirm that it would not disband until Congress did it justice (in effect a passive mutiny) or the more hotheaded junior officers might pull off a mutiny against their leadership. The latter possibility could hardly be ruled out, since Gates, Hamilton's old enemy, was in cahoots with an anti-Washington cabal of potential mutineers headed by Colonel John Armstrong.[96] Such a contingency alarmed the nationalists, who were prepared to incite a mutiny and then see it snuffed out before Gates could take over. Otherwise, if Washington would not prove helpful, perhaps even he would have to be shelved.

This was the kind of reckless double game that Hamilton was playing. To cover his traces, he had to tip off Washington. Some time in the second week of February, 1783, he alerted the General to the necessity of directing or controlling the protest movement in the army. Washington was urged "not to discountenance their endeavours to procure redress, but rather by the intervention of confidential and prudent persons *to take the direction of them*." Hamilton added a caution, both to protect his own ambiguous relation with the anti-

Washington plotters and out of concern for the kind of broth that might be brewing: "This however must not appear: it is of moment to the public tranquillity that your Excellency should preserve the confidence of the army without losing that of the people. This will enable you in case of extremity to guide the torrent, and to bring order, perhaps even good, out of confusion."[97]

While tipping off Washington, Hamilton at the same time contributed as much as any man to creating a climate of crisis which heartened the Gates forces. Reporting a conversation with Hamilton and other members of Congress on February 20, James Madison recounts that Hamilton warned that "a public declaration" would soon be made of the army's intention not to lay down their arms until their demands were met, while reminding his listeners that Washington was becoming increasingly unpopular with all ranks in the army, and that there was a move to supplant him. What Madison added casts further light on the complex Hamilton-Washington relationship. "Mr. Hamilton said that he knew General Washington intimately and perfectly, that his extreme reserve, mixed some time with a degree of asperity of temper, both of which were said to have increased of late, has contributed to the decline of his popularity." True, he had lessened his popularity by bringing "unfit and indiscreet persons into his family," but Hamilton reminded his hearers that the General's virtue and character would never consent to his yielding to dishonorable plans. Hamilton indicated that he wanted Washington to act as spokesman for the army, in order to moderate and legitimate their objectives and obviate having to supplant him by a troublemaking leader.[98] If Hamilton put patriotism and a grasp of Washington's central importance to the nation above his own sour evaluation of the General's liabilities and his personal pique that through his own fault he was no longer at the right hand of his former chief, he was proposing a solution that was nothing more than a devious connivance, completely out of character with Washington's forthrightness.

And Washington did not choose to walk tightropes. Less impulsive than Hamilton, he was utterly devoid of some of the latter's Machiavellian instincts. He would not encourage the army to act as a dangerous pressure group, he wrote Hamilton on March 4, although he did warn of the need for "doing justice to the army,"[99] and then he confounded the army plotters by appearing before the assembled officers and attacking them for "sowing the seeds of discord and separation between the civil and military powers of the Continent."

Washington's strong stand in behalf of the supremacy of civilian authority caused Hamilton to cover his traces and abruptly change his tune. When, in June of '83, a detachment of mutineers moved east toward Philadelphia while Congress was in session, Hamilton made a strenuous effort to head them off. When that proved impossible because of the lack of cooperation on the part of state officials, and Congress was obliged in its humiliation to withdraw to Princeton, Hamilton defended the move. On that occasion he wrote: "The licentiousness of an army is to be dreaded in every government; but in a republic it is more particularly to be restrained, and when directed against civil authority to be checked with energy and punished with severity."[100] Verily, Hamilton had learned a lot from the way in which Washington had handled the Newburgh crisis, and considering Hamilton's own devious role in that incident, his loud professions of virtue could easily have been prompted in part by a haste to clean his own muddied boots.

Hamilton's propensity for military solutions and his desire to achieve military glory found little opportunity for expression in peacetime, but as Washington's right hand in the new federal government, he was bent on forcing the issue against the whiskey remonstrants, stoutly maintaining, as Secretary of State Randolph implied, that "Government can never be said to be established until some signal display has manifested its power of military coercion." Advocating military suppression, Hamilton even took the field against the whiskey insurrectionaries, and justified his role on the ground that he who proposes a measure involving danger to his fellow citizens should himself "partake in that danger."[101] Aroused by the turn that the French Revolution took, Hamilton was first and foremost in beating the war drums. At the time of the quasi-war with France he was named inspector general of the army with the rank of major general. As a senior field general he revealed himself to be a dangerous expansionist, dreaming dreams of military glory, planning expeditions against Louisiana and Florida, and even urging that "we ought to squint at Latin America."[102] Regrettably for Hamilton but fortunately for the nation, Adams settled for peace, and Hamilton slumped into ironic despondency.[103]

Hamilton's special talent for praising men to their face and then knifing them in the back found numerous opportunities for display. In the Congress he attacked the peace commissioners for their separate negotiations apart from the French as well as for the separate and secret article about Florida. He tartly observed that although John Jay "was a man of profound sagacity and pure integrity, yet he was of a suspicious temper," a trait which "might explain the extraordinary jealousies which he professed." With Madison's backing, he proposed a compromise resolution, which, while commending the commissioners, would have authorized the Secretary for Foreign Affairs to communicate the separate article to the French. Fortunately, as events turned out, Hamilton's motion was rejected, and a committee resolution of like purport, whose passage would have amounted to a vote of no confidence in the commissioners, was held up. Then the Janus-faced delegate from New York turned right around and dispatched a congratulatory message to Jay, in which he asserted that the peace exceeded "in the goodness of its terms, the expectations of the most sanguine," and that it did "the highest honour to those who made it."[104]

When peace was won, Hamilton did not turn over a new leaf. He now combined devious dealings toward close associates with a curious penchant for leaking confidential information to a foreign power. Two notorious instances may be cited. At the beginning of Washington's presidency Gouverneur Morris was dispatched to Great Britain to secure a favorable trade treaty. Perhaps fearful that Morris would wield the one club he possessed—the threat to adopt high tariffs on British goods—Hamilton informed George Beckwith, a British confidential agent operating in America, that he was opposed to such discriminatory duties.[105] He behaved in a similarly unconscionable manner when President Washington dispatched John Jay to the Court of St. James's to settle outstanding issues with England. By gratuitously assuring George Hammond, the British minister to the United States, that there was little danger of America's joining the Armed Neutrality against Britain, Hamilton deprived the American envoy of a major weapon which could conceivably have brought the British government to terms.[106] It is difficult even today at a time so remote from these negotiations to justify Hamilton's conduct on any ground. With all due charity, Hamilton, although a man of overpowering talent, was a difficult if not treacherous collaborator.

That Hamilton was consumed with ambition was the one aspect of the man on which friend and foe agreed. But of what kind? As Washington generously observed, Hamilton's ambition was "of that laudable kind, which prompts a man to excel in whatever he takes in hand."[107] Indubitably, Hamilton had himself in mind when he denounced Aaron Burr, a political adversary whom he resembled in a number of respects, as one who never seemed to be "solicitous for fame." To Hamilton's mind this was a deficiency in character, because "great ambition, unchecked by the principle or love of glory is an unruly tyrant."[108] In that jealousy of his reputation Hamilton was markedly different from Burr. A true disciple of David Hume, Hamilton paid the Scottish philosopher silent tribute in the 72nd *Federalist* paper, wherein he invoked "the love of fame, the ruling passion of the noblest minds." Fame, indeed, was the secret passion that mobilized all his energies and ultimately devoured him.

In that quest for fame and in the guarding of his reputation Hamilton at times appeared desperate, if not ruthless, and prepared to sacrifice those nearest and dearest to him. Consider his marriage. As Hamilton confessed to his dear friend John Laurens in the spring of 1779, the kind of wife he was seeking would have to be a paragon, young, beautiful, shapely, "sensible (a little learning will do)," well bred, chaste, and tender. Getting down to money, Hamilton added:

> But as to fortune, the larger stock of that the better. You know my temper and circumstances and will therefore pay special attention in this article of the treaty. Though I run no risk of going to Purgatory for my avarice; yet as money is an essential ingredient to happiness in this world—as I have not much of my own and as I am very little calculated to get more either by my address or industry; it must needs be, that my wife, if I get one, bring at least a sufficiency to administer to her own extravagancies.[109]

Hamilton wrote in a spoofing tone, but he was deadly serious. He was not the kind of man who would lose his head and marry the barmaid. A year later he did wed a young lady who met some, if not all, of his exacting specifications,[110] particularly the last. She was Elizabeth Schuyler, daughter of the controversial general Philip Schuyler. That one stroke attached Hamilton to a powerful and affluent landed family, a connection he had so sorely missed up to then.

Hamilton loved Elizabeth after his fashion, and there were eight children of the marriage. Moments of connubial bliss were not allowed to interfere with a long-term flirtation he carried on with his sister-in-law, Angelica Schuyler Church. Worldly, witty, frivolous, and possessive, Angelica had a girlhood crush on dashing Alexander which she never lost. It was to Angelica that Hamilton wrote shortly before his marriage, praising his sweetheart's beauty and perfection. She was a veritable heartbreaker, he confessed, concluding: "It is essential to the safety of the state and to the tranquillity of the army that one of two things take place; either that she be immediately removed from our neighbourhood, or that some other nymph qualified to maintain an equal sway come into it. By dividing her empire it will be weakened and she will be much less dangerous when she has a rival equal in charms to dispute the prize with her. I solicit your aid."[111]

Hamilton was spoofing, but to Angelica, the supreme coquette, this was a challenge. Thereafter, she never withheld her affection and admiration from her *"petit fripon."* Typical of her correspondence with the Hamiltons was a note she penned from London, April 25, 1788, in which she mentioned reports that "our dear Hamilton writes too much and takes no exercise, and grows too fat." This was deplorable, she pointed out. "He will be unable to flirt as Robert Morris." After advising Elizabeth to get him to exercise, she added: "Embrace poor dear Hamilton for me, it is impossible to know him, and not to wish him health and pleasure, and then I am really so proud of his merit and abilities, that even you, Eliza, might envy my feelings."

When the Churches moved from England to America, their relationship to the Hamiltons was a source of discomfiture to the latter's friends. John Barker Church was a promoter and a gambler, mostly up to no good. Harrison Gray Otis described to his wife a dinner party he attended in Philadelphia. "After dinner," he related, "Mrs. C[hurch] dropped her shoe bow." Her younger sister Peggy picked it up and put it in Hamilton's buttonhole, saying, " 'There, brother, I have made you a Knight.' 'But of what order,' asked Mrs. Church. 'He can't be a Knight of the Garter in this country.' "

" 'True sister,' replied Peggy, 'but he would be if you would let him.' "[112]

When gallantry passed the bounds of flirtation, Hamilton and his adoring Eliza paid dearly for his indiscretions.

The scandal first erupted when Hamilton was at the height of his reputation as Secretary of the Treasury and in effect prime minister. In 1792 John Beckley, a Jeffersonian Republican politician and Hamilton-hater, rushed to James Monroe with a story, third hand, involving Hamilton in allegedly criminal operations. Beckley got the story from a man named Jacob Clingman, to whom a clerk in the Treasury named Andrew G. Fraunces had reputedly boasted that "he could, if he pleased, hang Hamilton." Fraunces insisted that Hamilton had given him the power of attorney to purchase a Revolutionary War veteran's certificate for back pay at a substantial discount and just before the enactment of the bill providing for redemption of these certificates at par. In addition to the small sums that Fraunces allegedly was paid, another friend of Clingman's named James Reynolds asserted that Hamilton had paid him $1,100 for services rendered.

The credibility of Clingman and Reynolds should have been dubious even to one so blind as a Hamilton-hater. Both men were under arrest and faced with prosecution for suborning a witness to commit perjury in an attempt to embezzle Treasury funds. Three congressmen, Monroe, Muhlenberg, and Venable, visited Reynolds, and with the data in their pockets, confronted Hamilton in his office. Hamilton asked them to meet him at his home that evening and took the precaution of requesting Oliver Wolcott, the comptroller, to be there as a witness.

The congressmen and the comptroller heard a weird story that night. Hamilton confessed that in the summer of 1791, while his wife was away from Philadelphia, he had had an affair with Reynolds's wife, Maria, who had come to him for financial aid. Hamilton had fallen into the trap, and thereafter was blackmailed by a scoundrel, aided and abetted by the scoundrel's wife. He paid Reynolds a thousand dollars, and some further small sums. The visitors were dumbstruck and agreed to treat the affair in strictest confidence.

But one of Hamilton's enemies did not keep his word. In 1797, some years after Hamilton left office, James T. Callender, a Republican hatchetman, published his so-called *History of the United States for the year 1796*. The hidden tale of 1792 was now exposed to the public eye. Hamilton's integrity as a public man was at stake, including his disinterested sponsorship of his key programs of funding and assumption of the public debt. Agonizing though the decision must have been, he made it nonetheless. By publishing the entire story, with the sordid disclosure, "My real crime is an amorous connection with his wife," Hamilton sacrificed his private life to his public reputation. Although there were some then and still today who doubt the story, it is evident that, true or fictional, Hamilton was prepared to go the limit to protect his public honor.[113]

The affair with Mrs. Reynolds could not help but deepen Hamilton's pessimistic views about women, as well as the rest of mankind. Ever fearful that men could not prove impregnable to corruption, Hamilton had come to regard sex as a great corrupter, a cynicism that indubitably sprang from his relationship toward the first "loose woman" he had ever known—his own mother. In his sixth *Federalist* paper he had made a point of blaming three loose women for leading their countries astray: the "prostitute" Aspasia, who induced Pericles to attack the Samnians, and Mesdames de Maintenon and de Pompadour, mistresses of Louis XIV and XV respectively, whose political intrigues led to religious persecution or foreign adventurism. Now, Hamilton's quondam mistress had besmirched his own career, but at least the Republic was safe.

The immigrant waif never made a complete adjustment to America, never lost a certain sense of alienation from his adopted country. At times this alienation manifested itself in fits of despondency, as when Hamilton confided to John Laurens in 1780, "I hate Congress—I hate the army—I hate the world—I hate myself. The whole is a mass of fools and knaves."[114] This despondency and alienation deepened when Hamilton left office, only to see his foreign program scuttled by President Adams and his domestic program threatened by Jefferson's election. Despite his phenomenal rise, he could write to a relative, the Laird of Cambuskeith, in 1797: "Public office in this country has few attractions." Far more money could be made in one of the professions, he pointed out, and the opportunity for "doing good" was too limited "to warrant a long continuance of private sacrifices." Not only had the party spirit dampened the impulses of a "virtuous man" to make such personal "sacrifices," but, Hamilton complained, "the prospect was even bad for gratifying . . . the love of fame, if that passion was to be the spring of action."[115] Despondent over the death of his eldest son, Philip, killed in a duel he fought to defend his father's reputation, disheartened by the ebb in the fortunes of his own party, Hamilton wrote a despairing letter to Gouverneur Morris in the winter of 1802:

> Mine is an odd destiny. Perhaps no man in the United States has sacrificed or done more for the present Constitution than myself; and contrary to all my anticipations of its fate, as you know from the very beginning, I am still laboring to prop the frail and worthless fabric. Yet I have the murmurs of its friends no less than the curses of its foes for my reward. What can I do better than withdraw from the scene? Every day proves to me more and more, that this American world was not for me.[116]

In his last days Hamilton dissented from the secessionist chatterings of the High Federalists, just as earlier he had condemned as constitutional aberrations the notions of nullification and interposition advanced by Jeffersonian Republicans. As always, to Hamilton, the real disease in the body politic was the "poison" of "democracy."[117]

Disappointed and disillusioned though he was at the end, Hamilton had done as much as any man to weld the states into a nation and thereby fulfill some of the noblest aspirations of that Revolution to whose success he had committed his life, his fortunes, and, above all, his sacred honor.

WHAT'S PAST IS PROLOGUE

If ever there was a conspiracy to revolt against British rule, as the Tories steadfastly insisted, it was indeed an extraordinary affair. One can point to no single moment between the convening of the First Continental Congress in September of '74 and the signing of the Definitive Peace with Great Britain in September, 1783, when the seven notable revolutionary activists who are the subjects of this book were ever discovered together in the same room and at the same time.

Of the Seven, only Washington, Adams, and Jay served in the First Continental Congress, where collective revolutionary measures were initially adopted. They were joined by Franklin and Jefferson in the Second Congress, and save for John Jay, a nonsigner, the first four named were the only ones of the Seven Founders to affix their signatures to the Declaration of Independence. Their revolutionary ardor notwithstanding, Madison and Hamilton were latecomers in the higher councils of the Revolutionary party. The two last served together in the Congress during 1782 and 1783, but Madison previously had made his impact on the state level, while Hamilton's most noteworthy Revolutionary service was as an aide to General Washington between March, 1777, and February, 1781.

In fact, the war pulled the leaders physically apart, dispatching them to areas where it was felt they could make their most effective contribution to victory—to the battlefield, to the emergent states where they could carry out the congressional mandate to establish state governments, or across the Atlantic on missions of war and peace.

In retrospect, it seems extraordinary that the Seven should have been able to make their presence felt in the councils of the nation and felt so forcefully even when they were absent from the seat of Congress, whether that happened to be Philadelphia, or New York, or Princeton, or Annapolis. It was their skill with the pen, their indefatigable role as drafters of state papers, framers of key legislation and state constitutions, not to speak of their superb talents as letter writers, that continually augmented their prestige. It would hardly be too much to say that the authority of the Seven in Revolutionary councils stemmed as much from their literary effusions as it did from their direct impact on men and events. One is continually astonished not only at the high literary level the Founding Fathers managed to maintain, but at their resourcefulness in finding time to write so much so well. Not only did they write their own copy, but they exhibited a special talent for phrasemaking. Aware that they were principal actors on the great stage of history, they took special pains to keep the record straight and to preserve it.

In an age of great oratory it is noteworthy that the Seven proved more articulate on paper than in public address. Great conversationalists all without exception, only three of the seven, John Adams, John Jay, and Alexander Hamilton, achieved any reputation as orators. Jefferson and Madison were painfully shy in public, Franklin was diffident if not inscrutable, and Washington saved his best oratorical efforts for a few choice occasions when his temper outran his prudence.

One cannot discount the ideological element that entered into the making of these Seven revolutionaries; one must recognize that these were principled men who were convinced of the rightness and necessity of their course. Granted their conversion from principle, one is still entitled to speculate on what might have been.

Let us suppose George Washington had got the commission in the British army that he pursued with such tenacity, or that Benjamin Franklin's land deals in the Old Northwest had been validated by the Crown and that he had not been stripped of his prestigious post and publicly humiliated. Assume that George Washington and John Jay had married into Loyalist families, which in either case was not beyond possibility. Suppose Jay's quest for a royal judgeship had been crowned with success, an event which might have posed a serious dilemma for a man who actively sought such preferment at the very time he was serving as a delegate to the subversive Continental Congress. Suppose John Adams, who, despite his large law practice, was unable to save money, had yielded to temptation and accepted the lucrative advocate generalship that the Crown party proffered him. With Patriots of this stature defecting from the Revolutionary cause, one might have legitimate ground for conjecturing how very different that cause might have been in character, in goals, and in durable consequences.

Granted the commitment of all Seven to the cause of independence out of both principle and interest, one cannot discount the factor of association or connections in their ultimate decision to break with the Crown. To a man the Southerners were part of a Whig elite that governed Virginia's counties and dominated her legislature. Washington's close ties with the Fairfaxes were an aberration, and clearly did not override the countervailing influence of so many active ideologists like his closeby neighbor, George Mason, to cite one example. Jay's marriage tied him to a foremost Whig ideologist and Northern political leader, William Livingston. Adams's Puritan associations were overwhelmingly anti-Tory, with one or two notable exceptions. The Whigs cultivated Hamilton on his arrival in America, and his marriage into the family of a foremost Whig landowner in New York cemented the Whig connection, if his military career under Washington had not already done so. In short, all Seven were guilty of subversion by association as well as from conviction and overt acts.

If it was extraordinary that the Seven exerted so much collective influence although often remote from the seat of power, what was even more extraordinary was their ability to work together to win a war and build a nation despite extreme disparities in age, physique, temperament, ethical values, religious attitudes, and even in wealth, family origins, and social status. As different physically as the tall, angular Jefferson was from the chubby, rotund Adams, they fought in a common cause without each finding it necessary to sacrifice his own striking individuality or to scuttle diverse opinions ardently advocated and clung to with tenacity.

Between the eldest and the youngest of the Seven stood an age gap of two generations. On July 4, 1776, Franklin was in his seventy-first year; Washington, already in command of the Continental army for a full year, was in his forty-fifth; Adams nearing forty-one; Jefferson just past thirty-three, and John Jay two years his junior. In an era when leaders in Parliament began their public careers at precociously early ages—Shelburne at twenty-six, "Champagne Charlie" Townshend at twenty-four, and Lord North at the venerable age of twenty-seven—the American Revolutionary leadership seems positively senescent in comparison. Even young James Madison, age twenty-five when the Revolution began, or still younger Alexander Hamilton, a probable twenty-one years of age in 1776, seem less precocious than the younger Pitt, who assumed the British prime ministership at the advanced age of twenty-four. Neither Madison nor Hamilton held comparable positions of power or influence for another decade and a half.

Instead of the Revolutionary leadership being divided by reason of age, as might well be the case today, the records of the Seven make it abundantly clear that in an era of elitist governance the more mature leaders encouraged and even propelled their younger activist compatriots forward on the basis of merit. Truly, a powerful argument against the seniority system that has for so long throttled change and reform in the American Congress! Thus, the committee that was responsible for the preparation of the Declaration of Independence turned to its second-youngest member to do the drafting, while on the important Committee on Foreign Relations and other committees of Congress James Madison was usually junior in years but senior in authority and influence.

Complex individuals, all Seven underwent one or more identity crises at various stages of their respective careers, and suffered the neuroses associated with ambitious, driving, and talented people. Jefferson, whose violent headaches coincided with the receipt of bad news, and Madison, with his seizures, tensions, and inhibitions, seem the most neurotic of the Seven, but Washington's temper tantrums were legendary. Adams, Jay, and Hamilton, and even Washington in his earlier years, appeared to derive undisguised pleasure from open quarrels, while, contrariwise, Franklin and Jefferson had a talent for avoiding head-on collisions and for backing away from confrontations.

Of the Seven, five came from a propertied and established elite, but John Adams was of distinctly lower-middle-class origins and Hamilton could not bury his humiliating origins quickly enough and climb the ladder of social respectability by marriage into a prominent Whig family.

Despite their elitist connections arising either from birth or at early stages of their respective careers, all Seven had to prove themselves. Franklin, a youngest son in a large family, bullied and browbeaten by an older brother, had every motive to seek a new life in a new place on his own. His dowdy lower-middle-class marriage provided an additional spur to escape to less drab surroundings. Washington as a younger son was overshadowed by a talented older brother and dominated by a matriarch, with whom he never developed a relationship of true affection. Thomas Jefferson had to show that the Jeffersons were the equal of the Randolphs, his mother's family, while Adams had to show that the Adamses were just as good as the disapproving but more prominent Smiths, Abigail's family. Hamilton, whose illegitimacy was a matter of notoriety in the tight gossipy West Indian islands, had an understandable craving for respectability. Madison, overshadowed at the start by a prestigious father and a dominating grandmother, and handicapped by afflictions psychological if not physical, had perhaps, more than all the rest, the need to demonstrate that he could succeed in the life of action as well as that of the mind. Perhaps the most neurotic of the Seven, Madison, by demonstrating creative statesmanship of a high order, supports the view of modern psychiatry that men and women can overcome psychoneurotic afflictions, the rejection of Senator Thomas Eagleton as a vice-presidential candidate in 1972 to the contrary notwithstanding.

In short, one would be hard put to come up with a combination of such clashing temperaments that managed to serve this country in common effort and with such effectiveness. The explosive John Adams found Franklin's deviousness infuriating, while the latter had reservations about the mental balance of his New England colleague. That the prim and proper Mr. Jay could strike it off so well with the cosmopolitan Franklin is a tribute to the unusual charm and sagacity of the Old Doctor while revealing as well certain hidden depths in Jay himself—his delight in anecdotal gossip even of the off-color variety and his fair-mindedness in evaluating the enormously important role played by Franklin abroad and played so superbly, despite his heedlessness of proper security measures, his contact with shady characters, and the huge amount of time he spent in cultivating his own image. Hamilton's open if temporary breach with Washington reveals much about the younger man's self-esteem and glory seeking and still more about the General's forbearance toward a talented junior whom he held in both affection and esteem.

When one considers their practices and professions on the score of sexual morality, it would be difficult to pick seven men who conformed so little to a stereotype. Franklin, the least bound by convention and the only one of the seven, save Jefferson, believed to have sired illegitimate offspring, could observe with approval that all cats look gray in the dark, a sage remark, voicing Franklin's casual attitude toward sexual affairs. Nevertheless, as a septuagenarian diplomat his French romances, as with Jefferson's pursuit of Maria Cosway, assumed an almost ritualistic character. Both men seemed relieved at the opportunity of transforming a physical relationship into a literary exercise. In contrast, no other Founding Father made so stark a confession of premarital innocence as John Adams felt obliged to do. When asked by Benjamin Rush late in life to champion "national, social, domestic, and religious virtues," Adams responded:

> If I should inculcate "fidelity to the marriage bed," it would be said that it proceeded from resentment to General Hamilton, and a malicious desire to hold up to posterity his libertinism. Others would say that it is only a vainglorious ostentation of my own continence. For among all the errors, follies, failings, vices, and crimes, which have been so plentifully imputed to me, I cannot recollect a single insinuation against me of any amorous intrigue, or irregular or immoral connection with woman, single or married, myself a bachelor or a married man.[1]

Or consider the matter of wives. Only two of the Seven Founders appeared to have had fully satisfying marriages. John Adams found Abigail the perfect helpmate, and John Jay adored his Sally. Both marriages were crowned with numerous progeny. Contrast their experiences with Benjamin Franklin's devious devices to escape from marital companionship by keeping the ocean between himself and his wife for exceptionally lengthy periods. Or consider Jefferson's various misogynist outbursts, his revealing comment on the brevity of the romantic ardor of the honeymoon, and his refusal to marry again even though he outlived his wife by forty-two years. The blighted romance of James Madison indubitably deepened a feeling of insecurity he long possessed in the presence of the opposite sex, and although his marriage to Dolley Payne was successful from all outward appearances, it does not appear to have been completely fulfilling. Washington's concern about his fatherless status and his remarkable profession of affection toward a woman other than his wife made toward the end of his life suggests that his marriage lacked romantic ardor even if it provided him with an eminently congenial spouse.

Capable of enduring friendships, the Seven were also stout controversialists, who could write with a drop of vitriol in their pens. John Adams dismissed John Dickinson, who voted against the Declaration of Independence, as "a certain great fortune and piddling genius." Washington castigated his critic General Conway as being capable of "all the meanness of intrigue to gratify the absurd resentment of disappointed vanity." And Hamilton, who felt it "a religious duty" to oppose Aaron Burr's political ambitions, would have been a better actuarial risk had he shown more literary restraint. Aside from an enthusiasm for controversy, the Seven guarded their reputations as zealously as the Romans protected the Vestal Virgins.

What set the Seven apart was far less significant than what bound them together. In their private lives they demonstrated a capacity for growth, an ability to emerge from their respective identity crises more purposeful, better balanced, and more effective, whether in human relations or as political operatives. All Seven possessed that sense of dedication to the public service which characterized the majority of the Revolutionary leadership. Franklin, who managed to be immersed in public affairs without being completely absorbed in them, and who maintained a detachment while in the midst of great controversies, a detachment which proved so infuriating to some of his associates, retired at the age of forty-two and for the next forty-two years devoted himself to public, scientific, and philanthropic affairs, even managing to keep a weather eye on his business interests. Jefferson and Jay abandoned attractive law practices on the eve of the Revolution, at considerable financial sacrifice to themselves and their families. John Adams handled one or two cases once the war began, but never practiced law again. Hamilton, poorest of the Seven, postponed his law career until the war was drawing to a close, and then worked at it sporadically, interrupted as he was by constant calls upon his time by his state and nation. Never completely abandoning his land, farming, and canal-building activities, Washington could spare no time whatsoever for them during the years of fighting. "My life has been so much a public one," Madison once ruefully remarked.[2] Aside from managing his plantation during his years of retirement, Madison never practiced a profession. Such selfless dedication on the part of the Seven may serve to redeem that streak of philistinism which all bore, along with their attachment to property, and their conformity to the social values of their age.

Ideological bonds tied all Seven together—their dedication to the American Revolutionary cause, their conviction that republican institutions were superior to monarchical, their keen perception of the national interest which set them apart from provincial leaders whose vision often failed to transcend their respective town, county, or state. All Seven possessed a profound faith in America's destiny; all were fired by the conviction that America had a unique role as a symbol of freedom.

Products of the American Enlightenment, they stamped upon republican institutions their own personal and often variant interpretations of what they themselves had wrought. First of all, they believed with almost religious fervor in the power of science. Franklin, the most distinguished man of science produced in America in pre-Revolutionary times, held that science should, as Sir Humphry Davy epitomized the American's contribution, be made "a useful inmate and servant in the common habitations of man," rather than preserved "merely as an object of admiration in temples and palaces."[3] Convinced of the "progressive" nature of science, Jefferson regarded it as an essential tool in reshaping social institutions.[4]

With equal enthusiasm did the Seven expound the value of general education in a republican society. All Seven were voracious readers. "From a child I was fond of reading, and all the little money that came into my hands was ever laid out in books," Franklin tells us in his autobiography. Adams collected the best law library in New England. After Jefferson sold his personal library to the government, he confessed: "I cannot live without books,"[5] and proceeded to acquire more.

All Seven possessed some of the versatility and encyclopedic range of knowledge associated with the European philosophes of that day. None could equal Franklin, whose volume on electricity was the most influential book to come out of America in the eighteenth century, but Jefferson achieved noteworthy results as an architect, inventor, and gadgeteer, and Washington combined proficiency in surveying, plantation management, civil engineering skills, and business administration with talents as a warrior and statesman.

"Let every sluice of knowledge be opened and set a-flowing," wrote Adams.[6] Two of the Seven, Franklin and Washington, were largely self-educated; the other five, college-trained. Hence, we would expect from the former more stress upon self-instruction and self-improvement, and in Franklin's case, even when he proposed a plan of formal education, that it would have a utilitarian bearing.[7] In view of his own experience, Washington recognized that "a knowledge of books" was not enough, and that a knowledge of "men and things" could be acquired in ways other than by formal education.[8] Nevertheless, conscious of his own educational limitations,[9] he urged as President, with Hamilton's collaboration, that the government promote "science and literature," along with the establishment of a national university, whose primary purpose would be the education of youth "in the science of *government*," and was prepared to back his proposal with a substantial personal contribution.[10] The federal government has in more recent years only done by indirection what Washington wished it to do by direct operation. Significantly, Washington in his will left a bequest to a free school for the support of orphans and poor children.[11]

Of the college-trained Founding Fathers Jefferson expressed the most pervasive interest in general as well as higher education. Insisting that government could not be "trusted to the rulers of the people alone" and that "the people themselves" were "its only safe depositories," Jefferson was to argue that "to render even them safe, their minds must be improved to a certain degree," even if that meant adopting a constitutional amendment empowering the federal government to contribute to public education.[12] Although Jefferson expressed these views fairly late in life, he had, between 1776 and 1779, set forth in his proposed legislative package the sweep of the ideas on education he would later espouse. To Jefferson, these educational proposals constitute the heart of his code.[13] Jefferson based his education bill on the assumption, as his preamble put it, that "those persons, whom nature hath endowed with genius and virtue, should be rendered by liberal education worthy to receive, and able to guard the sacred deposit of the rights and liberties of their fellow citizens, and that they should be called to that charge without regard to wealth, birth or other accidental condition or circumstance." Since the poor could not educate their children "at their own expence," it was appropriate, Jefferson argued, that "those of their children whom nature hath fitly formed and disposed to become useful instruments for the public" should be educated "at the common expence of all." The alternative was to have "the happiness of all" confided "to the weak or wicked."[14]

What Jefferson proposed was a selective system of public education, which would weed out the brighter students and give them precollege training to prepare them for the College of William and Mary. By his program, all children would be taught how to read, write, and cipher, but those "of superior genius" would be exposed to Greek, Latin, geography, and advanced arithmetic; and a still more advanced group given still more advanced education. Succinctly, he described the general objects of his bill as providing an education "adapted to the years, to the capacity, and the condition of everyone, and directed to their freedom and happiness." This was as far as he was prepared to go. Nor was he prepared to admit blacks into this program.

Toward the end of his life he founded the University of Virginia, an achievement he ranked with his authorship of the Declaration of Independence—an overly generous estimate, some might think today. More than any statesman of his age did Jefferson formulate an educational philosophy for a democratic society, a society not yet in being, a society more democratic perhaps than he himself envisaged. "Enlighten the people," he wrote in 1816, "and tyranny and oppressions of both body and mind will vanish like evil spirits at the dawn of day."[15]

How much enlightenment the people required remained to be spelled out. For universal education on all levels there existed no body of support whatsoever among the Founding Fathers. These worthies would have regarded "open admission" college programs of the present day with shocked disapproval.

In the controversial area of religious conviction, the Seven varied in the degree to which they paid obeisance to rational currents and in their display of outward piety. True, they were united in their devotion to the principles of religious toleration, but one can detect subtle shadings of difference in their attitude toward the separation of church and state, to touch on a crucial issue.

"I never told my own religion, nor scrutinized that of another," Thomas Jefferson once remarked, adding that he had "ever judged" the religion of others by their lives "rather than their" words.[16] Franklin, with his characteristic preference for the cryptic, would doubtless have subscribed to these views. The Old Doctor diverged widely from the dogmas of Presbyterianism, the faith in which he had been educated, and encouraged every variety of sect that sought subscriptions to build places of worship in Philadelphia, even venturing to tell the Vatican whom to appoint as first Catholic bishop in America.[17] By paying his respects to all denominations, Franklin was in fact saying that he did not want one denomination to prevail or gain authority over all others. A few weeks before he died he expressed doubts about the divinity of Jesus; his religious views could best be categorized as Deistic.[18]

Like Jefferson and Franklin, George Washington did not adhere to the dogmas of any single denomination. He attended church without formal affiliation, accepted Christianity in the sense that he did not question the teachings of Jesus, which he commended to the Indians,[19] but fitted into the Deistic pattern to which so many of the Founding Fathers conformed. The fact that he took no communion once the American Revolution began may have larger political than religious significance, considering the tight bonds of the Church of England to the Crown. Yet on matters of religious toleration no one of the Seven held more enlightened views. As he eloquently expressed them in a communication to the members of the New Church in Baltimore: "In the enlightened Age and in this Land of equal liberty it is our boast, that a man's religious tenets will not forfeit the protection of the Laws, nor deprive him of the right of attaining and holding the highest Offices that are known in the United States."[20] To date the very highest office in the land still eludes non-Christians.

The religious convictions of the Seven cover a broad spectrum. At one end range the Deistic positions of a Washington, a Franklin, a Jefferson, or a Madison; at the other end, the orthodox piety of John Jay; and somewhere in between the religious views of John Adams and Alexander Hamilton. His later years found John Jay absorbed in the propagation of the Bible, whose literal truths he accepted without question.[21] There is every ground to doubt that Jay would have agreed with his prestigious chief about the eligibility for the highest offices of non-Christians. In his closing years he questioned whether "our religion" permits Christians to vote for "infidel rulers." As for Jay himself, he reminded his correspondent of what the prophet had said to Jehoshaphat about his attachment to Ahab. "Shouldst thou help the ungodly, and love them that hate the lord?"[22] In truth, the Deistic positions of a Franklin, a Washington, a Jefferson, or a Madison seem quite at variance with the orthodox piety of Jay.[23] Nor would John Adams have endorsed the Deistic position of a majority of the Seven. While he did not subscribe to Calvinist dogma, he was a Puritan through and through.

It is with Hamilton that one observes the most extreme oscillation of religious opinion, from adolescent piety to freethinking, and then a reversion to orthodoxy in his last days. He was launched on his upward-bound career by a public letter he wrote describing a hurricane that hit St. Croix, a letter dripping with piety that appealed to the religiosity of a local Presbyterian minister. On coming to America he won no laurels for his religious orthodoxy, and even opposed, with heavy sarcasm, the motion offered by the Deistic-minded Franklin at the Constitutional Convention to have prayers introduce each session.[24] Notwithstanding, the radical ideology of the French Revolution and the formation of the Democratic-Republican Societies of the 1790's, in whose organization the hands of Jefferson and Madison were barely concealed, prompted Hamilton to propose a Christian Constitutional Society, which, fortunately for the future of the Republic, died aborning. Hamilton died attesting to the principles of Christianity.[25] On his deathbed he was accepted into the Episcopal Church and received the sacraments.

While the Seven, despite their diversity of religious outlooks and the pronounced anti-Catholic bias of several of their number, stood united on the issue of complete religious toleration, it is by no means clear that they would have agreed on how the First Amendment to the Constitution should be interpreted or that they would have been unanimous in supporting the more recent Supreme Court's imposition upon the states as well as the federal government of the restrictions laid down in the establishment-of-religion clause. Although Jefferson cordially endorsed James Madison's "Memorial and Remonstrance," Washington was troubled that the issue of assessment should be raised, while John Adams stoutly defended the establishment of the Congregational Church in Massachusetts, for which his own state constitution had made provision, and the Bay State clung to vestiges of church establishment until 1833.

Although three of the Seven came from the South and four were Northerners, in which category we must place the West Indies–born Hamilton, they were as one in their detestation of slavery. Shadings of difference there were between the Southerners and the Northerners, both as to how far they would risk their political necks in ending the institution and as to the genuineness of their commitment to curbing discrimination on grounds of race. As early as 1779, Hamilton proposed setting up several battalions of Negroes, who would be given "their freedom with their muskets." He argued that such a gesture would open the door to a general emancipation of the slaves. The Massachusetts Constitution of 1780 which John Adams drafted was interpreted by the courts of that state as ending slavery. John Jay, founder of the New York Society for Promoting the Manumission of Slaves, had the genuine satisfaction of signing as governor a bill for providing for the gradual emancipation of slaves in New York. He lived to see his own sons in the forefront of the antislavery battle. Franklin's last public act was to sign a memorial to Congress for the abolition of slavery.

Washington felt strongly on the subject of slavery, but was prudent about repossessing his own slave property, and carefully avoided a direct confrontation on the subject. For a Virginia politician Jefferson went as far as he could go on the slavery question. Had Congress adopted his territorial report of 1784, slavery would have been forbidden in all the western territory after 1800, not only in the Northwest as it was by the Ordinance of 1787, and the grounds for the Civil War, one could argue, might have been removed. He also had the satisfaction of signing the congressional act abolishing the foreign slave trade. He never was ready to accept racial amalgamation, and Madison, in his backing for African colonization of the American blacks, inferentially revealed the same bias against blacks, the same reservation about accepting the blacks into full citizenship. Egalitarianism they all professed, but only a few were color-blind.

All Seven recognized that independence was but the first step toward building a nation. "We have now a national character to establish," Washington wrote in 1783. "Think continentally," Hamilton counseled the young nation. "I wish to see our people more

Americanized, if I may use that expression," wrote Jay in 1797, thereby coining a new verb.[26] This new force, love of country, super-imposed upon—if not displacing—the affectionate ties to one's own state that characterized the complex federal structure that evolved out of the Revolution, was epitomized by Washington. His first inaugural address speaks of "my country whose voice I can never hear but with veneration and love." By that date when he alluded to "my country" he did not mean Virginia.

All sought the fruition of that nationalism in a federal government with substantial powers. Save Adams and Jefferson, all participated in the framing or ratification of the federal Constitution. They supported it, not as a perfect instrument, but as the best obtainable. Historians have traditionally regarded the great debates of the 1790's as polarizing the issues of centralized versus limited government, with Hamilton and the nationalists supporting the former and Jefferson and Madison upholding the latter position.

The states' rights position was formulated by Jefferson and Madison in the Kentucky and Virginia Resolves drafted in 1798, but in their subsequent careers as heads of state the two proved themselves better Hamiltonians than Jeffersonians. In purchasing Louisiana, Jefferson had to follow Hamilton's broad construction of the Constitution, and so did Madison in advocating the rechartering of Hamilton's bank, which he had so strenuously opposed at its inception, and in adopting a Hamiltonian protective tariff. Indeed, the old Jeffersonians in their liberalized construction of the Constitution and their conversion to nationalism were far more atune to the Hamilton-oriented Whigs than they were to the Jacksonian Democrats.

As patriots and nationalists the Seven Founders were convinced that the new nation boasted a better set of values than obtained in the Old World. Jefferson characterized Europe as a society where "every man must be hammer or anvil," and felt that a comparison of the American government with those abroad was "like a comparison of heaven and hell."[27]

As early as 1775, John Adams warned Americans to avoid alliances "which would entangle us." Years later, Jefferson was to repeat the injunction in almost identical phraseology in his first inaugural address. When the American peace commissioners in Paris were instructed by Congress to take no step without the approval of France, Jay vigorously protested against "casting America into the arms of France." Aware of Franco-Spanish efforts that would have confined the United States chiefly to lands east of the Appalachians, he deliberately ignored his government's instructions. "We have no rational dependence except on God and ourselves," he wrote Robert R. Livingston, the American secretary of foreign affairs, in a letter defending his direct negotiations with Great Britain.[28]

This general agreement among the Founding Fathers on the necessity for keeping politically and culturally aloof from Europe found expression in Washington's Farewell Address, which recognized the need for temporary alliances, but warned aganst permanent ones, and was epitomized in Hamilton's later comment: "We are laboring hard to establish in this country principles more and more *national* and free from all foreign ingredients, so that we may be neither 'Greeks nor Trojans,' " but "truly American."[29]

No dewy-eyed innocents they, the Seven Founders were realists. Convinced though they were that government must rest on the consent of the governed, they shared a deep concern about the frailty of human nature, about the virtue and wisdom of the propertyless masses, and the dangers of a tyranny of the majority over the minority. Franklin excepted, they were unanimous in their lack of enthusiasm for universal manhood suffrage. Only Adams even alluded to the possibility of woman suffrage, considered the proposition, and then rejected it. By an ingenious system of checks and balances and a division of powers the Founding Fathers made doubly sure that the federal Constitution would protect interests not necessarily endorsed by a majority.

Egalitarians in theory at least, they were prepared to provide guarantees that equal opportunities must be open to all, blacks excepted. It was *equality of opportunity* to which they were committed. The more recent demands for *equality of result,* with its bloc view of American life, its emphasis on quotas by age, sex, and racial or ethnic origin, would have been inconceivable and abhorrent to them.

The Seven Founders recognized that in the final analysis the republican system for which they had fought so long and so hard must secure the endorsement of an informed public in order for it to prove durable. Deeply committed though they were to the principle that governments derive their just powers "from the consent of the governed," the Founding Fathers did not keep their ears to the ground for every minor seismic disturbance, nor would they conceivably have approved national policies shaped by casual political polls. Since the people often lacked the necessary background information for informed opinions, and still do, it was the statesman's duty, as Jefferson put it, to "reclaim them by enlightening them."

Only after time had been given for cool and deliberate reflection could "the *real* voice of the people" be known, Washington insisted. While it was to be regretted, he confessed, that democracies "must always *feel* before they can *see,*" he reassured Lafayette that "the people will be right at last."[30] Even Hamilton, least sympathetic of any of the Seven with the goals of democracy, whose turbulence and imprudence he distrusted, denounced the "false calculation that the people of this country can ever be ultimately deceived."[31]

"At last," "ultimately," but not necessarily from the start, for that was the point at which the leaders were expected to form public policy. Quite different indeed from the folk hero, sometimes placed in Paris during the upheaval of 1848, or more recently by Gandhi in India. The leader is standing in a window. His people rush by in the street. He cries, "I must hurry and catch up with them, for I am their leader." Only in the sense that the ground swell of independence emboldened the Revolutionary leadership to move all out for independence has the tale the slightest relevance to the behavior of the leadership of the American Revolution. What made the Seven so effective was the fact that they were prepared to run ahead of public opinion, to articulate goals that would lift the people out of their parochial preoccupations, carry them above the conflicts that tear society apart, and unite them in pursuit of objectives worthy of their noblest efforts.

What gave the American Revolution its distinctive character was its sense of legality and moderation. The Seven Founders rested their cause upon charter rights, the English common law, and the British constitution. As a last resort they appealed to "Nature and Nature's God." Without a leadership committed to government by due process of law and to paying a "decent respect to the opinions of mankind," the American Revolution could have taken a more ominous turn; it might well have drifted down the road pursued not long thereafter by the French Revolution, whose initial thrust it had inspired. France's revolution was also rooted in legality, but it soon repudiated moderation and made a shambles of that very legality. The American leadership eschewed both the Terror and Thermidor, managing to fashion a durable constitution in the process. In France the very notion of constitutionalism was discredited beyond recognition. With its streak of demagoguery, its implacable spirit, its taste for bloodletting, its conviction that it had a corner on virtue, the French Revolutionary leadership could not, happily for America, be matched by the more moderate, responsible, and less vindictive stewardship of the American Revolution.[32]

Opinionated the American leaders indubitably were, but none could be accused of that fanatical dogmatism that has so often been the stamp of the revolutionaries who followed. Theirs was indeed a fortuitous conjunction of character and destiny, which left its stamp of moderation and legality both on the Revolution and on the Constitution which was its ultimate achievement.[33]

Without exception all Seven detested mobs and mobbism. Accepting force only as the ultimate weapon, they would have condemned the mindless massacres and assassinations associated with so-called wars of liberation of our own time. All considered the resort to first principles an extraordinary step to be taken only under extraordinary circumstances, although Jefferson, perhaps tongue in cheek, suggested drawing up a new constitution every twenty years. The reaction of all Seven, again save Jefferson, to the Revolutionary veteran-led Shays' Rebellion of 1786–87 made it clear that they wanted to consolidate the gains achieved by the War for Independence and move toward orderly reform rather than provoke change by further revolutions.

John Adams made this point in a conversation in the late spring of 1783 with the Conde de Aranda, Spain's ambassador to Versailles. Aranda remarked to Adams, as the latter recorded it, *"Tout, en ce monde a été Revolution."* Adams replied didactically: "History is but a string of them," but as for himself, he confessed, "One revolution is quite enough for the life of a man." He hoped he never would "have to do with another." Aranda laughed heartily, and declared, "I do believe you."[34]

That the American Revolution had a message and meaning for the whole world, that it was but the start of a new era, all Seven Founding Fathers would have ardently affirmed. They had launched and brought to successful conclusion the first great revolution of modern times, one that was both a war of decolonization and a movement of broad social change and reform, change and reform rooted in legality.

Franklin, master propagandist of revolution, felt that mankind's hopes would be determined by the character and events of the American Revolution. "God grant that not only the love of liberty, but a thorough knowledge of the rights of man, may pervade all the nations of the earth," he declared, "so that a philosopher may set his foot anywhere on its surface and say, 'This is my country.' "[35]

Franklin gave eloquent evocation to that profound faith in America's destiny shared by the other Founding Fathers. All Seven asserted America's unique position as a symbol of freedom, or, in Jefferson's felicitous phrasing, "an empire for liberty." They knew, with John Adams, that "freedom is a counter-balance for poverty, discord and war," or, as Washington phrased it in that inaugural address which ended one era and ushered in another: "The preservation of the sacred fire of liberty, and the destiny of the republican model of government are justly considered as deeply, perhaps as finally staked, on the experiment entrusted to the hands of the American people."[36]

What held this nation together was not the durable Constitution so artfully conceived by the Founding Fathers but a promise made to the whole world in 1776, a promise to which Abraham Lincoln attested, that "the weights should some day be lifted from the shoulders of all men." They have still not been lifted, but we ourselves may not honorably repudiate the ultimate goals of the Seven who shaped our destiny.

NOTES

I. DOCTOR FRANKLIN: THE SENIOR CITIZEN
AS REVOLUTIONARY

1. John Adams, *Works*, ed. by C. F. Adams (10 vols., Boston, 1850–56), III, 75–76.
2. D. H. Lawrence, *Studies in Classic American Literature* (New York, 1923), pp. 19, 27, 31.
3. See, e.g., V. S. Pritchett in *New Statesman and Nation*, Sept. 27, 1941; Robert E. Spiller, "Franklin on the Art of Being Human," American Philosophical Society, *Proceedings*, C (1956), 304–315; John W. Ward, "Who Was Benjamin Franklin?" *American Scholar*, XXXII (1963), 541–553.
4. BF to Arthur Lee, April 4, 1778, in Carl Van Doren, ed., *Benjamin Franklin's Autobiographical Writings* (New York, 1945), p. 442.
5. See Richard L. Bushman, "On the Uses of Psychology: Conflict and Conciliation in Benjamin Franklin," in *History and Theory*, V (1966), 229–239.
6. See Leonard W. Labaree, ed., *The Papers of Benjamin Franklin* (New Haven, 1959–   ) (hereinafter *BFP*), I, 182–183.
7. *BFP*, III, 120–125.
8. John Adams to James Warren, April 13, 1783, in *Warren-Adams Letters*, II (Massachusetts Historical Society, *Collections*, XLLIII), 209.
9. See Verner W. Crane, ed., *Benjamin Franklin's Letters to the Press, 1758–1775* (Chapel Hill, N.C., 1950).
10. J. G. Rosengarten, *American History from German Archives* (Lancaster, Pa., 1904), pp. 26–31.
11. Albert H. Smyth, ed., *The Writings of Benjamin Franklin* (10 vols., New York, 1905–7), VIII, 437–447.
12. *BFP*, I, 99, 100.
13. June 11, 1722, *BFP*, I, 8–23.
14. *Ibid.*, pp. 281–282.
15. *Ibid.*, III, 102, 336, 337.
16. *Ibid.*, II, 217 (1739).
17. *Ibid.*, II, 138 (1736).

18. *Pennsylvania Gazette,* July 29, 1731.
19. See Paul L. Ford, *Who Was the Mother of Franklin's Son?* (New Rochelle, N.Y., 1936).
20. Republished in *BFP,* III, 27–31.
21. *Poor Richard,* 1736, *BFP,* II, 138–142.
22. *Poor Richard,* 1737, *BFP,* II, 169, 171.
23. Smyth, ed., *Writings,* I, 373–374.
24. Paul W. Conner, *Poor Richard's Politicks* (New York, 1965), p. 217.
25. Smyth, ed., *Writings,* IV, 182.
26. See Claude-Anne Lopez, *Mon Cher Papa: Franklin and the Ladies of Paris* (New Haven, 1966).
27. BF to Mme. Brillon, Dec. 25, 1781. French original in Smyth, ed., *Writings,* VIII, 349–351; translation in Van Doren, ed., *Franklin's Autobiographical Writings,* pp. 511–512.
28. Lopez, *Mon Cher Papa,* p. 58.
29. Smyth, ed., *Writings,* VII, 375.
30. Sainte-Beuve, *Causeries du lundi* (Paris, n.d.), VII, 136–138. For a new unabridged translation of the "Elysian Fields" bagatelle, see Lopez, *Mon Cher Papa,* pp. 265–267.
31. See "Appeal for the Hospital," *Pennsylvania Gazette,* Aug. 8, 15, 1751.
32. BF to Peter Collinson, May 9, 1753, *BFP,* IV, 479–480.
33. See Adrienne Koch, *The American Enlightenment* (New York, 1965), pp. 15–18.
34. Delightfully conveyed in a letter to his intimate correspondent Catherine Ray, Oct. 16, 1755, in W. G. Roelker, *Benjamin Franklin and Catherine Ray Greene* (Philadelphia, 1949), p. 20.
35. *Observations Concerning the Increase of Mankind,* 1751; reprinted in *BFP,* IV, 227–234.
36. Matthew T. Mellon, *Early American Views on Negro Slavery* (New York, 1969), pp. 5–28.
37. For Franklin's early experiments in electricity, see *BFP,* IV, 82–83.
38. For Franklin the scientist, see Robert A. Millikan, "Benjamin Franklin as a Scientist," The Franklin Institute, *Meet Dr. Franklin* (Philadelphia, 1943), pp. 11–26; I. Bernard Cohen, "Franklin and Newton," American Philosophical Society, *Memoirs,* XLIII (Philadelphia, 1956). See also *BFP,* IV, 198; Peter Kalm, "Conversations with Franklin," in A. B. Benson, ed., *Peter Kalm's Travels in North America: The English Version of 1770* (2 vols., New York, 1937), I, 59.
39. BF to Joseph Huey, June 6, 1753, *BFP,* IV, 503–506.
40. See "Doctrine to be Preached" (draft, 1731), *BFP,* I, 212, 213; BF to Ezra Stiles, March 1, 1790, in Koch, *American Enlightenment,* pp. 108, 109.
41. *Plain Truth* (1747), *BFP,* III, 198–204.
42. See Nolan J. Bennett, *General Benjamin Franklin: The Military Career of a Philosopher* (Philadelphia, 1936), pp. 35–37, 60–62, 72, 83; William S. Hanna, *Benjamin Franklin and Pennsylvania Politics* (Stanford, 1964). For the Paxton Boys' grievances, see *Minutes of the Provincial*

Council of Pennsylvania (10 vols., Philadelphia, 1852), IX (1762–1771), 138 et seq.

43. *New England Courant*, Feb. 18, 1723.
44. *Poor Richard*, 1751, BFP, IV, 97–98.
45. H. G. R. de Mirabeau, *Considerations sur l'ordre de Cincinnatus, ou imitant d'un pamphlet Anglo-Américain* (London, 1784).
46. See, e.g., BFP, I, 273, 318, 359; II, 144, 225, 254, 298, 334; III, 9.
47. See *A Modest Enquiry into the Nature and Necessity of a Paper Currency* (Philadelphia, 1729).
48. BFP, I, 141.
49. See James Parton, *Life and Times of Benjamin Franklin* (2 vols., Boston, 1882), I, 332, 333; Verner W. Crane, *Benjamin Franklin and a Rising People* (Boston, 1954), pp. 30, 31.
50. BF to Thomas Clap, Aug. 20, 1753, *BFP*, V, 22.
51. See T. P. Abernethy, *Western Lands and the American Revolution* (New York, 1959 ed.), pp. 14–58; S. E. Slick, *William Trent and the West* (Harrisburg, Pa., 1947), chs. XI, XII.
52. BF to Thomas Walpole, Jan. 12, 1774, Harkness Collection, New York Public Library.
53. BF to Thomas Walpole, July 14, 1778, Harkness Collection, New York Public Library.
54. See Richard B. Morris, *The Peacemakers: The Great Powers and American Independence* (New York, 1965), p. 247.
55. A recent highly critical analysis of Franklin's conduct of his mission in France, one that seeks to substantiate by circumstantial evidence the accounts of Franklin's enemies and British espionage agents, as well as by inference, will be found in Cecil B. Currey, *Code Number 72: Benjamin Franklin: Patriot or Spy* (New York, 1972).
56. BF to James Parker, March 20, 1751, *BFP*, IV, 118.
57. *Ibid.*, p. 119n.
58. Richard B. Morris in *Times of Trial*, ed. by Allan Nevins (New York, 1958), pp. 25–39.
59. Lansdowne Papers, vol. 165, William L. Clements Library, University of Michigan; reprinted in Richard B. Morris, *The American Revolution, 1763–1783* (New York, 1970), pp. 12–20.
60. Cecil B. Currey, *Road to Revolution: Benjamin Franklin in England, 1765–1775* (New York, 1968).
61. BF to John Hughes, Aug. 6, 1765, Smyth, ed., *Writings*, IV, 392.
62. *A Collection of Scarce and Interesting Tracts Written by Persons of Eminence upon the Most Important Political and Commercial Subjects* (4 vols., London, 1787).
63. BF to Thomas Cushing, March 9, 1773, Smyth, ed., *Writings*, VI, 21–22.
64. "The Colonist's Advocate," No. 8, in Verner W. Crane, ed., *Franklin's Letters to the Press*, p. 197.
65. Benjamin Vaughan, ed., *Political, Miscellaneous, and Philosophical Pieces . . . written by Benjamin Franklin* (London, 1779), p. 341. For

a variant and more temperate version, see Israel Mauduit, ed., *Letters of Governor Hutchinson and Lt. Governor Oliver . . . with the Speech of Mr. Wedderburn* (London, 1774), reprinted in Israel Mauduit, ed., *Franklin Before the Privy Council* (Philadelphia, 1861), pp. 80–82, 93–94, 102–103.

66. Benjamin Franklin, *The Autobiography of Benjamin Franklin,* ed. by Leonard W. Labaree (New Haven, 1964), p. 271.
67. For the facts versus fiction, see Morris, *The Peacemakers,* p. 381.
68. Smyth, ed., *Writings,* VI, 408.
69. Parton, *Life and Times,* II, 209.

II. GEORGE WASHINGTON: SURROGATE FATHER TO A REVOLUTIONARY GENERATION

1. Elkanah Watson, *Men and Times of the Revolution* (New York, 1857), p. 39. Watson insisted that he was quoting Washington as accurately as possible.
2. GW to Reverend Jonathan Boucher, May 21, 1772, John C. Fitzpatrick, *The Writings of George Washington* (39 vols., Washington, D.C., 1931–44), III, 84 (hereinafter cited as *GWF*).
3. Gustavus A. Eisen, *Portraits of Washington* (3 vols., New York, 1932); Frances D. Whittemore, *George Washington in Sculpture* (Boston, 1933).
4. James Biddle, ed., *Autobiography of Charles Biddle* (Philadelphia, 1883), p. 285.
5. John Allen Murray, *George Washington's Rules of Civility and Decent Behaviour in Company and Conversation* (New York, 1942), p. 26.
6. GW to Thomas Jefferson, August 1, 1786, *GWF,* XXVIII, 504.
7. Worthington C. Ford, et al., eds., *Journals of the Continental Congress, 1774–1789* (34 vols., Washington, D.C.), XXIV, 494, 495; Papers of the Continental Congress, no. 19, VI, fol. 441.
8. Quoted in Daniel J. Boorstin, *The Americans—The National Experience* (New York, 1965), p. 355.
9. Seth Ames, ed., *Works of Fisher Ames* (2 vols., Boston, 1854), II, 73–88.
10. For Washington's enthusiasm for Addison's *Cato,* see Samuel Eliot Morison, *By Land and by Sea: Essays and Addresses* (New York, 1953), pp. 169–171; for Washington and his Roman counterparts, see the brilliant analysis in Marcus Cunliffe, *George Washington: Man and Monument* (London, 1959), pp. 21, 116, 154–155, 171. For the popular view of Washington as a demigod, see Marshall W. Fishwick, "Virginian on Olympus," *Virginia Magazine of History and Biography,* LIX (Jan., 1951), 51–71.
11. Douglas Southall Freeman, *George Washington* (7 vols., New York, 1948–54), I, 18–21, citing the mutilated Westmoreland Deeds and Patents, 1665–77.

12. Most biographers of GW, especially the most recent, are unsympathetic toward his mother. See, e.g., Freeman, *Washington*, I, 190–193; Morison, *By Land and by Sea*, p. 164; John Corbin, *The Unknown Washington: Biographical Origins of the Republic* (New York, 1930), pp. 29 passim; Paul Leicester Ford, *The True George Washington* (Philadelphia, 1896), pp. 17–18. Rising to her defense are Washington Irving, *Life of George Washington* (5 vols., New York, 1857), I, 25; Henry Cabot Lodge, *George Washington* (2 vols., Boston, 1889), I, 40–41; and the iconoclastic Bernhard Knollenberg's *George Washington: The Virginia Period, 1732–1775* (Durham, N.C., 1964), p. 4. For the financial arrangements between GW and his mother, see Freeman, *Washington*, III, 595–598, citing GW's diaries and ledgers.

13. Quoted in Freeman, *Washington*, I, 198–199.

14. A. P. C. Griffin, ed., *A Catalogue of the Washington Collection in the Boston Athenaeum* (Boston, 1897). See also H. Trevor Colbourn, *The Lamp of Experience* (Chapel Hill, N.C., 1965), pp. 152–154.

15. GW to Reverend Jonathan Boucher, July 9, 1771, *GWF*, III, 50–51.

16. *GWF*, II, 114, and GW to Major Anthony Lewis, May 21, 1758, *GWF*, II, 203.

17. GW to Lafayette, May 28, 1788, *GWF*, XXIX, 506–507.

18. GW to Joseph Reed, Dec. 12, 1778, *GWF*, XIII, 383.

19. GW to Hebrew Congregation of Newport, Aug. 17, 1790, *GWF*, XXXI, 93, n. 65.

20. GW to David Humphreys, July 25, 1785, *GWF*, XXVIII, 203.

21. Washington lifted this phrase from a memorial to him from Yeshuat Israel Congregation of Newport. See Morris Schappes, ed., *A Documentary History of the Jews in the United States* (New York, 1950), p. 79.

22. See Richard B. Morris, *Great Presidential Decisions* (Philadelphia and New York, 1960), pp. 32–33.

23. Worthington Chauncey Ford, *Wills of George Washington and His Immediate Ancestors* (Brooklyn, 1891), p. 91.

24. Philadelphia *Daily American Advertiser*, Sept. 19, 1796.

25. John C. Fitzpatrick, ed., *The Diaries of George Washington* (4 vols., Boston and New York, 1925), I, 25.

26. *Washington Diaries*, I, 5–10. In later years Washington came to estimate the Germans more highly. See GW to the Commissioners of the District of Columbia, Dec. 18, 1792, *GWF*, XXXIV, 268–272.

27. Washington came to regret his deficiency in French. See GW to Lafayette, Sept. 30, 1779, *GWF*, XVI, 372.

28. Ford, *Wills of George Washington*, pp. 53–55.

29. J. M. Toner, ed., *Journal of Colonel George Washington* (Albany, 1893).

30. GW to Lt. Col. Adam Stephen, Oct. 23, 1756, *GWF*, I, 484.

31. GW to Robert Dinwiddie, n.d., but endorsed May 29, 1754, *GWF*, I, 69. For the French translation of GW's Journal, see Freeman, *Washington*, I, 540–545. The British government chose to regard the incident as evi-

dence of France's hostile movements. See L. H. Gipson, *The British Empire Before the American Revolution*, V (New York, 1942), 324.

32. GW to John Augustine Washington, May 31, 1754, *GWF*, I, 70.
33. *London Magazine*, XIII (1754), 370–371, and Freeman, *Washington*, I, 423.
34. Quoted in John Corbin, *The Unknown Washington* (New York, 1930), p. 50.
35. GW to Robert Dinwiddie, June 3, 1754, *GWF*, I, 73.
36. *Washington Diaries*, I, 74, n. 2.
37. Freeman, *Washington*, I, 404–411; the capitulation is reproduced as the frontispiece of vol. II. Conceivably "L'assassin" could have been mistaken for "L'assaillir," an error which would have required a very poor light and a very hurried reading indeed. Sée also Lawrence C. Wroth, *An American Bookshelf 1755* (Philadelphia, 1934), pp. 40–41. Back in the colonies Washington was severely criticized by Governor Sharpe of Maryland. See Sharpe to Baltimore, Aug. 8, 1754, *Archives of Maryland, Correspondence of Governor Horatio Sharpe*, VI, 79–80; and recently by Knollenberg, *Washington*, p. 23.
38. That Washington was aware that the French would attack with superior numbers was clear from GW to Joshua Fry, May 29, 1754, and GW to Dinwiddie, May 29, 1754, *GWF*, I, 58–63.
39. GW to Dinwiddie, June 12–c. 15, 1754, *GWF*, I, 83.
40. *Ibid.*
41. GW to William Fitzhugh, Nov. 15, 1754, *GWF*, I, 105.
42. Freeman, *Washington*, II, 13.
43. Mary Washington to Joseph Ball, July 26, 1759, in Historical Society of Pennsylvania; GW to Robert Orme, June 30, 1755, *GWF*, I, 146; GW to Orme, April 2, 1755, Jared Sparks, ed., *The Writings of George Washington* (12 vols., New York, 1847–52), II, 71.
44. GW to John Robinson, April 20, 1755, *GWF*, I, 114.
45. GW to John Augustine Washington, May 14, 1755, *GWF*, I, 124. Noted as "not sent."
46. See Freeman, *Washington*, II, 77, n. 90.
47. GW's narrative, written in response to questions from Col. David Humphreys and published in *Scribner's Magazine* (May, 1893), appears in *GWF*, XXIX, 42–44. For GW's contemporary account, see GW to Dinwiddie, July 18, 1755, *GWF*, I, 148–150.
48. GW to John Augustine Washington, July 18, 1755; GW to Mary Ball Washington, July 18, 1755, *GWF*, I, 150–153.
49. GW to Robert Dinwiddie, July 18, 1755; GW to Mary Ball Washington, July 18, 1755, *GWF*, I, 148–151.
50. GW to Mary Ball Washington, *GWF*, I, 159.
51. Freeman, *Washington*, II, 113.
52. Charles Henry Lincoln, ed., *Correspondence of William Shirley* (2 vols., New York, 1912), II, 412–413.

53. Adam Stephen to GW, March 29, 1756, Stanislaus Murray Hamilton, *Letters to Washington and Accompanying Papers* (5 vols., Boston, 1898–1903), I, 203; see also *GWF*, I, 298–299; Freeman, *Washington*, II, 155–168.

54. GW to Robert Dinwiddie, April 22, 1756; GW to Robert Dinwiddie, Nov. 9, 1756, *GWF*, I, 324–325, 492–499.

55. GW to Peter Hogg, Dec. 27, 1755, *GWF*, I, 260; Peter Hogg to GW, Hamilton, *Letters*, I, 182–185.

56. GW to Robert Dinwiddie, Nov. 9, 1756; Nov. 24, 1756; Dec. 2, 1796, *GWF*, I, 497, 508, 511, 514; Robert Dinwiddie to GW, Nov. 16, 1756; Dec. 10, 1756, Hamilton, *Letters*, II, 2–5, 17–20; John Baylis to GW, Jan. 30, 1758, *ibid.*, p. 258.

57. GW to Richard Washington, April 15, 1757, GW to Robert Dinwiddie, April 29, 1757, *GWF*, II, 22, 32–33; John Robinson to GW, Dec. 31, 1756, Hamilton, *Letters*, II, 31–33; the original Washington letter is at Sulgrave Manor, Northamptonshire, England; a copy is at Mount Vernon; it is cited in James Thomas Flexner, *George Washington: The Forge of Experience 1732–1775* (Boston, 1965), p. 175.

58. GW to Brig. Gen. John Stanwix, April 10, 1758, *GWF*, II, 173.

59. Historians are agreed on the superiority of Forbes's route over Washington's. See J. W. Fortescue, *A History of the British Army* (14 vols., London, 1899–1930), II, 270–271; Flexner, *Forge of Experience*, 209n.

60. Kenneth P. Bailey, *The Ohio Company of Virginia* (Glendale, Calif., 1939), pp. 35, 147, 216, 229.

61. GW to Major Francis Hackett, Aug. 2, 1758, *GWF*, II, 260–261.

62. Alfred Procter James, ed., *Writings of James Forbes* (Menasha, Wis., 1938), pp. 171–173.

63. GW to John Robinson, Sept. 1, 1758, *GWF*, II, 276–278.

64. He later reported that the new road was "indescribably bad." GW to Francis Fauquier, Oct. 30, 1758, *GWF*, II, 300.

65. *GWF*, XXIX, 47–48.

66. Mary Ball Washington to Joseph Ball, July 26, 1759, copy in the Historical Society of Pennsylvania. Quoted in Flexner, *Forge of Experience*, p. 228.

67. See GW to Burwell Bassett, June 20, 1773, *GWF*, III, 138.

68. See, e.g., GW to his nephew George Augustine Washington, Oct. 25, 1786, *GWF*, XXIX, 28–29, where he talks about the remote possibility of having an heir of his body.

69. Nathaniel E. Stein, "The Discarded Inaugural Address of George Washington," *Manuscripts*, X, 2 (Spring, 1958), 10.

70. Quoted in Kenneth Umbeit, *Founding Fathers: Men Who Shaped Our Tradition* (New York and London, 1941), p. 267.

71. George Mercer to GW, Aug. 17, 1757, Hamilton, *Letters*, II, 174–175; Capt. Chevalier de Peyrouncy to GW, Sept. 5, 1754, *ibid.*, I, 39; see also GW to Charles Armand-Tuffin, Aug. 10, 1786, *GWF*, XXVIII, 514–515.

72. GW to Rev. William Gordon, Dec. 20, 1784, *GWF*, XXVIII, 15.

73. GW to Lafayette, May 10, 1786, *GWF*, XXVIII, 423; GW to Richard Sprigg, June 28, 1786, *GWF*, XXVIII, 471.

74. GW to Mrs. Annis Boudinot Stockton, Sept. 2, 1783, *GWF*, XXVII, 128.

75. John C. Fitzpatrick, *George Washington Himself* (Indianapolis, Ind., 1933), p. 44; *GWF*, I, 15–16, 19; George Parke Custis, *Recollections and Private Memoirs of Washington* (New York, 1861).

76. GW to William Fauntleroy, Sr., May 20, 1752, *GWF*, I, 22.

77. See Joseph Chew to GW, March 4, 1756, Hamilton, *Letters*, I, 201; Freeman, *Washington*, II, 160, 161; see also Joseph Chew to GW, July 13, 1757, Hamilton, *Letters*, II, 140.

78. Compare GW to Mrs. George William Fairfax, April 30, 1755, with GW to Mrs. George William Fairfax, June 7, 1755, Sept. 23, 1756, *GWF*, I, 117, 137–138, 473.

79. For the evidence that Washington ordered a ring from Philadelphia on May 4, 1758, see Joseph Jackson, "Washington in Philadelphia," *Pennsylvania Magazine of History and Biography*, LVI (1932), 115.

80. Flexner, *Forge of Experience*, pp. 197, 198.

81. GW to Mrs. George William Fairfax, Sept. 25, 1778, *GWF*, II, 292–294.

82. GW to Bryan Fairfax, March 1, 1778, *GWF*, XI, 2.

83. GW to George William Fairfax, Feb. 27, 1785, *GWF*, XXVIII, 83.

84. GW to Sarah Cary Fairfax, May 16, 1798, *GWF*, XXXVI, 263.

85. See John C. Fitzpatrick, *The George Washington Scandals* (Alexandria, Va., 1929); Allen French, "The First George Washington Scandal," Massachusetts Historical Society, *Proceedings*, LXV (1940), 460–474.

86. GW to Arthur Young, Nov. 1, 1787, *GWF*, XXIX, 298.

87. GW to Robert Cary and Company, Merchants, London, May 1, 1759, *GWF*, II, 319–321.

88. *Washington Diaries*, I, 122 (1760), 338, 339 (1769); Richard B. Morris, *Government and Labor in Early America* (New York, 1946), pp. 38, 39. For his employment of white labor as overseers and craftsmen, see W. C. Ford, *Washington as an Employer and Importer of Labor* (Brooklyn, 1889), pp. 28–32 (1762), 41–43 (1771); Morris, *Government and Labor*, pp. 220, 221.

89. See GW to Robert Cary, Sept. 28, 1760; to John Didsbury, Oct. 12, 1761; to Joshua Pollard, Aug. 22, 1766; to Robert Cary, June 20, 1768, *GWF*, II, 350, 369–370, 441–442, 491. See also Curtis P. Nettels, *George Washington and American Independence* (Boston, 1951), pp. 64–72.

90. Fairfax County Resolves, July 18, 1774, Robert A. Rutland, ed., *The Papers of George Mason, 1725–1792* (3 vols., Chapel Hill, N.C., 1970), I, 207.

91. See John Hancock, President of Congress, to GW, Dec. 2, 1775, in Peter Force, ed., *American Archives: Consisting of a Collection of Authentick Records, State Papers, Debates, and Letters and Other Notices of Publick Affairs* (9 vols., Washington, D.C., 1837–53), 4th ser., IV, 155.

92. GW to Joseph Reed, Dec. 15, 1775, William Reed, ed., *Life and Cor-*

respondence of Joseph Reed (2 vols., Philadelphia, 1847), I, 135; GW to Richard Henry Lee, Dec. 26, 1775, *GWF*, IV, 186.

93. GW to the President of Congress, Dec. 31, 1775, *GWF*, IV, 195.
94. GW to Henry Laurens, March 20, 1779, *GWF*, XIV, 267.
95. GW to John Laurens, July 10, 1782, *GWF*, XXIV, 421.
96. See GW to Brig. Gen. Rufus Putnam, Feb. 2, 1783, *GWF*, XXVI, 90.
97. GW to Daniel Parker, April 28, 1783, *GWF*, XXVI, 364–365.
98. GW to Robert Morris, April 12, 1786; GW to Lafayette, May 10, 1786, *GWF*, XXVIII, 407–408, 424.
99. GW to John Sinclair, Dec. 11, 1796, *GWF*, XXXV, 328; GW to Lawrence Lewis, Aug. 4, 1797, *GWF*, XXXV, 2.
100. GW to David Stuart, March 28, 1790, *GWF*, XXXI, 30. For GW's instructions to his private secretary, Tobias Lear, to send Mrs. Washington's slaves back to Mount Vernon if it seemed likely they would "attempt their freedom" when in the North, see GW to Tobias Lear, April 12, 1791, *GWF*, XXXVII, 573–574. See also Paul F. Boller, Jr., "Washington, the Quakers and Slavery," in James M. Smith, ed., *George Washington: A Profile* (New York, 1969), pp. 186–192.
101. Paul Leland Haworth, *George Washington, Country Gentleman* (Indianapolis, Ind., 1915), p. 217.
102. *GWF*, XXXVII, 276–278.
103. On Lawrence's death, in 1752, his share was purchased by Lunsford Lomax, Freeman, *Washington*, I, 264–267, and Knollenberg, *Washington*, p. 193, n. 45.
104. Bailey, *The Ohio Company of Virginia*, pp. 39–60. Fulfillment of these conditions would add 300,000 acres to the original grant.
105. GW to Lord Botetourt, Dec. 8, 1769, *GWF*, II, 530.
106. March [10], 1784, *GWF*, XXVII, 353.
107. GW to Presley Neville, June 16, 1794, *GWF*, XXXIII, 407. For the journey, see *Washington Diaries*, I, 401–452.
108. GW to George Muse, Jan. 29, 1774, *GWF*, III, 179–180.
109. For a highly critical analysis of GW's role, see Knollenberg, *Washington*, pp. 91–100. Since Dunmore seemed prepared to annul this grant on still another technicality—the qualifications of the surveyor—Washington, once the Revolution began, had the Virginia legislature validate these surveys. W. W. Hening, *The Statutes at Large: Being a Collection of All the Laws of Virginia* (13 vols., Richmond, Va., 1819–23), X, 36, 1779. GW to Benjamin Harrison, Dec. 18[–30], 1778, *GWF*, XIII, 463.
110. GW to Charles Washington, Jan. 31, 1770, *GWF*, III, 2–3.
111. C. W. Alvord, *The Mississippi Valley in British Politics* (2 vols., Cleveland, 1916), I, 95; C. H. Ambler, *George Washington and the West* (Chapel Hill, N.C., 1936), pp. 134, 209; C. W. Alvord and C. E. Carter, *Great Britain and the Illinois Country, 1763–1774* (Washington, D.C., 1910), pp. 165 et seq.
112. GW to William Crawford, Sept. 21, 1767, *GWF*, II, 467–471.

113. *Virginia Gazette,* July 29, 1773.

114. William S. Baker, *Early Sketches of George Washington* (Philadelphia, 1894), p. 32.

115. Leonard W. Labaree, *Royal Instructions to British Colonial Governors* (2 vols., New York, 1935), II, 580.

116. Knollenberg, *Washington,* p. 85; Freeman, *Washington,* III, 93–95, 102–103.

117. The papers of the Potomac Company which Washington headed in post-Revolutionary years are in the National Archives. See also Cora Bacon-Foster, *Early Chapters in the Development of the Potomac Route to the West* (Washington, D.C., 1912), pp. 45–51 et seq.

118. *GWF,* III, 144–146; GW to John David Wolper, Nov. 30, 1773, *ibid.,* XXXVII, 502.

119. Ambler, *Washington and the West,* p. 209; Ford, *Wills of Washington,* pp. 83–147.

120. Lucille Griffith, *The Virginia House of Burgesses, 1750–1774* (rev. ed., University, Ala., 1970), pp. 64, 93, 96, 143.

121. GW to Robert Stewart, May 2, 1763, *GWF,* II, 399–400; Col. Thomas Moore to GW, Oct. 21, 1766, Hamilton, *Letters,* III, 288–290.

122. GW to Francis Dandridge, Sept. 20, 1765, *GWF,* II, 425–426.

123. *Washington Diaries,* I, 325; Freeman, *Washington,* III, 219–224. For the probable authorship of this agreement, which historians have erroneously attributed to Mason, see Rutland, ed., *Mason Papers,* I, 93–96.

124. Samuel Johnson, *Taxation No Tyranny* (3d ed., London, 1775), pp. 2, 55, 66–68.

125. *Pennsylvania Gazette,* Sept. 16, 1756.

126. GW to George Mason, April 5, 1769, Rutland, ed., *Mason Papers,* I, 96–98.

127. GW to Robert Cary and Company, July 25, 1769, *GWF,* II, 513.

128. GW to George William Fairfax, June 10, 1774, *GWF,* III, 224.

129. GW to Bryan Fairfax, July 30, 1774, *GWF,* III, 232–233.

130. The copy in the Washington Papers is in Mason's hand. While the style is Mason's the ideas represent a consensus. See Rutland, ed., *Mason Papers,* I, 199–201.

131. David S. Lovejoy, *Rhode Island Politics and the American Revolution, 1760–1776* (Providence, 1958), pp. 167–168. See also Merrill Jensen, *The Founding of a Nation* (New York, 1968), pp. 474–479.

132. Rutland, ed., *Mason Papers,* I, 201–209.

133. GW to Bryan Fairfax, July 20, 1774, *GWF,* III, 233.

134. L. H. Butterfield et al., eds., *Diary and Autobiography of John Adams* (4 vols., Cambridge, Mass., 1961), II, 117.

135. *Ibid.,* II, 109.

136. Curtis Nettels, *George Washington and American Independence* (Boston, 1951), pp. 92–93.

137. GW to Capt. Robert Mackenzie, Oct. 9, 1774, *GWF,* III, 244–247.

138. GW to George William Fairfax, May 31, 1775, *GWF,* III, 292.

139. GW to George Mason, April 5, 1769, *GWF*, II, 501; GW to John Augustine Washington, June 20, 1775, *ibid.*, III, 299.

140. *Journals of the Continental Congress*, II, 91.

141. GW to Joseph Reed, Feb. 10, 1776, *GWF*, IV, 321.

142. GW to Henry Laurens, April 30, 1778, *GWF*, XI, 327.

143. GW to Bryan Fairfax, July 4, 1774, *GWF*, III, 229.

144. The original text of the speech is in the hand of Edmund Pendleton, a fellow delegate who also drew up Washington's will. Papers of the Continental Congress, lib. LII, Library of Congress.

145. Flexner cites one minor instance when Washington tried to purchase for his plantation some worn-out cavalry horses. See James Thomas Flexner, *George Washington in the American Revolution, 1775–1783* (Boston, 1967), p. 540.

146. For a tongue-in-cheek analysis, see Marvin Kitman, *George Washington's Expense Account* (New York, 1970).

147. GW to Joseph Reed, Dec. 12, 1778, *GWF*, XIII, 383.

148. See GW to Philip Schuyler, June 25, 1775, *GWF*, III, 302–304.

149. Force, *American Archives*, 4th ser., VI, 1119–1120.

150. GW to the Commissioners for Redressing the Grievances of the New Jersey Line, Jan. 27, 1781, *GWF*, XXI, 147–148.

151. Freeman, *Washington*, V, 218.

152. Henry Steele Commager and Richard B. Morris, *The Spirit of 'Seventy-Six* (2 vols., New York, 1958), II, 885–887.

153. See, e.g., GW to Lt. Gen. Thomas Gage, *GWF*, III, 416–417, 430–431.

154. Julian U. Niemcewicz in M. J. E. Budka, ed., *Under Their Vine and Fig Tree*, New Jersey Historical Society, *Collections*, XIV (Elizabeth, N.J., 1965), p. 102.

155. GW to Col. Lewis Nicola, May 22, 1782, Worthington Chauncey Ford, *The Writings of George Washington* (14 vols., New York, 1891), X, 21–24. See also Louise Burnham Dunbar, *A Study of "Monarchical" Tendencies in the United States from 1776 to 1801* (Urbana, Ill., 1920), pp. 46–53.

156. *Journals of the Continental Congress*, XXIV, 291–293.

157. Alexander Hamilton to GW, April 18, 1783, Harold C. Syrett et al., eds., *The Papers of Alexander Hamilton* (17 vols., New York, 1961–   ), III, 318–319.

158. "Brutus" to Knox, Feb. 12, 1783, Knox Papers, XI, 120, Massachusetts Historical Society. For an identification of "Brutus," see Richard H. Kohn, "The Inside History of the Newburgh Conspiracy; America and the Coup d'état," *William and Mary Quarterly*, 3d ser., XXVII (April, 1970), 197, n. 34.

159. GW to Alexander Hamilton, March 12, 1783, Syrett, ed., *Hamilton Papers*, III, 287.

160. *Journals of the Continental Congress*, XXIV, 306–310.

161. Kohn, *loc. cit.*, p. 210.

162. Thomas Jefferson to GW, April 16, 1784, Julian P. Boyd, ed., *The Papers of Thomas Jefferson* (18 vols., Princeton, 1952–   ) III, 106–107.

III. JOHN ADAMS: THE PURITAN
AS REVOLUTIONARY

1. JA to Benjamin Rush, April 4, 1790, March 23, April 12, 1809, *Old Family Letters: Copied from the Originals for Alexander Biddle* (2 vols., Philadelphia, 1892), I, 55, 226; John Adams, *Works*, ed. by C. F. Adams (10 vols., Boston, 1850–56), IX, 616–619.
2. JA to Abigail Adams (AA), July 1, 1774, *The Adams Papers; Adams Family Correspondence,* ed. by L. H. Butterfield (hereinafter *AFP*), (2 vols., Cambridge, Mass., 1963), I, 119.
3. *The Diary and Letters of His Excellency Thomas Hutchinson,* ed. by Peter O. Hutchinson (2 vols., Boston, 1884–86), I, 163.
4. *The Adams Papers: Diary and Autobiography of John Adams,* ed. by L. H. Butterfield (hereinafter *AP*) (4 vols., Cambridge, Mass., 1961), II, 251, 252.
5. See JA to AA, Sept. 18, 1774, *AFP*, I, 159.
6. See *Diary*, March 14, 1759, *AP*, I, 78.
7. See, e.g., JA to AA, n.d., *Familiar Letters of John Adams and His Wife Abigail during the Revolution,* ed. by C. F. Adams (Boston, 1876), p. 380; JA to Mrs. Mercy Warren, Nov. 25, 1775, *Works*, IX, 368.
8. *Diary*, April 24, 1756, *AP*, I, 22.
9. JA to Benjamin Rush, April 12, 1809, *Old Family Letters*, I, 228.
10. JA to AA, May 22, 1777, *AFP*, II, 245.
11. *Diary*, Feb. 16, 1756, *AP*, I, 7–8.
12. Novanglus, *The American Colonial Crisis: The Daniel Leonard–John Adams Letters to the Press, 1774–1775,* ed. by Bernard Mason (New York, 1972), pp. 156, 157.
13. See, e.g., JA to George Washington, June, 1775, *Works*, IX, 360n., for special recognition in the army for his brother-in-law William Smith.
14. JA to AA, June 23, 1775, *Familiar Letters*, I, 226. "Oh that I was a soldier!" he confessed to Abigail a few weeks earlier. JA to AA, May 29, 1775, *ibid.*, p. 207.
15. JA to James Warren, March 16, 1780, Massachusetts Historical Society, *Collections*, vol. 73, *Warren-Adams Letters* (2 vols., Boston, 1917–25), II, 129–130.
16. *Diary*, May 29, 1760, *AP*, I, 127, 128.
17. *Diary*, March 15, 1756, *AP*, I, 14.
18. JA to Patrick Henry, June 3, 1776, *Works*, IX, 387–388.
19. JA to Samuel Adams, Sept. 17, 1776, *ibid.*, p. 445.
20. JA to Benjamin Rush, Aug. 28, 1811, *ibid.*, pp. 635–640.

21. See Warren Hasty Carroll, "John Adams: Puritan Revolutionist" (unpublished Ph.D. dissertation, Columbia University, 1959).
22. Novanglus Paper, No. V (1775), *The American Colonial Crisis*, ed. by Mason, p. 151.
23. Novanglus Paper, No. I (1774), *ibid.*, p. 105.
24. AA to JA, Oct. 22, 1775, *AFP*, I, 311.
25. JA to John Quincy Adams, July 27, 1777, *AFP*, II, 290.
26. For this broad definition of virtue JA drew upon Joseph Butler's *An Apology of Religion* (1740), which he copied in his notebook in 1765, JA microfilm, reel 187, Massachusetts Historical Society. See also JA to Zabdiel Adams, June 21, 1776; to John Quincy Adams, April 8, 1777; to AA, Aug. 24, 1777, *AFP*, II, 21, 204, 328.
27. JA to AA, Aug. 24, 1776, *AFP*, II, 96, 97.
28. JA to Thomas Jefferson, Dec. 16, 1816, *The Adams-Jefferson Letters*, ed. by Lester J. Cappon (2 vols., Chapel Hill, N.C., 1959), II, 502–503; JA to John Trumbull, Jan. 1, 1817, *The Autobiography of Colonel John Trumbull*, ed. by Theodore Sizer (New Haven, 1953), p. 311.
29. JA to AA, April 27, 1777, *AFP*, II, 225.
30. JA to AA, April 12, 1778, *Letters of John Adams, Addressed to His Wife*, ed. by C. F. Adams (2 vols., Boston, 1841), II, 241.
31. JA to AA, June 3, 1778 (April, 1780), *ibid.*, II, 24–25, 70; JA to Thomas Jefferson, Dec. 21, 1819, *Adams-Jefferson Letters*, II, 551; JA to John Jay, Dec. 6, 1785, Jay Papers, Columbia University Special Collections (copy). See also Wendell D. Garrett, "John Adams and the Limited Role of the Fine Arts," *Winterthur Portfolio*, I (Winterthur, Del., 1964), 243–253.
32. JA to William Tudor, March 29, 1817, *Works*, X, 245.
33. JA to William Tudor, April 15, 1817, *ibid.*, pp. 251–252.
34. JA to Thomas Jefferson, Feb. 17, 1786, Julian P. Boyd, ed., *The Papers of Thomas Jefferson*, IX, 286.
35. *Diary*, Feb. 21, 1765, *AP*, I, 253–255, 256, 257. In revised and expanded form the essay appeared in the Boston *Gazette*, Aug. 12, 19, Sept. 30, Oct. 21, 1765.
36. JA to Thomas Jefferson, Aug. 24, 1815, May 29, 1818, *Adams-Jefferson Letters*, II, 455, 525.
37. The analogy of the Revolutionary Americans to the children of Israel was also made by Franklin and Jefferson in their proposal to Congress for a seal. See JA to AA, Aug. 14, 1776, *AFP*, II, 96.
38. JA to AA, May 17, 1776, *AFP*, I, 410. For AA's comforting reference to the "God of Israel" at the time of Bunker Hill, see AA to JA, June 18, 1775, *ibid.*, p. 222.
39. JA to F. A. Van der Kemp, Dec. 31, 1808, reprinted in I. S. Meyer, American Jewish Historical Society, *Publications* (1947), pp. 185–201. JA to Van der Kemp, Feb. 15, 1809, *Works*, IX, 608–610.
40. See JA to AA, March 28, 1777, *AFP*, II, 188, 189; also Alfred Iacuzzi, *John Adams, Scholar* (New York, 1952), pp. 177 et seq.

41. C. F. Adams, *A College Fetich: An Address Delivered before the Harvard Chapter of the Phi Beta Kappa, June 28, 1883* (Boston, 1884), pp. 22–23.

42. JA to AA, Oct. 9, 1774, *AFP*, I, 167; JA to Richard Price, April 19, 1790, *Works*, IX, 563–565.

43. JA to Thomas Jefferson, Jan. 23, 1825, *Adams-Jefferson Letters*, II, 607–608. See also Norman Cousins, ed., *The Religious Beliefs and Ideas of the American Founding Fathers* (New York, 1958), pp. 105, 111; Robert B. Everett, "The Mature Religious Thought of John Adams," South Carolina Historical Association, *Proceedings* (1966), pp. 51–55.

44. *Works*, II, 208.

45. JA to Isaac Smith, Jr., April 11, 1771, *AFP*, I, 75.

46. See Zoltan Haraszti, *John Adams and the Prophets of Progress* (Cambridge, Mass., 1952), pp. 17 et seq.

47. For his early efforts at translation, see JA to AA, March 16, 1763, *AFP*, I, 3. See also JA to AA, Feb. 18, 1776, *ibid.*, p. 349; JA to James Lovell, Dec. 21, 1777, *Works*, IX, 471.

48. *Works*, II, 201.

49. Abigail Smith to JA, April 12, 1764, *AFP*, I, 25. See also April 20, 1764, *ibid.*, p. 37.

50. JA to Abigail Smith, May 7, 1764, *ibid.*, pp. 44–47.

51. JA to Abigail Smith, May 7, 1764; Abigail Smith to JA, May 9, 1764, *ibid.*, I, 44–47.

52. AA to Mary Smith Cranch, Oct. 6, 1766, *AFP*, I, 56.

53. AA to JA, June 23, 1777, *AFP*, II, 270.

54. AA to JA, Sept. 16, 1774, Oct. 16, 1774, June [16?], 1775, *AFP*, I, 152, 172, 219.

55. JA to Cotton Tufts, July 20, 1776; to AA, Aug. 10, 1776, June 10, 1777, *AFP*, II, 54, 55.

56. JA to AA, July 7, 1775, *AFP*, I, 242.

57. AA to JA, May 27, 1776, *AFP*, I, 418.

58. AA to Hannah Quincy Lincoln Storer, c. March 1, 1778, *AFP*, II, 398.

59. JA to Benjamin Rush, April 12, 1809, Biddle, *Old Family Letters*, I, 229.

60. AA to JA, June 17, 1776, *AFP*, II, 16.

61. See *AFP*, I, xxxv, 407.

62. AA to JA, March 31, May 7, 1776, *AFP*, I, 370, 402, 403. See also AA to John Thaxter, Feb. 15, 1778, *AFP*, II, 391, 392.

63. JA to AA, April 14, 1776, *AFP*, I, 382.

64. JA to James Sullivan, May 26, 1776, *Works*, IX, 375 et seq.

65. See JA to AA, Aug. 25, 1776, *AFP*, II, 109, 110. See also Jean Fritz, *Cast for a Revolution: Some Friends and Enemies, 1728–1814* (Boston, 1972).

66. *Diary* [Jan. 1759], *AP*, I, 73.

67. *Diary*, March 14, 1759, *AP*, I, 78.

68. JA to AA, Sept. 30, 1764, *AFP*, I, 48.

69. A respectable number of Adams's law cases have been skillfully assembled and reconstructed in *Legal Papers of John Adams* (3 vols., Cambridge, Mass., 1960), ed. by L. Kinvin Wroth and Hiller B. Zobel.

70. *Doughty* v. *Little, Adams Legal Papers* (1768), I, 286.
71. *Gray* v. *Pitts, ibid.,* (1771), I, 157–161.
72. *Basset* v. *Mayhew, ibid.,* (1762–68), I, 87–195. *AP,* III, 285.
73. *Penhallow* v. *The Lausanna,* 1777–95, *Adams Legal Papers,* II, 352–395.
74. *Ibid.,* II, 105; Leonard W. Labaree, *Boston Tea Party* (New York, 1964), pp. 118–137.
75. *Longmans* v. *Maine; Wright & Gill* v. *Mein, Adams Legal Papers,* I 199–230 (1770–71).
76. *Ibid.,* III, 226.
77. *King* v. *Stewart,* 1773–74, *ibid.,* I, 106–140; JA to AA, July 7, 1774, *AFP,* I, 131. King had been awarded damages in 1766, which he later sought to increase. The jury saw fit to augment King's recovery by a modest sum, which his widow as late as 1790 was still trying to recover.
78. *AP,* III, 326.
79. See Richard B. Morris, *The Peacemakers: The Great Powers and American Independence* (New York, 1965), p. 361; *John Jay, the Nation, and the Court* (Boston, 1967), pp. 73–96.
80. *Sewall* v. *Hancock,* 1768–69, *Adams Legal Papers,* II, 173–209; O. M. Dickerson, *The Navigation Acts and the American Revolution* (New York, 1963); Lovejoy, "Rights Imply Equality: The Case Against Admiralty Jurisdiction in America, 1764–1776," *William and Mary Quarterly,* 3d ser., XVI (1959), 459 et seq.
81. See *Adams Legal Papers,* III, passim; Hiller B. Zobel, *The Boston Massacre* (New York, 1970).
82. For the pretrial depositions, see F. Kidder, *History of the Boston Massacre, March 5, 1770* (Albany, N.Y., 1870); Richard B. Morris, *Government and Labor in Early America* (New York, 1946), pp. 190–192.
83. *AP,* II, 73, 74.
84. Josiah Quincy, *Memoirs of Josiah Quincy, Jr., of Massachusetts,* 1774–1775 (2d ed., Boston, 1874), p. 29n.
85. JA to William Tudor, March 29, 1817, *Works,* X, 244–249. Similarly, earlier, JA to AA, July 3, 1776, *AFP,* II, 29. But cf. J. W. Ellsworth, *Huntington Library Quarterly,* XXVIII (1964–65), 294–295.
86. *Massachusetts Spy,* April 29, 1773.
87. The documents in Petition of Lechmere, 1761, are in *Adams Legal Papers,* II, 106–147; O. M. Dickerson, "Writs of Assistance as a Cause of Revolution," in Richard B. Morris, ed., *The Era of the American Revolution* (New York, 1939), p. 40; cf. Frese, "Otis and Writs of Assistance," *New England Quarterly,* XXX (1957), 496; Richard B. Morris, "Then and There the Child Independence Was Born," *American Heritage* (February, 1962).
88. *AP,* I, 271.
89. *Diary,* Dec. 18, 1765, *AP,* I, 265.
90. *Works,* III, 465–467.
91. Josiah Quincy, Jr., *Reports of Cases Argued and Adjudged in the Superior Court of Judicature of the Province of Massachusetts Bay, between*

1761 and 1772, ed. by Samuel M. Quincy (Boston, 1865), pp. 200–209.

92. *AP,* I, 311.
93. *Diary,* Dec. 18, 1786, *AP,* I, 263.
94. *Works,* I, 326–332, 365; II, 174–176; III, 477–483.
95. *Ibid.,* III, 484–497, passim.
96. *Ibid.,* III, 508–509; Boston *Gazette,* May 15, 1769.
97. *Diary,* Dec. 23, 1769, *AP,* I, 347; *Rex* v. *Corbet* (1769), *Adams Legal Papers,* II, 276–335.
98. Quincy, *Reports,* p. 411.
99. *Works,* II, 150, 151. See also Richard B. Morris, "Legalism versus Revolutionary Doctrine in New England," *New England Quarterly,* IV (1931), 195–215.
100. *Works,* X, 194, 321.
101. *AP,* III, 288, 289.
102. *The history of the Colony and province of Massachusetts, by Thomas Hutchinson,* ed. by Lawrence Shaw Mayo (3 vols., Cambridge, Mass., 1936), III, 213–214.
103. Preface to *Novanglus and Massachusettensis* (Boston, 1819), pp. vi, vii.
104. *Works,* I, 57, 58n.
105. *AP,* III, 289–290.
106. *Works,* III, 456, 464.
107. *Ibid.,* I, 389; IV, 18–28; *AP,* I, 90. For the conspiratorial interpretation advanced by the Whig ideologues, see Bernard Bailyn, *The Ideological Origins of the American Revolution* (Cambridge, Mass., 1967), pp. 144–159.
108. *Works,* III, 540–559.
109. For JA's role in the drafting of these papers, see JA to William Tudor, March 8, 1817, *ibid.,* II, 311–313.
110. *Ibid.,* IX, 333, 335–337; *Diary,* Dec. 17, 1773, *AP,* II, 86; JA to James Warren, Dec. 17, 1773, *Warren-Adams Letters,* II, 403.
111. JA to Mercy Warren, Jan. 3, 1774, *Warren-Adams Letters,* I, 22.
112. JA to William Tudor, Jan. 24, 1817, *Works,* X, 237–238.
113. JA to William Tudor, Jan. 24, 1817, *ibid.,* p. 241.
114. The family tradition is recorded by Charles Francis Adams in *Works,* I, 146–147. See also *Boston Town Records, 1770–1777,* p. 176.
115. *Diary,* June 20, 25, 1774, *Works,* II, 338; *AP,* II, 96, 97.
116. JA to James Warren, June 25, 1774, *Works,* IX, 339.
117. JA to AA, July 3, 9, 1774, *AFP,* I, 123, 135.
118. Timothy Pitkin, *A Political and Civil History of the United States of America* (New Haven, Conn., 1828), I, 277, for the report of a conversation between John and Samuel Adams in the presence of John's law clerk, John Trumbull. See also JA to James Warren, July 17, 1774, *Warren-Adams Letters,* I, 29. Cf. John W. Ellsworth, "John Adams: The American Revolution as a Change of Heart?" *Huntington Library Quarterly,* XXVIII (Aug., 1965), 293–300, for a gradualist interpretation of Adams as a revolutionary.

119. JA to AA, Sept. 25, 1774, *AP*, I, 164.
120. *Diary*, Sept. 17, 1774, *AP*, II, 134, 135.
121. JA to Joseph Palmer, Sept. 26, 1774, Burnett, *Letters*, I, 48.
122. JA to AA, Sept. 20, 1774, *AFP*, I, 161; JA to AA, Sept. 29, 1774, *AFP*, I, 164; *Diary*, Sept. 22, 1774, *AP*, II, 136.
123. *Works*, II, 258–539; *AP*, II, 152n.
124. *Diary*, Oct. 28, 1774, *AP*, II, 157.
125. *Works*, IV, 68–69. The "Novanglus" letters were written in reply to a series of "Massachusettensis" letters, which Adams erroneously attributed to Jonathan Sewall, whereas in fact they had come from the pen of Daniel Leonard. L. M. Sargent, "The Author of Massachusettensis," *New England Historical and Genealogical Magazine*, XVIII (1864), 354–356.
126. JA in his autobiography takes full credit for nominating Washington, *AP*, III, 322.
127. *AP*, III, 323.
128. JA to James Warren, June [July] 6, 1775, *Warren-Adams Letters*, I, 75.
129. JA to James Warren, July 24, 1775, *ibid.*, I, 88.
130. JA to James Warren, July 24, 1775, *ibid.*, I, 89; *Massachusetts Gazette and Boston Weekly News Letter*, Aug. 17, 1775; *Works*, I, 178–180; *AP*, II, 174n.; III, 318, 319.
131. See *AP*, II, 162n.
132. *Ibid.*, III, 342, 343, 346.
133. *Ibid.*, pp. 346–349.
134. *AP*, III, 350.
135. *Ibid.*, pp. 351, 352.
136. *Ibid.*, II, 354–356.
137. JA to Horatio Gates, March 23, 1776, Edmund C. Burnett, ed., *Letters of Members of the Continental Congress* (8 vols., Washington, D.C.), I, 406.
138. JA to AA, April 15, 1776, *AFP*, I, 383.
139. John Adams to James Warren, April 16, 1776, *Warren-Adams Letters*, I, 227.
140. JA to AA, May 17, 1776, *AFP*, I, 410. The resolve was voted May 10; the preamble, written by JA, the 15th, *JCC*, IV, 351, 357–358; *AP*, II, 238–241; III, 335, 382–386.
141. JA to James Warren, May 20, 1776, *Warren-Adams Letters*, I, 251.
142. *Ibid.*
143. JA to Patrick Henry, June 3, 1776, *Works*, IX, 386–388.
144. JA to John Winthrop, June 23, 1776, *ibid.*, pp. 409–410.
145. *AP*, III, 396.
146. JA to Timothy Pickering, Aug. 6, 1822, *Works*, II, 513–514n. JA's memory was faulty on this score, as Jefferson's first draft of the Declaration attests.
147. P. L. Ford, ed., *Writings of Thomas Jefferson* (10 vols., New York, 1892–98), IX, 377–378.

148. JA to AA, July 3, 1776, *AFP*, II, 30, 31.
149. JA to AA, July 3, 1776, *ibid.*, pp. 29–31.
150. JA to Nathanael Greene, March 9, 1776, *AP* microfilm, reel 9.
151. JA to AA, March 19, 1776, *AFP*, I, 363.
152. *Works*, IV, 193–200; JA to John Penn, Jan. 1776, *ibid.*, p. 205.
153. See S. E. Morison, "The Struggle Over the Adoption of the Constitution of Massachusetts of 1780," Massachusetts Historical Society, *Proceedings*, L (1917), 353–411.
154. *Works*, IX, 376.
155. Robert Brown, *Middle Class Democracy and the Revolution in Massachusetts* (Ithaca, N.Y., 1955), pp. 393–406.
156. JA to Edward Biddle, Dec. 12, 1774, *Works*, IX, 349; to Benjamin Hichborn, May 29, 1776, *ibid.*, p. 379; AA to Mary Smith Cranch, Oct. 6, 1766; to JA, Nov. 27, 1775, *AFP*, I, 55, 329; JA to Samuel Adams, Oct. 18, 1790, *Works*, VI, 414–420.
157. John Disney, *Memoirs of Thomas Brand-Hollis* (London, 1808), pp. 32–33.
158. JA to Rufus King, June 14, 1786, Adams microfilm, reel 113.
159. JA to John Taylor, April 15, 1814, *Works*, VI, 487.
160. Compare Gordon S. Wood, *The Creation of the American Republic, 1776–1787* (Chapel Hill, N.C., 1969), pp. 586, 587, with Zoltan Haraszti, *John Adams and the Prophets of Progress*, pp. 26, 27, and Timothy H. Breen, "John Adams' Fight Against Innovation in the New England Constitution, 1776," *New England Quarterly*, XL (1967), 501–520.
161. JA to James Warren, Jan. 9, 1787, *Warren-Adams Letters*, II, 281.
162. JA to Benjamin Rush, Jan. 8, 1812, *Old Family Letters*, I, 369.
163. Cf. JA to John Winthrop, June 23, 1776, *Works*, IX, 410, and JA to James Warren, Jan. 9, 1787, *Warren-Adams Letters*, II, 280–281. See also JA to Benjamin Hichborn, Jan. 27, 1787, *Works*, IX, 551.
164. Haraszti, *Adams*, pp. 82–91.
165. JA to Robert J. Evans, June 8, 1819, *Works*, X, 379–380. See also AA to JA, Sept. 22, 1774, *AFP*, I, 161.
166. JA to AA, July 9, 1774, *AFP*, I, 135.
167. JA to Rev. Henry Colman, Jan. 13, 1817, *AP* reel 123.
168. See John R. Howe, Jr., "John Adams's Views on Slavery," *Journal of Negro History*, XLIX (1962), 201–205.
169. JA to AA, May 17, 1776, *AFP*, I, 411.
170. AA to Mercy Otis Warren [Jan.?, 1776], *AFP*, I, 422.
171. JA to Samuel H. Parsons, Aug. 19, 1776, *Works*, IX, 432.
172. *Diary*, May 3, 1785, *AP*, III, 176.
173. JA to James Warren, June 17, 1782, *Works*, IX, 511–513. See also JA to AA, Oct. 29, 1775, Aug. 4, 1776, *AFP*, I, 318, 319; II, 76.
174. JA to John Winthrop, June 23, 1776; to James Warren, April 27, 1777, *Works*, IX, 409, 463; JA to John M. Jackson, Dec. 30, 1817, *ibid.*, X, 269 See also *ibid.*, II, 488–489.

175. *Diary,* Nov. 11, 18, 1782, *AP,* III, 52, 61; Cobenzl to Kaunitz, July 29, 1783, Staatskanzlei, Diplomatische Korrespondenz, Russland 39: 0015–0017, Haus-, Hof-, and Staatsarchiv, Vienna.

176. JA to AA, March 17, 1797, *Letters of John Adams to His Wife* (2 vols., Boston, 1841), II, 251–252.

177. See R. B. Morris, *Great Presidential Decisions* (New York, 1960), pp. 49–55. R. B. Morris, in *Hearings Before the Committee on Foreign Relations,* U.S. Senate, 92nd Cong., 1st Sess., pp. 75, 85.

178. JA to Samuel Chase, July 1, 1776, *Works,* IX, 416.

179. JA to John Quincy Adams, April 18, 1776, *AFP,* I, 388.

IV. THOMAS JEFFERSON: THE INTELLECTUAL
AS REVOLUTIONARY

1. TJ to François Jean, Chevalier de Chastellux, Nov. 26, 1782, in Julian P. Boyd, ed., *The Papers of Thomas Jefferson* (18 vols., Princeton, 1952–   ), VI, 203 (hereafter cited as *TJP*).

2. *Autobiography of Thomas Jefferson,* in Andrew A. Lipscomb and Albert Ellery Bergh, eds., *The Writings of Thomas Jefferson* (20 vols., Washington, D.C., 1907), I, 2.

3. TJ to Thomas Adams, Feb. 20, 1781, *TJP,* I, 62.

4. TJ to Governor James Monroe, Jan. 13, 1803, in H. A. Washington, ed., *The Writings of Thomas Jefferson* (9 vols., Philadelphia, 1853–55), IV, 455. For TJ's removal of the Federalist elite, see Carl E. Prince, "The Passing of the Aristocracy," *Journal of American History,* LVII (Dec., 1970), 563–595.

5. Lipscomb and Bergh, eds., *Writings,* I, 426. *The Anas,* April 13, 1798.

6. See TJ to George Clinton, May 17, 1801, in Paul Leicester Ford, ed., *The Writings of Thomas Jefferson* (10 vols., New York, 1892–98), VIII, 52–53, where TJ questions some of Clinton's appointments, and TJ to the Secretary of State (James Madison), July 31, 1803, in Ford, ed., *Writings,* VIII, 260, where Jefferson suggests Thomas Sumter of South Carolina for the post of governor of Louisiana because, among other things, of his "standing in society."

7. In his old age Jefferson made reference to the "near relationship of blood" of certain girls, "for by ascending to my great grandfather and to their great great grandfather, we come to a common ancestor"—second cousins twice removed. TJ to Mrs. Joseph Coolidge, June 5, 1826, Ford, ed., *Writings,* X, 390.

8. See C. Ray Keim, "Primogeniture and Entail in Colonial Virginia," *William and Mary Quarterly,* 3d ser., XXV (Oct., 1968), 545–586.

9. Dumas Malone, *Jefferson the Virginian* (Boston, 1948), pp. 31–32.

10. Bernard Mayo, ed., *Thomas Jefferson and His Unknown Brother Randolph* (Charlottesville, Va., 1942).

11. See Richard B. Morris, *Studies in the History of American Law* (New York, 1930), ch. 2, and *TJP*, II, 391.

12. TJ to John Harvie, Jan. 14, 1760, *TJP*, I, 3.

13. On Jefferson's competitive urges, see John Dos Passos, in Merrill D. Peterson, ed., *Thomas Jefferson: A Profile* (New York, 1967), p. 79; on the search for a father figure, Carl Binger, *Thomas Jefferson: A Well Tempered Mind* (New York, 1970), pp. 20, 68, 157.

14. Merrill D. Peterson, *Thomas Jefferson and the New Nation* (New York, 1970), p. 1006.

15. TJ to William Fleming, March 20, 1764, *TJP*, I, 15–17.

16. TJ to Martha Jefferson, March 28, 1787, *ibid.*, XI, 250–251.

17. TJ to John Page, Feb. 21, 1770, *ibid.*, I, 34–35; TJ to James Ogilvie, Feb. 20, 1771, *ibid.*, pp. 62–63; TJ to Robert Skipwith, Aug. 3, 1771, *ibid.*, pp. 76–80; Thomas Nelson, Sr., to TJ, March 6, 1770, *ibid.*, p. 37; Thomas Nelson, Jr., to TJ, March 6, 1770, *ibid.*, p. 37. For the contents of the library with its enormous range of subjects, see Millicent Sowerby, *Catalogue of the Library of Thomas Jefferson* (5 vols., Washington, D.C., 1959). After the sale, TJ acquired another library, which, though bequeathed to the University of Virginia, was dispersed at an auction sale owing to the insolvency of his estate. See Frederick R. Goff, "Jefferson the Book Collector," *Quarterly Journal of the Library of Congress*, XXIX (Jan., 1972), 32–57.

18. See TJ to John Walker, Sept. 3, 1769, *TJP*, I, 32. For the acquisition of a library to serve as "the scene of every evening's joy," see TJ to Robert Skipwith, Aug. 3, 1771, *ibid.*, pp. 76–80.

19. See William Peden, ed., Thomas Jefferson, *Notes on the State of Virginia* (Chapel Hill, N.C., 1954), pp. 97–100, and C. W. Ceram, *The First American* (New York, 1971), pp. 3–10.

20. TJ to Martha Jefferson, May 21, 1787, *TJP*, XI, 370.

21. Agreement with John Randolph, Oct. [i.e., April?] 11, 1771, and John Randolph to TJ, Aug. 31, 1775, *ibid.*, I, 66–67, 244.

22. TJ to Thomas Adams, June 1, 1771, *ibid.*, pp. 71–72.

23. TJ to Giovanni Fabbroni, June 8, 1778, *ibid.*, II, 196.

24. See James A. Bear, ed., *Jefferson at Monticello* (Charlottesville, 1967); Frederick D. Nichols, *Thomas Jefferson's Architectural Drawings* (Boston, 1960).

25. TJ to John Page, Dec. 25, 1762, *TJP*, I, 3.

26. See Gilbert Chinard, *The Commonplace Book of Thomas Jefferson* (Baltimore, 1926).

27. TJ to George Wythe, March 1, 1779, *TJP*, II, 235.

28. *Virginia Reports of the Supreme Court of Appeals—Jefferson* (1730–40, 1768–72).

29. For notice concerning legal fees (May 20, 1773), *TJP*, I, 98–99. On TJ's difficulty in collecting fees, see Malone, *Jefferson*, I, 122–123.

30. Joseph Henry Smith, *Appeals to the Privy Council from the American Plantations* (New York, 1950), pp. 607–626.

31. Emory G. Evans, "Planter Indebtedness and the Coming of the Revolution in Virginia," *William and Mary Quarterly*, 3d ser., XIX (Oct., 1962), 511–533; Richard B. Morris, *John Jay, the Nation, and the Court* (Boston, 1967).

32. For changing political alignments, see Thomas P. Abernethy, *Western Lands and the American Revolution* (New York, 1937), ch. XI. For the Robinson scandal, see David J. Mays, *Edmund Pendleton, 1721–1803* (2 vols., Cambridge, Mass., 1952), I, ch. XI.

33. Lipscomb and Bergh, eds., *Writings*, I, 5, and William Wirt, *Sketches of the Life and Character of Patrick Henry* (Philadelphia, 1818), p. 41.

34. Bernard Bailyn, *Origin of American Politics* (New York, 1968), pp. 96, 97.

35. Resolutions for an Answer to Governor Botetourt's Speech [May 8, 1769], *TJP*, I, 26–27.

36. Virginia Nonimportation Resolution, 1769. For Jefferson's signature to this agreement and the 1770 agreement as well, see *TJP*, I, 30, 46.

37. Resolution of the House of Burgesses Designating a Day of Fasting and Prayer, May 14, 1774, *ibid.*, pp. 105–107. For TJ's distortion of history, see H. Trevor Colburn, "Thomas Jefferson's Uses of the Past," *William and Mary Quarterly*, 3d ser., XV (1958), 60–65.

38. Association of Members of the Late House of Burgesses, May 22, 1774, *TJP*, I, 107–109.

39. Proceedings of a Meeting of Representatives in Williamsburg, May 30, 1774, *ibid.*, pp. 109–111.

40. Edmund Randolph, quoted *ibid.*, p. 671.

41. *Ibid.*, p. 143. The restriction Jefferson claimed to have been in the original draft does not appear in the final instructions.

42. *Ibid.*, pp. 117–137 and 669–676.

43. TJ to Archibald Cary and Benjamin Harrison, Dec. 9, 1774, *ibid.*, pp. 154–156.

44. TJ to William Small, May 7, 1775, *ibid.*, pp. 165–166.

45. TJ to James Madison, Dec. 16, 1786, *ibid.*, X, 604; see TJ to James Madison, Feb. 20, 1784, *ibid.*, VI, 549, regarding "six sentences of offensive bagatelles," in Chastellux's *Voyage de Newport à Philadelphie, Albany, etc.* (Newport, 1781), which he recommended to be expunged; see also Bernard Bailyn, "Boyd's Jefferson: Notes for a Sketch," *New England Quarterly*, XXXIII (Sept., 1960), 386–387; Winthrop Jordan, *White Over Black* (Chapel Hill, N.C., 1968), pp. 462–464.

46. TJ to Walker Maury, Aug. 19, 1785, and TJ to John Banister, Jr., Oct. 15, 1785, *TJP*, VIII, 409, 636.

47. TJ to John Page, Dec. 25, 1762, and Jan. 20, 1763, *ibid.*, I, 3–9.

48. TJ to John Page, Oct. 7, 1763, *ibid.*, pp. 11–12.

49. TJ to John Page, Jan. 19, 1764, and TJ to William Flemming, March 20, 1764, *ibid.*, pp. 13–14, 15–17.

50. TJ to Robert Smith, July 1, 1805, in *Thomas Jefferson Correspondence Printed From the Originals in the Collections of William K. Bixby* (Bos-

ton, 1916), p. 115. For this affair, see the analysis in Malone, *Jefferson the Virginian*, 153–155, 447–451, and Dumas Malone, *Jefferson the President* (Boston, 1970), 216–223.

51. Translation in John Dos Passos, *The Head and Heart of Thomas Jefferson* (New York, 1954), p. 249. See also Sarah N. Randolph, *The Domestic Life of Thomas Jefferson* (New York, 1958), pp. 63–64.

52. TJ to James Monroe, April 17, 1791, Ford, ed., *Writings*, V, 318.

53. TJ to Edward Rutledge, Dec. 27, 1796, Washington, ed., *Writings*, IV, 152.

54. Peterson, *Jefferson and the New Nation*, p. 385.

55. TJ to Governor Page, June 25, 1804, in Henry S. Randall, *The Life of Thomas Jefferson* (3 vols., Philadelphia, 1871), III, 103.

56. TJ to Mrs. William Bingham, May 11, 1788, *TJP*, XIII, 151–152.

57. See Helen Duprey Bullock, *My Head and My Heart* (New York, 1945).

58. Memoir of Madison Hemings in *Pike County Republican*, March 13, 1873. The births of each of the six other children of Sally Hemings were as follows: *Harriet (1)*, Oct. 5, 1795, Pearl Graham, "Thomas Jefferson and Sally Hemings," *Journal of Negro History*, XLIV (1961), 89–103. She died shortly thereafter (*loc. cit.*, p. 52). *Edy* (1796), died in 1797. *Beverly*, April 1, 1798. *Harriet (2)*, May, 1801. *Madison*, Jan. 19, 1805. *Eston*, May 21, 1808. Edwin M. Betts, *Thomas Jefferson's Farm Book* (Princeton, 1953), pp. 31, 50–51, 57, 128. For Jefferson's presence at Monticello nine months before each of these births, see Lipscomb and Bergh, eds., *Writings*, ix–x, 293 (Dec. 28, 1794); Dumas Malone, *Jefferson and the Ordeal of Liberty* (Boston, 1962), pp. xxiii–xxiv; Ford, ed., *Writings*, VIII, 320–321 (July 24, 1797), 14, 137 (July, Aug., 1804); Lipscomb and Bergh, eds., *Writings*, XI, 21 (April 16, 1804); XI, 336–348, *passim* (Aug., 1807). See also Jordan, *White Over Black*, p. 466.

59. *Pike County Republican*, March 13, 1873.

60. Ellen Randolph to Joseph Coolidge, Oct. 24, 1858, quoted in Malone, *Jefferson the President*, p. 498. These charges are dealt with in detail in Malone, *ibid.*, 212–216, and appendix II, "The Miscegenation Legend," 494–498; Merrill Peterson, *The Jeffersonian Image in the American Mind* (New York, 1960), pp. 181–187; Jordan, *White Over Black*, pp. 461–469. But see *contra* Fawn M. Brodie, "The Great Jefferson Taboo," *American Heritage* (June, 1972), pp. 50, 98, where the point is made, on the basis of family letters at the University of Virginia, that Peter and Samuel Carr were elsewhere during most of the years that Sally Hemings was bearing children at Monticello.

61. Peden, ed., *Notes on State of Virginia*, pp. 138–139, 288n.

62. TJ to Mrs. William Bingham, May 11, 1788, Ford, ed., *Writings*, V, 9.

63. See TJ to Martha Jefferson, Nov. 28, 1783, and TJ to Nathaniel Burwell, March 14, 1818, *TJP*, VI, 359–361, and Ford, ed., *Writings*, X, 104–106.

64. TJ to the Secretary of the Treasury (Albert Gallatin), Jan. 13, 1807, Ford, ed., *Writings*, IX, 7.

65. William Livingston to William Alexander (Lord Stirling), July 4, 1775,

Worthington C. Ford, et al., eds., *Journals of the Continental Congress, 1774–1789* (34 vols., Washington, 1904–37), II, 128.

66. See Julian P. Boyd, "The Disputed Authorship of the Causes and Necessity of Taking Up Arms, 1775," *Pennsylvania Magazine of History and Biography*, LXXIV (1950), 51–73, and *TJP*, I, 187–192.

67. *TJP*, I, 225–230.

68. TJ to John Randolph, Aug. 25, 1775, *ibid.*, p. 241.

69. TJ to Frances Eppes, Nov. 7, 1775, *ibid.*, p. 252.

70. TJ to John Randolph, Nov. 29, 1775, *ibid.*, pp. 268–270.

71. Refutation of the Argument that the Colonies were Established at the Expense of the British Nation (after Jan. 19, 1776), *ibid.*, pp. 277–285.

72. See James McClung to TJ, April 6, 1776, and John Page to TJ, April 6, 1776, *ibid.*, pp. 286–287.

73. John Page to TJ, April 26, 1776, *ibid.*, pp. 288–290.

74. *Ibid.*, pp. 290–291, 298.

75. *Ibid.*, pp. 299–308.

76. *Ibid.*, pp. 299–308. John Hazelton, *The Declaration of Independence* (New York, 1906).

77. Hazelton, *Declaration*, p. 120. Lyman H. Butterfield, et al., eds., *Diary and Autobiography of John Adams* (4 vols., Cambridge, Mass., 1961), III, 335.

78. Carl L. Becker, *The Declaration of Independence* (New York, 1940), ch. V.

79. Franklin attributed the phrase to one of the regicides. See Malone, *Jefferson the Virginian*, pp. 226, 242. See also TJ to Edward Everett, Feb. 24, 1823, Lipscomb and Bergh, eds., *Writings*, XV, 415.

80. TJ to James Madison, Jan. 30, 1787, and TJ to William Stephens Smith, Nov. 13, 1787, *TJP*, XI, 93, and XII, 356.

81. Bennett M. Rich, *The Presidents and Civil Disorder* (Washington, 1941), p. 5.

82. James M. Smith, *Freedom's Fetters* (Ithaca, N.Y., 1956), pp. 297–300.

83. TJ to L. Lomax, March 12, 1799, Washington, ed., *Writings*, IV, 300–301.

84. A. B. Hart, ed., *The Virginia and Kentucky Resolves, with the Alien, Sedition and Other Acts, 1798–1799* (New York, 1894).

85. See *TJP*, XV, 391, 392.

86. See note to the debt to Farrell and Jones in *ibid.*, pp. 642–677.

87. *Ibid.*, II, 168–171.

88. TJ to John Jay, April 11, 1783, *ibid.*, VI, 260–261.

89. TJ to James Madison, Sept. 6, 1789, *ibid.*, XV, 392–397, and cf. A Bill for Establishing Religious Freedom, *ibid.*, II, 546.

90. TJ to John Adams, Oct. 28, 1813, Lipscomb and Bergh, eds., *Writings*, XIII, 399.

91. For his views on the Order of the Cincinnati, see TJ to George Washington, Nov. 14, 1786, *TJP*, X, 531–533.

92. TJ to Edward Carrington, Jan. 16, 1787, *ibid.*, XI, 49.

93. John Adams, *A Defense of the Constitutions of the Government of the United States of America* (Philadelphia, 1787).

94. TJ to Joseph Milligan, April 6, 1816, Lipscomb and Bergh, eds., *Writings*, XIV, 466.

95. TJ to John Adams, Sept. 4, 1823, *ibid.*, XV, 465.

96. TJ to John Adams, Sept. 12, 1821, *ibid.*, p. 334.

97. TJ to Roger Weightman, June 24, 1826, Ford, ed., *Writings*, X, 391.

98. On the moral element in republicanism, see Gordon Wood, *The Creation of the American Republic* (Chapel Hill, N.C., 1969), pp. 91–124.

99. TJ to Benjamin Franklin, Aug. 13, 1777, *TJP*, II, 26.

100. Similarly rejected was TJ's draft proposal making county or borough representation proportional to the numbers of qualified voters, a necessary consequence of his egalitarian views, again a half-century ahead of his time. See J. R. Pole, *Political Representation in England and the Origins of the American Republic* (New York, 1966), pp. 286–289. Edmund Pendleton to TJ, Aug. 10, 1776, TJ to Pendleton, Aug. 26, 1776, *TJP*, I, 488–491, 503–506, and 344, 352, 362.

101. TJ to Edmund Pendleton, Aug. 26, 1776, *TJP*, I, 503.

102. Hart, *Virginia and Kentucky Resolves*.

103. For a comparison of TJ with Blackstone as regards the suffrage, see Daniel Boorstin, *The Mysterious Science of the Law* (Cambridge, Mass., 1941), p. 160, and Boorstin, *The Lost World of Thomas Jefferson* (New York, 1948), pp. 190–191.

104. TJ to Roger Weightman, June 24, 1826, Ford, ed., *Writings*, X, 391–392.

105. Jefferson originally wrote "inalienable," meaning not transferrable to another by law; but it was changed to "unalienable," or unalterable.

106. See note in Robert A. Rutland, ed., *The Papers of George Mason, 1729–1792* (3 vols., Chapel Hill, N.C., 1970), I, 274–276, 279–282, 291; Irving Brant, *James Madison* (6 vols., New York, 1941), I, 244–250.

107. *Mason Papers*, I, 289.

108. See *TJP*, I, 329–386.

109. *Ibid.*, IX, 195.

110. See Leonard Levy, *Jefferson and Civil Liberties: The Darker Side* (Cambridge, 1963).

111. William Hening, ed., *The Statutes at Large; Being a Collection of all the laws of Virginia from the First Session of the Legislature in the year 1619* (13 vols., Richmond, Va., 1819–1823), X, 264–270 (1780), and *TJP*, III, 493.

112. TJ to James Innes, May 2, 1781, *TJP*, V, 593.

113. Peden, ed., *Notes on Virginia*, p. 155.

114. Hening, ed., *Statutes*, IX, 549; X, 22–23; *TJP*, II, 219, 222, 590.

115. *TJP*, II, 189–191. This bill clearly would have violated the original article in Mason's Declaration of Rights banning ex post facto legislation, but the article had been dropped under pressure from Patrick Henry. *Mason Papers*, I, 290.

116. TJ to L. H. Girardin, March 12, 1815, Lipscomb and Bergh, eds., *Writings*, XIV, 271–278; TJ to William Wirt, May 12, 1815, Ford, ed., *Writings*, IX, 472.

117. TJ to Thomas Sim Lee, Feb. 11, 1781, *TJP*, IV, 494.

118. TJ to William Preston, March 21, 1780, *ibid.*, III, 325.

119. On Jefferson's conduct toward Burr see Richard B. Morris, *Fair Trial* (New York, 1952), pp. 119–155; Thomas P. Abernethy, *The Burr Conspiracy* (New York, 1954).

120. *TJP*, III, 25, 26, 30–31, 40–41, 44–45, 61, 97, 98, 103 (July 5–Oct. 8, 1779).

121. TJ to James Brown, Oct. 27, 1808, Lipscomb and Bergh, eds., *Writings*, XII, 183.

122. Levy, *Jefferson and Civil Liberties*, p. 44.

123. *TJP*, VI, 304.

124. *Ibid.*, XV, 367.

125. Julian P. Boyd, *The Declaration of Independence: The Evolution of the Text* (Princeton, 1945), pp. 19, 29.

126. For TJ's view that the alterations had weakened the force of the original statement, see *TJP*, I, 423, 429.

127. See Peden, ed., *Notes on Virginia*, pp. 100–102; Boorstin, *Lost World*, pp. 75, 78.

128. See TJ to John Adams, June 11, 1812, in Lester J. Cappon, ed., *The Adams-Jefferson Letters* (2 vols., Chapel Hill, N.C., 1959), II, 307.

129. See Jordan, *White Over Black*, pp. 480–481.

130. See Peden, ed., *Notes on Virginia*, pp. 138–143. On Jefferson's correspondence with the Negro scientist Benjamin Banneker, see TJ to Banneker, Aug. 30, 1791, Ford, ed., *Writings*, V, 377–378. TJ's views on the Negro are analyzed in Matthew T. Mellon, *Early American Views on Negro Slavery* (new ed., New York, 1969), pp. 85–123; Jordan, *White Over Black*, pp. 429–481.

131. Hazelton, *Declaration of Independence*, p. 171.

132. Peterson, *Jefferson and the New Nation*, p. 44.

133. *TJP* [June 16, 1777], II, 22–23.

134. *Ibid.*, pp. 470–473.

135. Peterson, *Jefferson and the New Nation*, p. 283, and Ford, ed., *Writings*, IV, 181. For the role of others than Jefferson in the shaping of the Ordinance, see Robert F. Berkhofer, Jr., "Jefferson, the Ordinance of 1784, and the Origin of the American Territorial System," *William and Mary Quarterly*, XXIX (1972), 230–262.

136. James D. Richardson, ed., *A Compilation of the Messages and Papers of the Presidents* (11 vols., Washington, D.C., 1907), I, 396. See also Richard B. Morris, introduction to Matthew T. Mellon, *Early American Views on Negro Slavery* (New York, 1969), p. viii; Oliver Jensen, ed., *America and Russia* (New York, 1962), pp. 280–283; W. W. Freehling, "The Founding Fathers and Slavery," *American Historical Review*, LXXVII (Feb. 1972), 81–93.

137. See Jordan, *White Over Black*, pp. 375–386; Carl L. Lokke, "Jefferson and the Leclerc Expedition," *American Historical Review*, XXXIII (1927–28), 322–328.
138. Peden, ed., *Notes on Virginia*, p. 163.
139. TJ to Edward Coles, Aug. 25, 1814, Ford, ed., *Writings*, IX, 479.
140. Quoted in Peterson, *Jefferson and the New Nation*, p. 1001.
141. Madison to TJ, March 27, 1780, *TJP*, III, 335.
142. See, e.g., TJ to William Preston, June 15, 1780, *ibid.*, pp. 447–449.
143. TJ to Edmund Randolph, Sept. 16, 1781, and Edmund Randolph to TJ, Oct. 9, 1781, *ibid.*, VI, 118 and 128.
144. TJ to James Madison, Sept. 8, 1793, Ford, ed., *Writings*, VI, 419.

V. JOHN JAY AND
THE RADICAL CHIC ELITE

1. JJ to Robert Randall, Feb. 2 and 3, 1773, Jay Papers, Special Collections, Columbia University Libraries (hereinafter cited as SC, CUL).
2. Manuscript list of Members of the Dancing Assembly, by John Moore, copied in 1857 by Thomas W. C. Moore, New York Historical Society. See also James Grant Wilson, *The Memorial History of the City of New York* (4 vols., New York, 1892–93), II, 474, 475.
3. JJ's manuscript account of his ancestry has disappeared, but his son William Jay quoted from it. *The Life of John Jay* (2 vols., New York, 1833), I, 2–9.
4. JJ to Robert Goodloe Harper, Jan. 19, 1796, in Henry P. Johnston, ed., *The Correspondence and Public Papers of John Jay* (4 vols., New York, 1893), IV, 199–200.
5. See Richard B. Morris, *The Peacemakers: The Great Powers and American Independence* (New York, 1965), pp. 297–298.
6. Peter Jay to James Jay, July 3, 1752, Peter Jay Letterbook III, SC, CUL.
7. Peter Jay to David and John Peloquin, Oct. 24, 1753, in Peter Jay Letterbook III, SC, CUL.
8. Samuel Johnson to Peter Jay, Dec. 29, 1739, in SC, CUL.
9. Peter Jay to David Peloquin, April 14, 1763, in Peter Jay Letterbook III, SC, CUL.
10. Statutes of King's College, n.d. [March 2, 1763], SC, CUL.
11. New York *Mercury*, May 28, 1764.
12. *Ibid.*, June 1, 1767.
13. Thomas Jones, *History of New York During the Revolutionary War*, ed. by E. F. DeLancey (2 vols., New York, 1879), II, 224–225, 475–480; Sir James Jay, *A Letter to the Governors of the College of New York . . .* (London, 1771) and *A Letter to the Universities of Oxford and Cambridge . . .* (London, 1774).
14. JJ to Robert R. Livingston, Jr., Jan. 1, 1775, American Art Association

Collection, copy; also Livingston Letters (transcripts), I, 21–25, Bancroft Collection, New York Public Library.

15. Peter Jay to John Jay, April 15, 1765, Jay Papers, SC, CUL.

16. Peter Jay to John Jay, April 18, 1776: "I have discharged Jemmy's bond to the College and it is delivered up to me." *Ibid.*, SC, CUL.

17. Frederick Jay to John Jay, March 6, 1776, *ibid.*, SC, CUL.

18. Frank Monaghan, *John Jay* (New York, 1935), pp. 89–90.

19. *New York Senate Journal*, March 1, 1779; Richard Henry Lee to Henry Laurens, May 27, 1779, in Edmund C. Burnett, ed., *Letters of Members of the Continental Congress* (8 vols., Washington, D.C., 1928–36), IV, 237.

20. Jones, *History*, II, 225, 226, 524–538.

21. JJ to George Clinton, May 6, 1780, Jay Papers, SC, CUL.

22. See William Jay, *Life*, I, 113.

23. JJ to Frederick Jay, March 15, 1781, Jay Papers, SC, CUL.

24. Frederick Jay to JJ, Nov. 8, 1781, *ibid.*, SC, CUL; Gouverneur Morris to John Jay, June 17, 1781, *ibid.*, SC, CUL.

25. W. H. W. Sabine, ed., *Historical Memoirs of William Smith* (3 vols., New York, 1971), III, March 11, April 15, May 6–10, 11–13, 1782, pp. 458, 495, 503–506; New York *Royal Gazette*, April 17, 1782.

26. JJ to Peter Van Schaack, Sept. 17, 1782, Jay Papers, SC, CUL.

27. James Jay to Earl of Shelburne, June ?, 1782, Shelburne Papers, William L. Clements Library, University of Michigan.

28. Shelburne to Thomas Townshend, n.d., Additional Sydney Papers, III, 7, William L. Clements Library, University of Michigan.

29. Correspondance Politique, Etats-Unis, 24:222, 224, 229, 415, 416; 25:329–330, 332 (May 20–Sept. 28, 1783), Ministère des Affaires Etrangères, Paris.

30. Sarah Livingston Jay to William Livingston, June 24, 1781, Jay Papers, SC, CUL.

31. See Morris, *Peacemakers*, pp. 4 et seq.

32. Sarah Livingston Jay to William Livingston, June 24, 1781. For Carmichael's relations with dubious characters, see Morris, *Peacemakers*, p. 236, n. 58.

33. William Carmichael to Robert R. Livingston, Jr., Aug. 30, 1783, Carmichael Papers, Library of Congress.

34. James Madison to Thomas Jefferson, May 6, 1783, *The Papers of James Madison*, ed. by W. T. Hutchinson and W. M. E. Rachal (7 vols., Chicago, 1962–), VII, 18.

35. JJ, notation on Carmichael correspondence, n.d. [after Feb. 9, 1795], Jay Papers, SC, CUL. Carmichael's earlier role in Paris was tainted with suspicion of espionage, and he was reputedly sent back to America by Franklin and Deane. Paul Wentworth to William Eden, Jan. 6, 1778, Auckland Papers, BM Add. MSS. 34, 415, f. 18. See also Samuel Flagg Bemis, "The British Secret Service and the French-American Alliance," *Ameri-*

can Historical Review, XXIX (April, 1924), 471; he charges that Car-michael "went to the verge, if not over the edge of treason."

36. The John Jay–Littlepage correspondence is in Jay Papers, SC, CUL.

37. See JJ's lengthy pamphlet *Letters, Being the Whole of the Correspondence between the Hon. John Jay, Esquire, and Mr. Lewis Littlepage* (New York, 1786); Curtis C. Davis, *The King's Chevalier: A Biography of Lewis Littlepage* (Indianapolis, Ind., 1961), pp. 32–126.

38. Minutes of the Supreme Court of Judicature, 1766–69, p. 566; Roll of Attorneys, 1754–1847, Ledger J, Parchment Roll 1, New York County Clerk's Office.

39. Accounts of JJ with agents of New York and New Jersey, July 26–Dec. n.d., 1769, and c. Jan. 1770, Jay Papers, Box 6, Boundary Papers I, New York Historical Society.

40. JJ to Benjamin Kissam, Aug. 12, 1766, in William Jay, *Life,* I, 17–19.

41. Benjamin Kissam to John Jay, Aug. 25, 1766, Jay Papers, SC, CUL; also in William Jay, *Life,* I, 19–21.

42. Benjamin Kissam to John Jay, Nov. 6, 1769, Jay Papers, SC, CUL; also in William Jay, *Life,* I, 21–23, and Johnston, ed., *Jay,* I, 9–10.

43. See Catharine Crary, "The American Dream: John Tabor Kempe's Rise from Poverty to Riches," *William and Mary Quarterly,* XIV (1957), 176–195.

44. See Chancery Minutes, IV, 46, 64, 69, New York County Clerk's Office.

45. JJ to John Tabor Kempe, Dec. 27, 1771; Jan. 2, 1772; John Tabor Kempe to John Jay, Dec. 27, 1771, Sedgwick Papers, Massachusetts Historical Society.

46. New York Colonial MSS., Land Papers, XXV, 69, New York State Library.

47. JJ to Dartmouth, March 25, 1773, CO5/1103/440; CO5/1104/260–263, Public Record Office.

48. Sabine, *Smith Memoirs,* I, 137.

49. JJ to Egbert Benson, Aug. 26, 1782, Jay Papers, SC, CUL.

50. Sabine, *Smith Memoirs,* I, 51. For Jay's observation that the judges were picked from "among the farmers," see Jay to Reverend John Vardill, May 23, 1774, AO13/105/283, Public Record Office.

51. Sabine, *Smith Memoirs,* I, 129, 132.

52. JJ to John Vardill, May 23, 1774, *supra;* John Jay to John Vardill, Sept. 24, 1774, AO13/105/5022, Public Record Office.

53. Memorial of John Vardill to Loyalist Commission, Nov. 16, 1783, AO13/105/321, Public Record Office.

54. JJ to Egbert Benson, Dec. 15–16–18, 1783, Jay Papers, SC, CUL.

55. Peter Jay to David Peloquin, May 7, 1765, Peter Jay Letterbook III, Jay Papers, SC, CUL.

56. JJ's practice covered the Supreme Court, Chancery, the New York City Mayor's Court, and the inferior courts in Queens, Westchester, Dutchess, Ulster, and Orange counties.

57. John Tabor Kempe to John Jay, April 5, 1773, and John Jay to John

Tabor Kempe, April 22, 1773, Kempe Papers, New York Historical Society. See Minutes, Supreme Court of Judicature, 1772–76, pp. 101, 131, 153.

58. See also Jared Sparks, *The Life of Gouverneur Morris* (3 vols., New York, 1832), I, 20; Henry B. Dawson, *Westchester-County, New York, During the American Revolution* (New York, 1886), p. 4.

59. Jones, *History*, II, 223.

60. JJ to James De Lancey, Jan. 2, 1778; James De Lancey to John Jay, Jan. 14, 1778, Jay Papers, SC, CUL.

61. Sarah Livingston Jay to Susannah French Livingston, Aug. 28, 1782, *ibid.*, SC, CUL.

62. Sarah Livingston Jay to Susannah French Livingston, Aug. 28, 1780; to Susannah Livingston Symmes, Aug. 28, 1780; to Mary White Morris, Sept. 1, 1780, all in *ibid.*, SC, CUL.

63. JJ to Sarah Livingston Jay, March 31, 1776, *ibid.*, SC, CUL.

64. Monaghan, *Jay*, p. 88.

65. See Samuel Flagg Bemis, ed., *The American Secretaries of State and Their Diplomacy* (10 vols., New York, 1927–29), I, 240–241.

66. Peter Force, *American Archives*, 4th ser., I, 250, 251.

67. Originally Fifty, the Committee became Fifty-One when Francis Lewis was added with unanimous consent. *Ibid.*, p. 295.

68. The committee to draft the letter comprised Alexander McDougall, the firebrand, Isaac Low and James Duane, conservatives, plus Jay. Both Johnston, ed., *Jay*, I, 13–15, and Carl Becker, *The History of Political Parties in the Province of New York, 1760–1776* (Madison, Wis., 1909), p. 119n., attribute the letter to Jay, but in fact the final draft was written by Duane. McDougall Papers, New York Historical Society.

69. JJ to Vardill, May 23, 1774, cited *supra*.

70. Cadwallader Colden to the Earl of Dartmouth, July 6, 1774, Colden *Letter Book*, II, 346, New York Historical Society. Those eligible to vote for the congressional delegates were described as "not only the freeholders and freemen, but also persons who pay taxes." Force, *American Archives*, I, 318.

71. JJ to John Morin Scott, [July 20] 1774, Bancroft–Samuel Adams Papers II, 505 (copy), New York Public Library.

72. L. H. Butterfield, ed., *Diary and Autobiography of John Adams* (Cambridge, Mass., 1961), II, 124, 126, 128, 139.

73. *Ibid.*, pp. 385, 386.

74. *Ibid.*, p. 151.

75. Worthington C. Ford, et al., eds., *Journals of the Continental Congress, 1774–1789* (34 vols., Washington, D.C., 1904–1937), I, 25; for the debate of Sept. 6, 1774, on unit rule, see Burnett, *Letters*, I, 12–15, for Adams's and James Duane's notes of proceedings.

76. The Suffolk Resolves were passed unanimously, *JCC*, I, 39–40.

77. Joseph Galloway, *A Candid Examination of the Mutual Claims of Great-Britain, and the Colonies* (London, 1780).

78. *JCC*, I, 80.

79. Thomas Jefferson to William Wirt, Aug. 4, [1805], in Burnett, *Letters,*
I, 79.

80. Johnston, *Jay,* I, 17–31; *JCC,* I, 82–90.

81. William Laight to John Vardill, March 27, 1775, AO 13/105, Public
Record Office.

82. William Laight to John Jay, Oct. 3, 1775, Museum of the City of New
York.

83. Force, *American Archives,* 4th ser., I, 330.

84. William Laight to John Vardill, March 27, 1775, *supra.*

85. JJ's draft letter, April 17, 1775, Jay Papers, SC, CUL.

86. Extract from the Committee's Proceedings, *Broadsides,* I (cited by
Becker, *Political Parties,* p. 186n.).

87. JJ to Alexander McDougall, April 11, 1776, Jay Papers, SC, CUL.

88. "Letter to the Oppressed Inhabitants of Canada," Johnston, *Jay,* I, 32–36.

89. *JCC*, II, 52.

90. JJ's draft is in the Dickinson Papers, Library Company of Philadelphia,
now on deposit with the Historical Society of Pennsylvania. See also
The Olive Branch Petition of the American Congress to George III, 1775
(New York, 1954), original in the New York Public Library (second
copy).

91. JJ to Alexander McDougall, Oct. 17, 1775, McDougall Papers, Box 1,
New York Historical Society.

92. Arthur Lee to BF, Feb. 13, 1776, with enclosure to Lt. Gov. Colden, Feb.
14, 1776, Force, *American Archives,* 4th ser., IV, 1127; JJ to Robert R.
Livingston, Feb. 25, 1776, Jay Papers, SC, CUL. JJ reputedly conducted
secret conversations with Lord Drummond, a Scottish peace emissary,
along with JJ's father-in-law, his friend Livingston, and Thomas Lynch,
Sr., of South Carolina, all moderates. The conversations were aired in
Congress, and the intermediary's efforts failed. The Drummond Plan,
originally in Drummond Castle, Scotland, is in the Scottish Record Office
(microfilm, Rutgers University Library). See Milton M. Klein, "Failure
of a Mission: The Drummond Peace Proposal of 1775," *Huntington Library Quarterly,* XXXV (1972), 343–380.

93. Thomas Jefferson to William Wirt, Aug. 4 [1805], *supra.*

94. Butterfield, ed., *Adams,* II, 204–206, Oct. 12, 1775.

95. Burnett, *Letters,* I, 386, 395.

96. *Ibid.,* I, 303; *JCC,* III, 404.

97. *New Jersey Archives,* 1st ser., X, 691.

98. John Durand, *New Materials for the History of the American Revolution*
(New York, 1889), pp. 2–16.

99. *Journals of the Continental Congress,* III, 463; IV, 25–28.

100. JJ to Alexander McDougall, Dec. 23, 1775, McDougall Papers, Box 1,
New York Historical Society.

101. JJ to Alexander McDougall, March 27, 1776, *ibid.,* Box 1, New York
Historical Society.

102. JJ to Alexander McDougall, April 27, 1776, *ibid.*, Box 1, New York Historical Society.
103. JJ, Commission as Colonel of the Second Regiment of Militia of Foot, Nov. 3, 1775, Jay Papers, SC, CUL.
104. James Duane to JJ, May 11, 1776, Royal Archives, Windsor Castle, England.
105. *Journals of the Provincial Congress*, I, 461.
106. JJ to Robert R. Livingston, May 29, 1776, Jay Papers, SC, CUL.
107. *Journals of the Provincial Congress*, I, 490.
108. James Duane to JJ, May 18, 1776, Jay Papers, SC, CUL.
109. JJ to Gouverneur Morris, April 29, 1778, *ibid.*, SC, CUL.
110. Edward Rutledge to JJ [June 8, 1776], *ibid.*, SC, CUL.
111. Edward Rutledge to JJ, June 29, 1776, *ibid.*, SC, CUL.
112. JJ to Edward Rutledge, July 6, 1776, Johnston, *Jay*, I, 68–70.
113. JJ to George Alexander Otis, Jan. 13, 1821, Jay Papers, SC, CUL.
114. *Journals of the Provincial Congress*, I, 517, 518.
115. JJ to Robert Morris, Oct. 6, 1776, Johnston, *Jay*, I, 85–89.
116. *Journals of the Provincial Congress*, I, 526–527. See "Powers Granted to John Jay by Secret Committee," July 22, 1776, and "John Jay's notes of trip to Connecticut for Secret Committee for Defense of Hudson River, June 22–24, 1776," in Jay Papers, SC, CUL, and John Jay to the Secret Committee for obstructing the Channel of Hudsons River, Aug. 7, 1776, Newburgh Free Public Library, Washington's Headquarters Papers.
117. JJ to Robert Morris, Oct. 6, 1777, *American Book Prices Current*, Jan. 16, 1917.
118. JJ to Alexander McDougall, March 21, 1776, McDougall Papers, New York Historical Society.
119. *Journals of the Provincial Congress*, I, 527.
120. On Thomas Hickey, see *Journals of the Provincial Congress*, I, 495, 496, Force, *American Archives*, 4th ser., VI, 1084–1086, 1118, 1119–1120. On David Matthews, see *ibid.*, p. 1158, *Journals of the Provincial Congress*, I, 530, II, 280.
121. New York *Royal Gazette*, Jan. 23, 1779.
122. JJ to Peter Van Schaack, Sept. 17, 1782, *supra.*
123. James Fenimore Cooper, ed., *Correspondence of James Fenimore-Cooper* (2 vols., New Haven, 1922), I, 42.
124. JJ to Alexander McDougall, March 13, 1776, Union College, Schenectady, New York; Alexander McDougall to John Jay, March 20, 1776, Jay Papers, SC, CUL.
125. JJ to Alexander McDougall, Dec. 4, 1775, McDougall Papers, Box 1, New York Historical Society; John Jay to Alexander McDougall, March 23, 1776, Jay Papers, SC, CUL.
126. Nathaniel H. Carter and William L. Stone, *Reports of the Proceedings and Debates of the Convention of 1821* (Albany, 1821), pp. 691, 692.
127. Edward Rutledge to John Jay, Nov. 24, 1776, Jay Papers, SC, CUL.

128. See Richard B. Morris, *John Jay, the Nation, and the Court* (Boston, 1967), pp. 10–14.
129. See Richard B. Morris in Matthew T. Mellon, *Early American Views on Negro Slavery* (New York, 1969), pp. ix, x.
130. JJ to Leonard Gansevoort, June 5, 1777, Jay Papers, SC, CUL; also in Johnston, *Jay*, I, 140–141.
131. JJ, "A Hint to the Legislature of the State of New York," n.d. [1778], Jay Papers, SC, CUL.
132. JJ, Report on "An Act for raising a further Sum by Tax to be applied towards the Public Exigencies of this State," Nov. 5, 1778, in Library of Congress Microfilm, Records of the States of the U.S.: New York, reel 50.
133. JJ, "Address of the Convention of the Representatives of the State of New York to Their Constituents," Dec. 23, 1776, published in Johnston, *Jay*, I, 102–120.
134. JJ to John Adams, Aug. 2, 1782, Adams Papers, Massachusetts Historical Society; draft in Jay Papers, SC, CUL.

VI. JAMES MADISON: THE REVOLUTIONARY AS A MAN OF CONSCIENCE

1. This is the view of Irving Brant, *Madison* (6 vols., Indianapolis, Ind., 1941–61), I, 105–109.
2. Ralph Ketcham, *James Madison* (New York, 1971), p. 51. See also William Bradford to JM, Oct. 13; JM to Bradford, Nov. 9, 1772, *The Papers of James Madison*, ed. by W. T. Hutchinson and W. M. E. Rachal (7 vols., Chicago, 1962–   ), I, 72–76, 164 (hereinafter *MP*).
3. He was deterred from entering military service by "a constitutional liability to sudden attacks, somewhat resembling Epilepsy." Although he was commissioned a colonel of militia in Virginia's Orange County, Oct. 2, 1775, Madison rarely served with the militia, was not a veteran of the American Revolution, and never claimed to be. Brant, *Madison*, I, 106; *MP*, I, 163, 164.
4. See *MP*, I, xv–xxiv.
5. Gaillard Hunt, ed., *The Writings of James Madison* (9 vols., New York, 1900–10), V, 123, 165, 198, 203, 208, 216, 224.
6. Brant, *Madison*, I, 57 ff.
7. John C. Payne to J. Q. Adams, Aug., 1830, Adams MSS., Massachusetts Historical Society; Brant, *Madison*, I, 60.
8. *An Account of the College* (Woodbridge, N.J., 1764), pp. 25–29.
9. *The Works of John Witherspoon* (4 vols., Philadelphia, 1802), IV, 214–215.
10. V. L. Collins, *President Witherspoon* (2 vols., New York, 1969), I, 217–221.

11. For the argument that JM's MS. "Brief System of Logic" was written while a Princeton undergraduate, see *MP*, I, 32–36.
12. *Ibid.*, p. 41.
13. See Benjamin Rush to James Rush, May 25, 1802, Rush Papers, Library Company of Philadelphia, cited by Ketcham, *Madison*, p. 35n.
14. See *MP*, I, 61–67.
15. Brant, *Madison*, I, 87, 88.
16. William Bradford to JM, Oct. 13, 1772, *MP*, I, 73.
17. JM to William Bradford, Nov. 9, 1772, *ibid.*, p. 75.
18. Philip Freneau to JM, Nov. 22, 1772; William Bradford to JM, May 27; JM to Bradford, June 10, 1773; *ibid.*, pp. 77–79, 86, 89.
19. Bradford to JM, March 4; JM to Bradford, April 1, 1774, *ibid.*, pp. 109–112.
20. Bradford to JM, Aug. 12, 1773; JM to Bradford, Sept. 25, 1773, *ibid.*, pp. 91–97.
21. JM to Bradford, Dec. 1, 1773, *ibid.*, p. 100.
22. JM to Bradford, Dec. 1, 1773, *ibid.*, pp. 101, 102.
23. An account of the event was sent to JM by Bradford from Philadelphia, on Christmas day, 1773, telling of the part Bradford's father played in having the tea turned back. *Ibid.*, pp. 103, 104.
24. JM to Bradford, Jan. 24, 1774, *ibid.*, pp. 104, 105.
25. JM to Bradford, April 1, 1774, *ibid.*, pp. 111–113.
26. JM to Bradford, July 1, 1774, *ibid.*, pp. 114, 115.
27. JM to Bradford, Aug. 23, 1774, *ibid.*, p. 121.
28. [May 9, 1775], *ibid.*, p. 147.
29. [May 9], *ibid.*, p. 147; Patrick Henry to James Madison, Sr., May 11, 1775, *ibid.*, pp. 146–147.
30. "Edmund Randolph's Essay on the Revolutionary History of Virginia, 1774–1782," *Virginia Magazine of History and Biography*, XLIV (1936), 45.
31. Robert A. Rutland, ed., *The Papers of George Mason* (3 vols., Chapel Hill, N.C., 1970), I, 278, 279n.
32. "Randolph's Essay," *loc. cit.*, p. 47.
33. Rutland, ed., *Mason Papers*, I, 289.
34. Julian P. Boyd, ed., *The Papers of Thomas Jefferson* (18 vols., Princeton, 1952–　), I, 345n.
35. David J. Mays, *Edmund Pendleton* (2 vols., Cambridge, Mass., 1952), II, 637–646.
36. Brant, *Madison*, I, 298–300.
37. Boyd, *TJP*, I, 329–386.
38. Brant, *Madison*, II, 322–323.
39. Hunt, ed., *Madison Writings*, II, 89.
40. Thomas Jefferson to JM, Dec. 8, 1784, Boyd, *TJP*, VII, 558.
41. JM to Monroe, Nov. 14, 1784, Thomas Jefferson to JM, Dec. 8, 1784, *ibid.*, VII, 557–560; JM to TJ, Jan. 9, 1785, *ibid.*, VII, 597.

42. JM to Monroe, Nov. 27, Dec. 4, 1784, Madison Papers, Library of Congress.

43. *Journal, Virginia House of Delegates*, Dec. 11, 18, 22, 23, 24, 1784; JM to Thomas Jefferson, Jan. 9, 1785, Boyd, *TJP*, VII, 594–595.

44. Hunt, ed., *Madison Writings*, II, 183–191; Rutland, ed., *Mason Papers*, II, 831n.; JM to Thomas Jefferson, Aug. 20, 1785, Jan. 22, 1786, Boyd, *TJP*, VIII, 415–416, IX, 194–196.

45. George Washington to George Mason, Oct. 3, 1785, Rutland, ed., *Mason Papers*, II, 832. So great a civil libertarian as Richard Henry Lee was unsympathetic to Madison's arguments. R. H. Lee to JM, Nov. 26, 1785, James C. Ballagh, ed., *Lee Papers* (2 vols., New York, 1970), II, 304.

46. Everson *v.* Board of Education, 330 U.S. 1 (1947), at pp. 33 et seq. Cf. also Reed, J., Dissent in Illinois *ex rel.* McCollum *v.* Board of Education, 333 U.S. 203 (1948).

47. That Madison opposed *any* establishment of religion, as an unwarranted exercise of power in a domain forbidden to government, is the view of Leonard Levy, *Judgment: Essays in American Constitutional History* (Chicago, 1972), pp. 203–205. Among the more recent treatments of this moot issue, see Paul G. Kauper, *Religion and the Constitution* (Baton Rouge, 1964); Robert F. Drinan, *Religion, the Courts and Public Policy* (New York, 1963); Wilbur Katz, *Religion and American Constitutions* (Evanston, Ill., 1964); Leo Pfeffer, "Church and State: Something Less than Separation," *University of Chicago Law Review*, XIX (1951), 1–29; Arthur E. Sutherland, "Due Process and Disestablishment," *Harvard Law Review*, LXII (1949), 1306–1344; and Paul M. Butler and Alfred Scanlan, "The Wall of Separation—Judicial Gloss on the First Amendment," *Notre Dame Lawyers*, XXXVII (1962), 288–308; William G. McLoughlin, "The Role of Religion in the Revolution," in *Essays on the American Revolution*, ed. by Stephen G. Kurtz and James H. Hutson (Chapel Hill, N.C., 1973).

48. Worthington C. Ford *et al.*, eds., *Journals of the Continental Congress* (34 vols., Washington, D.C., 1904–37), April 23, 1785, XXVIII, 293–296.

49. JM to James Monroe, May 29, 1785, cited by Brant, *Madison*, I, 353; Library of Congress, Madison Papers.

50. JM, "Essay on Monopolies," *William and Mary Quarterly*, 3d ser., III (Oct., 1946), p. 554; *Harper's Magazine*, CXXVII (March 1914), 487.

51. Douglas Southall Freeman, *George Washington, a Biography* (7 vols., New York, 1948–57), II, 320–321.

52. Charles S. Sydnor, *American Revolutionaries in the Making* (New York, 1962), pp. 53, 57, 59.

53. *MP*, I, 193.

54. See JM to GW, Dec. 2, 1788, Madison Papers, Library of Congress; also JM to TJ, Dec. 8, 1788, Boyd, *TJP*, XIV, 339–342. In the 1790's JM became a more aggressive candidate.

55. *Journal of the House of Delegates*, Oct., 1777, pp. 25, 29.

56. JM to JM, Sr., Jan. 23, 1778, *MP*, I, 223.
57. For the issues that came before the Council, see *ibid.*, p. 216 passim.
58. Told by N. P. Trist as having been heard July 17, 1827; recorded in Henry S. Randall, *The Life of Thomas Jefferson* (3 vols., New York, 1858), II, 326n. For advertisement of the missing horse, see *MP*, I, 310.
59. *MP*, I, 318.
60. Worthington C. Ford, et al., eds., *Journals of the Continental Congress, 1774-1789* (34 vols., Washington, D.C., 1904-37), XVI, 268.
61. *Ibid.*, XV, 1052-1062; XVI, 262-267.
62. JM to William Bradford, July 17, 1779, *MP*, I, 300, 301.
63. *Ibid.*, pp. 302-310.
64. *National Gazette* (Philadelphia), Dec. 19, 22, 1791.
65. JM to Thomas Jefferson, May 6, 1780, *MP*, II, 20.
66. Adopted April 26, *ibid.*, VI, 487-488. For Hamilton's supporting paper, which he drafted for Congress on the refusal to ratify the proposed impost amendment to the Articles of Confederation, see Harold C. Syrett, et al., *The Papers of Alexander Hamilton* (17 vols., New York, 1961-), III, 213-223.
67. JM to Joseph Jones, Nov. 21, 1780, *MP*, II, 190-191.
68. "Autobiography," *William and Mary Quarterly*, 3d ser., II (April, 1945), p. 204.
69. Draft of a letter to John Jay, explaining instructions, Oct. 17, 1780, *MP*, II, 127-136; motion on navigation of the Mississippi (Feb., 1781), *ibid.*, pp. 302-303. See also R. B. Morris, *The Peacemakers: The Great Powers and American Independence* (New York, 1965), pp. 238 et seq. For Madison's later views amplifying his reluctance to accede to the waiver of the navigation of the Mississippi, see H. B. Adams, *The Life and Writings of Jared Sparks* (2 vols., Boston, 1893), II, 34-35; *Journals of the Continental Congress;* XIX, 152-153; Morris, *Peacemakers*, pp. 237-241.
70. For the miniatures, see illustration following p. 146.
71. The JM–Kitty Floyd romance was related for the first time by Brant, *Madison*, II, 283-287. See also Katherine Anthony, *Dolly Madison* (New York, 1949), pp. 66-68. The related JM–Jefferson correspondence is found in Boyd, *TJP*, VI, 263, 271, 273-274, and in *MP*, VII, 270.
72. JM to TJ, Aug. 11, 1783, *MP*, VII, 268.
73. Aaron Burr to James Monroe, March 10, 1796, Monroe Papers, Library of Congress, cited by Ketcham, *Madison*, p. 387.
74. W. W. Crosskey's conversations in July, 1960, are cited by Ketcham, *ibid.*, p. 704n, without substantiation.
75. Hubbard Taylor to JM, Aug. 9, 1795, Brant, *Madison*, III, 357-358.
76. JM to Thomas Jefferson, April 4, 1785, Aug. 12, 1786; TJ to JM, Dec. 16, 1786, Boyd, *TJP*, X, 234-236, 605; Brant, *Madison*, II, 341-342.
77. JM to George Washington, Nov. 5, 1788; to Henry Lee, Nov. 30, 1788, Hunt, ed., *Madison Writings*, V, 301-302, 306-307; Ketcham, *Madison*, p. 148.

78. JM to William Bradford, Nov. 26, 1774, *MP*, I, 130. For a confirmation of JM's fears of a British plot to arm the slaves, see William Bradford to JM, Jan. 4, 1775, *ibid.*, p. 131. JM to William Bradford, June 19, 1775, *ibid.*, p. 153.

79. JM to Joseph Jones, Nov. 28, 1780, *ibid.*, II, 209.

80. Joseph Jones to JM, Dec. 8, 1780, *ibid.*, pp. 232, 233.

81. JM to JM, Sr., March 30, 1782, *ibid.*, IV, 127.

82. JM to JM, Sr., Sept. 8, 1783, *ibid.*, VII, 304.

83. JM to Edmund Randolph, July 26, 1785, Hunt, ed., *Madison Writings*, II, 154; Boyd, *TJP*, II, 470–473; *Journals, House of Delegates*, pp. 10, 11, 70.

84. Max Farrand, *Records of the Federal Convention* (4 vols., rev. ed., New Haven, 1966), I, 476; II, 9–10.

85. Jacob E. Cooke, ed., *The Federalist* (Middletown, Conn., 1961), pp. 367–369.

86. Jonathan Elliot, *The Debates in the Several State Conventions on the Adoption of the Federal Constitution* (5 vols., Philadelphia [1941]), V, 477.

87. JM to Mr. Pleasants, Oct. 30, 1791, Hunt, ed., *Madison Writings*, VI, 60.

88. Gaillard Hunt, "Thornton," American Antiquarian Society, *Proceedings*, N.S., XXX (1920), 51–52; *Journal of Negro History*, VI (1921), 74–102; Matthew T. Mellon, *Early American Views on Negro Slavery* (New York, 1969), pp. 133–148, 153–159; Winthrop Jordan, *White Over Black* (Chapel Hill, N.C., 1968), pp. 552–553.

89. Hunt, ed., *Madison Writings*, IV, 264–265, 268, 269.

90. See JM's will, April 19, 1835, *ibid.*, IX, 548–552.

91. JM to William Bradford, early March, 1775, *MP*, I, 141.

92. JM to William Bradford, July 28, 1775, *ibid.*, p. 161.

93. W. W. Hening, *The Statutes at Large: Being a Collection of All the Laws of Virginia* (13 vols., Richmond, 1819–23), IX, 170–171.

94. JM to JM, Sr., March [29], 1777, *MP*, I, 190–192 and n. 6.

95. JM to William Bradford, June 19, 1775, *ibid.*, p. 151. Italics added. Bradford tried to clear up the suspicions in a follow-up letter to Madison [July 18, 1775], *ibid.*, p. 158.

96. JM to William Bradford, Jan. 20, 1775, *ibid.*, p. 135.

97. JM, "Vices of the Political System," Hunt, ed., *Madison Writings*, II, 363, 366; JM to Thomas Jefferson, Oct. 17, 1788, Feb. 4, 1790, Julian P. Boyd, ed., *The Papers of Thomas Jefferson* (18 vols., Princeton, 1952–   ), XVI, 146–150.

98. Farrand, *Records of the Federal Convention*, I, 214, 421–423; JM to Thomas Jefferson, Oct. 24, 1787, Boyd, *TJP*, XII, 277–278.

99. JM, "Advice to My Country," 1834, facsimile in JM's hand in Brant, *Madison*, VI, 530. See Ketcham, *Madison*, pp. 641–643.

100. JM to Thomas Jefferson, Feb. 4, 1790, Boyd, *TJP*, XVI, 146–150.

101. See also JM to W. T. Barry, Aug. 4, 1822. Madison Papers, Library of

Congress. For JM's earlier hopes that the French Revolution would be patterned after the American, see JM to Edmund Randolph, Oct. 17, 1788, Hunt, ed., *Madison Writings*, V, 276.

VII. ALEXANDER HAMILTON
AND THE GLORY ROAD

1. Harold C. Syrett, et al., eds., *The Papers of Alexander Hamilton* (17 vols., New York, 1961–   ), I, 1–3 (hereafter designated *AHP*).
2. Also "Lewine" and "Lavien."
3. Allan M. Hamilton, *Intimate Life of Alexander Hamilton* (New York, 1911), p. 8.
4. Quoted in Broadus Mitchell, *Alexander Hamilton: Youth to Maturity, 1755–1788* (2 vols., New York, 1957), I, 8.
5. See *ibid.*, p. 15.
6. The principal authorities for the island origins of AH are Gertrude Atherton, *The Conqueror* (New York, 1902), and Holger Utke Ramsing, "Alexander Hamilton og hans møderne stoegt Tidsbilleder fra Dansk Vestindiens barndom," *Personalhistorisk tidsskrift*, 24 cm., 10 Raekke, 6 bd. (Copenhagen, 1939), pp. 229–231.
7. AH to Elizabeth Hamilton [178], *AHP*, III, 235. See also AH to Nathanael Greene, Oct. 12, 1782, *ibid.*, pp. 183–184.
8. AH to James Hamilton, Jr., June 22, 1785, *AHP*, III, 617; to Robert Troup, July 25, 1795, to Alexander Hamilton, Laird of Cambuskeith, May 2, 1797, Hamilton Papers, 1st ser., Library of Congress; also in Richard B. Morris, *Alexander Hamilton and the Founding of the Nation* (New York, 1957), pp. 571–573.
9. At that time he gave his age as seventeen, *The Royal Danish American Gazette* [April 6, 1771], in *AHP*, I, 6.
10. AH to Edward Stevens, Nov. 11, 1769, *ibid.*, p. 4.
11. Thomas Jefferson to Benjamin Rush, Jan. 16, 1811, Paul L. Ford, ed., *Writings of Thomas Jefferson* (10 vols., New York, 1892–99), IX, 296.
12. For his business correspondence, see *AHP*, I, 8–34.
13. *The Royal Danish American Gazette* [April 6, 1771, Oct. 17, 1772], *ibid.*, pp. 6–7, 38–39.
14. *The Royal Danish American Gazette*, April 10, 1771. Broadus Mitchell (*Hamilton*, I, 28) attributes the article to Hamilton.
15. *The Royal Danish American Gazette*, Oct. 3, 1772, in Mitchell, *Hamilton*, I, 30–31.
16. For the details of Knox's efforts, see Broadus Mitchell, "The Man Who Discovered Hamilton," New Jersey Historical Society, *Proceedings*, LXIX (1951), 88–114.
17. See "The Soul ascending into Bliss," in *AHP*, I, 38–39.
18. Compare Madison's version in *Documents Illustrative of the Formation*

of the Union of the American States (Washington, D.C., 1927), p. 296, with Jonathan Dayton to William Steele, Sept., 1815, *National Intelligencer,* Aug. 25, 1826.

19. Henry Cabot Lodge, ed., *The Works of Alexander Hamilton* (12 vols., New York, 1904), X, 434.

20. See Douglass Adair and Marvin Harvey, "Was Alexander Hamilton a Christian Statesman?" *William and Mary Quarterly,* 3d ser., XII (April, 1955), 308–329.

21. Mulligan's recollections are in Hamilton Papers, Library of Congress. See also *William and Mary Quarterly,* 3d ser., IV (April, 1947), 209 et seq.

22. MS. *The Matricula or Register of Admissions and Graduations, and of Officers employed in King's College at New-York,* Columbiana Collection, Columbia University.

23. Livingston's dismay was justified on still another ground. King's College was a Tory stronghold. Of the twenty-one young men enrolled in the classes, 1772–74, thirteen are known to have been Loyalists, while only three joined Patriot military units. Richard H. Greene, "King's College and Its Earliest Alumni," *The New York Genealogical and Biographical Record,* XXVI (July, 1895), 120–125, 186; XXVII (April, 1896), 35–37, 106–108. William Livingston, et al., *The Independent Reflector,* ed. by Milton M. Klein (Cambridge, Mass., 1963).

24. J. B. Pine, *King's College and the Early Days of Columbia College* (New York, 1917), pp. 6–9.

25. See Hamilton's account with Harpur [Sept. 20, 1774], in *AHP,* I, 44.

26. Cf. J. C. Hamilton, *Life of Alexander Hamilton* (7 vols., Boston, 1879), I, 21–23, with Carl L. Becker, *The History of Political Parties in the Province of New York, 1760–1776* (Madison, Wis., 1909), p. 124.

27. Both pamphlets are republished in *AHP,* I, 45–165; in abridged form in Morris, *Hamilton,* pp. 1–19.

28. Sir William Blackstone, *Commentaries on the Laws of England* (4 vols., London, 1809), I, 250.

29. "The Farmer Refuted," *AHP,* I, 122.

30. Hugh Knox, *Discourses on . . . Truth of Revealed Religion* (2 vols., London, 1768), II, 243.

31. John Jay to Alexander McDougall, Dec. 8, 1775, New-York Historical Society.

32. "A Full Vindication," *AHP,* I, 48.

33. For Madison's account, see *Documents,* pp. 215–225; for Robert Yates, "Secret Proceedings," *ibid.,* pp. 776–783; Lansing in Joseph Strayer, ed., *The Delegate from New York* (Port Washington, N.Y., 1939), pp. 64–70.

34. Max Farrand, *Records of the Federal Convention* (4 vols., New Haven, 1911), I, 381; *AHP,* V, 36, 85.

35. "A Full Vindication," *AHP,* I, 51. For a perceptive analysis of Hamilton's ideas about self-interest, see Gerald Stourzh, *Alexander Hamilton and the Idea of a Republican Government* (Stanford, 1970).

36. *Federalist*, No. 73.
37. AH to the Provincial Congress of New York [May 26, 1776], *Journals of the Provincial Congress of the State of New York* (2 vols., Albany, 1842), I, 108–109; *AHP*, II, 184–186; *Journals of the Provincial Congress*, I, 462.
38. *The Continentalist* (1782), III, 70.
39. *AHP*, V, 42.
40. *Ibid.*, p. 43.
41. *Federalist*, No. 85.
42. *Documents*, p. 261.
43. See examples cited in Morris, *Hamilton*, pp. 74–76.
44. LVI, 326–327. Various accounts of the rescue appear in Nathan Schachner, "Alexander Hamilton Viewed by His Friends: The Narratives of Robert Troup and Hercules Mulligan," *William and Mary Quarterly*, 3d ser., IV (April, 1947), 211, 219. See also *Documents Relative to the Colonial History of New York*, VIII, 297–298; see also Robert Troup to Timothy Pickering, March 17, 1828, Columbia University Libraries.
45. AH to John Jay, Nov. 26, 1775, Hamilton Manuscripts, New York Public Library; Morris, *Hamilton*, pp. 475–477.
46. See AH to the New York Committee of Correspondence, April 20, 1777; to William Livingston, April 21, 29, 1777, in *AHP*, I, 233–236, 242–244.
47. See AH to Robert Morris, April 13, 1782, Morris, *Hamilton*, p. 459; *AHP*, III, 132–143.
48. AH to Robert R. Livingston, Aug. 13, 1783, Livingston Papers, New-York Historical Society; Morris, *Hamilton*, pp. 459–460; *AHP*, III, 431–432.
49. *Laws of the State of New York*, I, 6th sess., 1783 (Albany, 1886), p. 283.
50. AH to Gouverneur Morris, Feb. 21, 1784, *AHP*, III, 512.
51. *The New-York Packet, and the American Advertiser*, March 18, 1784.
52. See Richard B. Morris, *Select Cases of the Mayor's Court of New York City, 1674–1784* (Washington, D.C., 1935), pp. 57–59; Julius Goebel, Jr., et al., *Law Papers of Alexander Hamilton* (2 vols., New York, 1964–   ), I, 309–310. See also E. S. Corwin, *The Doctrine of Judicial Review* (Princeton, 1914), p. 73; B. Coxe, *Judicial Power and Unconstitutional Legislation* (Philadelphia, 1893), p. 233; L. B. Boudin, *Government by Judiciary* (2 vols., New York, 1932), I, 56–58.
53. Morris, *Hamilton*, p. 460.
54. New York *Journal*, March 25, 1784.
55. AH to the U.S. Senate, Jan. 16, 1795, *American State Papers*, V, 336; "Camillus," No. 18 (1795–96), draft in AH's hand, Hamilton Papers, 1st ser., Library of Congress.
56. See AH's speech in the New York Assembly, Jan. 24, 1787, *AHP*, IV, 22–24.
57. E. Wilder Spaulding, *New York in the Critical Period, 1783–1789* (New York, 1932), pp. 129–133.
58. See G. P. Anderson, "Pascal Paoli, An Inspiration to the Sons of Liberty,"

Colonial Society of Massachusetts, *Publications,* XXVI (1924–26), 180–210. The company was later called "Hearts of Oak."

59. For Mulligan's account, see Nathan Schachner, "Alexander Hamilton Viewed by His Friends," *William and Mary Quarterly,* p. 210.

60. *Journals of the Provincial Congress, Provincial Convention, Committee of Safety and Council of Safety of the State of New York* (2 vols., Albany, 1842), I, 359.

61. Hamilton Pay Book, Aug. 31, 1776–March 1, 1777, Hamilton Papers, Library of Congress.

62. Historians differ on Burr's help. Cf. F. S. Drake, *Life and Correspondence of Henry Knox* (Boston, 1837), p. 30, with Mitchell, *Hamilton,* I, 521, n. 23.

63. Washington Irving, *Life of George Washington* (5 vols., New York, 1856–59), II, 88, quoting a "veteran officer."

64. The military phases of AH's career are found in Broadus Mitchell, *Alexander Hamilton: The Revolutionary Years* (New York, 1970).

65. *AHP,* I, 196.

66. John J. Fitzpatrick, ed., *The Writings of George Washington* (39 vols., Washington, D.C., 1931–44), X, 201.

67. *Ibid.,* V, 361, 362.

68. *Ibid.,* VI, 28.

69. AH to Robert R. Livingston, June 28, 1777, Robert R. Livingston Collection, New-York Historical Society; *AHP,* I, 274–277.

70. Fitzpatrick, ed., *Writings of Washington,* VI, 106–111. Similarly in a letter to Lund Washington, Sept. 30, 1776, *ibid.,* pp. 136–139.

71. AH to George Clinton, *AHP,* I, 439–442.

72. *Ibid.,* pp. 414–421.

73. George Washington to Gouverneur Morris, Oct. 4, 1778, Gouverneur Morris Papers, Special Collections, Columbia University Libraries.

74. George Washington to Joseph Reed, Dec. 12, 1778, Fitzpatrick, ed., *Writings of Washington,* XIII, 383.

75. Sept. 3, 1780, Hamilton Papers, 1st ser., Library of Congress; *AHP,* II, 400–418.

76. *AHP,* II, 236–251. Robert Morris, John Sullivan, or Philip Schuyler have been suggested by various historians as the probable addressee. Cf. John C. Miller, *Alexander Hamilton, Portrait in Paradox* (New York, 1959), p. 52; Mitchell, *Hamilton: Youth to Maturity,* I, 190; Nathan Schachner, *Alexander Hamilton* (New York, 1946), pp. 97–98, 444.

77. *AHP,* II, 604–635.

78. Fitzpatrick, ed., *Writings of Washington,* XXI, 181.

79. For the itinerary of AH's journey to Gates's headquarters, see Hamilton's expense account, *AHP,* I, 412–413. For correspondence on the mission, see Morris, *Hamilton,* pp. 34–38.

80. *AHP,* II, 421.

81. AH to Governor George Clinton, Feb. 13, 1778, *AHP,* I, 428; to James Duane, Sept. 6, 1780, *ibid.,* II, 420–421. For the Conway Cabal, see

Douglas Southall Freeman, *George Washington, a Biography* (7 vols., New York, 1948–54), IV, 571; James T. Flexner, *George Washington in the American Revolution* (Boston, 1967), pp. 241–277.

82. The accounts of AH's confrontation with Lee at Monmouth are found in "Proceedings of a General Court Martial for the Trial of Major Charles Lee," New-York Historical Society, *Collections*, VI (1873), 5–6; AH to Elias Boudinot, July 5, 1778, *AHP*, I, 510–514; AH to Lord Stirling, July 14, 1778, *ibid.*, pp. 522–523; Morris, *Hamilton*, pp. 42–47.

83. AH to George Washington, [Sept. 25, 1780], *AHP*, II, 438–439.

84. AH to Elizabeth Hamilton, Sept. 25, 1780, *ibid.*, pp. 441, 442.

85. See Morris, *Hamilton*, pp. 52–61; Carl Van Doren, *Secret History of the American Revolution* (New York, 1968), pp. 366–367; *AHP*, II, 446n., wherein the editors express doubts about AH's authorship of the "AB" letter. (In the Reynolds affair, AH also wrote in a disguised hand.)

86. See James T. Flexner, *The Traitor and the Spy: Benedict Arnold and John André* (New York, 1962), pp. 383–387.

87. AH to Major General Henry Knox [June 7, 1782], *AHP*, III, 91–93.

88. See Fitzpatrick, ed., *Writings of Washington*, XXIV, 217–218; Francis Wharton, ed., *The Revolutionary Diplomatic Correspondence of the United States* (6 vols., Washington, D.C., 1889), V, 462–463, 617–618, 634–636; Elias Boudinot, *Life, Public Services, Addresses, and Letters* (2 vols., Boston, 1896), I, 249–251.

89. See Lt. Col. John Brooks to AH, July 4; AH to Francis Dana, July 11; AH to David Henley, July 12; AH to Brooks, Aug. 6; AH to John Laurens, Sept. 11; William Gordon to AH, Sept. 23, 1779, *AHP*, II, 60–188, passim; Massachusetts Historical Society, *Proceedings*, LXIII (1931), 425–426.

90. AH to Philip Schuyler, Headquarters, New Windsor, Feb. 18, 1781. Original draft in Lloyd W. Smith Collection, Morristown National Historical Park. *AHP*, II, 563–568.

91. See Mitchell, *Hamilton: The Revolutionary Years*, II, 270–278; Morris, *Hamilton*, pp. 61–65.

92. AH to James Duane, Sept. 3, 1780, *AHP*, II, 404.

93. See James Madison, "Notes on Debates," Dec. 24, 1782, W. T. Hutchinson and William M. E. Rachal, eds., *The Papers of James Madison* (Chicago, 1962–   ), V, 442.

94. Madison, "Notes on Debates," Jan. 28, 1783, Gaillard Hunt, ed., *The Writings of James Madison* (9 vols., New York, 1900–10), I, 335–336n.

95. "Brutus" to Knox, Feb. 12, 1783, Henry Knox Papers, Massachusetts Historical Society. For an identification of "Brutus," see the capital article by Richard H. Kohn, "The Inside History of the Newburgh Conspiracy," *William and Mary Quarterly*, 3d ser., XXVII (1970), 197n.

96. See Rufus King, "Notes on a Conversation with William Duer," Oct. 12, 1788, in Charles R. King, ed., *The Life and Correspondence of Rufus King* (6 vols., New York, 1894–1900), I, 621–622.

97. Hamilton Papers, 1st ser., Library of Congress. The letter is dated Feb. 7, but the New York Public Library copy is endorsed Feb. 13, the date adopted in *AHP*, III, 253–255.

98. Madison, "Notes on Debates," Feb. 18–20, 1783, Hunt, ed., *Writings of Madison*, I, 370–371, 374–378.

99. Fitzpatrick, ed., *Writings of Washington*, XXVI, 187, 214–216.

100. AH to John Dickinson [Sept. 25–30], *AHP*, III, 451.

101. See Edmund Randolph to George Washington, Aug. 5, 1794, Washington Papers, CCLXVIII, Library of Congress; AH to George Washington, Aug. 2, Sept. 19, 1794, J. C. Hamilton, *Hamilton*, IV, 575–578, V, 30–31. AH to Thomas Mifflin, Sept. 20, 1794, *Pennsylvania Archives*, 2d ser., IV, 334.

102. AH to James McHenry, June 27, 1799, Hamilton Papers, Special Collections, Columbia University Libraries.

103. See AH to William Smith, March 11, 1800, Lodge, ed., *Works*, X, 364.

104. AH to John Jay [July 25, 1783], *AHP*, III, 416. Richard B. Morris, *The Peacemakers: The Great Powers and American Independence* (New York, 1965), pp. 442–444.

105. See Julian P. Boyd, *Number 7* (Princeton, N.J., 1964).

106. See Samuel Flagg Bemis, *Jay's Treaty* (New York, 1923).

107. George Washington to John Adams, Sept. 25, 1798, Fitzpatrick, ed., *Washington*, XXXV, 460–461.

108. AH to James A. Bayard, Jan. 16, 1801, Lodge, ed., *Works*, X, 417.

109. AH to John Laurens [April, 1779], *AHP*, I, 34–38.

110. AH to John Laurens, June 30, 1780, *AHP*, II, 348, wherein he described Elizabeth as neither a "genius" nor a "beauty," but "a good hearted girl," adding: "I do not speak of the perfections of my Mistress in the enthusiasm of Chivalry."

111. AH to Angelica Schuyler [Feb., 1780], *AHP*, II, 269–271, wherein it is suggested that the letter was written to Margarita Schuyler.

112. A. M. Hamilton, *Intimate Life*, p. 73. Morris, *Hamilton*, pp. 579–580.

113. *Observations on Certain Documents contained in Nos. V and VI of "The History of the United States for the year 1796," in which the charge of Speculation against Alexander Hamilton, late Secretary of the Treasury, is fully refuted* (Philadelphia: printed for John Fenno by John Bioren, 1797). See also Morris, *Hamilton*, pp. 579–587.
    Julian P. Boyd infers from a review of the evidence that Jefferson was correct in his surmise that Hamilton's willingness to plead guilty to adultery seemed "rather to have strengthened than weakened the suspicions that he was in truth guilty of the speculations." TJ to John Taylor, Oct. 8, 1797, cited by Julian P. Boyd, ed., in *The Papers of Thomas Jefferson* (18 vols., Princeton, 1952–   ), XVIII, 685, where the entire Reynolds affair is reexamined at length (pp. 611–688).

114. AH to John Laurens, Sept. 12, 1780, *AHP*, II, 428.

115. AH to Alexander Hamilton, Laird of Cambuskeith, May 2, 1797, draft in AH's hand, Hamilton Papers, 1st ser., Library of Congress.

116. AH to Gouverneur Morris, Feb. 27, 1802, draft in AH's hand, *ibid.*, 1st ser., Library of Congress.
117. AH to Theodore Sedgwick, J. C. Hamilton, *Hamilton*, VI, 567–568.

WHAT'S PAST IS PROLOGUE

1. JA to Benjamin Rush, Aug. 28, 1811, John Adams, *Works*, ed. by Charles Francis Adams (10 vols., Boston, 1850–56), IX, 637.
2. JM to J. K. Paulding, April, 1831, Gaillard Hunt, ed., *The Writings of James Madison* (9 vols., New York, 1900–10), IX, 452.
3. *Collected Works of Sir Humphry Davy*, ed. by John Davy (9 vols., London, 1839–40), VIII, 264–265.
4. TJ to JA, Oct. 28, 1813, *The Adams-Jefferson Letters*, ed. by Lester J. Cappon (2 vols., Chapel Hill, N.C., 1959), II, 391.
5. TJ to JA, June 10, 1815, Cappon, ed., *Adams-Jefferson Letters*, II, 443.
6. "A Dissertation on the Canon and Feudal Law" (1765), John Adams, *Works*, ed. by C. F. Adams (10 vols., Boston, 1850–56), III, 463.
7. "Proposals Relating to the Education of Youth in Pennsylvania," (1749), Leonard W. Labaree, ed., *The Papers of Benjamin Franklin* (New Haven, 1959–), III, 404.
8. GW to Rev. Jonathan Boucher, July 9, 1771, John C. Fitzpatrick, ed., *The Writings of George Washington* (39 vols., Washington, D.C., 1931–44), III, 50–51.
9. GW to David Humphreys, July 25, 1785, *GWF*, XXVIII, 202.
10. James D. Richardson, ed., *Compilation of the Messages and Papers of the Presidents* (Washington, D.C., 1896): First Annual Address, Jan. 8, 1790, I, 65; Farewell Address, Sept. 19, 1796, I, 213; Eighth Annual Address, Dec. 7, 1796, I, 199; GW to the Commissioners of the Federal District, Philadelphia, Jan. 28, 1795, I, 150.
11. Last Will and Testament, July 9, 1799, *GWF*, XXXVII, 278.
12. Jefferson's explanation of education in *Notes on Virginia* (1782), Paul Leicester Ford, ed., *The Writings of Thomas Jefferson* (10 vols., New York, 1892–98), III, 252.
13. TJ to George Wythe, Aug. 13, 1786, Julian P. Boyd, ed., *The Papers of Thomas Jefferson* (18 vols., Princeton, 1952–), X, 244–245.
14. "A Bill for the More General Diffusion of Knowledge," *ibid.*, II, 527.
15. TJ to Du Pont De Nemours, April 24, 1816, Johns Hopkins Studies in International Thought, *The Correspondence of Jefferson and Du Pont De Nemours* (Baltimore, 1931), p. 259.
16. TJ to Mrs. M. Harrison Smith [1816], H. W. Washington, ed., *The Writings of Thomas Jefferson* (9 vols., Philadelphia, 1853–55), VII, 28.
17. From the Pope's Nuncio to BF, July 28, 1783, John Bigelow, ed., *The Works of Benjamin Franklin,* (12 vols., New York, 1904), X, 148.
18. BF to Ezra Stiles, March 9, 1790, *ibid.*, XII, 185–187.

19. GW, Speech to the Delaware Chiefs, May 12, 1779, *GWF*, XV, 55.
20. GW to the Members of the New Church in Baltimore [Jan. 27, 1793], *GWF*, XXXII, 315.
21. See JJ to Jedidiah Morse, Feb. 28, 1797, Jay Papers, Special Collections, Columbia University Libraries (copy); Henry P. Johnston, ed., *The Correspondence and Public Papers of John Jay* (4 vols., New York, 1893), IV, 225; William Jay, *The Life of John Jay* (2 vols., New York, 1833), II, 280.
22. JJ to Jedidiah Morse, Jan. 1, 1813, draft in Jay Papers, Special Collections, Columbia University Libraries; *HPJ*, IV, 365; *WJ*, II, 351. This quotation appears as a postscript in William Jay's handwriting.
23. *Ibid.;* Annual Address as President of the American Bible Society, May 9, 1822, Jay Papers, Special Collections, Columbia University Libraries.
24. Jonathan Dayton to William Steele, Sept. 1825, *National Intelligencer* (Washington, D.C.), Aug. 25, 1826. For the earlier version, see James Madison, "Debates" in *Documents Illustrative of the Formation of the Union of the American States,* 69th Cong., 1st Sess., House Doc. No. 398 (Washington, D.C., 1927), p. 296.
25. AH to Elizabeth Hamilton, July 10, 1804; Tuesday evening, 10 o'clock, 1804, Henry Cabot Lodge, ed., *The Works of Alexander Hamilton* (12 vols., New York, 1904), X, 475, 476.
26. JJ to John Trumbull, Oct. 27, 1797, *HPJ*, IV, 232.
27. TJ to Mr. Bellini, Washington, ed., *Writings*, I, 444.
28. JJ to Robert R. Livingston, Nov. 17, 1782, *HPJ*, II, 451; Francis Wharton, ed., *The Revolutionary Diplomatic Correspondence of the United States* (6 vols., Washington, D.C., 1889), VI, 49. See also Richard B. Morris, *The Peacemakers: The Great Powers and American Independence* (New York, 1965), p. 310.
29. AH to Rufus King, Dec. 16, 1796, J. C. Hamilton, *Life of Alexander Hamilton* (7 vols., Boston, 1879), VI, 187–188.
30. GW to Lafayette, July 25, 1785, *GWF*, XXVIII, 208.
31. "Camillus," No. 9 (1795), draft in AH's hand, Hamilton Papers, 1st ser., Library of Congress.
32. These points are spelled out in Richard B. Morris, *The American Revolution Reconsidered* (New York, 1967), pp. 43–91; *The Emerging Nations and the American Revolution* (New York, 1970), pp. 53–67.
33. For a recent emphasis on the moderation and rationality of the American Revolutionary movement, see Pauline Maier, *From Resistance to Revolution* (New York, 1972).
34. L. H. Butterfield, et al., eds., *The Adams Papers: Diary and Autobiography of John Adams* (4 vols., Cambridge, Mass., 1961), III, 138.
35. BF to David Hartley, Dec. 4, 1789. Carl Van Doren, ed., *Benjamin Franklin's Autobiographical Writings* (New York, 1945), p. 778.
36. 1st Inaugural Address [April 30, 1789], *GWF*, XXX, 294–295.

INDEX

Achard de Bônvouloir, Julien, 179
Adams, Abigail Smith, 73, 78, 80, 87, 106, 110, 112, 113, 133, 168, 263, 264; on Benjamin Franklin, 17; romance and marriage, 82–84
Adams, Elihu, 77
Adams, John, 1, 5, 67, 116, 121, 124, 139, 140, 157, 168, 171, 178, 187, 196, 198, 224, 252, 257, 260, 261, 262, 263, 264, 265, 266, 272, 275; on Benjamin Franklin, 6, 11, 75; character, 73–75; Puritanism, 73, 75, 76, 77, 78, 80, 110, 111; education, 77, 81; humor, 75, 78, 79; "Dissertation on the Canon and Feudal Law," 79; on American Revolution, 76, 79, 80; on religion, 80–81, 269, 270; romance and marriage, 82–84; on women in civic affairs, 84–85; lawyer, 85–87, 91, 94–95, 160; Boston Massacre trial, 87, 88, 89, 90, 91, 95; on mobbism, 87, 88, 98, 99, 110; 1782–83 peace negotiations, 88, 104; John Hancock smuggling case, 88–89, 94; Writs of Assistance case, 91, 122; on Stamp Act, 92–94; "Clarendon" letters, 94; and Jonathan Sewall, 96–97; "Novanglus" letters, 98, 102; revolutionary, 96, 98–99, 102, 103, 104, 105, 106; in Continental Congress, 99–106; proposal for setting up state governments, 104–105, 109, adopted by Congress, 106; for independence in Continental Congress, 106–108, 111; on committee to draft Declaration of Independence, 107–108, 135; "Thoughts on Government," 109,
110; on committee to draft Massachusetts Constitution, 109–110, 271; *The Defence of the Constitutions of Government of the United States of America*, 110, 111; author of Massachusetts Bill of Rights, 111; on slavery, 111, 271; as President, 113; as nationalist, 112–113; on Thomas Jefferson and drafting of Declaration of Independence, 136; on committee for seal of the United States, 137; on John Jay, 172; on Alexander Hamilton, 221; "Massachusettensis" letters, 229; in 1st Continental Congress, 259; premarital innocence, 264; woman suffrage, 273; *Diary and Autobiography*, 74, 77, 88, 99, 100, 101, 136
Adams, John, father of John Adams, 76–77
Adams, John Quincy, 77, 112, 114
Adams, Peter Boylston, 77
Adams, Samuel, 2, 63, 67, 72, 80, 86, 98, 100, 172; on Boston Massacre, 89; and Hutchinson-Oliver letters, 28; radical, 94, 100
Adams, Susanna Boylston, 76
Addison, Joseph, 33
Adler, Alfred, 74
Albany Plan of Union, 25
Alexandria, Va., 66, 204
Alien and Sedition Acts, 145, 218, 219
Allen, Bennet, on George Washington, 60–61
Allen, Moses, 194
Alsop, John, 171
Amber, Jacquelin, 126, 127
American Colonization Society, 216, 271

321